Networking Personal Computers

3rd Edition

AF576591

Michael Durr
Mark Gibbs

Networking Personal Computers

3rd Edition

Copyright © 1989 by Que® Corporation

All rights reserved. Printed in the United States of America. No part of this book may be used or reproduced in any form or by any means, or stored in a database or retrieval system, without prior written permission of the publisher except in the case of brief quotations embodied in critical articles and reviews. Making copies of any part of this book for any purpose other than your own personal use is a violation of United States copyright laws. For information, address Que Corporation, 11711 N. College Ave., Carmel, IN 46032.

Library of Congress Catalog No.: 89-60844

ISBN 0-88022-417-7

This book is sold *as is*, without warranty of any kind, either express or implied, respecting the contents of this book, including but not limited to implied warranties for the book's quality, performance, merchantability, or fitness for any particular purpose. Neither Que Corporation nor its dealers or distributors shall be liable to the purchaser or any other person or entity with respect to any liability, loss, or damage caused or alleged to be caused directly or indirectly by this book.

92 91 90 8 7 6 5 4 3 2

Interpretation of the printing code: the rightmost double-digit number is the year of the book's printing; the rightmost single-digit number, the number of the book's printing. For example, a printing code of 89-1 shows that the first printing of the book occurred in 1989.

ABOUT THE AUTHORS

Michael Durr

Michael Durr received his B.A. in Business and Technical Communications and his M.A. in Marketing Communications from California State University. He has worked as a communications security specialist in the U.S. Navy, as managing editor of *Personal Computer Age*, and as director of strategic marketing for Novell, Inc. He is the author of numerous magazine articles and books including *Micro to Mainframe* and *Using NetWare*.

Mark Gibbs

Mark Gibbs is a former architect and graphics designer. He has been in computer networking for over eight years and has established technical support departments for several computer companies. He is a frequent speaker and presenter at computer conferences and seminars and works for Novell, International in England.

Publishing Manager

Lloyd J. Short

Product Director

David Maguiness

Production Editor

Kelly D. Dobbs

Editors

Jo Anna Arnott
Fran Blauw
Kelly Currie
Alice Martina Smith
Richard Turner

Technical Editor

Thomas Neuburger

Index

Brown Editorial Service

Editorial Assistant

Stacie Lamborne

Book Design and Production

Dan Armstrong
Dave Kline
Jennifer Matthews
Jon Ogle
Cindy L. Phipps
Joe Ramon
Dennis Sheehan
M. Louise Shinault
Peter Tocco

Composed in Garamond and Excellent #47
by Que Corporation

Contents at a Glance

Part VI Security and Reliability

Table of Contents

III Applications on the Network

Trademark Acknowledgments

Que Corporation has made every effort to supply trademark information about company names, products, and services mentioned in this book. Trademarks indicated below were derived from various sources. Que Corporation cannot attest to the accuracy of this information.

1-2-3, Lotus, and Framework are registered trademarks of Lotus Development Corporation.

3+ is a trademark of 3M Company.

3Com is a registered trademark and EtherLink, EtherMail, EtherNet, and EtherTalk are trademarks of 3Com Corporation.

ANSI is a registered trademark of American National Standards Institute.

Apple, AppleTalk, Lisa, and Macintosh Plus are registered trademarks and System and AppleShare are trademarks of Apple Computer, Inc.

ARCnet and Datapoint are registered trademarks of Datapoint Corporation.

Ashton-Tate and dBASE III Plus are registered trademarks of Ashton-Tate Corporation.

AT&T is a registered trademark and UNIX is a trademark of AT&T.

CompuServe is a registered trademark of CompuServe Corp.

Constellation is a registered trademark and Corvus and Omninet are trademarks of Corvus Systems, Inc.

CP/NET is a registered trademark and GEM Draw is a trademark of Digital Research Inc.

DaVinci and eMail are trademarks of DaVinci Systems.

DEC, DECnet, and CP/M are registered trademarks of Digital Equipment Corporation.

DESQview is a trademark of Quarterdeck Office Systems.

G-Net is a trademark of Gateway Communications.

IBM and Personal System/2 are registered trademarks and PC XT, OS/2, PS/2, IBM RT/PC, NETBIOS, VM/XA, SQL/DS, and Systems Application Architecture are trademarks of International Business Machines Corporation.

MCI Mail is a registered servicemark of MCI Communications Corporation.

MicroPro and WordStar are registered trademarks of MicroPro International Corporation.

Microsoft, Microsoft BASIC, MS-DOS, and Microsoft Windows are registered trademarks of Microsoft Corporation.

Motorola is a registered trademark of Motorola, Inc.

Net/One Personal Connections is a trademark and Ungermann-Bass is a registered trademark of Ungermann-Bass, Inc.

NetWare and Novell are registered trademarks of Novell, Inc.

NFS is a trademark of Sun Microsystems, Inc.

PCnet BLOSSOM is a trademark of Orchid Technology.

Printronix is a registered trademark of Printronix.

Proteon and ProNET are registered trademarks of Proteon, Inc.

SideKick is a registered trademark of Borland International, Inc.

The Source is a service mark of Source Telecomputing Corporation, a subsidiary of The Reader's Digest Association, Inc.

Telenet is a registered trademark of GTE Telenet Communications Corporation.

TOPS is a registered trademark of Centram Systems West, Inc.

Tymnet is a registered trademark of Tymnet, Inc.

WordPerfect is a trademark of Satellite Software International.

Xerox is a registered trademark of Xerox Corporation.

Introduction

With each edition of *Networking Personal Computers*, personal computer networking has changed dramatically. In the first edition (published in 1984), the underlying issue was that personal computers actually could be connected and share information. The local area network (LAN) had emerged as a useful technology, loaded with immediate practicality and a promising future. At the time, one of the biggest concerns for people considering the large-scale use of LANs was the lack of standardization. LAN companies were doing many things in many ways and virtually every aspect of networking was the subject of controversy.

By the second edition, which came out in 1987, the maverick tendency of the local area network marketplace had begun to diminish. Standards were being adopted by vendors. LANs were beginning to be connected to mainframes and, with communications to various systems being demanded by users, the LAN industry was forced to provide integration strategies.

The Evolution of LANs

The standardization and maturity of LAN technology have caused wide-ranging changes in networking. These changes are reflected in this third edition of *Networking Personal Computers*.

LANs are defined as local systems that support personal computer workstations. Today, LAN technology does not fit that narrow definition. LAN technology, which provides a means of managing distributed intelligent workstations and distributed resources, now is being used on minicomputer and mainframe networks and soon will become common on wide area networks (WANs). The distinctions among LANs, premises networks, and WANs are becoming blurred. For these reasons, the terms "network" and "distributed processing system" are used more than in previous editions of this book.

Also included in the third edition are discussions of workstations besides IBM PCs and operating systems besides DOS. LAN operating systems now support Apple Macintoshes and Unix workstations in addition to IBM PCs. OS/2, a multitasking operating system for personal computers, has joined other multitasking operating systems for Apple and Unix machines. All of these workstation options can be networked together. This edition includes discussions of the differences among these options and how to choose the right products for specific needs.

Applications development also has progressed since the second edition. New types of applications, such as groupware and SQL databases, are helping to integrate the distributed operations as never before. Besides the impact on management and organization, the new applications are increasing the power and reach of the networked personal computer.

Who Should Use This Book?

Networking Personal Computers, 3rd Edition, is designed as a guide for network users and managers. The discussions in this book concentrate on topics that are practical for people who are selecting, installing, managing, and using personal computer networks. Technology may be beautiful in its own right, but this book tells you how to use that technology—cost-effectively to improve productivity.

What Is in This Book?

This book is divided into six parts that follow a logical progression from the theories behind networking to how to keep your system secure.

Part I, "Network Theory," introduces you to LANs, describes the standards that today's LANs are based on, compares the types of networks you can use, and concludes with a discussion of application-processing options. If you are trying to decide whether networking is right for you, the first part of this book presents the information necessary for you to make the best decision.

Part II, "Choosing a System," describes the hardware involved in networking personal computers, the different network operating systems, workstation and server choices, and how you can evaluate the basic network components.

Part III, "Applications on the Network," discusses the applications software available for use on a network, applications programming interfaces, electronic mail, groupware, and distributed data services.

Part IV, "Communications," provides detailed information about internetworking and the PC-to-mainframe link that permits distributed resources to be accessed from any point on the network.

Part V, "Network Management," focuses on management strategies, how to create and use batch files, how to install a network, and how to maintain your network.

Part VI, "Security and Reliability," tells you how to protect your data from unforeseen risks and viruses. This section also discusses network security systems, risk analysis, and data recovery.

I

Network Theory

Includes

The Development of LANs

Communications and Standards

Examining the Alternatives

Application Processing

1

The Development of LANs

Shortly after the introduction of the personal computer, a system was developed for attaching the PC to an office network. That system is the *local area network*, or LAN. The impact of the LAN-and-PC combination is still producing major changes in the way work is performed and in office automation.

The Growth of Office Automation

The goal of office automation is to use computers to make office functions easier. Although that goal sounds simple, it has been difficult to achieve.

First, office functions had to be analyzed. Some functions should be mimicked exactly in the automated environment. The change from typing to word processing is a good example of successful mimicking in an automated approach. Every office needs some means of creating textual material, and doing that job with a computer rather than a typewriter is much more efficient.

Other office functions have a long tradition but are becoming outdated. Perhaps the best examples of such functions are the ways in which people send messages. Paper memos and telephones often fail as communications tools because the systems are overburdened with too many messages. Therefore, in automating the message function, designers have had to rethink the office communications process, taking into account large, dispersed employee populations, and potentially enormous volumes of messages.

While the office functions were being analyzed, computer technology also had to be examined and improved. The trend has been to move data closer to the end user and give that person greater control over the data. This movement has been accomplished through the introduction of smaller computers called minicomputers. These machines were dedicated first to departments and then to workgroups within departments. The ultimate step was achieved with the personal computer—a machine that serves only one person.

The Local Area Network Defined

A local area network is a communications system much like a telephone system. Any connected device can use the network to send and receive information. Most of the information on LANs is text and graphics, assembled as structured data that can be manipulated by computers. A new but increasingly important use of LANs is the passing of unstructured data, such as facsimile messages and pictures, that cannot be readily manipulated but can be stored and retrieved efficiently.

As the name implies, a LAN is a system that covers relatively short distances. Usually, a LAN is limited to a department or perhaps one building. Whether used in large corporations or small businesses, LANs tend to be small for functional reasons. The most common network for PC users contains from 7 to 15 personal computers, various data storage devices, printers, and other specialized peripherals (see fig. 1.1).

Speed is an important characteristic of LANs. Ideally, a person passing and receiving data over a LAN experiences the same rapid response time as if the data were coming from a local machine rather than from some place on the network. To get this kind of response time, most LANs operate at 1 to 16 megabits per second (Mbit/sec).

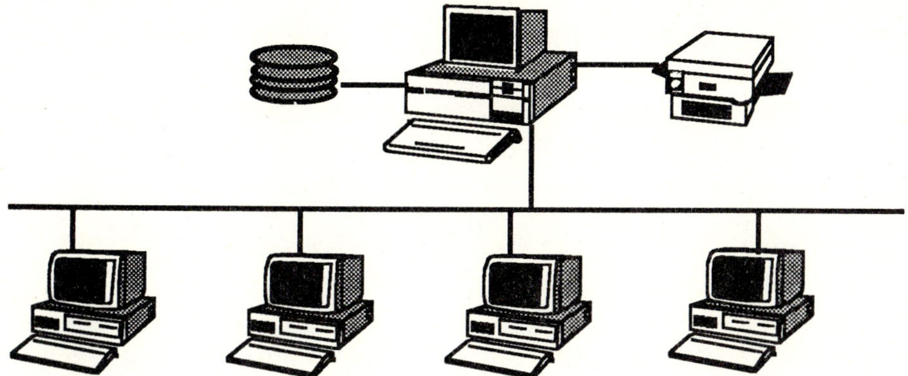

Fig. 1.1. A PC local area network.

Besides being fast, a LAN must be adaptable. A LAN should have a flexible architecture that permits PC workstations to be located wherever they are needed. Users also should be able to add or remove PCs or peripherals to or from the system easily, without causing any extended interruption in network operation.

A LAN also must be reliable. One of the major benefits of a stand-alone personal computer is that if the computer breaks down or malfunctions in some way, the effect is limited. The rest of the office work is not interrupted. When PCs are linked into a LAN, the system should retain this kind of reliability. The failure of one PC should not cause the entire network to shut down.

Finally, a LAN is essentially a network designed for intelligent workstations (PCs). The PCs attached to the network can use the processing capability of other intelligent devices for certain shared processing functions, such as network management, batch processing, and so on. In most applications, however, the PCs use their own computing power.

The network just described might be called a small, high-performance, local area network for personal computers. In common usage, the term *local area network* can involve a much broader definition. LAN can mean everything from large corporate terminal networks to networks based on PBX telephone systems. In this book, however, the terms local area network, LAN, and network all refer to the high-performance PC network described in the previous paragraphs.

Components of the Network

A LAN is a system made from building blocks that can be added and configured as needed. The following is a list of the basic LAN components:

- ❑ Cable
- ❑ Network adapter
- ❑ Network servers
- ❑ Central mass storage
- ❑ Workstations

Cable

Each device on the network is attached to a transmission cable so that messages can be sent from one device to another. LANs are run on cables varying from low-cost, twisted-pair telephone wire, to single- or multichannel coaxial cable, to high-performance fiber-optic cable.

Network Adapter

PCs are attached to a LAN through a circuit board called a *network interface card* (NIC) or *network adapter* (see fig. 1.2). The NIC is plugged into one of the available slots on the PC expansion bus, and the transmission cable is attached to the connector on the NIC.

Network Servers

LANs use special systems to manage the shared resources on the network. These systems are called servers. A *server* is a combination of hardware and software. The hardware may be a personal computer or a computer designed specifically as a server.

Although LANs may have a variety of different servers to manage various hardware and software resources (for example, a communications server to manage shared modems), every LAN must

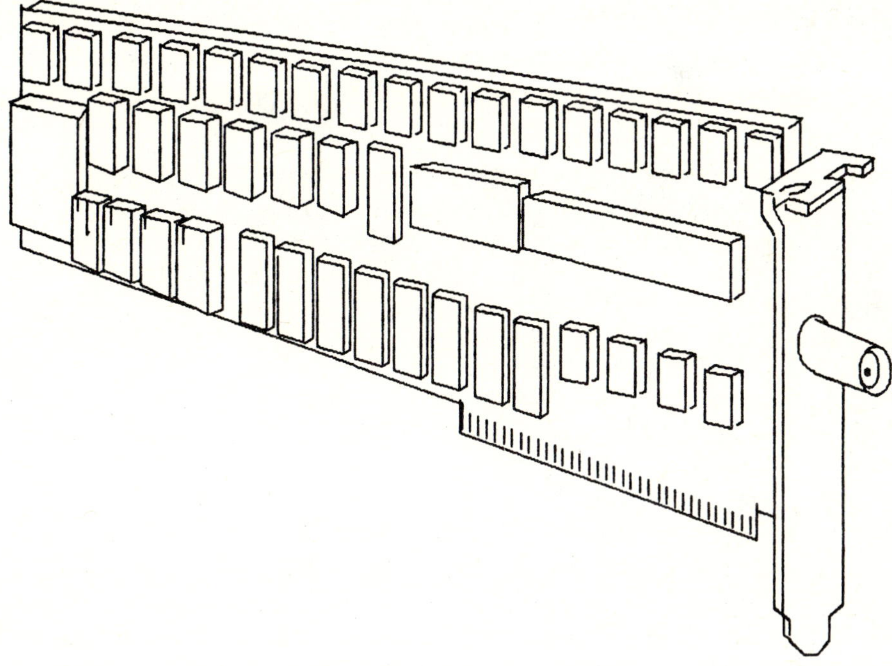

Fig. 1.2. The network interface card (NIC), or network adapter, provides the physical connection between the PC and the LAN.

have a *file server*. The file server manages the shared hard disk and makes sure that multiple requests—especially write requests—do not conflict with each other. To protect the data and prevent unauthorized access, the file server also maintains lists of privileges and authorizations associated with the data files.

Network servers, conceptually and in network diagrams, resemble host machines. One of the primary differences between a LAN and a shared processing system (host-to-terminal system) is that in a shared processing system, all processing occurs in the central host machine; attached terminal workstations cannot process information because they lack intelligence (a microprocessor). A server on a LAN is similar to a host machine in that the server supplies some shared functions, such as disk management. On a LAN, however, processing is distributed among all the intelligent machines, including PC workstations.

Central Mass Storage

Central mass storage is provided in the form of a hard disk that contains the files and programs shared by people using the network. Often one network is supported by several hard disks. The storage capacity of LANs has risen dramatically since their introduction. Network operating systems designed to implement the features of the Intel 80286 microprocessor can manage several gigabytes of data on a hard disk. An operating system that uses the 80386 microprocessor capabilities can manage several terrabytes of data on disk.

(A *byte*, the basic computer measurement term, is a unit of measurement equal to 8 characters. A *kilobyte* (K) is 1,024 bytes. A *megabyte* (M) is 1,000 kilobytes. A *gigabyte* (G) is 1,000 megabytes, and a *terabyte* (T) is 1,000 gigabytes. A terabyte, therefore, is equal to one trillion bytes. The terms gigabyte and terrabyte are still somewhat unreal to most computer users, but these measures undoubtedly soon will become a familiar part of the jargon. Computer users always can find a need for more speed and more storage.)

The limitations on network storage are related more to memory and hard disk technology than to CPU limitations. As a rule of thumb, the maximum amount of storage that 15M of RAM (random-access memory) can manage is about 2G. With today's technology, getting enough RAM in a microcomputer to manage more than 2G is impossible. The inevitable next step is higher-capacity RAM chips. Similarly, the physical size of a few terabytes of disk storage is so great that the size is impractical. But disk technology, such as the optical disk, will move the terabyte from the possible to the practical and, eventually, to the affordable.

The network normally uses each hard disk as one or more independent volumes (logical storage units). Several LAN database management programs, however, permit the combining of multiple hard disks to create large storage systems. Part of the database can be stored on one disk, another part on another disk, and so on. When the database is accessed, these distributed parts can be assembled and manipulated as if they all are on one disk. The *distributed database* is a major breakthrough in LAN technology. This capability simplifies data management and security and enhances network growth and configuration options. (See Chapter 4, "Application Processing.")

Workstations

The workstations on a LAN are personal computers, including IBM PCs, IBM PS/2s, and any of a dozen or more IBM PC-compatible personal computers. Many LANs also support computers that are not IBM PC-compatible, such as the Apple family of personal computers. LANs do not support so-called "dumb" terminals that rely on a host processor for intelligence.

The Network as a Communications System

When PC users think of networking or plan a network, they usually think of the LAN as a device-sharing scheme. Device sharing is certainly one of networking's benefits, but device sharing is not the total picture. LANs are communications systems that enable users to send messages, letters, memos, and files from one PC to another. A LAN also can be connected to wide area networks so that users can communicate with remote PCs and with other LANs, mainframe networks, and public service networks.

PCs and LANs have changed communications significantly. Now, a user can communicate directly from one workstation to another without going through a host machine. This direct link speeds up the communications and reduces or eliminates the need for an expensive host machine.

Communicating and sharing information have a side benefit that may be the best inducement of all for networking: A network promotes an organized computing environment. In many businesses, even small ones, the personal computer can be a disruptive force. The personal computer may encourage a kind of "maverick" behavior among users because everyone does things differently. The text files generated by one user may not be readily usable by another user because each person has a different word processor. Formats of company documents tend to vary from machine to machine.

If information generated on a personal computer must be read by other machines or stored on a mainframe, much of the work may need to be redone before the data can be moved to a new system. The situation is reminiscent of the Tower of Babel, where cooperative work was stopped by communication problems. Is it any wonder that many data processing professionals have resisted PCs? Unlike the stand-alone PC, the LAN, with its shared central storage and channels of communication, requires user cooperation, and cooperation results in better organization and continuity of effort.

LANs in Action

To illustrate how LANs work, suppose that a user is working on a PC attached to a network, and the user issues the DOS or other workstation operating system command to load a word processor package. The network intercepts and routes the command to the file server.

The server checks to see whether it can comply with the request. The word processor is stored as a shareable, read-only file. *Shareable, read-only* means that many people can read the file at the same time, but no one can modify the file. Because the user's request does not conflict with the restrictions, the word processor is sent down to the user's PC and loaded in memory. Now, the PC can perform word processing.

Next, suppose that the user wants to modify an existing text file also stored on the server's hard disk; the user requests the file, which is stored as a nonshareable, read/write file. *Read/write* means that the file can be modified, and *nonshareable* means that only one person at a time can work on the file. The technique of setting up nonshareable files is known as *file locking*.

The text file is loaded into the computer's memory, and the user makes the necessary changes. While the file is being modified, several other people on the network also can load and use the word processor. If they try to load the same text file that the first user is modifying, they are denied access.

After making the changes, the user decides to print the text. The request to print the file is routed to the network printer. Because another job is being printed, the text file is placed in a queue maintained by the server. When the first job is finished, the user's text file is printed.

Meanwhile, other people on the network are using a database management system (DBMS). The database application is stored as shareable, read-only, like the word processor, but the database itself is stored as shareable, read/write, which means that several people can use and modify the database simultaneously.

Suppose that one of the database users requests a record—the address of a customer whose name is in the database. Although other users can be using and updating the database at the same time, if someone else tries to modify the customer address while the first modification is in progress, the modification is denied. This technique is known as *record locking* (see fig. 1.3).

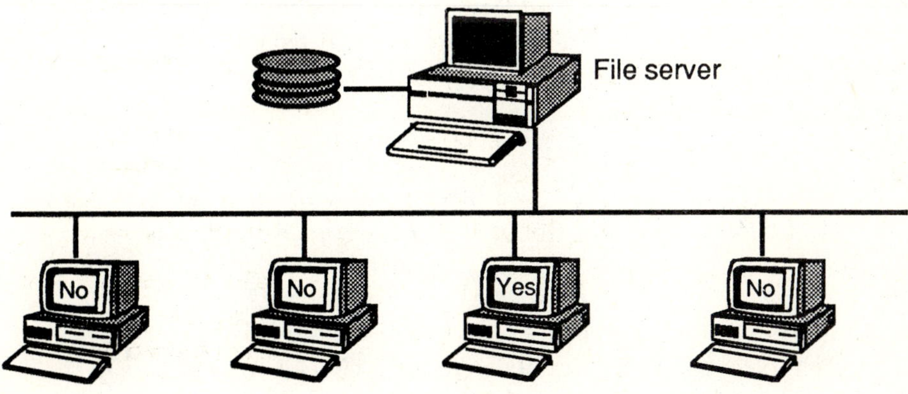

Fig. 1.3. When a record is locked, other users cannot update the record.

The word processor user and database users finish their work and store the data back on the hard disk. As the requests to write to disk are received, the file server gathers and answers them one at a time. In this way, data is stored safely.

In this example, the LAN has operated mostly in the background as an extension to the users' PC workstations. The LAN provides many of the capabilities of host-to-terminal systems, but the LAN connection does not force the PC to act as a terminal. PC workstations continue to function as personal computers, with the LAN providing extensions to the familiar PC environment.

The Development of Network Applications

The LAN was created as a cost-reduction tool for sharing expensive peripherals among PCs and reducing the overall cost of managing the resources of a computer system. The technology that evolved, however, resulted in broader implications for PCs in a networking environment.

In 1979, the price of the hard disk dropped significantly. Almost immediately, PC users began attaching their PCs (predominantly Apple computers) to the fast, convenient peripherals. Because many people did not need the high capacity offered by the hard disk, manufacturers were asked to provide a means of enabling several PCs to share a hard disk.

This need led to the introduction of a multiplexer device from Corvus called Constellation—the forerunner of today's LANs. Using a polling scheme to regulate PC access to a central hard disk, Constellation enabled several users to share that disk, dividing among them the disk's storage capacity and cost. (*Polling* is a mechanism in which machines are queried sequentially on the network to see whether they have requests.) The multiplexer polls each computer to which it is attached. When a transmitting computer is found, the message is taken and passed to the shared cable and hard disk (see fig. 1.4).

The next logical step was to share files on the same hard disk. The relatively simple sharing of equipment turned into the more complex process of sharing information. In fact, many people tried sharing files before the protections were created to allow for such activity. Some major problems had to be resolved concerning the way in which files could be shared.

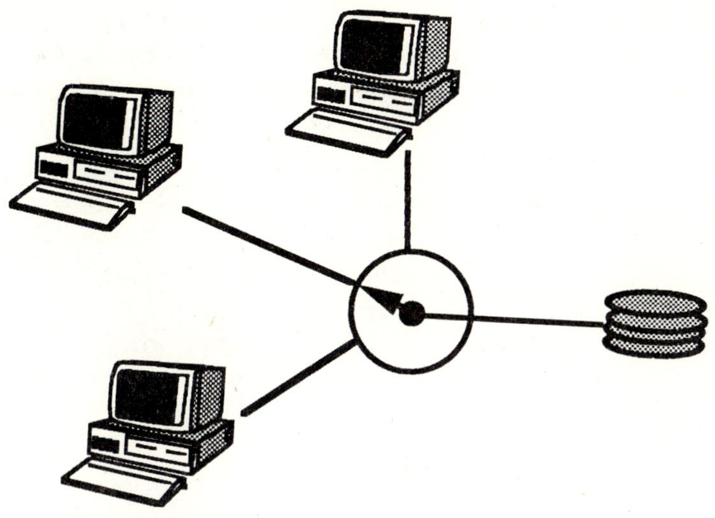

Fig. 1.4. The multiplexer was an early network scheme for sharing a hard disk among the attached personal computers.

The polling process gives several people access to one hard disk. A polling scheme, however, does not have a mechanism for security or data integrity. If one user places a file on the hard disk, another user can go in, read that information, and modify or delete the file. Such concepts as data organization, disk management, and information sharing are nearly impossible in this kind of free-for-all, shared environment.

Some of these issues were addressed when the disk server was introduced in the early 1980s. The *disk server* is a software program that runs on top of PC DOS (the IBM operating system for PC workstations) and provides a level of network management. Many LANs used this management approach before 1985. In a disk-server environment, PC workstations access the shared hard disk as if the disk is their own dedicated device. Input/output (I/O) requests to disk storage are redirected by disk server software to go out onto the network to the shared hard disk. The workstation operating system is tricked into thinking that it is talking to a local disk when, in reality, the disk is somewhere on the network.

Disk servers include many information-sharing facilities. In a multiuser environment in which people share information, two users cannot modify the same information at the same time without somebody's data being lost or corrupted. Methods were needed to enable people to work on the same information—but not simultaneously. Updating had to occur in a sequential manner.

One scheme to prevent simultaneous access is *file locking*. For most applications, only one person at a time needs to work on a particular file. In word processing, graphics, spreadsheets, and so forth, one person usually creates or modifies the data file and then offers the file to others to make modifications. File locking takes care of this situation. You can open and lock a file, and other users have to wait until you finish and unlock the file before they can access the data.

Another scheme that was developed for disk servers was *record locking*. An important concept in data management is availability. Data should be available for as much time as possible to all authorized users. File locking, of course, limits the amount of time that data is available. With many applications, that limitation is necessary. But with some applications—especially database applications—multiple users need access to the same file. For example, an inventory database file or a customer database file has many records, which are small, organized blocks of information. A person safely can modify one record in a database application while another person modifies another record. The integrity or reliability of the data is not threatened by such use.

These information-sharing schemes, new to PC LANs, held promise. Unfortunately, because of the inherent design of the disk server, sharing information without losing data integrity still was not possible. Disk servers are unable to synchronize disk access reliably in a multiuser environment. Each PC on the disk server network manages I/O down to the sector and block level on the shared hard disk. When the PCs write to disk, they write to the next available block. A common occurrence in a disk server network is for two or more machines to try to write to the same next available block. In that situation, the data written first is overwritten by the next write to the same block. No amount of file locking or record locking can prevent this problem, which is a *disk* management problem rather than a *data* management problem.

In 1983, Novell introduced a new management approach for LANs called *file service*. The file server software is a centralized system for managing disk I/O. While in a disk server environment, each PC manages its own disk I/O through low-level sector calls to disk. In the file server environment, PC workstations make high-level calls to the file server. A high-level call can be, for example, "open this file" or "write this data." The file server's job is to translate that call into a low-level call to the disk. For example, a low-level call can be a read or write to a particular sector on the disk.

The file server approach offers several advantages over the disk server. One advantage is that by forcing all disk I/O requests to go through the file server, the system can synchronize disk I/O. Data integrity is maintained because only one device is controlling the disk, and writes occur in a safe, sequential manner. Another advantage is that security is much better in a file server environment. All disk I/O requests must go through the file server software that maintains the security structure of the network. (Disk server systems enabled you to circumvent the security scheme and go directly to disk.)

Another important advantage of the file server is that its architecture enables dissimilar workstation operating systems to access the same disk and to share information. The file server accepts only high-level calls that provide a common language for operating systems; for example, "open this file" is a concept generally understood by all operating systems. This common language access scheme has led to the elimination of inconvenient disk partitions and to the capability of having a variety of workstations on the LAN. Disk partitions logically divide the disk into separate storage areas, often to accommodate dissimilar operating systems. This division permits hard disk sharing, but not information sharing, among the dissimilar systems.

In 1984, IBM and Microsoft adopted the file server approach to network management. Soon, most other vendors committed to this approach, giving LANs a level of data integrity equal to the data integrity of host-based systems.

The broad acceptance of file-server operating systems also had a major impact on network applications. Before the file server, applications developers were forced to include operating system-type functionality in their network applications, which required complex communications programming. Because every network vendor used a different channel to access the disk, developers had to write a different version of their application software for each network that they wanted to support.

IBM and Microsoft included features in PC DOS, beginning with Version 3.1, that forced the use of file server management and required the use of one specified channel between the application and the network. Any network vendor who wanted to be DOS-compatible had to follow these requirements that quickly became standards. From then on, applications developers could rely on a sturdy network operating system platform for their applications and no longer had to include low-level communication's codes in the applications. The result was an increase in the number of applications for PC networking. Tens of thousands of applications software packages currently run on LANs.

Chapter Summary

Local area networks are high-speed communication systems. These systems are designed to support intelligent workstations, commonly known as personal computers. LAN technology has matured to provide secure ways of handling multiple PCs, each of which is processing data. The access to a shared hard disk is controlled by management software called the file server, which ensures coordinated access.

Data sharing is enabled by locking mechanisms to prevent simultaneous updates that might destroy some data. File locking enables only one user at at time to update a locked file. Record locking permits users to work within the same file, such as a database, but when a user locks a record within the file, only that user can modify the locked area.

In the development of LANs, the popularity of the PC workstation was the initial catalyst. The file server operating system provided good security and data integrity. Standardization, the topic of Chapter 3, gave LANs yet another critical component—high-quality applications—as LANs began to challenge host-based computer systems.

2

Communications and Standards

LANs today are based on important standards. If you are going to be involved in selecting and maintaining a LAN, you need to be familiar with these standards and the way they fit with the overall communications design.

Understanding the Types of Computer Systems

The rules by which communication takes place in a computer system are called *protocols*. A protocol specifies who talks to whom, what they can say to each other, and how they can say it. Speed of communications, electrical characteristics, use of shared resources, message length and addressing, and many more variables are all defined within computer protocols.

The protocols that have the most visible influence on computer systems are the high-level, application protocols. These protocols define the relationships of nodes on the network. Perhaps the best analogy to how protocols work is a political system. Consider three political systems: a monarchy, a democracy, and a republic.

In a monarchy, one person rules. The ruler usually allows a few high-ranking subordinates a little power to accomplish limited tasks, but all real power resides at the top. Another way to describe the system is as strictly hierarchical, with controlling power at the top, limited power at the middle layer, and almost no power at the bottom.

A democracy, in its purest form, makes everybody equal. Nobody has more power than anybody else. Everybody is considered equally intelligent and equally capable. In a democracy, no rank exists, and any citizen might do any job.

A republic is a representative system. The people choose certain individuals with special capabilities to act on their behalf. These representatives serve the people.

Not surprisingly, computer systems have been designed along lines similar to these familiar political systems. The three most common computer systems are host-to-terminal, peer-to-peer, and client-server, and they closely resemble their political counterparts.

A *host-to-terminal* system is like a monarchy. The host has nearly all the power. Intelligent subordinates, such as departmental minicomputers, can do some jobs, but the host runs the network. The lowest entity in this hierarchical system is the terminal workstation. It has no intelligence (or very little) and must rely on the host machine for all its processing, even down to interpreting the simplest keystroke.

A *peer-to-peer* system is the computer version of a democracy. Nodes are treated as intelligent equals. When mainframes or minicomputers pass data back and forth, they use peer-to-peer protocols.

Because they are networks of intelligent machines, LANs used to be referred to as peer-to-peer systems. Some LANs are designed to let every node participate in network management. Some of these systems also enable nodes to share their resources with any other node.

Another type of LAN environment, however, has become much more popular. This LAN uses the *client-server* system, the "representative" system in the political example. In a client-server network, clients typically are intelligent workstations (PCs) that perform many of their own processing functions. When the client needs additional resources, such as data not stored locally or some special processing capability, the client sends a request onto the network to a server. The server answers the request for the client.

Each of these computer systems has a different impact on how computing resources are used. In most cases, the client-server protocol is the most efficient for several reasons.

Host-to-terminal protocols were created at a time when computer processors were extremely expensive. To be economical, one processor had to support many people using dumb terminals. Today, the cost of processors has declined to the point that intelligent workstations are as inexpensive as dumb terminals. The cost efficiency of host-to-terminal protocols, therefore, has diminished. In a host-to-terminal system, every request must exit the workstation and use some communication resources of the network. The requests go to the host computer where they add to the overhead on the mainframe.

By contrast, client-server protocols are designed for optimal use of distributed intelligent workstations. The workstation, or client, uses its own resources for most processing. Only when the workstation's local resources are not sufficient does it send a request to the network.

The typical peer-to-peer protocol was designed for transferring large files from one host computer to another. Such communications involve one request and one response. But, this type of traffic is not what you see in a true distributed environment with intelligent workstations. When intelligent workstations are generating requests, many requests usually go to a few machines. Where peer-to-peer types of protocols have been used on LANs, performance has suffered because the protocols were not optimized for handling multiple requests. Reliability also declines when no special-purpose machine is placed in control of shared resources (see Chapter 1's discussion of the disk server and file server).

Seeking a Hardware Standard

Until 1985, most of the focus for standardization in LANs had been on a *hardware standard*. Several LAN vendors were able to point to relatively large installed bases and claim that their hardware would become the industry standard, but no LAN hardware system emerged as the clear-cut winner. IBM's minimal presence in the LAN business further complicated the situation. Even if Omninet, EtherNet, and ARCnet were widely used, IBM was quite capable of coming out with a new system and establishing it as the LAN standard. Large corporations and systems integrators found this situation unstable. If they adopted a particular type of hardware, which then proved to be nonstandard, the mistake could cost many thousands of dollars in hardware, wiring, and labor.

For example, suppose that a large company decided to install a single-channel coaxial cable LAN throughout the firm's building. A short while later, IBM introduces a hardware system based on twisted-pair cable and an entirely different wiring design. If the LAN industry and third-party hardware and software developers accept the IBM system as the new standard, they will produce few or no technological upgrades for the coaxial system. In a short time, the company would be forced to install a new system compatible with the new hardware standard. This potential problem prevented many companies from installing a LAN until a standard was declared.

As a hardware standard was being sought, however, people began to notice the shortcomings of such a standard. A hardware standard, as defined by its proponents, means that everyone uses the same type of LAN cable, the same topology (cable layout scheme), the same cable-access method, and the same message format. If such a standard became a reality, everyone would use this generalized LAN hardware solution. The many other LAN hardware alternatives would disappear.

The problem is that LAN hardware cannot be cross-optimized—no one type of hardware is best for all situations. One department may find that ARCnet gives adequate performance and is preferable because of its reliability and relatively low cost. Another department in the same company may be willing to pay more for a token-ring network because it delivers faster performance and is somewhat easier than ARCnet to manage in large sites.

LAN vendors confirmed the need for multiple types of LAN hardware by starting to offer their systems with a choice of cabling. Novell began supporting its NetWare operating system to run on LAN hardware from other vendors. IBM, which had been slow to enter the LAN market, became active and within a year was selling several different cabling schemes. Other vendors followed suit. Today, almost all LAN vendors support more than one type of cable. Some generic standards, however, do exist. For example, most hardware topologies that run on coaxial cable also can run on twisted-pair cabling. Rather than adopt a single, general-purpose LAN hardware as part of a hardware standard, LAN vendors began to provide *hardware independence*.

Hardware independence sounds like an idea that is exactly the opposite of standards. Much of the credit for hardware independence and for other types of independence, however, must be given to the standardization bodies, especially the International Standards Organization and the Institute of Electrical and Electronic Engineers (IEEE). Members of these groups come from industry, government, academia, and large user organizations. To see how this situation has come about, you need to understand the International Standards Organization's Open System Interconnection (OSI) Reference Model. The model is the basic framework for LAN design, and most LANs are designed in accordance with the model.

The International Standards Organization, ISO, exists to produce international specifications. Because communications always have been an important area for ISO, the organization developed a model to define a conceptual architecture of communications systems: the OSI Reference Model.

Understanding the OSI Reference Model

The OSI Reference Model divides the communication process into a hierarchy of seven interdependent functional layers (see fig. 2.1). Each layer is responsible for carrying out different functions. The services that each layer supplies are defined by a range of standards. A range of standards allows for different ways of performing the same service, which is vital if different users' needs are to be met.

The layers of the Reference Model define the functions of a complete communications network from the cable (Physical Layer) to the network application software (Application Layer). Each layer has a built-in interface to the adjacent layer. Layer 2 can pass data

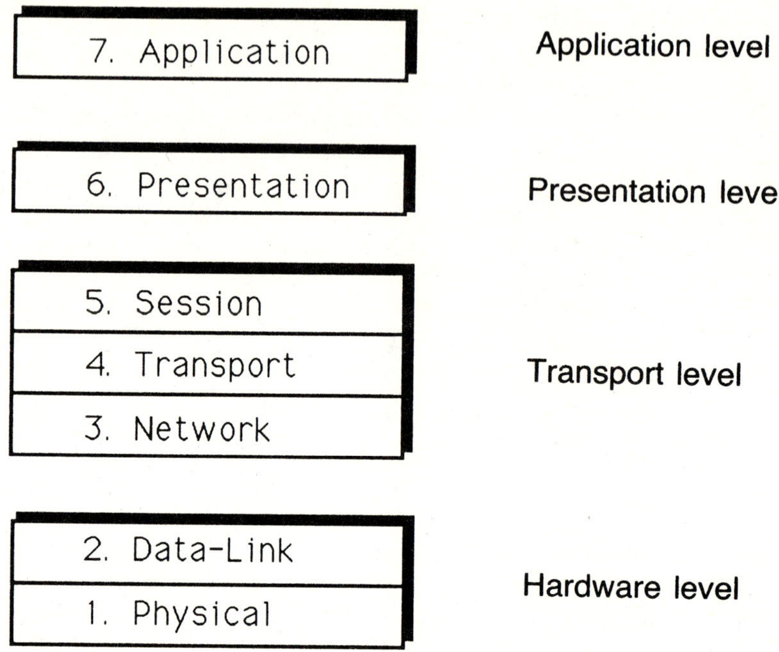

Fig. 2.1. The seven-layer OSI Reference Model.

to Layer 3 or Layer 1, but Layer 1 cannot communicate directly with Layer 3.

The OSI Reference Model does not establish or promote any particular communication technique (protocol). The model's definitions are broad enough to include many protocols.

Layer 1: Physical

The Physical Layer defines the *physical connection* between the PC and the network communications system. This connection is partly mechanical, including the cables and connectors. The connection also is electrical, with specified modulation techniques and voltages. The *bandwidth* (speed) of the cable transmission is defined at this layer, as is the *topology* (physical layout). (Topologies are discussed in detail in Chapter 5, "LAN Hardware.")

Layer 2: Data-Link

The Data-Link Layer defines the network *access-control mechanism*. The formats used in network message units also are defined in this layer. LANs do not send messages as a continuous stream but break them up into one or more *packets*, or message units. Each packet carries the address of its source and destination, along with some error-detection mechanisms.

Layer 3: Network

The Network Layer defines the *switching and routing* of information between networks. *Network management*, including the relay of status information to PCs, and the regulation of packet flow also are established in Layer 3.

Layer 4: Transport

The Transport Layer defines *network addressing* (the physical location of devices on the network) and the way in which connections between parties can be linked and unlinked. Layer 4 also defines the way in which guaranteed message delivery takes place on the network—by numbering packets (message units) and ensuring that they arrive in order with no omissions or duplications. Internetwork routes are managed at this level.

Layer 5: Session

The Session Layer's primary function is to define an application interface to the Transport Layer. One of the services handled at this layer is the mapping of names to network addresses so that applications can use names to communicate with devices.

Layer 6: Presentation

The Presentation Layer defines the *translation* of formats and syntax from an application to the network. Layer 6 specifies the manner in which software applications can enter the network.

Layer 7: Application

The Application Layer defines the *network applications* that support end-user applications. The network operating system is defined primarily at this level, as are many network utility programs. User applications, such as word processing, are not part of this layer; in fact, that level of functionality is not defined within the OSI Reference Model.

Using the Model

A layered architecture usually is not the most efficient choice, in terms of performance, for system design. A single, monolithic communications system can be designed with less code, fewer redundant activities, and faster speed.

The reasons for following the OSI layered approach are migration and flexibility. The layered modularity has led to *hardware independence*, as mentioned earlier. You no longer need to change everything in a communications system just because one component of the system has been superseded by newer technology.

Using the layered model, new technology can replace old technology with a minimum of other changes and cost. For example, if a new type of cable (Physical Layer) is superior to the old cable, you can replace the old cable without making other modifications to the layers above the Physical Layer. This feat is possible because products that follow the OSI model must include the same functionality in a particular layer.

Although this example mentions replacing one implementation at the Physical Layer with another, the Physical Layer and the Data-Link Layer are seldom separated in practice. Most products that provide the communications functions defined by the model cover multiple layers. For this reason, the layers of the model are frequently grouped according to their general functions. This grouping is a closer representation of real products.

Layers 1 and 2 are the hardware layers, providing the fundamental connection on which more sophisticated services are built. At the hardware level, the three general protocols in common use are *EtherNet*, *token-bus*, and *token-ring*. They have been defined by the

802 Committee of the Institute of Electrical and Electronic Engineers (IEEE). Often, a protocol is referred to by its IEEE 802 classification: 802.3 for EtherNet, 802.4 for token-bus, and 802.5 for token-ring. ARCnet is not defined by an 802 specification but is nonetheless a popular, widely used hardware topology. (See Chapter 5 for more information on topologies.)

Layers 3, 4, and 5 combine to form the network's *transport level* that contains the software controlling network communications. This level also is known as the *subnet* (see the discussion in the following section).

In a network, cables are attached to every device, creating a web of physical connections. Actual communications, however, usually involve only two devices: the sender and the receiver. Software at the transport level establishes and manages the temporary link between sender and receiver. This temporary link is called a *virtual connection* to distinguish it from a physical connection.

The transport level defines one of two critical application-to-network interfaces. An *application-to-network interface* is a point at which an application can attach to the network. Some applications, especially communications-intensive ones such as communications gateways, need point-to-point communications services. These applications usually attach to the network at Layer 5.

The Presentation Layer, Layer 6, is the other application-to-network interface. Almost all software application programs should attach to the network through this layer. Layer 7, as discussed earlier, defines network applications.

Seeking Software Standards—the Subnet

Several subnet implementations are prevalent on PC LANs, and the number appears to be growing. Each of these subnets has its own set of advantages. Novell's IPX/SPX (Internet Packet Exchange/Sequenced Packet Exchange) is based on Xerox Network Systems (XNS) and is the most widely used PC LAN subnet. IPX/SPX's primary advantage is its high performance. Designed for communications among multiple networks (internetworking),

IPX/SPX also is a small program that takes approximately 30K of memory at the workstation. The program is not, however, supported outside the PC LAN environment.

IPX/SPX was developed at a time when no LAN subnet standard existed. (XNS was a specification but not a usable product.) IBM's NetBIOS (Network Basic Input and Output System) was announced in 1984. At that time, IBM declared that future network products from IBM also would support NetBIOS. Given this endorsement, many LAN companies began offering NetBIOS-compatibility as their only subnet solution or as an option.

NetBIOS's main advantage is its endorsement as an IBM standard. NetBIOS is slow, difficult to write to, inefficient for internetworking, and requires significant amounts of memory in the workstations (approximately 80K). NetBIOS is supported mainly in the PC LAN environment.

IBM has another subnet implementation called LU6.2, or Application-Program-to-Program Communications (APPC). LU6.2, like NetBIOS, is strategic among IBM's products and will be supported in future IBM product releases. The difference is that LU6.2 is supported outside the PC LAN environment with implementations on IBM mainframes and minicomputers. The large size of LU6.2 (280K at the workstation) limits its value within a LAN because little memory is left for applications.

LU6.2's advantage is its capability for use between the LAN and other systems. LU6.2 is one of the first subnet protocols designed for communications among intelligent processes outside the LAN. By assuming intelligence at either end of the communications link, LU6.2 eliminates terminal control codes, reducing the amount of traffic and significantly lowering the overall cost of wide-area communications. (Terminal control codes instruct the terminal in how to handle and display data. Because PCs, with their built-in intelligence, know much of the information provided by the control codes, they can be omitted in host-to-PC communications.)

As LANs enter big corporations, the trend is to replace LAN-based subnets with mainframe subnets such as DECnet, TCP/IP, and IBM DLC (Data Link Control). This movement enables user organizations to standardize on one subnet protocol. This trend has led vendors to support multiple subnets. Many companies in the LAN industry are moving toward protocol independence of their operating systems so that the services they create will run across whatever subnet the user wants.

Understanding Systems Application Architecture (SAA)

IBM has two issues in dealing with protocols; one is external, and the other is internal. Externally, IBM products do not make any overt concession to other companies' protocols for compatibility. Users, therefore, must rely on third-party developers to provide interconnection strategies or on companies to develop IBM-compatible products. Because of the size of IBM's presence in the marketplace, these strategies have resulted in widespread integration of IBM and non-IBM products.

The Open Systems Interconnection (OSI) protocols have been the one non-IBM technology with which IBM has sought compliance. As noted in the following section, OSI now is well-defined and well-supported by users, and IBM appears intent on not being excluded from this new market. IBM supports several OSI protocols, including X.25 and X.400.

The other protocol issue for IBM is the internal one. IBM manufactures many hardware platforms, and few of them are compatible with each other. IBM has many communication and data format protocols and, again, few of these are compatible with each other. The growing, distributed computing market has made this lack of compatibility a major problem for IBM customers. Customers who buy IBM computers often move to mainframes, or other minis and PCs, only to discover that the systems cannot communicate with each other.

To handle internal compatibility, IBM announced Systems Application Architecture (SAA) in 1987. The goal of SAA is to provide a framework for the development of consistent applications across future offerings in the three major IBM computing environments: System/370 (TSO/E under MVS/VA, and CMS under VM), System/3X, and OS/2.

Unlike the other protocols discussed in this chapter, SAA is not a single protocol. Instead, SAA is a collection of software interfaces, conventions, and protocols that IBM says will be part of this new architecture.

SAA compatibility is aimed at the following four areas:

- ❑ Programming interface
- ❑ User access
- ❑ Communications support
- ❑ Applications

For the common programming interface, certain languages are specified. These languages include C, COBOL, and FORTRAN. If developers want to be SAA compliant, they must use one of these languages to build applications. (The fact that several languages are included in the standard, and that they cannot communicate directly with each other points to the difficulty of achieving standardization.)

The common user access (CUA) in SAA offers a standard for the machine/application and the user to communicate with each other. Key selection and mouse movements are part of the CUA as are the way in which information is displayed to the user. CUA requires physical consistency (keyboard layout and other input devices), syntactical consistency (sequence of display elements and user requests), and semantic consistency (words and commands). To be consistent in each area, the definitions and designs need to be identical across all systems.

Common communications support (CCS) is the plan for interconnecting applications, systems, networks, and devices. While IBM indicates that new architectures may be selected in the future, the ones now part of CCS are Systems Network Architecture (SNA) and specified international standards.

The types of support under CCS are data streams (3270 Data Stream, Document Content Architecture, and Intelligent Printer Data Stream), application services (SNA Distribution Services, Document Interchange Architecture, and SNA Network Management Architecture), session services (LU type 6.2), network (Low-Entry Networking Nodes type 2.1), and data-link controls (Synchronous Data Link Control, Token-Ring Network, and X.25).

Common applications, under the SAA standard, are applications written by IBM that conform to all other aspects of SAA. Like other parts of SAA, the conforming applications will be consistent across all systems.

SAA specifies four types of interfaces: database, dialog, presentation, and query. The database interface is Structured Query Language (SQL). SQL already is an important standard recognized by ANSI and supported by many vendors including IBM. (IBM's reinforcement of this standard through SAA acceptance is standardization at its best.) The query manager is related directly to the database interface, providing the services to build queries and the resulting reports.

The *dialog interface* manages the way that information is used by the application and displayed or made available. The presentation interface expands upon the user interface definition. Actual implementation of the presentation interface is seen in the Presentation Manager of OS/2 and is consistent with other user interfaces now seen throughout IBM systems. Many third-party developers have endorsed the Presentation Manager interface. The Presentation Manager's icons, pull-down menus, windows, and other data presentation techniques are workstation standards. The success of the popular Apple Macintosh user interface, which the Presentation Manager closely resembles, confirms that users want this kind of interface. The Presentation Manager interface probably will remain the standard through many evolutions of technology and into the 21st century.

IBM describes SAA as an emerging set of specifications. Many of SAA's current goals probably will not be realized until the mid-1990s, but SAA already has become a powerful force in computing through such technologies as LU6.2 and the Presentation Manager.

OSI Protocols

The OSI Reference Model has been an important force in the standardization of how communications networks are designed. Adherence to the reference model, however, does not mean that one vendor's products can communicate with another vendor's products. The reference model specifies only a layered architecture and defines functions at each layer. The model does not specify how those functions must be performed. That level of definition requires a defined implementation (protocol) for each layer. The OSI committees around the world have begun to recommend specific protocols with the goal of interoperability (the capability to operate among all compliant systems).

Complete OSI compliance requires adoption of a full suite of protocols, from the Physical Layer up to the Application Layer of the OSI Reference Model. A suite of protocols also is called a profile. Europe has led the way in the definition and adoption of OSI profiles. Many other governments, however, including the United States, are committed to OSI migration.

When governments make such a commitment, they often require civilian contractors to comply. With the endorsements of governments, their militaries, and civilian contractors, OSI has become a major standard of the 1990s. Realizing the size of the market, many computer vendors have begun to supply OSI-compliant products and strategies. Many other vendors promise to move in that direction.

Several standards groups are evaluating and approving OSI profiles. Those groups with the most influence on the ultimate profile selection are the Government Open Systems Interconnection Profile (GOSIP) groups sponsored by various governments around the world. Over time, the other standards groups probably will migrate their profiles to GOSIP compliance.

Understanding the UK GOSIP Architectural Model

The United Kingdom GOSIP committee is among the most influential of all the GOSIP groups. This committee is issuing specifications every four years to update OSI progress and to provide a direction for organizations committed to OSI compliance. In the 1988 specification, UK GOSIP published the architectural model shown in figure 2.2. This model shows the relationships of the major OSI components that are defined and those components that are under study.

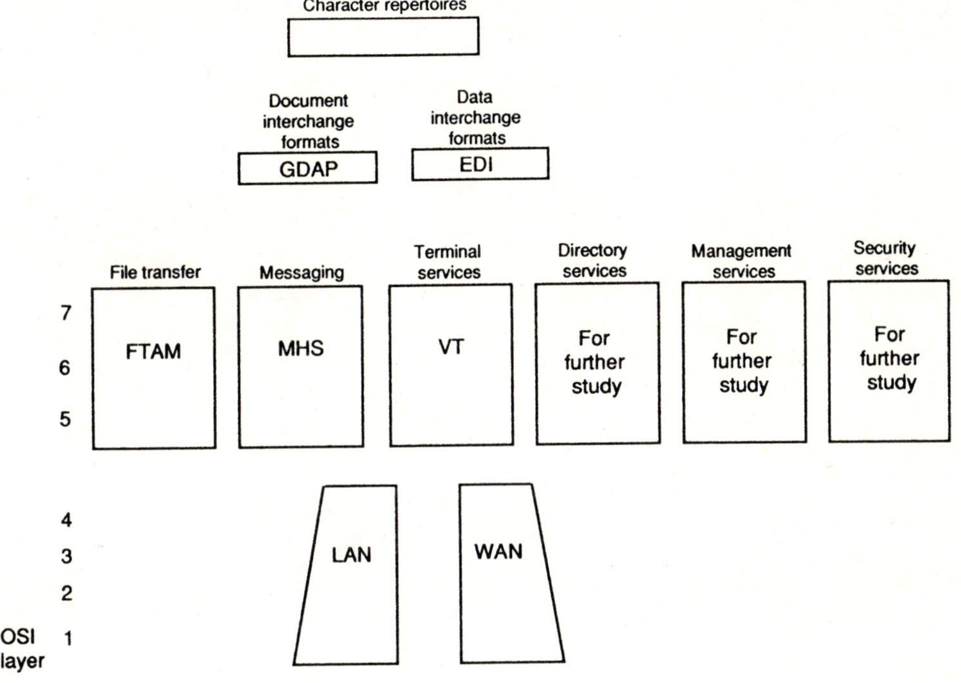

Fig. 2.2. The UK GOSIP Architectural Model.

Character Repertoires

At the highest level of the model are the character repertoires, including semantic specifications, character encoding, and control functions. Character repertoires are tied to support interchange formats and the transfer mechanisms. Character repertoires should be designed so that characters can be carried by the transfer mechanisms without the necessity of character conversion at any stage.

Interchange Formats

The next level of the model contains the interchange formats. Government Document Application Profile (GDAP) is one of the two approved formats. GDAP is based on the ISO standard for Office Document Architecture (ODA) and Office Document Interchange Format (ODIF). Standardization at this level permits documents to be passed among compliant environments and processed or revised as necessary. Precise layout standards are not defined in the current specification, but layout specifications, desktop publishing specifications, and graphics standards will be part of future standards.

Electronic Data Interchange (EDI) is the other approved format, although this format is classified as "not fully specified" in the 1988 specification. The GOSIP-approved definition of EDI is "the transfer of structured data, by agreed message standards, from computer to computer, by electronic means." Structured data is intended for further computer processing and usually is character-based text. Unstructured data is intended for direct interpretation by end users; the format does not permit easy manipulation by computers. Facsimile is an example of unstructured data. Unstructured data may eventually be included in the EDI specification.

The purpose of the EDI specification is to standardize business communications for transactions such as trade data interchange, electronic funds transfer, and interactive applications (for example, reservation systems). Through EDI standardization, most forms of business communications can occur across data networks, which will improve speed and efficiency of the communications.

File Transfer Access and Management Systems

The levels so far are above and beyond the scope of the OSI Reference Model. In the GOSIP architectural model, the next level encompasses the top three layers of the OSI Model (Layers 5, 6, and 7). The services at this level are file transfer, messaging, terminal, directory, management, and security services.

The GOSIP protocol for file transfer is File Transfer Access and Management (FTAM) systems. FTAM does not define the user interface; FTAM has no component that corresponds to IBM's SAA Presentation Manager. FTAM defines a file transfer utility program, a programmatic interface, and an integrated application. The file transfer utility program enables the system to store and forward transfers, such as screen transfers, common in host-to-terminal environments and other batch-oriented transfers.

The programmatic interface under GOSIP is concerned primarily with maintenance of security. Issues such as language selection are considered outside the GOSIP FTAM specification. The application programs specification states that access control and other FTAM compliant issues must be satisfied by the application. The issues of functionality, user interface, machine control, and so forth, are unspecified.

Messaging

Messaging is defined by the Message Handling Systems (MHS). GOSIP MHS is based on the CCITT X.400 specification that has been stable since 1984. MHS is designed to support an electronic messaging service based on store-and-forward messaging. MHS's primary functions include delivery to one or multiple recipients, notification to originator of delivery or non-delivery, automatic forwarding, and redirection.

Figure 2.3 shows the functional model of MHS that contains several agents designed to package, transfer, and unpackage the message at the recipient's station. The process is included in the MHS environment separated from electronic-mail applications. Because these applications use MHS functions as an underlying communications service, developers do not need to develop these services.

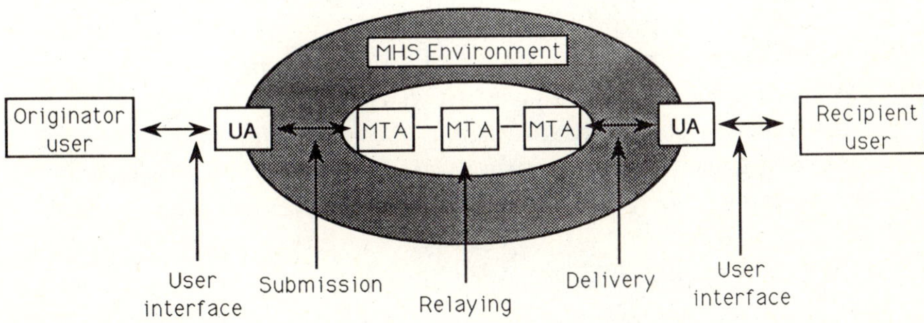

Fig. 2.3. The MHS Model includes several interface and transfer points. Processing is handled by user-agents (UA) and message-transfer agents (MTA).

Developers must write an interface to the set of MHS services—a process that in the current MHS specification is complex and time consuming. GOSIP MHS (the CCITT X.400 specification) is still one of the most important of all modern standards. As the application programming interface is standardized and simplified and as applications begin to support the interface, MHS will improve greatly the world's ability to communicate via data-based electronic mail. (X.400 also is discussed in Chapter 11, "Electronic Mail.")

Terminal Services

Terminal services in the GOSIP architecture are defined in the ISO Virtual Terminal (VT) protocol. Virtual terminal supports two modes of operation. One mode is Forms—a paged, full-screen display. The other mode is Paged—a subset of the Forms mode. Under Paged mode, data display is not restricted to a set number of lines as in Forms mode but may be of any length supported by the terminal display.

Directory, Management, and Security Services

Listed at the same level of the GOSIP Architecture Model are directory services, management services, and security services. None of these specifications are defined completely as of the 1988 specification. The fact that these services are included in the model, however, shows what area GOSIP eventually will cover.

Directory services are probably the best defined of this group. When these services are completely defined, they will be published as CCITT X.500 and adopted as an OSI protocol. The primary function of this protocol is a common addressing scheme to simplify the finding and using of network information. This protocol also will isolate the user from physical changes in network addresses of resources. This latter capability is enabled by referring to objects by name rather than by network address. Mapping is performed by the directory.

The Network Level

The next level of the GOSIP architecture, the network level, includes OSI Reference Model Layers 1 through 4. Two types of systems are noted at this level, LANs and wide area networks (WANs).

On the wide area network side of the model, X.25 is the dominant protocol. X.25 is a network subnet standard presented in 1980 and extensively used for wide area communications.

On the LAN side of the model, GOSIP has approved two fundamental standards: Carrier Sense, Multiple Access with Collision Detection (CSMA/CD); and Token Ring. CSMA/CD in this specification conforms to the IEEE 802.3 EtherNet specification.

One of the major issues at the network level is the use of connection-oriented or connectionless protocols. Connection-oriented protocols commonly are known as virtual circuit service. (X.25 is a connection-oriented protocol.) With connection-oriented protocols, stations set up a circuit prior to the actual broadcast of the message. Two station circuits are most common, but multiple stations also can communicate. Broadcasting also is supported by connection-oriented protocols. The connection-oriented service provides for correct sequencing of data, guaranteed delivery through error recovery, and data flow control.

Connectionless protocols also are known as datagram systems. In this type of service, delivery of message packets is not guaranteed and confirmations are not sent. The responsibility for proper message receipt rests on the particular sender and receiver.

A connectionless protocol is particularly useful in a local environment where the cable and hardware in the system are of high-quality. A connectionless protocol is much faster in a high-quality network than a connection-oriented protocol, because the connectionless protocol sends fewer messages. In a system of poor or varying quality, however, the connection-oriented system is preferable.

Complying with OSI Protocols

The decision of whether to move a company's data processing networks and computers to OSI protocol compliance is a major issue with long-term ramifications.

The broad government and international support for OSI does not mean that end users should abruptly move to OSI. Governments have good reasons for needing OSI—reasons that do not necessarily have similar importance within businesses. Governments' computing needs are so complex that they need standards to avoid total confusion. Businesses, on the other hand, have more narrowly defined objectives and fewer people with policy-making authority. These differences may make it feasible for businesses to avoid generic solutions in favor of optimized ones.

The OSI Protocol suite is a group of generic communications solutions, aimed at covering a broad range of requirements. Because many of these standards are thorough and rigorously defined to improve the likelihood of computer interoperability, the result is high software overhead and usually slow performance. These elaborate requirements also can increase the cost of hardware and software by necessitating faster processors, more memory, and so forth.

OSI's primary benefit is in connecting dissimilar systems. These systems may be computers or communications networks. For example, the need to integrate with several other companies' electronic mail systems or with public data networks for wide area communications is much easier to satisfy using OSI systems. Within a company or a department, however, OSI compliance may be inappropriate.

A small-to-mid-sized company probably can avoid OSI compliance and concentrate instead on price/performance issues. A larger company or any company that needs data communications with the outside world also may avoid complete OSI compliance.

Today and probably for years to come, the most practical strategy for organizations to adopt an OSI compliance is a migration plan. While many organizations should not implement OSI protocols for a variety of price, performance, and functionality reasons, every organization should have a plan in place to achieve OSI compliance.

Almost any organization abruptly could find itself in the position of needing OSI compliance. Without a planned migration path in these situations, the cost of non-compliance and the cost of replacing an entire system would both be unacceptable.

Fortunately, many computer and systems vendors offer useful strategies for connecting existing hardware and software into an OSI-compliant system. As OSI installations become commonplace, more and more vendors will follow suit. End users should make sure that such a migration strategy is available to them.

The speed with which OSI protocols are adopted by end users faces several roadblocks. A lack of full specification, lack of applications, and lack of desired functionality are some of the problems that must be overcome. One of the biggest shortcomings of OSI protocols to date is the focus on host-to-terminal architectures. FTAM and OSI standardization began in an era where host-to-terminal systems were the only widely used computer networks. OSI protocols, therefore, have been designed to support large numbers of transmissions, short-length transmissions, and relatively slow transmission speeds.

These specifications are very different from the conditions in a client-server network. In a client-server network, transmissions usually are fewer in number, but larger in size and much faster.

3

Examining the Alternatives

Does your office need a local area network? Can stand-alone personal computers perform the same functions as networked PCs but without the expense of a LAN? You should examine these and other important issues before you start installing cables in your office.

Why Connect to a Network?

Sharing expensive peripherals is often given as the primary reason for networking, but expense alone may not be sufficient reason to install a LAN. With today's rapidly declining hardware costs, you easily can dedicate inexpensive peripherals.

Small PC-mounted hard disk drives are getting less expensive as their capacities increase. As a result, the local hard disk is becoming commonplace and frequently is dedicated to a single PC. Printers also are more affordable. Some dot-matrix printers are so inexpensive that many companies automatically buy a printer with every PC they purchase.

The basic issue of sharing also is questionable. Do people really want to share? A large part of the appeal and acceptance of the personal computer has been that the computer is not shared—it is available for *personal* use. You may like the idea of having a large, fast hard disk, and sharing the disk may seem an ideal way to justify the expense. When three or four people start using that hard disk, however, its speed quickly can slow to that of a local floppy drive.

These considerations are serious, but they are only part of the picture. When viewed as a system, a LAN has some powerful arguments in its favor. In most cases, organizations with multiple PCs should network them for the following reasons:

- *Sharing peripherals reduces their per-user cost.* Frequently, a higher-quality peripheral can be justified as a shared resource, resulting in improved speed and quality and increased mean time between failures. Sharing in a properly designed LAN improves the entire system's reliability. When a device fails, another one is ready to fill the void while repairs are being made.

- *Excellent response times can be achieved through a properly selected and configured LAN.* The LAN's performance always should equal or surpass that of a stand-alone PC.

  The cable speeds (bandwidths) of all the LANs discussed in this book far exceed the speed of the PC with its Intel 8088 or 80286 microprocessor. For many applications, the PC, not the LAN, is the bottleneck. Because a LAN is by definition a multiple-processor system, sharing the processing load across several microprocessors—a version of parallel processing—is possible. For example, many people in a workgroup may work on the same report or the same database, with each person using a dedicated processor. The result is that the aggregate processing power of the LAN is applied to the workgroup's activity. You may not be able to speed up a single processor, but you can speed up the results. This advantage of distributed processing is unique and highly significant.

  The speed with which a request is answered is a crucial factor in computing. After all, most jobs performed by a computer can be done with pencil and paper. When you buy a computer, you are buying speed more than capability.

  Keep in mind, though, that better response time through a LAN is not guaranteed. In fact, inefficient implementation of

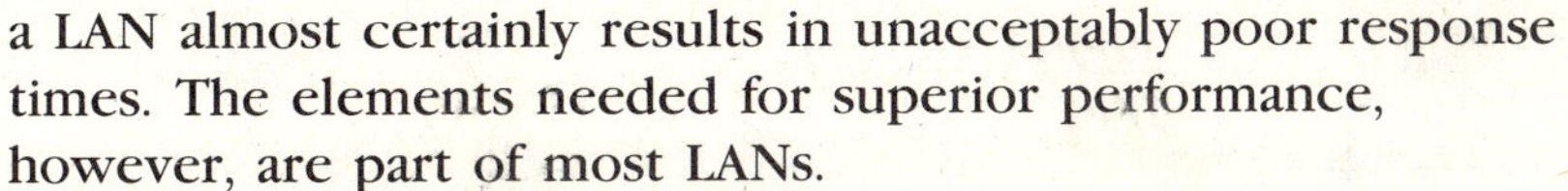

a LAN almost certainly results in unacceptably poor response times. The elements needed for superior performance, however, are part of most LANs.

- *In addition to sharing peripherals, the PC LAN enables users to share applications software.* First, this sharing offers a cost advantage. Many software vendors offer network versions that can be shared legally by several people on the LAN. Usually, the per-user cost is much lower than the cost of buying individual packages.

  Second, when applications software is stored on a central hard disk, supporting and maintaining that software is much easier. When a new version of a software program is adopted in the office, the old version is removed from the hard disk and replaced by the new version. Making the same change on many stand-alone PCs is more time-consuming, and the transition often is confusing and only partially implemented. Some users invariably continue to use their old software, a practice that may complicate support and reduce compatibility.

- *LANs permit users to share information and communicate.* Sometimes this communication occurs without the user being aware of the process. For example, several people may be working on the LAN with an inventory program—stocking, selling, and shipping goods. As each entry is updated, the information instantly is available to every person on the network.

- *Networking is a communications mechanism that ties the isolated PC into the organization.* The organizational benefit of LANs often is overlooked during evaluation. Departments, companies, corporations, and institutions are all organizations—a term that implies interaction and teamwork. Without a LAN, a PC is a powerful but isolated device. Because a PC's output is difficult to integrate into the organization's mainstream, its value is limited.

  The capability to integrate PCs through the LAN encourages continuity and compatibility so that administrative chores can be systematized. For example, the task of backing up data can be assigned to a particular individual rather than left as an afterthought to each employee.

What Kind of Network Is Best?

The preceding discussion illustrates the reasons for connecting PCs into a network. The next question is what kind of a network is best? You can partially answer this question by examining the issue of resource management.

Where computers are concerned, people sometimes get too heavily involved in the "miracles" of the technology. In business, a primary consideration usually is the net cost of the output. The manager of a computing system manages three resources for cost efficiency: processors, peripherals, and personnel.

You can reduce the use of any one of these resources by increasing the use of one or both of the other two resources. For example, the processor (PC) was brought into businesses to increase the efficiency of personnel. The same job can be done with more people and fewer processors or with fewer people and more processors. Additional peripherals also reduce personnel downtime, incurred as people wait for a report to be printed or for data to be delivered to the local PC from the hard disk.

The relative costs of these three resources change continually. A few years ago, units of processing power were quite expensive. Now the evolution of the microprocessor has made processing perhaps the least expensive of the three resources. Processing is certainly cheaper than personnel. For this reason, using intelligent, processor-equipped PCs as workstations is possible and cost-effective.

As processors have declined in cost, so have peripherals. Each character-per-second printer output and each byte of hard disk storage are much less expensive than they were just a few months ago.

In the computing system, personnel time has become the most expensive resource, and the cost gap is widening. This expense generally justifies the purchase of more PCs and high-performance peripherals.

The ideal balance is unique to each organization. High performance is relative, as are the hourly costs of personnel. A LAN exploits the low cost of processors by permitting each user to have a dedicated processor (PC), thereby guaranteeing good and dependable response time. At the same time, a multiuser environment in which peripherals are shared reduces the total cost of those peripherals. Most importantly, a LAN enables you to tailor system performance to your organization's individual needs.

Using PCs in a Host System

The processing power of early computers was extremely expensive. To get the most value from the system, users attached many terminal-type workstations to the system. In that way, many people could share the expensive resource.

As processing power became less expensive, businesses brought processors closer to end users by installing relatively small departmental processors called minicomputers. Minicomputers, however, have limitations. Their applications software is expensive, and they are difficult for the average person to use. System performance often is inadequate because the minicomputer must provide all the processing power for the attached terminals.

When the personal computer appeared, it quickly became the workstation of choice. The intelligent PC frequently delivers better performance than a terminal attached to a minicomputer. The PC is supported by tens of thousands of applications programs designed to be used by nontechnical people. Thousands of hardware add-on products are available to customize the basic PC. Adding to the PC's desirability, the cost has declined to the point where PCs and dumb terminals cost approximately the same.

Early attempts to integrate the PC into an office network often involved attaching the PC to a minicomputer (see fig. 3.1). The PC attaches to a host processor, such as a minicomputer, in one of two ways. The PC can emulate a dumb terminal, or the PC can use the host only as a storage device—essentially a large hard disk—and download files for local processing. Neither system is optimized to its full potential.

When the PC emulates a dumb terminal, the PC's power is unused, and every additional workstation adversely affects system throughput. Emulation hardware must be purchased for each PC, and this hardware may cost more than the PC. The other drawback is that hardware emulation is never total. Some functionality is lost as the PC tries to emulate another type of workstation.

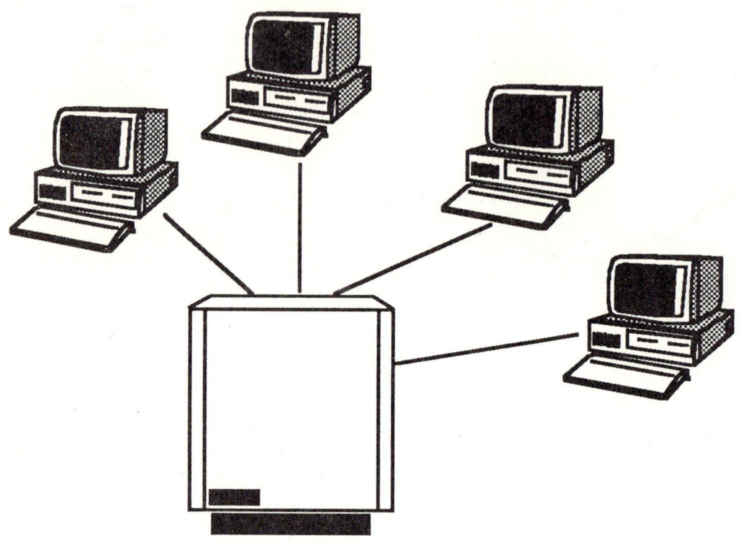

Fig. 3.1. PCs can attach into a host network, but the result is a PC that must emulate a dumb terminal or a host that must act like a large hard disk.

When the PC uses the host only as a storage device, the impact on the host communications system usually is severe. A terminal transfers data one screenful at a time. A PC uses the communications system differently—moving data in large blocks and overburdening the host. The processing capability of the expensive host machine also goes unused. Because the data is going from one environment to another (host to PC and back), data usually must go through several format translations. This factor significantly slows the file-transfer process.

Some important applications are better performed by shared-processing minicomputers than by LANs. Sites where large files routinely are processed may be better served by a minicomputer; this category includes scientific and engineering applications. The aggregate processing capability of a LAN is applicable only when the processing is divided into small individual jobs.

Using a PBX System

If you want to network several PCs, communicate among them, and share peripherals, several alternatives are available. One of these alternatives is to use a PBX (Public Branch eXchange) system rather than a LAN. Most large to mid-size companies have their own internal telephone system with a central control unit known as a PBX. PBXs and their telephone wiring systems can carry data traffic and interconnect attached PCs (see fig. 3.2).

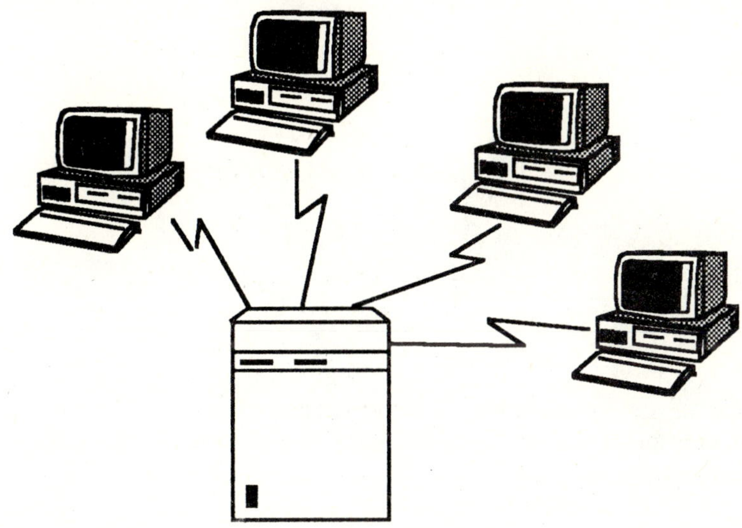

Fig. 3.2. PCs can be networked through a PBX telephone system.

If a PBX already is installed, and connectivity requirements are for infrequent file transfers, the PBX may be a practical solution. A PBX, however, is not a direct alternative to a LAN. The architecture of the PBX and the software to manage the system do not match the functionality normally expected in a high-speed LAN. The PBX is designed to service a high volume of short communications at low baud rates. Most data network traffic, on the other hand, involves lengthy work sessions at high baud rates, which the PBX does not handle well. Although PBXs can support simple file transfers, these systems usually are not equipped to provide file-handling services, such as security, data integrity, and disk management—all of which are important elements of a data network.

A more efficient way to use an existing telephone network may be to bypass the PBX and use just the wiring system. Most LAN topologies are capable of running on telephone-type, twisted-pair wiring, if the wire and junctions are in good condition and if the cable runs are not excessively long.

The PBX is most valuable in data communications when the PBX is attached to the LAN and can be accessed by PC workstations for wide area communications. The PBX-to-LAN connections are rare, but represent an important future application in data communications.

How Is a LAN Structured?

LAN architecture is different from shared-processor and PBX systems. Because the LAN was developed to support PC workstations, LAN architecture basically is a peer-to-peer system. Intelligent PC workstations handle their own processing and communicate as equals (peers) on the LAN. Individual PC workstations, however, cannot manage shared resources. One machine, the network server, is given the management function and provides all the services that a shared-processing machine offers, except for applications processing that usually occurs in the PC workstation.

LANs provide a smooth growth path. As new users and workstations are added to the system, new processing power also is added because the workstations have their own processors. More network servers eventually may be necessary to increase disk management capability. New servers can integrate smoothly into the system so that communication and resource sharing are not impeded. At no point during this growth does discarding hardware that has been outgrown become necessary.

The keyboard, screen, and CPU function efficiently as a unit on a LAN. The link to the hard disk is less efficient (see fig. 3.3). On a host system, the CPU and the hard disk function as a unit, with a slower connection to the user screen and keyboard (see fig. 3.4). CPU-to-disk operations are handled most efficiently.

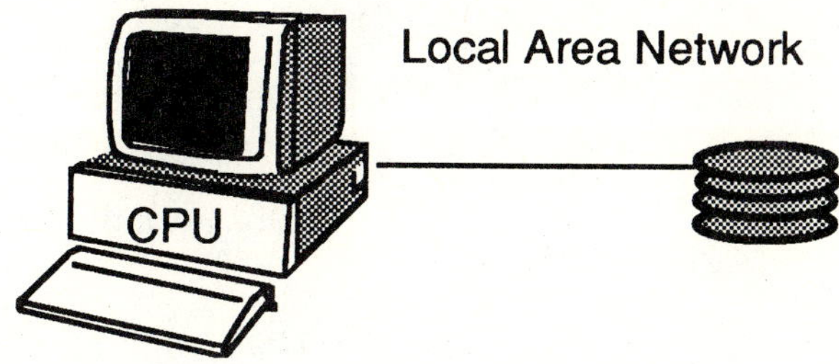

Fig. 3.3. The keyboard, screen, and CPU function efficiently as a unit on a LAN.

Fig. 3.4. On a host system, the CPU and the hard disk function as a unit, with a slower connection to the screen and keyboard.

Although the functions of a shared-processor system and a LAN are similar, on the LAN these functions have been distributed and given to many smaller machines rather than centralized in one large machine.

In addition to lower unit cost, this division or distribution of functions has another benefit. The distributed LAN architecture builds into the system a high degree of fault tolerance. If any PC workstation on the network fails, the other machines can continue to function. If the server or the network fails, the PCs can operate as stand-alone workstations until the fault is repaired.

As shown in tables 3.1 and 3.2, the LAN architecture tends to be more efficient for office applications.

Table 3.1
Office Applications on LANs

Resource	*Use*	*Configuration*
Display I/O Display-CPU interface	Heavy	Closely coupled
Transmission bandwidth	Low	High speed
Disk I/O Disk-CPU interface	Low	Loosely coupled
Workstation processor	Heavy	Dedicated

Table 3.2
Office Applications on Host Systems

Resource	*Use*	*Configuration*
Display I/O Display-CPU interface	Heavy	Loosely coupled
Transmission bandwidth	Heavy	Low speed
Disk I/O Disk-CPU interface	Low	Closely coupled
Central processor	Heavy	Shared

One of the LAN's biggest advantages is that it supports all or most of the software written for the PC. Several thousand DOS programs also have been enhanced with multiuser features to permit multiuser programs to run in the LAN's distributed environment.

Chapter Summary

Most offices will benefit from attaching their workstations to a network. Networks improve office communications, simplify organization, support functions, and can reduce peripheral and software costs.

A LAN is the best network solution if any of the following conditions is present:

- ❑ *When PCs are used as workstations.* LANs maintain the PC environment and fully use the PC's capabilities.

- *When file management and security are needed.* LANs provide management and security functions unavailable in PBX systems and lacking in some minicomputers.
- *When microcomputer-based applications are needed.* Microcomputer-based applications run as they do on stand-alone PCs, except that additional functionality may be available through the LAN.
- *When the network will grow.* LANs provide a low-cost, smooth growth path. Because each new workstation supplies its own processing power, the impact of additional workstations on system performance is minimal. Servers and other relatively low-cost LAN components also can be added as needed to support increased amounts of data traffic.

Application Processing

Application processing is the primary objective of all computer systems. They may have secondary goals, such as managing users, implementing security and data integrity, and so forth, but all of these functions are designed to support the real objective of reliable and efficient application processing. *Application processing* means loading a software application onto one or more machines and running the application, managing the user interface for keyboard input and screen display, and producing requested output.

Different systems tend to perform application processing in different ways. Traditionally, application processing occurs on a computer in a self-contained fashion: a computer, running an application, produces some output. In this model, the network acts solely to link user requests to computers or to transfer data. Now, however, new computer and communications technologies are altering this rigid view of application processing. Applications today can be processed anywhere on the LAN. An application can be divided into separate programs, and these programs can run on different machines—while still functioning as one application.

Systems administrators have to make a decision, with each application, as to where and how processing should occur. No simple formula is involved in making this decision. You must understand the needs of the application and the available options.

Understanding the Terminology

One of the first hurdles to cross is learning the terms used to describe elements of application processing. Many of the terms are ambiguous; the same term is used in different contexts to mean different things. The following key terms and definitions provide a basis for dealing with the concepts in application processing.

Shared processing—A single processor is used by several end users or even other computer processes. (A computer process is a discreet task running in a computer.) A host computer uses shared processing, for example, to support dumb terminals. One copy of the application is executed on the host, and all attached terminals can share the processing. Shared processing is synonymous with *centralized processing*.

Distributed processing—An application is processed on more than one machine in the network. An example of distributed processing is a LAN in which each PC workstation runs its own copy of the application. Two variations of distributed processing are client-based and server-based applications.

Client-based applications—Applications run in a network client that usually is a PC workstation. Most LAN applications are client-based.

Server-based applications—Applications run partially in a server machine and partially in a client. The programs running in the server are referred to as the application's *back end*. The programs that run in the client are called the *front end* of the application.

Server—A machine answers requests from one or more clients on a network. These requests typically are for access to some shared resource, such as files on a hard disk. Like all computers, servers are given a particular identity (functionality) by the software they run. A *file server* runs software that handles read/write requests to files on a shared hard disk and synchronizes the requests of multiple users to ensure that data integrity is maintained. An *application server* runs applications software for network clients.

Interprocess communications—Communications protocols permit programs to talk to each other.

Cooperative processing—Different tasks within the same application can be processed on different computers. The tasks communicate their results to each other to produce the final result.

Processing in the Distributed Environment

Personal computers began as simple, stand-alone machines. Even in this isolated condition, PCs are useful, especially in end-user computing in which computers are viewed as extensions of their users. In an end-user environment, the computer helps the user do his job. (The opposite of an end-user environment is a production environment in which operators input data and maintain the computer's data for various business uses.)

PCs are ideal for end-user computing because they answer the users' needs: accessibility, functionality, and performance. Functionality and performance are basic requirements in computing, but the PC is able to deliver these better and more reliably than the host systems used by end-users. Accessibility also is one of the biggest benefits of the PC. No other system makes starting up, using applications, and accessing data so easy.

Stand-alone PCs, however, still have limitations. Local area networks were developed to solve many of the problems. LANs enable users to share resources and information, something stand-alone PCs cannot do easily. When LANs are bridged together in an internetwork, they provide high-speed, transparent communications among large, dispersed communities of users. LANs also offer host gateways that can be shared among users and provide a cost-effective means of host access.

Maximizing Efficiency

The communications channels available with internetworked LANs and host connections are evolving as a powerful communications system. But some problems still need to be addressed—especially the problem of inefficiently used communications channels. The host system's hierarchical communication system has this problem, as discussed in Chapter 3, "Examining the Alternatives." LANs, however, have similar problems for certain types of applications. A database environment, for example, can place unnecessary traffic on a network and perform poorly on a LAN.

Figure 4.1 shows an example of using a database application on a LAN network. The typical LAN application runs a separate copy of the applications software in each workstation and is referred to as a client-based application.

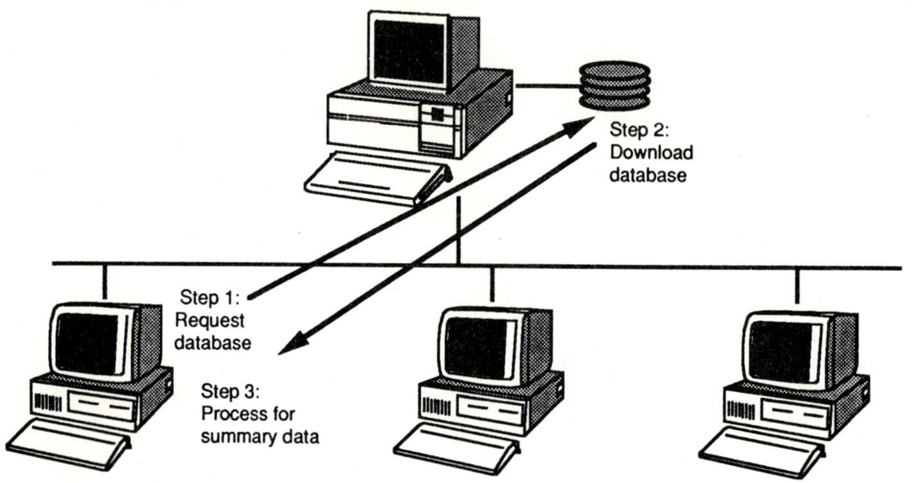

Fig. 4.1. A client-based application transfers the entire database to the client/workstation.

When a user wants to generate a report from the database, the user first must list criteria to create a subclass of database entries. An example of this type of criteria is all customers within a certain ZIP code who have not placed orders within the past six months. After the criteria are developed, the entire database must be downloaded. After the database is loaded into the memory of the client, the user applies the criteria and can generate a report. Typically, 1,000 or more records must be downloaded to generate a report that might contain only 5 records. In this example, downloading those 1,000 records just to get 5 records is a waste of network communications—the transfer is large, and most of the records are not even going to be used.

Cooperative processing is a way to improve the system's efficiency. The user interface, queries, and data input can be processed at the workstation. Database indexing, reporting, and any other manipulation of the data can be processed at the server.

The way to apply cooperative processing in a database environment is to use a server-based application (see fig. 4.2). This type of application has been designed to run with a server and a client component. When you perform the database task in the preceding example with a server-based application, the network usage is very different. The list of criteria is developed at the workstation and sent to the server. At the server, the criteria are applied to the database. The records that meet the criteria are sent to the workstation.

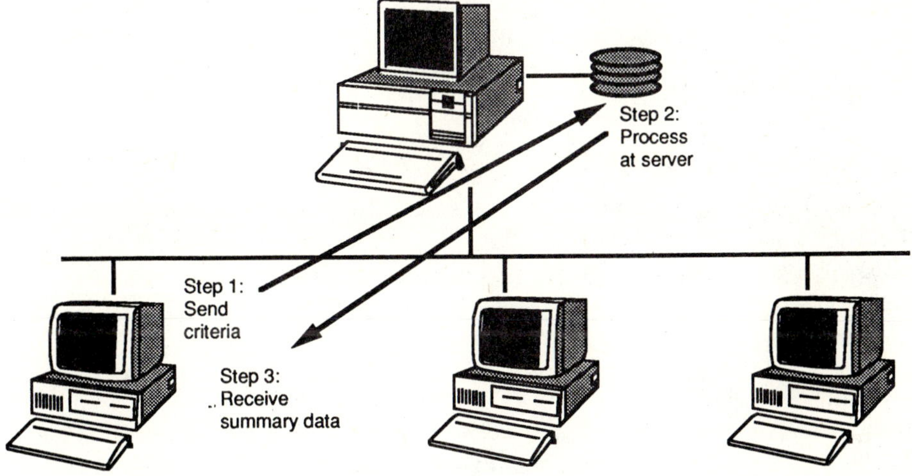

Fig. 4.2. A server-based application processes reports at the server.

This system is more efficient at two points. By sending the criteria to the server for processing, many of the transfers that take place during the processing occur at memory-transfer speeds within the server. These transfers are much faster than transfers across the network. The communications network also is used much more efficiently because only the required data is passed across the network. In this case, that data is the list of criteria and the resulting records.

Deciding Where To Run Server-Based Software

With these two examples of client-based and server-based applications, the term *server* has been used without any qualifiers. The server might be a file server or an application server, or the server might be a database server that does double-duty as a workstation. The new distributed processing environments enable you to run the server software anywhere appropriate.

When designing a distributed system, think of the server as a *virtual machine*. A virtual machine is independent of any particular piece of hardware. Because servers are software programs not tied to hardware, a file server (a machine running file-server software) also can be a communications server, a print server, or even a workstation. The server process, or function, is a virtual machine. The virtual machine concept helps in designing a new system and in planning and implementing a migration strategy. When the LAN grows in the number of users, functions, or activity, or when technology changes, a migration strategy should be in place to move the system as painlessly as possible to meet the new requirements.

For a midsize installation, you can install the server-based application on the network file server. The application is more efficient and performance is higher than if the application is client-based (all other things being equal). The database, therefore, runs faster. The application, however, now is sharing processing time with file-server software. If the application is used heavily, that use reduces the performance of the network file server. On the other hand, if the file server is used heavily, the application performance suffers.

The file server is a poor choice for the location of server-based application software, unless the network has few users or unless the machine running the file server software is extremely powerful. A full-size minicomputer might be a logical place to run the file-server software and the application software. Even in these situations, however, you should develop a migration plan.

One such plan is to put the server-based application on a workstation and run the server in nondedicated mode (meaning that the machine's processor does more than one job). That way, the machine can be used as a workstation while the application software is running in the background. This strategy is appropriate if the workstation is used lightly, leaving most of the processor's time available to the application. The workstation also should be a powerful machine (80286 or better). The application still is sharing processing time with another application, and reliability and security decline.

A dedicated server (one that performs only server functions) can be locked up and protected from careless users and intentional attackers. A workstation, by definition, must be accessible for use. Even if the user understands such rules as not turning off the machine to do a cold reboot if the application fails, other accidents can occur. The server/workstation (nondedicated) option is one that should be considered with caution.

The highest performance and most reliable solution is to run the server-based application in a computer dedicated to that application. Such a server might be called an application server or, if it is running a database application, a database server. If all the machines have compatible processors, you can move the same server-based software from one location to another as performance needs warrant and ultimately have the software run in its own machine.

This discussion about the efficiency of server-based applications does not mean that every LAN application should be server-based. Some applications, for example, do not benefit from being server-based.

Database applications are good candidates for the server-based approach because they are transactional. A *transactional application* is record-oriented; data is formatted in data sets (records). A *transaction* occurs when a record is created and written to the database, or when an existing record is locked, modified, written to disk, and unlocked. Transactional applications usually require simultaneous access of the file by multiple users and frequent disk I/O. Because several people may be using the same file at the same time, having the back-end processing of the application operate in a shared, or centralized, mode is more efficient than having the back-end processing distributed.

A nontransactional application, such as word processing, is file-oriented rather than record-oriented. For a user to work with this type of application, the entire file must be sent to the user's workstation for modification. If the file remains at a centralized location, you gain no performance advantage, because other users cannot effectively share a file in a file-oriented application. The result actually is a reduction in performance because network traffic would increase as the system performed host-to-terminal types of data transfers.

Considering Client-Based Applications

To benefit from a server-based application method, you must be using a transactional application. Not every transactional application, however, should be run as a server-based application. Client-based applications have advantages, even for transactional applications. Client-based applications are inherently more reliable because they avoid the problem of a single point of failure (see fig. 4.3). Copies of the application are being processed in each workstation, and if one of the stations or software packages fails, the other stations are unaffected. With a server-based application, if the server process fails, all workstations shut down until the problem is corrected.

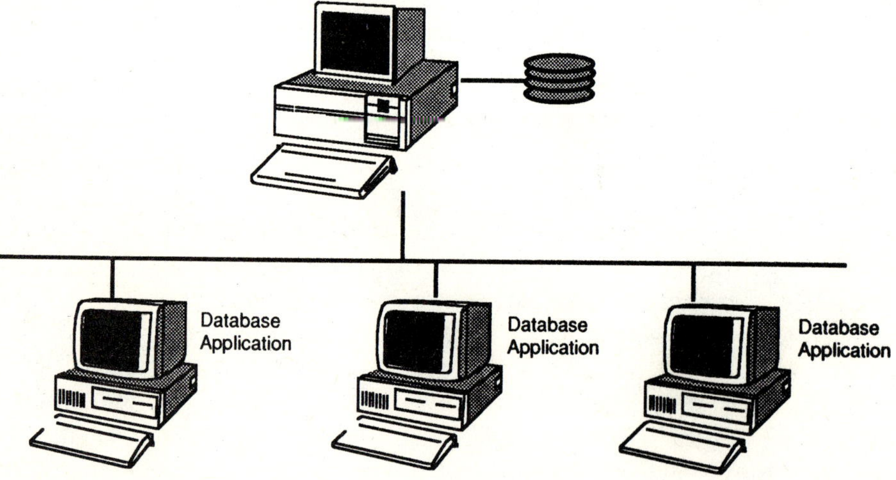

Fig. 4.3. Client-based applications are failure resistant because a complete copy of the application runs in each workstation.

Despite the clear performance advantage of server-based applications, a particular site may be getting completely satisfactory performance from its client-based application. In informal surveys, 90 percent or more of those surveyed are satisfied with the client-based application's performance. If a particular site is satisfied with its client-based application, but is considering migration to a server-based application, the migration should be delayed until better performance is truly needed. Buying new software provides no benefit if the old software is functioning well, particularly when the old software has its own significant advantages.

The percentage of sites satisfied with client-based applications, however, inevitably will decline. LANs are supporting increasingly larger databases in higher-activity environments. As this trend continues, the demand for the high performance of server-based applications also will increase. A new site without any existing software should seriously consider the server-based option if the anticipated size of the system and activity appear to warrant performance optimization. (You must consider whether the better performance justifies the cost.) You can effectively deal with the reduced reliability of a server-based application by using several reliability enhancement strategies (see Chapter 23, "Risk Analysis and Reliability").

Understanding Interprocess Communications

The mechanism that enables the cooperative processing which occurs in server-based applications is *interprocess communication* (IPC). A process completes its function and needs to pass information to another process through a communications channel. The channel is defined in an IPC protocol.

Standard IPCs

Four IPCs currently are considered industry standards. Each of these IPCs has advantages.

IPX/SPX (Internet Packet eXchange/Sequenced Packet eXchange) was developed by Novell and is supported on all Novell networks. The protocol originally was designed to support peer-to-peer communications on a LAN. When the PIX/SPX was designed, Xerox Network System (XNS) generally was accepted as a model for peer-to-peer communications, but XNS was only a design reference model. No standard XNS implementation was available. IPX/SPX is based on XNS and offers high performance, good internetwork capability, and support by the largest installed base of LAN operating systems. IPX/SPX, however, is not supported outside the micro-LAN environment.

NetBIOS (Network Basic Input/Output System) is an IBM protocol. NetBIOS has the advantage of IBM support but provides relatively poor performance and limited internetwork capability.

APPC (Advanced Process-to-Process Communications) is another IPC from IBM. APPC is a strategic protocol for IBM (one that IBM intends to support on various machines) and is likely to be a major standard for many years. This protocol is excellent at internetworking (communicating among networks) and is unique among all the IPC protocols because of its support in mainframe, minicomputer, and microcomputer environments as well as support by many different vendors. The APPC, however, is so large and demands so much memory that it is not practical for DOS LANs. OS/2's large memory capability overcomes this problem on OS/2 workstations.

Named Pipes/Mail Slots, from Microsoft, is the most recently introduced IPC. Named Pipes/Mail Slots handles internetworking and is widely supported, with significant support coming from IBM. In design, the biggest advantage of Named Pipes/Mail Slots is a relatively simple application programming interface (API) compared to other IPCs. (No IPC is truly easy to program because of the knowledge of low-level communications functions required of the programmer.)

Interfacing Multiple IPCs

The choice of IPC usually does not involve the end user. Whether an application uses Named Pipes/Mail Slots, APPC, or another IPC is not an issue when selecting the application. You must assume that the developer chose an IPC that properly supports the application. IPC compatibility is a significant consideration, however, when selecting a network operating system. Ideally, a LAN should be capable of supporting all the popular IPCs.

The IPC issue can be more critical for developers. Most LAN applications do not interface directly with the IPC. For these applications, the underlying IPC is transparent. The applications that do interface with the IPC need peer-to-peer communications with other processes on the network. One such application is the communication application that for optimized performance needs a direct link between workstation and the communications gateway. The gateway translates protocols so that dissimilar systems can communicate. To operate efficiently, the workstation should communicate directly with the gateway without going through the file server. Another application that uses the IPC directly is the server-based application.

For the developers of applications that interface with the IPC, the several IPC standards can cause problems. IPCs are not compatible with each other. Developers, therefore, often must port applications to multiple IPCs to cover the needs of the marketplace. Developers not only need to understand the low-level communications functions of IPCs, but also must learn the idiosyncrasies of several IPC protocols.

A new strategy is emerging to overcome these problems. A few companies, most notably Netwise, have developed a common interface to multiple IPCs. The Netwise product is called Netwise RPC (Remote Procedure Call). RPC prevents developers from being forced to write to low-level communications functions in an IPC and provides a common interface to most standard IPCs.

In most applications, a common function is to call and execute procedures. A word processor, for example, uses a procedure call to open a data file on the hard disk. The calling procedure issues an argument, or request, to the called procedure. The called procedure returns the results (see fig. 4.4). A developer can use this same model to send procedure calls across a network. But to do so, the developer must program the application to get the message onto the network through the IPC.

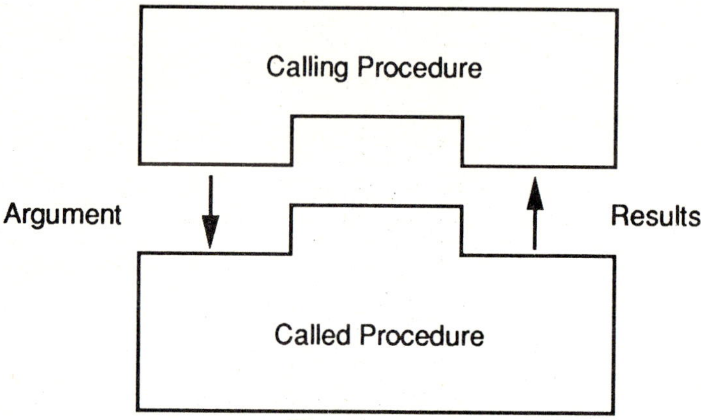

Fig. 4.4. A diagram of an IPC call (source: Novell, Inc.).

RPC simplifies the handling of remote procedures. With RPC, the developer writes the application as if the calling procedure and the called procedure were in the same machine. RPC provides a piece of software code that accepts and routes the call across the network. The code used to perform this task is called the *stub*. When the reply comes back through the network, the stub receives and passes the message to the calling procedure (see fig. 4.5). The calling procedure thinks that the stub is the called procedure. The stub has the same address as the called procedure and receives and passes information in the same way.

The network communications code is written by a code generator in Netwise RPC. The process is automated, although the developer can modify and customize the code after it is generated.

New tools like Netwise RPC continue the movement toward protocol independence in a multiple-protocol environment. Besides writing the communications code, Netwise RPC includes a library of transport interfaces. Among the transports supported are TCP/IP, DECnet, SNA/APPC, OSI/MAP, NetWare SPX, and Named Pipes/Mail Slots. With the library, developers do not have to rewrite their

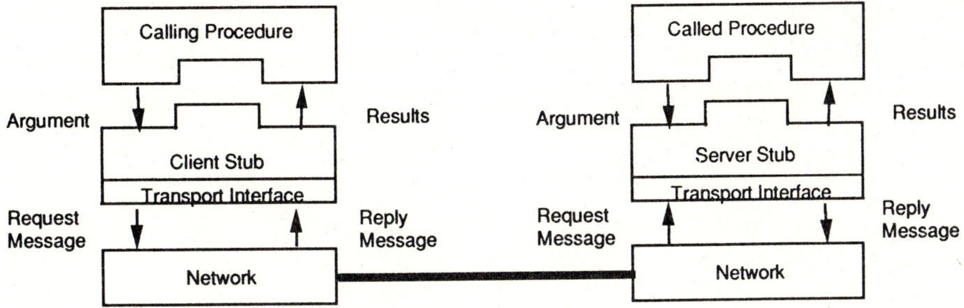

Fig. 4.5. The Remote Procedure Call adds a client stub and server stub that provide network communications codes.

applications for each transport. A developer can port an application and the stub to a different network transport by linking with the appropriate library (see fig. 4.6).

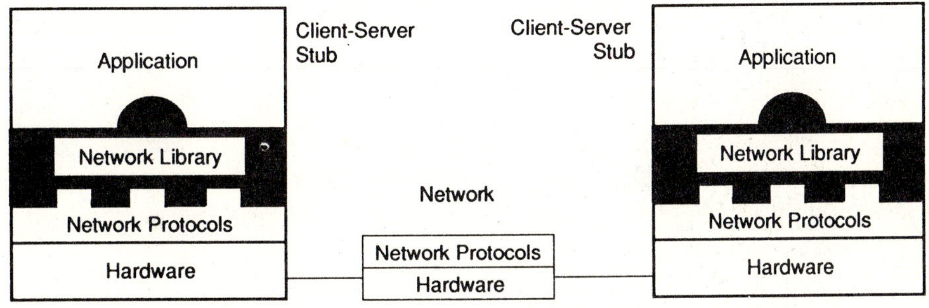

Fig. 4.6. Netwise RPC makes a set of network libraries available to the developer (source: Novell, Inc.).

Chapter Summary

Application processing is a highly flexible aspect of design on LANs. The application can be processed anywhere and in any mode that is cost efficient and cost effective. Options include client-based processing and server-based processing, and the hardware platform for the processing can be a workstation, a file server, an application server, or a combination of any of these.

Several IPC protocols enable cooperative processing in which two or more processors can work on pieces of the same application. Each of these IPCs has advantages. The direction of the LAN industry is to support multiple IPCs while providing a consistent and simple means of hooking into any specific IPC.

II

Choosing a System

Includes

LAN Hardware

Network Operating Systems

Workstation and Server Choices

LAN Evaluation

5

LAN Hardware

LANs probably are the most flexible communications systems ever created. The basic LAN technology can be shaped and adapted to fit any site where PC workstations must be connected. Interchangeable standards and the LAN's distributed architecture contribute to this flexibility. Another important factor in LAN adaptability is the availability of diverse LAN hardware.

LAN hardware can be defined as the LAN's physical components, along with the methods used to connect those components. Cables, topologies, and network interface cards are the primary pieces of LAN hardware. Your selection of each component depends on the physical site layout and on the performance requirements of users and applications.

To convert a stand-alone PC to a networked PC, you first plug a network interface card (NIC) into the PC's expansion bus. You then connect a cable to the NIC, giving the PC a physical connection to the network (see fig. 5.1).

When the person at the PC workstation sends a message to the network, the message is directed from the PC through the expansion bus and into the NIC. The NIC has onboard firmware that divides the message into units called *packets* and addresses the packets. Part of the firmware implements a cable-access scheme so that packets enter the network in an orderly manner without colliding with other packets on the network. When the network cable is available for the transmission, a transmitter on the NIC sends the packet on to the network cable. Incoming message packets are received by a receiver on the NIC, processed, and passed into the PC workstation.

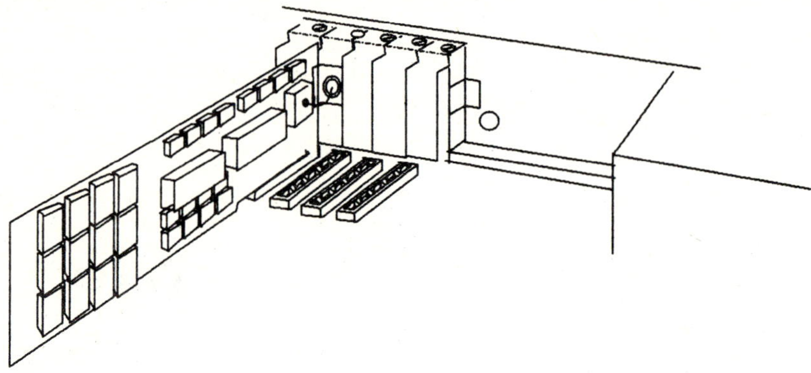

Fig. 5.1. Install the network interface card (NIC) in the PC's expansion bus.

This chapter looks at each of the LAN hardware components in more detail and gives you an idea of which components are appropriate for your network site.

Exploring Cable Alternatives

LANs are built with any of several types of cable: twisted-pair, baseband coaxial, broadband coaxial, and fiber-optic.

Defining Twisted-Pair Cable

The least expensive LAN cable is *twisted-pair*—the same medium used in telephone wire. Twisted-pair is multistrand wire, insulated and frequently shielded to reduce the possibility of interference (see fig. 5.2). Twisted-pair cable can support data transmissions up to 10 Mbits/sec, with some limitations on distances of cable runs.

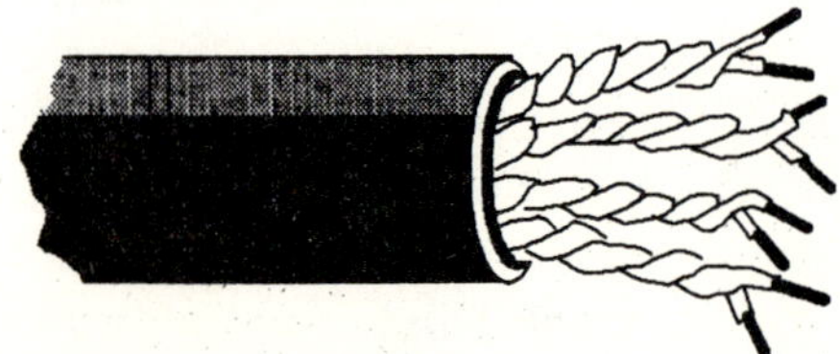

Fig. 5.2. The most common version of twisted-pair cable is standard telephone wire.

The IBM Cabling System, used in the IBM Token Ring network, uses a special type of shielded twisted-pair (IBM Type 1). The IBM twisted-pair is made with great precision and can support faster data transmission rates and longer cable runs than common twisted-pair. The IBM twisted-pair also is several times more expensive than common twisted-pair.

Defining Coaxial Cable

Coaxial cable, or *coax*, is made with a single-wire conductor surrounded by a stranded ground wire. The two wires are separated by a thick insulating core. Another insulating jacket protects the outside surface.

Two transmission systems are used with coax: baseband and broadband. *Baseband transmission* takes the digital signal as the signal comes from the computer and passes the signal directly through the cable to a receiving station. (Baseband transmission is used on coax and twisted-pair cable.) Baseband coax transmits a single channel at high data transmission rates (up to 10 Mbits/sec) and has a maximum range of approximately 4,000 meters.

Broadband transmission systems convert the digital signal to a radio frequency (analog) signal and pass it to the receiving station, where the RF signal is converted back to a digital signal. An RF modem (modulator/demodulator) handles the conversion; each station must have its own modem in a broadband system. Sometimes the modem is built into the NIC.

Broadband coax is a multichannel medium capable of carrying dozens of transmission channels within the same length of cable (see fig. 5.3). These transmissions can include voice, video, and data. The maximum recommended speed of broadband usually is 5 Mbits/sec. Cable runs can be as long as 50 kilometers.

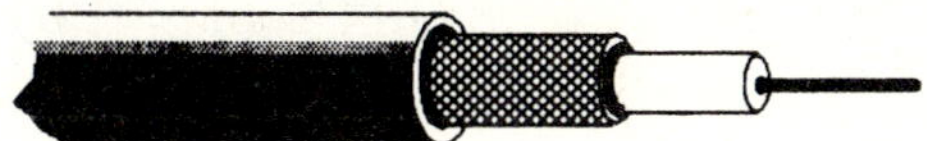

Fig. 5.3. Coaxial cable is designed with two wires separated by a thick insulating core.

Broadband is the same cable and transmission system as cable TV (CATV). At one time, many people thought that this relationship would lead to a general standardization on broadband systems, with video and data signals carried in the same network. The widespread use of broadband for data transmissions, however, has not materialized because of the differences in CATV and data traffic. CATV networks cannot be converted to broadband data easily because CATV is a one-way transmission system, and data requires two-way transmissions. The cost of conversion from one-way to two-way systems often is as much as installing a new cable plant.

A broadband usually is more expensive than a baseband installation. Although baseband systems are essentially maintenance-free, the broadband network must be tuned on a regular basis (at least annually). Despite the possible disadvantages, broadband remains a powerful technology and cabling option.

Defining Fiber-Optic Cable

Fiber-optic cable is the newest technology to be used in LANs. A light beam is carried through a glass thread running the length of the cable. The beam is modulated by the network to shape the signal.

Using fiber-optic cable has several advantages. Because light beams transmit the messages, the system is immune to outside electrical interference. Because cable-generated interference does not occur, extremely fast and error-free data transfers are possible. Additionally, because of the lack of interference, long cable runs are possible. For a given amount of space, the channel capacity of fiber-optic cable is enormous.

Fiber-optic cable is specified in the ANSI 100 standard, a cable specification with a transmission rate of 100 Mbits/sec. ANSI 100 also is known as fiber-optic distributed data interface (FDDI). Current uses for FDDI's high speed are in large, host-to-host transfers and in backbone cable plants for LANs. The uses for fiber optics undoubtedly will continue to expand.

Fiber-optic technology and expertise have increased dramatically since the introduction of fiber optics. The cable and its installation were prohibitively expensive at first, but its support by government and military users as well as standards organizations has brought down the cost.

Fiber-optic cable is less expensive than coaxial cable in most cases. The cost of installation for fiber-optic, however, is much more than for coax. Fiber-optic cable is more difficult to pull (run or install) because it is somewhat fragile and easily damaged in sharp bends. Fiber-optic also is more difficult to terminate, requiring a polishing and epoxy phase. A coax crimp connector can be completed in 30 seconds, but connecting fiber-optic cable takes 30 to 45 minutes. Currently, the total cost of the installations is approximately the same.

The other aspect of fiber-optic cable to consider is that the signaling equipment, such as hubs, transceivers, and concentrators, is much more expensive than comparable coaxial cable equipment. The signaling equipment can run in the range of $1,000 to $1,200 per fiber-optic station. With thin EtherNet coaxial cabling, the cost drops to almost nothing (see this chapter's section on EtherNet). Even with multiport repeaters for EtherNet, the connection cost is only $200 to $300.

Understanding LAN Topologies

LAN cabling is arranged in a predetermined configuration called a *topology*. The topology of a LAN is defined as part of the LAN hardware. After you select a particular type of hardware (cable and NIC), you must follow a specified topology precisely. The most common of these topologies are the linear bus, star, distributed star, and star-wired ring.

The *linear-bus* topology is a simple design with a single length of cable, known as the bus or trunk. All devices on the LAN are attached to the bus and share this single communications medium (see fig. 5.4).

The linear-bus topology is simple and economical. The only consideration in wiring a bus is that the cable must pass by each networked device, which is not the case in other topologies. Because all devices share the bus, the cost of the wiring may be

Fig. 5.4. The linear bus topology attaches all devices (PCs and other network nodes) to a common cable.

lower than with topologies that require lengths of dedicated cable. The failure of any networked device has no effect on network operation, but failure of the cable shuts down the network. Cable failures can be extremely difficult to locate on large linear networks.

The *star* topology is arranged like a star, with cables extending from the network server. Cables are not shared; each PC workstation has its own dedicated cable (see fig. 5.5). In this situation, more cable usually must be purchased when workstations are added. With a star topology, your chance of system failure is reduced because a cable fault affects only the workstation attached to that particular cable.

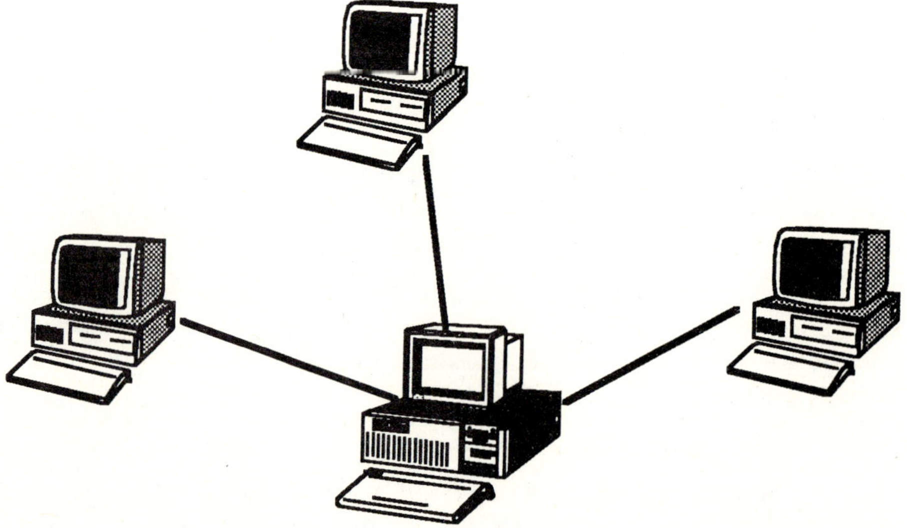

Fig. 5.5. The star topology is shaped like a star, with cables radiating from a central device such as a file server.

The *distributed-star* topology uses a dedicated cable to connect each PC workstation to a central point. The central point is a connection box, called a *hub*, attached to a shared linear cable. Usually, four to eight workstations can be connected to each hub (see fig. 5.6).

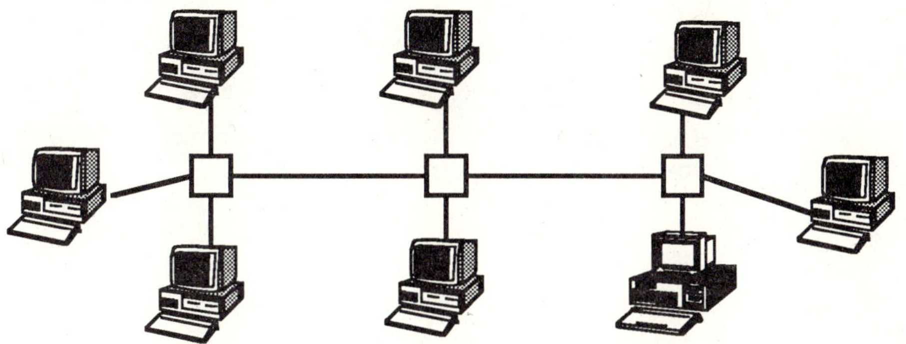

Fig. 5.6. The distributed star topology uses a shared linear bus cable to which clusters of star-wired cables are attached.

The *star-wired-ring* topology, like the distributed-star version, uses a combination of shared and dedicated cables (see fig. 5.7). Dedicated cables radiate from a central wiring concentrator. Control messages are passed from workstation to workstation as in a ring. (The ring is part of the LAN's logical design but is not physically evident.) On the other hand, in the star and the distributed-star topologies, messages are passed from the central point to the workstation.

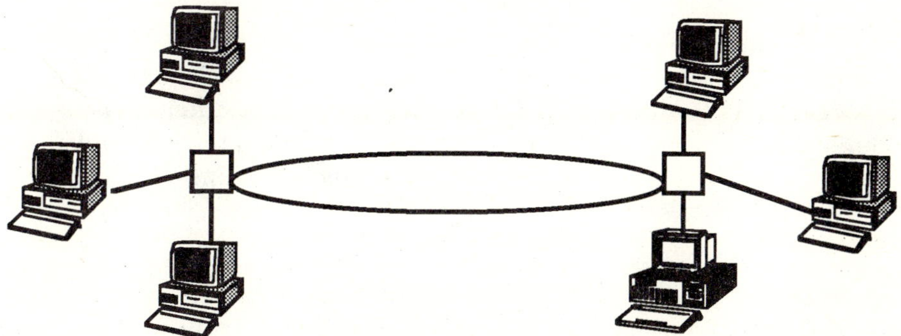

Fig. 5.7. The star-wired ring topology uses star-wired clusters attached to each other by a ring cable.

Linking Networks with Premises Wiring Schemes

LANs traditionally have been installed in workgroups. In these small sites, the types of wiring and layout make little difference. Systems, however, grow and spread. Many organizations have found that their LAN wiring is a mixture of several types of hardware.

In most cases, dissimilar networks can be bridged together in a *premises internetwork*. (A premises network usually covers an entire building but does not extend beyond the building to a campus or wide area network.) You can use any of several plans to wire a premises internetwork.

Building Internetworks

One method of building an internetwork is to link separate networks through bridges to form a daisy chain. A *daisy chain internetwork* is a robust system because of its modularity; if one network fails, the other networks can continue to operate. Usually, the only functionality lost is communications between the two network segments on either side of the downed network.

The daisy chain has two disadvantages, one of which is the lack of optimization. The various LANs in the internetwork may each meet the performance needs within their areas, but when linked and acting as a transport between LANs, each network may not have the bandwidth needed to handle such a specialized task. The potential result is slow internetwork communications.

The second problem with the daisy chain internetwork is its effect on *intranetwork* communications. Each network in the daisy chain supports communications within the network and internetwork communications that must cross the local network. This additional traffic can reach a level at which all communications on the local network are slowed.

Another premises solution is the *backbone-and-cluster* plan. This modular plan avoids the limitations of the daisy chain. In the backbone-and-cluster scheme, a high-speed network is installed to handle internetwork traffic. Workgroup and departmental LANs (cluster networks) are bridged onto the backbone. In this system, the amount of internetwork traffic has no effect on a cluster unless the transmissions specifically are addressed to that cluster. Most daisy chains can be turned into a backbone-and-cluster internetwork through the addition of the backbone network and reconfiguration of existing bridges.

Choosing the Wiring System First

So far the assumption has been that several small LANs were in place and gradually were bridged together to form the internetwork. This method commonly is referred to as *bottom-up networking*. When a new building is being wired, or an old one rewired, organizations have the option to implement a top-down plan. A *top-down plan* looks at the needs of the entire organization and the individual departments. Typically, a top-down plan is designed from the onset as a premises network, linking all groups within a building.

Top-down plans have numerous advantages, but cost and management are among the most important. Wiring a whole building usually is much less expensive than wiring the building in a piecemeal, ad hoc fashion. If a centralized network management software program is being implemented, one program may not be capable of monitoring a variety of LAN hardware.

Many of the major computer system vendors have developed their own premises wiring plans. Two of the most popular of these are IBM's Cabling System and AT&T's Premises Distribution System.

The IBM Cabling System is based on the concept that properly selected and installed wiring can be used to support a variety of current and future communications products. The wiring system is designed to last through many changes in computer technology—a desirable goal.

The Cabling System specifies cable, topology, connectors, and signaling equipment. In the Cabling System, a *wiring closet* is populated with wiring concentrators called *multistation access units* (MAUs). Dedicated wires connect workstations to the MAUs to form a star topology. The IBM system uses IBM data connectors.

Workstation cables lead into a *patch panel*, which is part of the wiring closet equipment. From there, the lines are patched into MAUs.

A *riser cable* is strung between wiring closets to interconnect them. The connecting riser cable must be configured as a ring to support token-ring networks; however, the general topology is that of a string of star-wired clusters. Cable types are shielded twisted-pair or fiber-optic, with various combinations bundled into the same sheath with optional sheathing material.

AT&T's premises wiring scheme is called the Premises Distribution System (PDS). The PDS is similar to the IBM Cabling System, but PDS specifies only cable, topology, and connectors. How the cables are connected with the signaling equipment is left to the particular vendors of the various protocol suites. PDS cabling is unshielded twisted-pair media, the DIW (D-Inside Wire) telephone wire, and fiber-optic. All the jacks are standard telephone jacks, RJ45 or RJ11C. Punchdown blocks are used in the wiring closets. The 110 punchdown blocks are specified and suitable for data and telephone.

(Although running voice and data through the same cables and into the same punchdowns is possible, you usually should separate the two. That way, telephone technicians can leave the data equipment alone, and data technicians can stay away from the telephone equipment.)

The PDS topology is a string of stars, identical to the IBM Cabling System. Riser cables that connect wiring closets usually are fiber-optic cable. Cable that runs to workstations for the PDS and the Cabling System are about 300 feet from wiring closet to end device.

The advantage of the PDS is cost. PDS is based on unshielded twisted-pair cable, which is approximately $.07 a foot in bulk quantities. PDS also uses the standard inexpensive telephone punchdowns. With the IBM Cabling System, the cost is $1 to $1.20 per foot for IBM Type 1 cable, and more for the other acceptable cable types.

IBM offers the use of standard telephone wire (unshielded twisted-pair) for its Token Ring product. The distances are limited severely, however, and a media filter is required for each workstation. (A *media filter* is a special cable with a built-in filter that limits the size of the ring and the number of stations on the ring.) Unshielded twisted-pair cable, however, currently is not part of the Cabling System.

The IBM Cabling System supports a wide variety of IBM hardware. For a site with many different types of IBM equipment, the Cabling System's cost may be justified.

An interesting feature of the IBM and AT&T premises-wiring schemes is the use of risers between wiring concentrators. In a diagram, the riser has the appearance of a backbone network in a backbone-and-cluster topology. A riser, however, is a more generic term, usually implying a cable that connects the networks on one floor of a high-rise building with networks on another floor. A backbone, on the other hand, is a complete, special-purpose network designed to carry internetwork traffic.

IBM and AT&T wiring schemes permit the network to be wired as a single network without bridges and segments. You also can use the backbone-and-cluster plan by giving the riser function to a backbone network and bridging to the clusters. Designers and installers with primarily host network experience tend to choose the single network configuration. In the distributed LAN environment, however, the backbone-and-cluster configuration usually is superior. The backbone-and-cluster network isolates traffic within the workgroup, thereby improving network performance and security. Backbone-and-cluster configurations also are more reliable, because each segment is an independent network capable of functioning on its own if other segments of the internetwork fail.

The single-network approach is appropriate only when all network users must interact with each other—communicating and sharing information and generally operating as a single workgroup. The reliability of segments is irrelevant because, by definition, segments require interconnectivity to support the application.

Integrating Wiring on a Network

The need to integrate services on a network is a constant consideration. IBM and AT&T premises wiring schemes support multiuse cable for the carrying of voice and data. Integrated wiring's greatest support is in the emerging Integrated Services Digital Networks (ISDN) standard.

ISDN originated in the early 1980s as the CCITT (International Telegraph and Telephone Consultative Committee) began to develop the design for an integrated services digital network. The CCITT's goal is to produce a network capable of using the same communications equipment for all types of communications traffic, with special emphasis on voice, data, facsimile, and video.

ISDN is still in its infancy. The few installations are pilot programs for the most part; however, ISDN's use is expected to expand through the 1990s. Although widespread use may not occur until the 21st century, ISDN represents an important movement that data communications planners should follow.

The integration of communications services requires a movement to all digital channels, away from the analog telephone services that dominate today. This movement already is underway, and digital telephone lines are an option in many areas of the world. Economical high-speed lines such as the 1.544 Mbits/sec T-1 standard, another necessary component of the technology, have gathered vendor support and now are widely available. On the data communications side, the movement of LAN protocols to support common cabling systems, such as telephone wire's unshielded twisted-pair and fiber-optic, facilitates the integrated concept. The Fiber Distributed Data Interface (FDDI), currently a high-speed data transfer option, is considered a part of the ISDN environment. Fiber also will be used for other communications that demand wide bandwidth, such as video conferencing.

The common cabling inherent in ISDN is only one part of its development. Standard interfaces for user access also are an important facet of ISDN. In some subscribers, premises are linked by using integrated digital access (IDA) to digital circuits. The objective is to provide digital switches that can control all types of communication transmissions, especially voice and data, across the same circuit.

Exploring Cable-Access Schemes

Any topology that uses a shared length of cable must employ some means of regulating access to that cable. Otherwise, nothing would prevent two PCs from making simultaneous transmissions and blocking one another. Two access schemes used on LANs are token passing and contention.

Token passing manages cable access by sending an access-granting message, called a token, to each workstation on the LAN. When a workstation wants to transmit, the workstation seizes control of the token and transmits. Other stations, before they can transmit, must wait until they control the token.

Contention LANs use a much simpler system than token passing. In contention LANs, each workstation monitors the network, and if no signal is detected, the workstation transmits. If a signal is detected, the workstation waits until the transmission is completed and the network is clear; then the workstation transmits.

Contention schemes are known by various names: Carrier Sense Multiple Access (CSMA), Carrier Sense Multiple Access with Collision Avoidance (CSMA-CA), and Carrier Sense Multiple Access with Collision Detection (CSMA-CD). Because these variations are similar, they can be classified under the generic name "contention."

Process control systems, such as those used in factory robotics, require a predictable access scheme so that they know the time between messages. These systems must use token-passing access. Otherwise, token passing and contention are of little importance from the end user's point of view. Neither scheme has a consistent performance advantage.

Selecting a Network Interface Card

The network interface card (NIC) establishes most of the LAN's hardware characteristics. These characteristics include the cable type, topology, access scheme, and data transmission (bit) rate. In the following paragraphs are descriptions of some of the most widely used NICs from major LAN vendors.

Using EtherNet

EtherNet networks are defined by the IEEE 802.3 specification, but in practice, many variations also are included. EtherNet networks have two points in common: a contention access scheme and a linear-bus topology. EtherNet has evolved so that it runs on most types of cabling and through baseband or broadband transmissions. Transmission rates of the various EtherNet implementations range from 1 Mbit/sec to 10 Mbits/sec, although the 802.3 specification is intended to support signal rates up to 20 Mbits/sec.

On EtherNet, access to the cable is controlled by Carrier Sense Multiple Access with Collision Detection (CSMA-CD). Every active EtherNet network interface card (NIC) monitors network traffic continuously, even when the NICs have nothing to transmit. If a workstation wants to transmit, and no one else is using the cable, the workstation begins transmitting. If the cable is in use, a workstation delays the transmission until the cable is free and then waits an additional period to ensure proper intermessage spacing.

Occasionally two or more workstations find the cable free of traffic and attempt to transmit at the same time. This situation causes the messages to have *collisions*, and they have to be retransmitted. To retransmit, the workstation waits a scheduled period determined by a process called *controlled randomization*. After the delay, the station can retransmit.

EtherNet wiring specifications include medium access units for connecting trunk cables to branch cables in a tree topology. The *trunk cable* is thick EtherNet (RG-11) and thin EtherNet (RG-58). Both are coaxial cables. The typical EtherNet installation for a local area network uses only thin EtherNet cable and is laid out as a linear bus—a one-cable network tapped at any point where a workstation is required. Thin EtherNet is much easier to handle and is cheaper than thick EtherNet.

The migration to cheaper media has continued with the adoption by the Institute of Electrical and Electronic Engineers (IEEE) of a specification for unshielded twisted-pair cable. The specification supports transmission rates of 10 Mbits/sec and is called 10Base-T. In overall configuration, 10Base-T EtherNet looks like a typical premises wiring plan, especially AT&T's Premises Distribution System (PDS). (AT&T was one of the developers of 10Base-T, along with Hewlett-Packard, Ungermann-Bass, and SynOptics.) The 10Base-T design calls for wiring closets, concentrators, transceiver cables, and so forth.

Many people have been concerned with the reliability of unshielded twisted-pair as a medium for high-speed data transmissions. Specifically, the problems that had to be addressed were cable attenuation, radio frequency emission, and protection from electromagnetic noise. The 10Base-T specification appears to have solved these problems by altering the transmission characteristics of the baseband EtherNet signal.

Many companies supply EtherNet LAN hardware, and the availability from such a large number of sources is one of EtherNet's most important advantages. 3Com, Novell, Taurus Systems, Western-Digital, and Digital Equipment Corporation are some of the suppliers.

Using ARCnet

ARCnet (Attached Resource Computer network) was developed by Datapoint Corp. ARCnet is a token-passing hardware protocol that runs at 2.5 Mbits/sec in its current implementation. Development is proceeding on new, optimized ARCnet that will run at 20 Mbits/sec.

ARCnet is not an approved standard of the IEEE, although this protocol does resemble the IEEE 802.4 specification. The 802.4 specification is the standard for the Manufacturing Automation Protocol (MAP) used primarily in factories. ARCnet, on the other hand, is widely used in office automation applications. ARCnet and 802.4 use token-passing, media-access schemes, and both use a shared-cable, bus topology. These LAN hardware protocols, therefore, are classed as token-bus systems.

With token-passing, a token controls the access to the network cable system. By taking possession of the token, a workstation can assume temporary control of the network. The token, which is a special-purpose message unit or packet, circulates the network from one workstation to the next. This transfer of the token creates a logical ring different from the physical topology, but that represents the movement of messages on the system.

A workstation sends a token by addressing the token to a specific workstation address. When a workstation receives the token and wants to transmit, a message is sent. The workstation then sends the token to the next workstation along the network.

The workstation that passes the token listens to make sure that the new token owner is active—passing the token or sending a message. When the new token recipient fails to respond, a second token is sent to that workstation. If the token recipient still fails to respond, the sending workstation broadcasts a message to learn the address of the next workstation in line after the apparently inactive workstation. When that workstation responds with its address, the token is sent to that workstation, bypassing the inactive workstation. In this way, each workstation is responsible for keeping the network in an operative state.

The physical topology of token-bus networks includes shared and dedicated media. The shared media are the connections from one hub to the next. (A *hub* is a signal repeater or conditioner to which several, normally four to eight, dedicated workstation lines can be attached.)

The primary media for ARCnet is RG-62 coaxial cable. Like most other physical protocols, however, ARCnet has expanded to support a variety of other media. RG-62 still has advantages, such as low attenuation at ARCnet frequencies, which permits cable runs between hubs of up to 600 meters. Shielded twisted-pair cabling that conforms to the IBM Cabling System supports runs of up to 200 meters. Unshielded twisted-pair supports runs of up to 100 meters.

Major vendors of ARCnet products include Datapoint, Standard Microsystems, Pure Data, and Novell.

Using Token-Ring Networks

Token-ring networks are defined by the IEEE 802.5 specification. These networks use a token-passing scheme for network access. The wiring plans are star-wired rings, and shielded twisted-pair wiring is the standard for workstation connection. Shielded twisted-pair or fiber-optic cable may be used to connect wiring concentrators. Current token-ring implementations are available in 4 Mbits/sec and 16 Mbits/sec.

The token-ring specification from IEEE defines the Physical Layer and the lower half of the Data-Link Layer, called the medium access control (MAC) sublayer. In a token-ring network, workstations are connected serially to the network cable that is configured logically as a ring. The physical design is that of a star (on a small network) or a series of stars attached to a ring. Messages are passed sequentially from one workstation to the next.

A workstation that needs to send a transmission first must gain control of the token, a special-purpose message unit that circulates the network when no active message is circulating. To control the token, the workstation modifies the token's start-of-frame sequence and builds a message packet onto the token. The new packet has delivery information, including control and status fields, address fields, the information field, frame-check sequence, and an end-of-frame sequence. The originating workstation completes its message and checks for proper transmission.

When a workstation receives a message, the workstation regenerates and sends the message to the next workstation in the network. When the message reaches the destination, the recipient recognizes its address in the message and copies the message. The message continues to circulate until it comes back to the message-originating station that removes the message from the network and generates a new token. The new token begins circulation and is available for the next station waiting to transmit. A process called a *token holding timer* regulates the maximum time during which one workstation can transmit so that no one station can monopolize the network.

If a token is lost, the token-ring protocol provides a means for a new token to be generated after a specific interval. Other error-detection routines can restore normal operation when errors or signal fluctuations occur. Error detection and recovery is accomplished by a network monitor function provided by the file server. Any workstation on the network can serve as a network monitor if the server is unable to provide proper monitoring.

The LAN hardware in a token-ring network includes the network interface card (also called the network adapter), the cable, the patch panel, and the multistation access unit (MAU). Several companies make MAUs, and the designs vary, but the typical MAU is a wiring concentrator that can connect as many as eight stations into the network with drop cables.

If your network has more than eight workstations, you can add multiple MAUs to the system by serially attaching one MAU to the next and adding a final cable that connects the out port of the last MAU in the chain to the in port in the first MAU in the chain. This design forms a ring topology. You can use patch panels within wiring closets to connect different cable types that may be used in the installation.

Major vendors of token-ring network interface cards and signaling equipment include IBM, Proteon, Ungermann-Bass, and 3Com.

Chapter Summary

LAN hardware consists of the physical equipment that interconnects PC workstations and other devices on the network. Network interface cards, cable, and cable layout plans (topologies) are the primary components of LAN hardware.

The choice of one type of LAN hardware over another should be based on the needs of the particular site. Because not all types of cable can support long cable runs, if long runs are necessary, the cable choices are limited. Transmission speeds, or raw bit rates, vary with NICs and should be chosen to match the needs of the application. (For more information on choosing hardware, see Chapter 8, "LAN Evaluation.")

The choice of LAN hardware generally is not a compatibility issue. Most operating systems and LAN software can run on several types of LAN hardware, and this flexibility is increasing. Although you should never ignore compatibility, price and performance present stronger concerns.

The layout of the LAN has long-term implications for the network. A good layout for a large facility probably should follow one of the premises wiring plans from IBM or AT&T or a generic backbone-and-cluster design. A top-down approach to design, in which the overall needs of the facility are considered, is less expensive to implement and easier to manage.

Network Operating Systems

The network operating system is the heart and soul of the network. System hardware provides the data paths and platforms on the network, but the network operating system controls nearly everything else. From the user's point of view, the network operating system is the single most critical element of networking. Functionality, ease of use, performance, management, data safety, and security all depend on the network operating system.

Several network operating systems commonly are available today. Among these are Novell NetWare, IBM LAN Server, 3Com 3+Open, Banyan Vines, and Apple AppleShare. Each of these systems serves a segment of the market, yet one of the clearest directions for the development of future systems is toward similar design strategies. Demands of end users have been heard by the vendors.

Examining the Basics

The network operating system has two basic components: the network server operating system itself, and the workstation. The network server operating system runs within the server machine and processes all the services. The network operating system usually is supplied by a manufacturer or OEM, sometimes building on a general-purpose operating system. The workstation components run in the workstation and establish the connection with the network and the network server and control the flow of communications. These components may be supplied by the workstation or network operating system vendor, or a combination of the two.

The network server operating system can be divided into five basic subsystems: the control kernel, the network interfaces, the file systems, system extensions, and system services. Figure 6.1 shows the conceptual relationship of these components.

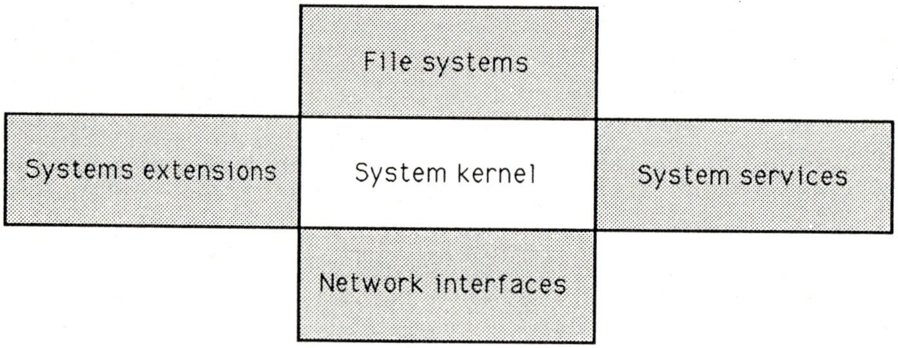

Fig. 6.1. A network server operating system is composed of five basic subsystems.

The *control kernel* is the heart of the system, coordinating the various processes in the other subsystems. Central in kernel design are the processes that optimize access to services for user activity. One of these areas is the user's interface to the disk subsystem. The kernel can distribute user activity as evenly as possible across the disk services and any input/output devices so that no user or group is favored by getting better performance, and perceived performance is consistent. The kernel also is responsible for maintaining the status information of many processes; the kernel is a component of the network management facilities. Error reporting, service initialization, and service termination commonly are mediated by the kernel services.

Some of the synchronization and multitasking support services may be supplied by a host operating system, on top of which the network operating system runs. Examples of hosted operating systems are Novell's Portable NetWare and Microsoft's LMX, both of which are targeted at implementation by OEMs. If the control kernel is targeted at a specific processor, significant performance improvements over implementation on a host operating system may result.

The *network interfaces* support the technologies that are the actual network media implementation. In sophisticated network operating systems, the network interfaces may be dynamically loaded and unloaded, and multiple interfaces of different types may be supported simultaneously. For example, a new network may be bridged into an active system without having to shut down the system and rebuild the operating system. The network interface components also handle the low-level subnet protocols and provide the basic translation among these protocols when bridging services are required (see fig. 6.2).

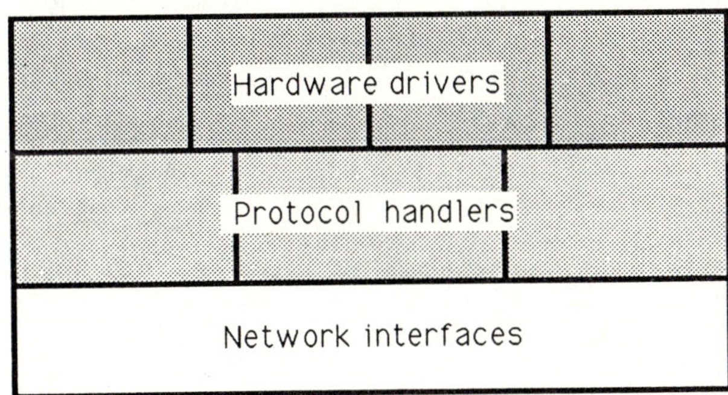

Fig. 6.2. Network interfaces frequently support not only the hardware, but also translate the transport and server protocols.

File systems are the mechanisms by which data is organized, stored, and retrieved from the data storage subsystems available to the network operating system. These file systems may be high-speed subsystems, such as hard disks or RAM disks, or they may be longer-term storage devices, such as Write Once Read Many (WORM) optical storage systems (see fig. 6.3). Current microcomputer-based network operating systems support total storage in the gigabyte range. Recent announcements propose to extend this capacity to terabytes.

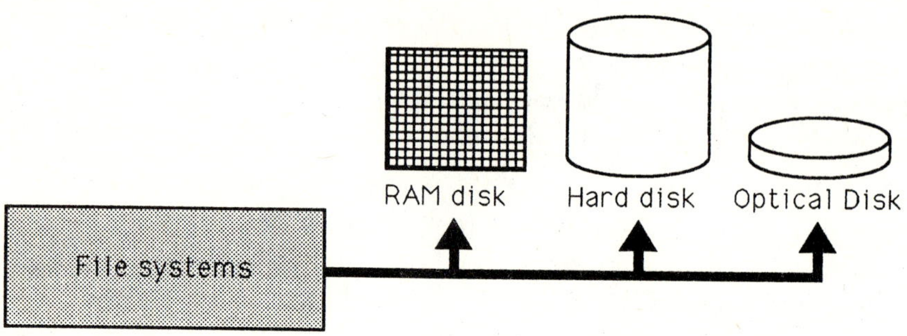

Fig. 6.3. Sophisticated server operating systems support many types of media and different file-handling methods.

File systems are frequently implemented with the concept of universal applicability, meaning that the file system can be presented as compatible with any application's expectation of file input/output protocol. Through adaptable interfaces, one file system is made to look like a variety of different file systems. This technique enables different clients to use a common data storage area.

Network operating *system extensions* define the openness of the system, and third-party developers use these extensions to develop add-on products. The extensions commonly offered by vendors usually are high-level protocol handlers that perform operations, such as the translation between file-access protocols required by the different client operating systems.

The extensions offered by developers cover network management, system tools that extend a range of applications support, and database services. SQL support engines (see Chapter 13, "Distributed Data Services and SQL") are a current focus for developers because distributed processing systems benefit from centralized data resources (see fig. 6.4).

The network *system services* cover all services that do not fit easily into any of the other categories of the model. These may be system-level store-and-forward services such as queuing protocols or resource accounting subsystems. Security and reliability features are often implemented within the network system services to ensure that they provide service at a true system level. Error conditions

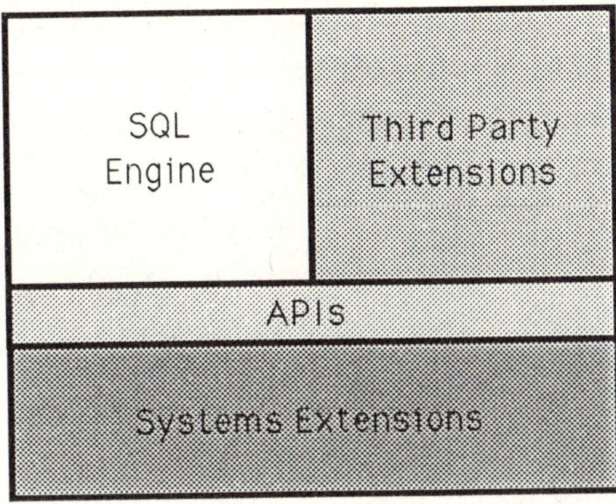

Fig. 6.4. Extensions to the server operating systems enable high-performance database engines to be integral parts of the OS.

and access violations, therefore, can be trapped before they can compromise subsystem integrity.

At the workstation, the network operating system services trap, or capture, calls from the workstation and then address them to a network resource. These calls may be redirected by the operating system if the system is aware of remote file services. OS/2, Unix, and Apple Macintosh OSs all provide this service. The alternative approach for operating systems that are not network-aware is to trap application I/O before the input or output reaches the local operating system. The software that uses this method, often referred to as a shell or redirector, examines and sends the request to the file server for action. This technique is used by the Novell NetWare shell and Microsoft MS-Net redirector for support of DOS workstations.

An important aspect of the relationship between the network operating system and the application executing on a workstation is the level at which requests occur. The now-obsolete disk server systems accepted I/O requests that were low-level accesses to the disk subsystem (for example, "read this sector"). Access from multiple workstations could cause competition for resources; this competition had to be resolved at the workstation level. This problem could be serious if a workstation chose not to obey the resolution rules. Sometimes even the rules were inadequate to guarantee data integrity, and the resulting disk directory corruptions could obliterate entire files, data sets, or even disks.

The file server was the development point for client-server protocols (see Chapter 3, "Examining the Alternatives"). In essence, these protocols carry a much higher level of information, and many low-level operations may be initiated by a request to perform one high-level operation. Issues such as access and conflict resolution are in many cases no longer a problem, because the high-level request is frequently a transaction in its own right. Applications can request an action with little or no knowledge of the state of the rest of the network and still carry out the required operations with complete reliability.

Establishing LAN Technology

Early local area network operating systems were weak communications tools designed mainly to enable hard disks and printers to be shared. In the early 1980s, however, few people were predicting the use of LANs in strategic applications, as replacements for host systems, or in end-user computing. (Strategic applications are regarded as long term and critical to the organization.)

Despite a lack of planning, those uses became the direction of LAN technology growth. The following technological advances paved the way for the following strategic uses of LANs:

- File server
- DOS 3.1
- Hardware independence
- User profile security
- Connectivity

File Servers

File server technology, discussed in Chapter 1, was a radical concept. The PC permitted fully distributed processing, which in most cases was highly advantageous. One place in which fully distributed processing was not beneficial, however, was in network and resource management. Distributed processing required a new management scheme, and the file server was the solution, a centralized system for management in an otherwise distributed environment.

In network architecture, as a general rule, any task that requires coordination benefits from centralized control. The result is increased efficiency. In some cases, efficiency is a secondary issue; centralization may be the only way to provide reliable services. The file server established the idea that a distributed processing environment could include a mixture of distributed and centralized functions. The idea has been extended today to encompass applications servers, batch processing servers, and communications servers and will, no doubt, continue to spawn many new centralized services.

DOS 3.1

DOS 3.1 gave the LAN industry a standard way for applications to access the network. Before that version of DOS, most vendors had their own, proprietary application-to-LAN interface (channel for connecting the application to the LAN). If developers wanted their products to run on a particular LAN, they had to make a special version of their software that used the proprietary interface. With the DOS 3.1 interface, developers can write one version of an application that runs on all DOS-compatible networks.

DOS 3.1 interfaces continue to be supported in new versions of DOS and in OS/2. Also important for LAN architecture is the design concept inherent in standard interfaces. Since the advent of DOS 3.1, networking applications have grown in number and in their level of sophistication. These new applications have needed to interface with applications at various points within the communications environment, such as the Session Layer or the Transport Layer.

Rather than argue over proprietary interfaces, as they did prior to DOS 3.1, LAN vendors today have accepted the necessity for supporting standard protocols and their APIs. Additionally, the fact that standard protocols and APIs are now available (they were not available in the early 1980s) has made acceptance possible.

Hardware Independence

Hardware independence was one of the first indications that supporting standards in local area networking did not necessarily mean supporting a single standard. LAN vendors have long supported a variety of hardware protocols and LAN hardware. Additionally, network interface card vendors now support multiple media and topology types.

From a cost standpoint, media and topology selection are among the most important decisions in networking. The cost of the cable system, especially in a large installation, is a major expenditure. A well-chosen, well-installed cable system can last for decades, a goal of every systems designer. When hardware is firmly tied to higher levels of the communications model (such as the subnet and operating system), the hardware's life expectancy is necessarily shortened.

Hardware independence separates the hardware from the higher layers to provide long-term flexibility and easy technology migrations. The effect of hardware independence is to reduce the life-and-death aspect of hardware selection by reducing the dangers of buying into a technological dead end. At the same time, hardware independence reduces the cost of cabling by increasing its useful life, thus spreading the cost over a longer period.

User Profile Security

User profile security is becoming a standard feature on LANs. Under this scheme, a user is defined and given specific authorization and access rights on the system. When the user logs on, all authorized resources become available. With object-name security, users are given the names and passwords of various resources. User profile security until recently was considered a minor issue in most LAN selection processes. Security itself was viewed by many users as an unnecessary inconvenience on a PC network. Again, the increased use of LANs in strategic and mission-critical applications has affected how various LAN characteristics are assessed. Today, security is a big issue that most LAN vendors try to address adequately (see Chapter 21, "Security").

The user profile system of security places the security checkpoint at the entrance to the system. Other systems, such as object-name security, allow people into the network, permitting them to communicate with various network resources to attempt to gain access. The user profile system bars all entrance to the network except to authorized users. Then, the user enters as a defined entity with specific rights to network resources. Resources to which the user has no authorization remain hidden while all authorized resources are readily available. All major network operating systems now use the user profile security system, in some cases with optional schemes such as object-name security.

Connectivity

Connectivity to other LANs, to host-based systems, and to remote systems is another of the prerequisites for LAN acceptance. The first physical connections provided primitive links to ship data from one point to another. Terminal emulation hardware and software enabled the PC to look like a dumb terminal, but the LAN was still excluded from the network. Gateways solved that problem by establishing connections between LANs and host systems.

As the connectivity technology was evolving, it became apparent that connectivity was only part of the goal. For connectivity to be useful, the connection needed to be transparent. Bridges that interconnected LANs provided partial transparency. But when dissimilar systems or remote systems were connected, the gateways or direct connection links were intrusive and not easy to use.

Connectivity needed to occur through extensions of the network operating system. The emergence of standard mechanisms, protocols, and interfaces to allow interprocess communication, subnet protocols, and common end-user interfaces supports this need. Connectivity has now moved into a new dimension—that of a transparent access to diverse services.

Examining the Current Phase of Development

The network operating systems are going into a new phase. This direction is so new from the previous technology that even the name local area network is becoming too limited to encompass the new technologies and architectures. Terms like network and network computing will increasingly replace the term LAN.

The network server is becoming an element in the computing environment that is truly distributed. Functionality that was centralized to improve efficiency now is being distributed to ensure reliability and improve performance. Rather than a simple distribution of server functionality, the network computing environment uses the facilities available to establish redundant and resilient services. This development is due partly to improved architectural concepts and partly to significant improvements in processing power.

The file server is becoming the control and coordination center, while network resiliency is a cooperative process among all units on the network. Communications are distributed, but the services are controlled through global databases provided by the servers. These databases may be scattered throughout an organization and contain information on access rights and profiles that network users are allowed access to when using services such as communications. The databases, therefore, provide a mechanism to organize and manage the distributed environment.

The concept of the server as a mere traffic cop is obsolete. The porting of server systems to multiple computer types, which in turn eases the transition to supporting a specific vendor protocol set, is providing networking strategies for vendors who traditionally had focused on only host-centric systems.

Support for native workstation protocols at the server is another important step for networking. The server "understands" the inherent network support provided by a client operating system. By minimizing or even avoiding the addition of software into the client environment, the integrity of the client is maintained. This design also ensures that problems of trying to keep pace with the evolution of the client system are minimized.

The great evolutionary pressure of the 1990s and beyond will be the trend to adoption of OSI-related standards. The issue for owners of existing network systems is how to maintain their investments and not be forced to replace systems prematurely. Because the systems used by organizations today cannot simply be thrown out, a migration path to allow for a gradual integration with OSI standards will be a critical business issue.

Most network operating system manufacturers are adopting a modular design that separates the components of the server OS. This design means that the file system or systems and the protocol handlers are replaceable. Flexible support of this kind allows for dynamic reconfiguration as well as upgrading and maintenance services with minimal impact on operations.

Looking to the Future

Developers are heading toward 12 key goals in the design of future network operating systems:

- ❑ Open architectures
- ❑ Standards compliance
- ❑ Embedded intelligence
- ❑ Distributed fault tolerant features
- ❑ Hybrid network management
- ❑ Platform independence
- ❑ Client independence
- ❑ Protocol independence
- ❑ Global services
- ❑ Support for distributed applications
- ❑ Platform performance
- ❑ Communications performance

Open Architecture

The issue of *open architecture* has been discussed briefly in this chapter. The impact of this feature, as far as users are concerned, should be to promote inherent interoperability from protocol levels right up to and including applications. Network applications will eventually include sophisticated features associated with workstation operating systems such as the Macintosh, in which data can be moved freely between applications through integrated applications, and system events can trigger processes in concurrent applications through the use of interprocess communications (see Chapter 4, "Application Processing").

Applications that support critical corporate endeavors, therefore, will become commonplace. These applications will intercommunicate data from different subfunctions in real time and allow records, such as financial performance records, to be accurate and up-to-date at all times. This communication of data will not be limited by the physical location or real-time availability of the information generator or consumer. Store-and-forward technologies will be an integral component of the open architecture and will ensure that critical data can reach a potential consumer when that consumer is available.

Standards Compliance

Standards compliance is being perceived at present only in the context of the major market de facto standards or internationally defined standards. The future will see not only these standards integrated within the same network systems, but also more opportunity for high-performance proprietary operating systems to coexist because of the open architecture.

An added advantage of a more open approach to standards compliance is the fact that companies having particular, specialized needs will be able to select nonstandard components but be ensured interoperability with standard environments.

Embedded Intelligence

A degree of *embedded intelligence* is already a component of some client-server architectures discussed in Chapter 2, "Communications and Standards." In the future, expert systems technology will allow for more efficient use of data-access protocols. SQL has no explicit relationship with expert systems, but future extensions may allow SQL inquiries to be directed at database systems that not only are integral parts of the network operating system but also understand the broader context of the inquiry.

Additionally, embedded intelligence combined with knowledge-based systems will enable autonomous network management and diagnostic facilities to act as built-in network supervisors. This structure obviously will require much greater processing power than is available today. Recent developments in processor technology and knowledge-engineering techniques, however, are likely to make these services a reality in the 1990s.

Embedded intelligence is especially important to increase the efficiency and lower the cost of wide area networking. Routing algorithms are already semi-intelligent as implemented in some network software. They can search to find optimal routings. Most of these algorithms currently look for optimal routings within a limited range of choices. The network systems of the future will be much bigger systems, and a network will often be part of a citywide, nationwide, or international system. If you are using an international network to link company offices and different companies, intelligent routing will be crucial.

A choice, for example, may be among routes that run through land lines with capacity problems, through very expensive satellite connections, or through microwave links or various other routes. Many of these routes will be tariffed according to the time of day and possibly traffic quantity. Given this situation, embedded intelligence in the server will allow much more sophisticated routing that will continuously monitor the path of the communications to ensure that the cost or quality of the service is optimized.

Distributed Fault-Tolerant Features

Distributed fault tolerance, characterized by multiple server redundancy, has been announced by Novell and other vendors, although this feature is already a reality on mainframe systems. As components within a network system fail, redundant subsystems and components on other network platforms (not necessarily from the same manufacturer) ensure that service continues without interruption.

At the application level, distributed fault tolerance will allow for redundant software elements that execute on multiple nodes. Current research and development into parallel processing environments will probably be key to providing these services. The technology of object-oriented views of processing also will have a significant impact. This technology encapsulates data objects and processes and provides an implicit modularity fundamental to parallel processes operating in a distributed fault-tolerant environment.

Hybrid Network Management

Hybrid network management covers the ability to control and modify the network and client environments across a broad range of vendors and technologies. In particular, the ability to integrate various network management strategies from different vendors is critical to flexible network servicing. Again, the impact of knowledge-based systems in enabling bridges between technologies will be immense.

In the future, the user interface for network management and the underlying management services will be separated into discrete components. The reason for this division is that network management services will become smarter. The underlying services provide such things as alerts, traffic monitoring, and statistics gathering. Often this information and the utilities that generate the information are specific to the hardware and software. The user interface, or front end, needs to be able to take information about various network events, analyze the information, and recommend action. When this capability is built into the front end, a consistent user interface can be developed, with the underlying system complexity hidden.

Platform Independence

Platform independence, the ability to run the network operating system on a wide range of computers, is required to meet the needs of the varied environments in which client-server networking is being used. In part, this issue is related to processing capacity. Network server platforms may need anything from moderate microcomputer performance to large minicomputer and even mainframe performance. Ideally, the network operating system also should run on platforms from a variety of vendors.

Even within this level of platform independence, another level is needed to address some specific requirements. Server platforms (computers that support and execute server software and functionality) come in two distinctly different shapes. One is a general-purpose platform with network services added; the other is a network-optimized platform targeted specifically for network services.

One benefit of the general-purpose platform is that such a platform often is already installed at the site. By supporting that equipment and its existing applications and filing system, the network operating system provides smooth integration of client-server networking into the installation. The general-purpose platform also may answer a special software requirement. For example, OS/2 requires ownership (control) of the hardware and will not run on top of another operating system. When server-based applications are designed for OS/2, the network operating system must be capable of running on top of OS/2.

Special-purpose server platforms are optimized for networking. The network operating system is closely integrated with a network-optimized filing system designed for multiuser activity. The operating system that has direct control over the hardware has better control over the security and management functions. Finally, performance of the network-optimized platform usually is better than the performance on a general-purpose platform of comparable size.

Both types of server platforms have their ideal uses, which is one reason that platform independence is important. The industry has seen some movement in platform independence with portable operating systems from Novell and Microsoft that have been ported to some minicomputers. (Portable software programs—applications or operating systems—are designed so that they can be adapted to multiple types of computer hardware.) This trend will continue as network operating systems are programmed in conformance with standard, portable languages such as the C POSIX standard.

Client Independence

Along with platform independence is *client independence*. The unique functionality of numerous client workstations, such as the IBM DOS or OS/2 workstation, the Apple Macintosh, and the Unix workstation, should be supported in the workstation's native environment. Each workstation should be permitted, through network operating system architectures, to attach to a heterogeneous/multivendor environment while maintaining its own unique characteristics.

Protocol Independence

Protocol independence is discussed in Chapter 2, "Communications and Standards." Independence is an important direction in network operating system design and differs significantly from a simple standards approach. Although the OSI standards are becoming more complete and robust, issues and omissions still exist in the area of functionality. In fact, decades of work may be required for the upper layers of the OSI protocols to mature. Additionally, in its pure form, OSI ignores the existence of large installed bases of non-OSI conforming systems.

The TCP/IP standard has been in use for many years and is a true standard. The existing investment in TCP/IP-related systems precludes its disappearance certainly until well into the 21st century. At a higher level of functionality, standards such as Microsoft's Server Message Block protocols and Novell's NetWare Core protocols will continue to be powerful client-server protocol strategies. Network operating systems of the future, therefore, must be able to integrate and to interoperate these diverse protocols.

Network operating systems should be designed to support multiple protocols at each level of the OSI Reference Model. The most practical way is through industry support for standard Application Global services also relate to resource acquisition. When an application requires a resource (for example, a new data file, batch processor, printer, and so forth) the network operating system should be able to locate the resource without user intervention. Global directory services, tables of available resources, and mappings to those resources are some of the network operating system features needed. Support through the network operating system for program-to-program communications or interprocess communications (IPCs), such as IBM's Application Program to Program Communications (APPC) protocol, is another part of the requirement.

Programming Interfaces (APIs). OSI does not specify such APIs except at the highest application level. Standard interfaces are emerging, however, including the IEEE 802.2 Media Access Control (MAC) interface layer supported by IBM and others, Netwise RPC for interprocess communications and transport layer access, and other evolving interfaces from network vendors. This approach differs from pure OSI but is consistent with many Government OSI Profile (GOSIP) specifications that allow for implementations of subsets of the total OSI model and integration with other non-OSI protocols.

Global Services

Global services include network management strategies, security, routing, and addressing schemes. These services need to be implemented on an internetwork basis and, as in the case of routing and addressing, may need to be standard on an intercompany as well as intracompany basis. Work is underway at the Massachusetts Institute of Technology and other institutions to develop global services standards that support networks with millions of nodes—systems far larger than even the huge ARPANET used by the U.S. Department of Defense, other government agencies, and civilian contractors. IBM, Sun Micro Systems, Banyan, and other vendors have developed proprietary protocols for global services, and some of these may form the basis for eventual global standards.

Support for Distributed Applications

Support for distributed applications is interrelated to global services. Parallel processing, for example, permits dynamic redistribution of work loads. This type of redistribution will be important for networks of the future as distributing processing tasks become more complex. Increasing the capacity of every node because of periodic, heavy processing loads on individual workstations or servers is an expensive solution. When one node is overburdened, others usually are running at a fraction of their capacity. Parallel processing will be able to distribute these loads to use the aggregate power of the distributed network more efficiently.

Platform and Communications Performance

As the functionality of networks evolves to encompass many of these new features, the performance of server platforms, network operating systems, and communications links will have to increase. For example, moving beyond the local area for distributed resources is a requirement of corporate networks of the future. For these resources to be useful and for the location to be transparent (that is, for their remote location to avoid affecting the user or the application), however, the whole system must support extremely high speed. Throughput in the 100 Mbits/sec range, although considered fast today, will no doubt be inadequate for certain network links toward the end of the 1990s.

Chapter Summary

The network operating system is the most important single component of the network. The operating system defines the functionality, ease of use, performance, management, data safety, and security for the network.

A large amount of consensus has developed among vendors about network operating system design. Most vendors currently support the same broad functionality, standards compliance, high performance, and services. The real difference in network operating systems is the manner in which these features have been implemented in existing products and the plans that vendors demonstrate to support tomorrow's technology.

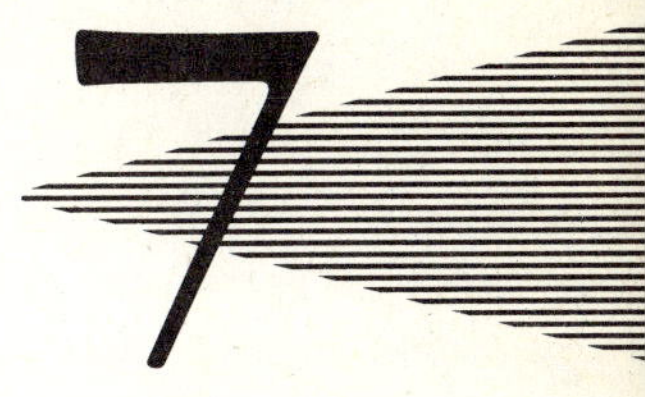

Workstation and Server Choices

As a user of computers, you are faced with a difficult decision: which type of workstation and which operating system do you use? The problems of selection are made more difficult by the need to make compromises on complex issues such as compatibility, performance, and price.

Most of the de facto standards are serviced by large markets. No single hardware, operating system, or application software, therefore, should limit growth, service, and application support unless you have exceedingly specialized needs.

Finding a Workstation that Matches Your Needs

Many different types of networkable computers are available in the PC and minicomputer markets. The main offerings include the following:

- Intel 808x- and 80x8x-based processors for IBM-compatible PC computers (8088, 80286, 80386)
- Motorola 680x0-based processors for Apple Macintosh computers
- RISC (Reduced Instruction Set Computers) computers

Knowing exactly which configuration meets a specific set of needs is a matter of getting enough information to make a realistic comparison. Many of the benchmarks and statistics relate poorly to the actual performance of a workstation when running a target application. The only certain way to benchmark a workstation is to use the system configured as it is intended to be used on the Network.

You need a workstation because you need to perform some computer-based tasks. By defining the tasks, in detail, you can develop a list of key features that will be part of the constraints for your workstation selection.

Setting objectives is vital to building a specification of required performance, implementation time scales, and features. Some of these features fall into the category of critical success factors—those objectives by which the workstation succeeds or fails.

The following sections cover the main aspects of workstation selection and provide a basic strategy for analyzing workstation choices.

Understanding the Processor

The *processor* choice is relevant in the areas of performance and, to some extent, compatibility. The Intel processor systems are by far the most common in the existing network market and commonly are found in IBM-compatible systems. These processors span a wide range of performance from the 8088 at less than 0.5 million instructions per second (MIPS) to the 80386 that delivers over 4 MIPS on a high-performance system. The Motorola processors, used in the Apple Macintosh, operate at between 1 and 4 MIPS.

Selecting the right processor is important from the standpoint of software. People buying new equipment should select their software first; the software determines which workstations to buy, or at least which processors.

Reduced Instruction Set Computers (RISC) technology is becoming available in the general-purpose workstation market. The best-known RISC chip sets are used in the IBM RT PC and the Sparc chip set developed by Sun. RISC technology promises enormous performance. The latest announcements from Intel covered the firm's response to this market, the i860, that is intended to exceed the performance of the 80x8x processors.

In terms of workstation performance as perceived by the user, the MIPS figures indicate how the workstation performs for a compute-bound task; the more MIPS available, the faster a task executes. In terms of network performance, the limiting factors are the performance of the network and the workstation interface rather than the MIPS of the workstation.

Understanding Memory

Memory configurations for most Intel-based computers usually include 640K of random-access memory (RAM) as standard. Many workstations have the capability to support up to 4M or even 8M on the system motherboard. The amount of RAM required is dependent on three factors:

- ❑ How much RAM the workstation operating system can use
- ❑ How much RAM any system extensions (such as multitasking add-on environments—MS Windows, DESQview, and so on) can use and what is needed by RAM disks and memory managers
- ❑ How much RAM the applications need

Understanding Clock Speed

Clock speed determines the rate at which the processor can carry out instructions. This speed can range from 4.77 MHz (million cycles per second) to the latest machines driven at 33 MHz. You should not base your workstation purchase solely on this factor. Clock speed indicates the performance potential of the system and also may affect cost.

Understanding the System Bus

The circuitry that connects all the subsystems in the workstation is called the *system bus*. In the IBM-compatible marketplace, workstations use the IBM PC, IBM MCA, and EISA bus types. The

Macintosh system configuration is unique and is supported by only one bus type, the NuBus.

Much discussion has been circulating recently about which bus is better, MCA (proprietary to IBM) or EISA (designed by a consortium). The performance differences actually are less critical than the marketing issues, because IBM's licensing is strict and costly. The EISA bus offers slots that accept IBM PC/AT-compatible circuit boards.

The system bus in some workstations may operate at a lower clock speed than the processor to ensure that the system experiences no compatibility problems with add-on hardware. This factor may reduce the performance of a system considerably. The amount of data that can be transferred during each clock cycle, called the *bus width*, also is an issue. The bus width may be 8, 16, or 32 bits. The bus width is determined by the processor and by specific bus design. Obviously the width of the bus limits the rate at which data can be transferred. Most systems allow for add-on hardware to be of any of the standard bus widths. If a potential system does not allow a mix, the possible configurations may be limited.

Understanding Local Storage

Two types of local storage are available: a local hard disk drive or a local floppy disk drive. Either storage may have its uses in particular applications. All applications and most data generally should be stored centrally at the file server. Central storage lowers cost and improves security and system manageability. With a high performance network operating system and a properly configured network, the throughput from a central storage system should equal or exceed the performance from a local storage system. A standard network workstation should be equipped with one floppy disk drive for installing remotely created data or possibly running security or software protection mechanisms.

Understanding Footprint

In many office environments, the amount of space that a workstation is allowed to take is minimal. The area consumed by a workstation is referred to as the *footprint*. This area includes the monitor, the keyboard, and the space required to use a mouse or other input device. Because some workstations have a much smaller footprint than others, footprint should be considered during workstation selection.

Understanding the Monitor

Whether an application requires color or monochrome display is often a function of the significance of the job function being performed by the workstation. For situations in which the information displayed is critical to the company or requires a fast response from the user, color can be an absolute necessity.

The *resolution* of the display refers to the number of points that can be displayed on-screen. This feature is crucial in determining how complex an image can be produced. The size of the screen is important from the user's point of view, because small screens can be tiring to look at if the image displayed is complex.

Understanding the Input Device

Many types of input devices can be used with a workstation, but some are useful for only special applications. The *keyboard* is by far the most common input device and comes in a wide variety of types to support different countries and key layouts.

The *mouse* is becoming the other major input device for workstations. A mouse is a box-like object that fits into the palm of your hand. When you move the mouse around on the desktop or table, a ball rotates inside the mouse and drives the position of a cursor, or pointer, on the monitor. The mouse usually is equipped with two or three buttons you use to indicate that an action should be performed on whatever item or object is located on-screen at the mouse cursor's position. The trackball is the equivalent of the mouse turned up-side down; you place your hand on top of the ball and rotate the ball against the palm of your hand to move the cursor.

The rise of the iconographic front end (uses symbols or icons to represent services) makes the mouse an ideal device for control of the computer environment, as is demonstrated by the Macintosh, the OS/2 Presentation Manager, and to a lesser extent by the front end for PC DOS 4.0.

The *light pen*, another input device, works similarly to the mouse but consists of a pen-like device that you place on-screen. To signal that an action is to occur, you press a button on the side of the light pen. Light pens are more common in CAD environments because these devices are a more natural device for drafting.

Voice input is a much-discussed technology but is not reliable enough to be a major benefit except in specific applications. The major drawback is the lack of speaker independence—the voice input system must be trained individually for each speaker. Companies such as British Telecom have used voice input to construct dial-in voting systems for game shows.

Understanding System Options

Many workstations can be extended, which allows you to upgrade the performance or available functionality. These upgrades may be available from the workstation vendor or a third-party supplier. Using products supplied by a third party may, in some cases, void the warranty on your workstation, as may allowing someone other than the vendor's authorized representative to perform an upgrade.

The most common enhancements are adding coprocessor support, memory expansion, and network support. *Coprocessors* handle specific processing tasks such as arithmetic operations, which reduces the workload on the computer's CPU. A coprocessor can give phenomenal performance increases in compute-bound applications such as computer-aided drafting and engineering. Coprocessors also are available to accelerate display performance and handle communications services.

Memory expansion is available for most machines and often represents a significant percentage of the workstation's value. As discussed earlier, many machines targeted as high-performance workstations come with 640K RAM as standard. Expansion on the system motherboard may allow up to 4M; additional hardware that plugs into the system bus is then required.

Network support is sometimes built into the workstation. In those cases, the workstation does not need to take up a slot on the system bus. Those workstations that do not have a built-in network adapter require one compatible with the bus design and system architecture.

Understanding Compatibility

Compatibility means that a hardware unit or software program performs exactly the same as another unit or program. If a PC is said to be IBM PC-compatible, that implies that the PC can run the same software and support the same add-on hardware as an IBM PC, but it may mean only that the PC can run most IBM PC-compatible software.

In these days of fast-moving technologies, issues such as forward and backward compatibility have become important. The Intel microprocessors' popularity is partly due to the ability of newer processors in the family to run most software written to run on earlier Intel processors. This feature is called *backward compatibility*. When a company such as IBM says that a particular protocol will run on its future machines, that is forward compatibility—also a good feature.

Sometimes, however, claims and intentions do not translate into fully compatible machines, and many networks are purchased as turnkey systems. Here, the system integrator has put the network together and made sure that everything works with everything else. If you are acting as the system integrator, always test your application on a new workstation before purchase or require a guarantee from the reseller that the workstation will work with your application.

Understanding a Diskless Network Workstation

In many cases the network user requires only the data storage services supplied through the file server. Local storage, in the form of floppy and hard disks, is therefore unnecessary. This situation allows significant savings in large networks.

A diskless workstation also enhances security. The lack of any simple means of unloading files from the network or, for that matter, loading files onto the network (such as security-breaking programs) adds an additional level of protection.

Networking with DOS Workstations

PC DOS (IBM) is the most widely used workstation operating system in PC networking. To be PC-compatible, a network operating system must support several PC DOS conventions. The system also must supply several layers of functionality to permit DOS applications to exist in a network environment.

The most important functions in a DOS network environment are related to disk directory and file handling. DOS-based network applications use these functions for synchronization in the multiuser environment. (Synchronization is the ability to coordinate requests from multiple users to the same file or other resource.)

Although DOS is limited in providing network services, the operating system specifies function calls for synchronization of disk access among multiple users. The channel used by applications to communicate with DOS is Interrupt 21h (see Chapter 10, "Applications Programming Interfaces"). DOS compatibility requires that the application and the network operating system use this channel.

Through Interrupt 21h and its underlying functionality, PC DOS can require the use of the file server environment (see the section on "Network Servers" in Chapter 1). This fact has given DOS-compatible networks centralized control of the shared disk, resulting in fully synchronized disk access and satisfactory data integrity.

PC DOS contains no internal means for using a remote (networked) resource such as a shared hard disk. DOS assumes that every request is being issued to and answered by a local hard disk. Network operating systems that support DOS workstations have to supply a network interface program, which is run in the workstation, to redirect I/O from the local operating system and storage to the network. This interface program is called a shell or a redirector.

A *shell* intercepts the application's requests for service before they are handled by the local operating system (see fig. 7.1). If they are local requests, they are sent to DOS for local processing. If the requests are for network services, the shell translates the requests from low-level, disk I/O requests to high-level file access requests. A *redirector* passes the application's request after DOS has determined that the system cannot supply the service (see fig. 7.2). With the shell and the redirector, the requests then are sent onto the network to be received by the file server and converted into appropriate disk I/O requests.

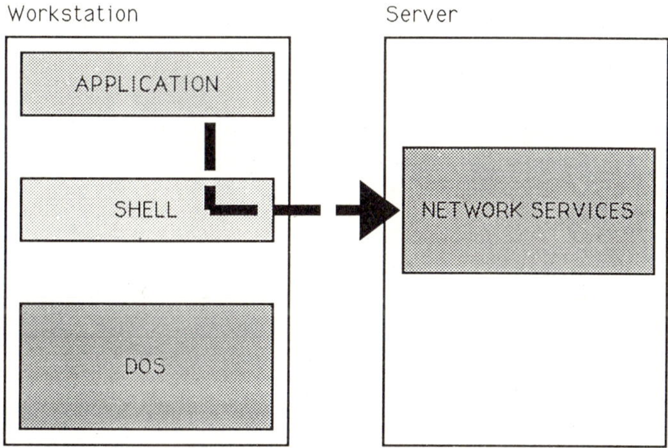

Fig. 7.1. The shell method of diverting network input/output relies on intercepting input/output requests with a software component.

Networking with OS/2 Workstations

In OS/2, IBM designed a workstation operating system to use the capabilities of Intel 80286-based microcomputers. Primarily, the improvements over DOS are the capability to use more than 640K of RAM, to support multitasking, and to implement the 80286's protected mode. (The protected mode segments memory so that if one process fails, other processes can continue to function.)

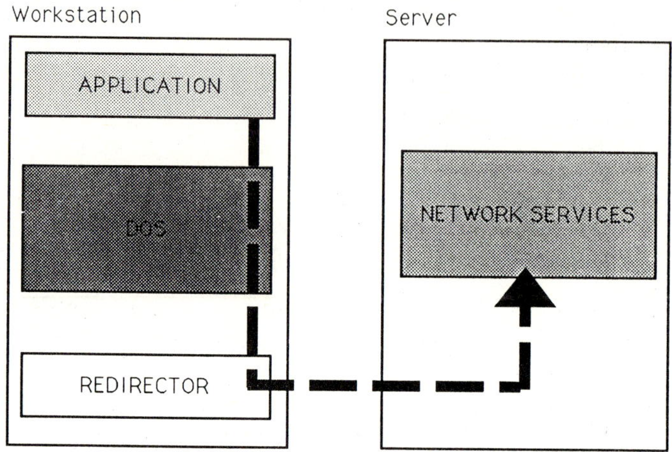

Fig. 7.2. The redirector method of diverting network input/output enables the local operating system to examine and send the request to a software component.

Increasing Memory Capacity

The 640K barrier of DOS has been a limit to applications developers for years. Although several schemes have been developed to get around this limitation, they present programming problems and a confused, nonstandard development and production environment. OS/2 overcomes this dilemma by supporting the 80286 chip that permits the addressing of up to 16M of RAM.

The added memory in OS/2 is becoming extremely useful as applications grow increasingly powerful, complex, and large. In a network environment, large memory is often crucial. Networked PC workstations must load at least one transport protocol and network interface program and then the application and the data file. Typically, users also want to load an electronic mail package or other task in the background. Add to these packages the programs that must be loaded to perform host or wide area communications, and little memory is left for the application. This type of configuration is not merely the wish list of a few power users but is necessary to enable user productivity. OS/2 effectively opens up this DOS roadblock to workstation system functionality.

Multitasking

Multitasking is the ability to run two or more operations simultaneously. Like DOS's limited memory capability, the fact that DOS does not support multitasking has slowed the growth of productivity among PC users. Third-party developers have overcome some of the problems with a profusion of terminate-and-stay resident programs that enable users switch from one task to another. True multitasking, however, allows multiple active tasks; that is, tasks that continue their processing and do not go into a suspended state even when another task is running. In a multitasking environment, activities such as batch processing and communications can occur in the background while the user works on a foreground application. On a network, OS/2's multitasking permits one machine to function as a client and a server at the same time.

OS/2 also can be used to support server-based applications through its multitasking capabilities. A server-based application has two components. One component runs in a server and provides back-end or centralized low-level functionality for multiple users. The other component runs in the PC workstation and provides the user interface (front end) to the application.

The alternative to a server-based application is the client-based application, which runs the entire application, back end and front end, in the PC workstation. Server-based applications are usually more efficient than client-based applications in running transaction-oriented programs such as database applications.

Server-based applications were possible in the DOS environment long before the appearance of OS/2. Novell NetWare supports them as value-added processes (VAPs). The IBM PC LAN program supported server-based applications as early as 1985. Only since the emergence of OS/2, however, has the server-based concept attained widespread attention. Other factors such as the growth of interprocess communication (IPC) technology and distributed processing techniques also have helped promote server-based applications, but the marketplace interest in OS/2 has been the strongest catalyst. Users are demanding, and developers will provide, more network-aware, server-based applications, which will increase the power of networking and distributed processing. OS/2 will play a key role in this process.

Using Protected Mode

The protected mode of the 80286 processor, which OS/2 supports, adds a new level of system integrity and reliability to PC-based workstations running multiple tasks. The 80386 chip can emulate this mode, enabling OS/2 to run on the more powerful 80386. The protected mode is a great enhancement in a networking environment where foreground and background tasks abound. In the protected mode with several applications running on the 80286, one application can fail without affecting the other active applications.

The 80286 was designed to force approved types of hardware access from applications. Developers have less ability to avoid standard access channels and go directly to the hardware. Such conformity also produces an overall better level of data integrity and system reliability. Under OS/2, most applications interface with the operating system kernel through dynamic linked libraries. The kernel then communicates with device drivers, which interface with the hardware.

OS/2 uses the hierarchical protections in the 80286. These protections follow a model of concentric rings (see fig. 7.3). The inner ring (ring 0) is the level at which the OS/2 kernel and device drivers run and where the drivers access the hardware interrupts. Ring 1 is not used. Ring 2 includes the dynamic linked libraries. Ring 3 is where most applications run. In this hierarchy, OS/2 applications are unable to threaten the integrity of the system. If an application fails, the operating system unloads the failed application and recovers without an overall system failure resulting.

Understanding the Advantages of OS/2

Part of the importance of OS/2 as a workstation choice is the system's strong support from IBM. OS/2 is a part of IBM's System Application Architecture (SAA), which means that the system is slated for a primary role in IBM's strategic planning. The foremost evidence of the SAA tie is the Presentation Manager. The Presentation Manager is an implementation of SAA's common user interface (CUI). All compliant CUI applications must conform to specified screen layouts, standardized user information, and other

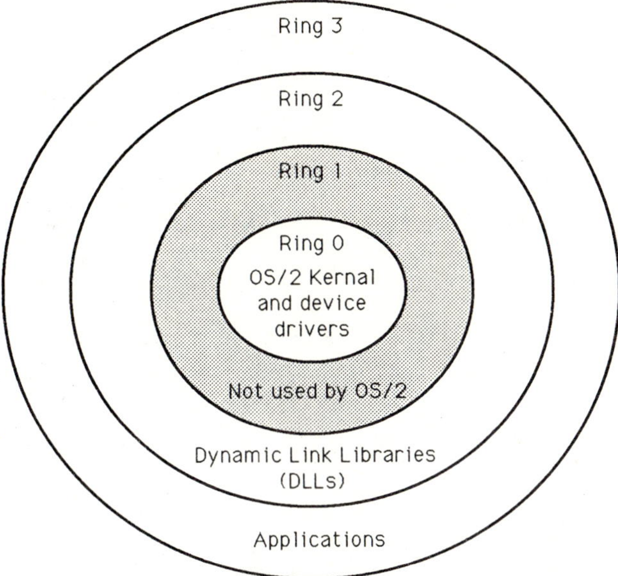

Fig. 7.3. The OS/2 hierarchical ring protection system limits access to sensitive areas.

user-interface techniques. An immediate advantage is the reduction in the retraining necessary when a user moves from one application to another. Graphics are a major aspect of the interface, offering users a presumably more appealing screen and a less intimidating way to control the machine.

Besides the functionality of OS/2, the operating system also is an upgrade in network awareness over DOS. OS/2 workstations are thus easier for network operating system vendors to support on the LAN. The network interface in an OS/2 workstation is called a *requester* rather than a shell or a redirector, and its function is different enough to warrant the different name. Included in the OS/2 kernel are redirector hooks to which you can attach a set of loadable device drivers (the requester). The significance of the requester is that OS/2 has the concept of remote file services as an integral component of its design. Therefore, unlike DOS, OS/2 does not have to be fooled about the nature of network resources.

Another aspect of OS/2 design that makes the system a good candidate for networking is its modularity. One of the goals of its designers was to allow easy upgrading by third parties who want to add special functionality. IBM, for example, is adding communications and database managers in its Extended Edition.

Understanding the Disadvantages of OS/2

OS/2 does have several drawbacks as a workstation standard. One drawback is its lack of speed. All the functionality has added significant overhead that results in OS/2 being slower than DOS. To get satisfactory speed, many users find that they must run OS/2 on high-end 80386 workstations, which adds to the cost of the solution. The relatively high cost of the OS/2 software and of the memory upgrades necessary to support the software add to the expense and force careful cost justification for any organization planning to migrate to OS/2.

Another drawback of OS/2 is its limited hardware support. Like PC DOS, OS/2 is essentially limited to Intel 808x- and 80x86-based machines. OS/2 is written to a large extent in assembly language, which is machine specific. IBM and Microsoft appear to have little interest in making OS/2 a more universal operating system. Even among PC-compatible machines, OS/2 is not well supported. Many so-called PC-compatible machines that run PC DOS satisfactorily cannot run OS/2 because of OS/2's more exacting compatibility requirements.

Networking with Unix Workstations

Unix is a multitasking, multiuser operating system of considerable vintage. Since its introduction in the early 1970s, Unix also has been used as an operating system for powerful graphics and scientific workstations. This market was relatively small when intelligent workstations were expensive. A typical configuration used the Unix host machine as a workstation for one user, and additional users were connected through dumb terminals, attached to the Unix machine with asynchronous cables. All users shared the host machine's single processor.

The PC workstation of the 1980s changed the positioning of Unix. Suddenly, running Unix on an inexpensive PC became possible, and Unix vendors and program developers began to push for Unix as a general-purpose workstation operating system. In the process, Unix implementations became smaller and more efficient, while Motorola 68030- and Intel 80386-based workstations came along with enough memory and processing power to be appropriate Unix hardware platforms.

Today, Unix is a popular and widely used operating system in networks of PC workstations. In many ways, Unix is similar to OS/2, and even though they compete directly, some significant differences focus Unix and OS/2 on distinct market segments.

Defining the Advantages of Unix

Unix is available on a greater variety of computer platforms than is any other operating system. In addition to the appeal of Unix's basic design, the availability is due to two factors. AT&T, the designers of Unix, chose to make Unix an open architecture, making source code readily available and increasing the amount of development that has been based on Unix. Additionally the Unix hardware interface is clearly defined, allowing Unix to be ported easily from one hardware platform to another. The Institute of Electrical and Electronic Engineers (IEEE) defines a set of system calls and library routines in its Portable Operating System Environment Standard (POSIX) but does not restrict enhancements to the basic set through support of proprietary services.

The use of large memory, multitasking, and protected areas of memory were standard in the Unix environment 20 years before OS/2 introduced them. What Unix has been slow to provide is a user-oriented iconographic windowing interface—a primary design feature of OS/2. Graphics and windowing, however, are available from several vendors, including the X Window System developed by Massachusetts Institute of Technology.

Although the user interface is only beginning to mature, the graphics and scientific applications available for Unix workstations are extensive. Often applications with similar functionality, aimed at narrowly defined markets, are unavailable outside the Unix environment. Similarly, many business applications have been written by developers who design systems for small businesses. These applications are intended for a multiuser system of host and terminals, but through Unix networking, they can become part of a distributed processing environment.

In the Unix world, two systems are the primary choices for networking: AT&T's Remote File System (RFS) and Sun Microsystems's Network File System (NFS). These products are generally incompatible.

Accessing Multiple File Systems

Like DOS, Unix uses a hierarchical file system, a tree-structured layout stemming from a root directory to which subdirectories link. Other subdirectories link to those subdirectories, and others to those, and so on to whatever limitations are imposed by system design (see fig. 7.4). A single Unix host can support a number of file systems, and a user may need to access two or more of these systems simultaneously. Unix supports this access by allowing a file system to be "mounted" at an arbitrary point in the hierarchical file structure. A subdirectory becomes a "mount point" at which the two directory structures merge (see fig. 7.5).

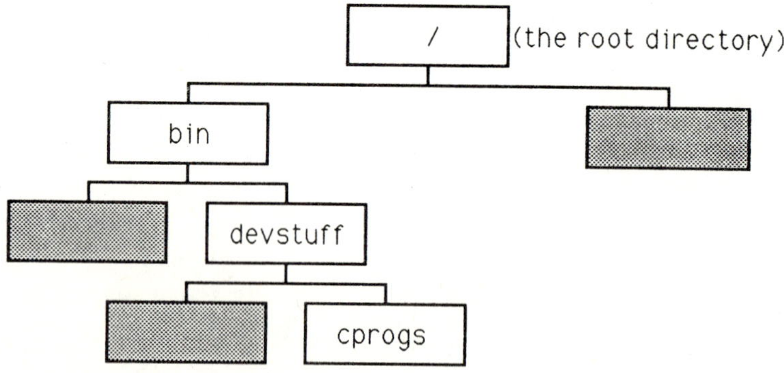

Fig. 7.4. Unix uses a hierarchical directory structure.

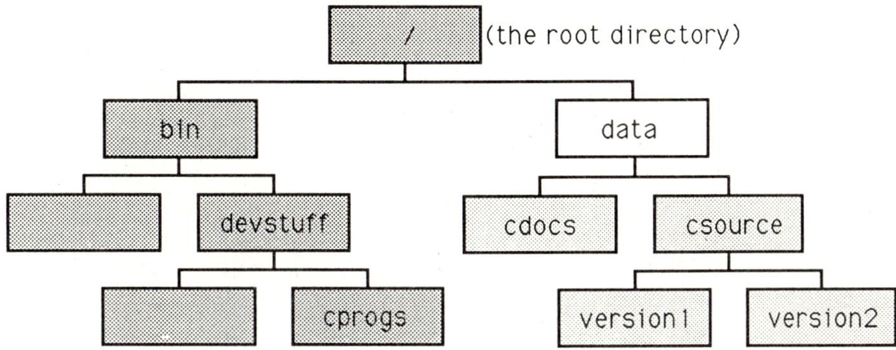

Fig. 7.5. The subdirectory data *is the mount point for the remote file system added to the directory tree.*

The limitation of a standard Unix system is that the user can access only file systems located on the machine where the user logged in. Accessing remote file systems must be accomplished through file transfer, such as the Unix-to-Unix copy program.

Using Unix network protocols such as AT&T's RFS and Sun's NFS, you can map a directory tree from one machine into the directory tree on another machine. This extension of a local file system into a server's file system, or vice-versa, is transparent to the user and applications.

Using RFS

AT&T's Remote File System (RFS) strictly follows native Unix command syntax as a transparent network extension of the basic multiuser system. Users have no need to know that they are on a network, because resources are all used as if they were local to the user's log-in station. The transparency of connection combined with the full support of Unix completely insulates users from the fact that they are on a network.

RFS runs on any of several transport protocols, through the Streams transport interface, an interface mechanism that supports connection to one of several network protocols. Usually, the transport in a Unix environment is TCP/IP or XNS (see Chapter 2, "Communications and Standards"). Streams accepts Unix requests (including RFS requests, because they are Unix compatible) and structures them for the underlying transport protocol. Through Streams, RFS becomes transport protocol independent. Streams uses mechanisms called protocol handlers, which translate transport layer protocols into the common Unix format.

In the RFS scheme, client and server machines are located in a *domain* (a defined group of machines). A machine becomes a server by advertising its file systems as a resource for other machines (clients). One machine can be a client and a server, offering its file system for client access and using the resources of other machines in the domain.

Every domain has one machine that acts as a central manager for the domain. This machine keeps a common list of domain resources and maintains security within the domain. Security includes the capability to limit the domain resources available to a specific machine, to a user name, and to a group name.

To configure the RFS environment, when the network is started, each machine advertises its available resources, if any, and mounts whatever remote file systems it requires. If the primary domain server fails, a machine previously designated as a secondary domain server assumes the primary machine's duties. Because all active machines already have mounted their required resources, including those of the primary server, the active machines are unaffected by the failure. Machines that subsequently come on-line cannot use any resources that they must get from the downed machine.

This structure does not mean that a downed machine has no effect on the network. On the contrary, an application that is accessing a file on a machine that goes off the network will find the service suspended or terminated. The file itself may become corrupted. The benefit of the RFS approach is that the view of the network is maintained over the period of a machine outage.

This environment is a powerful one for networking Unix systems but has several drawbacks:

- ❑ The network structure is not completely robust, because the maintenance of the Unix file access mechanisms does not allow for explicit knowledge of network conditions. All error conditions, therefore, are not seen as network errors but as file errors.

- ❑ The traffic on the network is higher than it would be for a tuned networking system, because the network supports a generalized view of input/output activity. A generalized view means that many confirmations and status reports are generated because the communications system supports a wide and nonspecific variety of messages between the client and the server. A tuned system would allow for the elimination of possibly redundant condition reports and thus offer higher performance.
- ❑ The directory structure is not necessarily consistent when viewed from different machines, because of the flexible nature of the RFS scheme.

Using NFS

Sun Microsystems's Network File System (NFS) permits a remote file system to be treated as if the system were local, much as RFS does. NFS differs from RFS, however, in that NFS is not a networking superset of Unix. NFS does not follow all Unix semantics of input/output.

At the level of network access and organization, NFS and RFS are similar. Both the advertising and mounting of remote file systems exist, but in NFS the Streams interface is replaced with Remote Procedure Calls (RPC) and External Data Representation (XDR). The file system access method also is different. NFS uses a virtual file system that masks the real file system. This design ensures that portability is maximized because no assumption is made about the client or server file architectures.

The RPC facility is central to this strategy. RPC enables the request for service to be transmitted across the network as a high-level I/O request rather than a low-level request. The RPC call links the components of the client and server NFS support as if they were in the same machine. XDR is a machine-independent low-level protocol that enables data represented under different OSs and processors to be carried in a common format. Machines of different types can therefore "talk" to each other, using data that is, as far as they are concerned, in their own formats.

NFS enables non-Unix operating systems to network and use the network's resources. PC DOS, OS/2, and other workstation OSs can be supported relatively easily as clients of an NFS server. Sun, a leading Unix/NFS systems vendor, offers a Unix-to-MS-DOS network support called PC-NFS.

The fact that NFS is in the public domain has a certain value, because the implementation of the protocol by various vendors has a defined common standard. NFS also has better error-recovery characteristics than RFS and a lower potential traffic because read-aheads and write-behinds can be performed.

Networking with Apple Workstations

Macintosh is the name of the personal computer and the operating system from Apple. The design of both is unique, and consequently, because of the system's popularity, the Macintosh has become a standard in its own right.

The Macintosh is based on previous Apple products, most notably the Lisa. Lisa differed from most PC configurations and was a complete, proprietary system, but one that was difficult to expand. Since its launch, the Macintosh has evolved from being a truly personal computer (friendly and portable) to having a configuration similar to an IBM PC. The overall design features that made the Macintosh so successful are still in place, but the system has given up some simplicity to permit expansion and easier third-party support.

The original Macintosh operating system was, for the PC world, revolutionary in its design. Macintosh OS was based on a user interface that was extremely well designed and implemented on a bit-mapped graphics system. The result was that the user saw applications that had a consistent, generic interface in all aspects of presentation. This system was arguably the first real WYSIWYG (What You See Is What You Get) environment on a personal computer. Documents were shown on-screen as they appeared when printed, and they could contain pictures, charts, and other graphic items.

The building blocks of the Macintosh are managers and support subsystems that control different areas of service. All interaction with each manager is event-driven, ensuring that applications are capable of optimal performance with respect to the operating system and multiple system process.

The Macintosh is now a multitasking system that handles up to 8M of memory. One of the key features of the Macintosh has always been its desk accessories (DAs), programs that can be selected from a pull-down menu while any application is executing.

The basis of all Macintosh network communication is AppleTalk, the protocol set that integrates Macintoshes with a network system. This set of services is built into the Macintosh operating system. The heart of AppleTalk is a proprietary peer-to-peer architecture that can be split into layers equivalent to the OSI Reference Model. The peer-to-peer aspect of AppleTalk enables the Macintosh network scheme to be self-configuring—no central controller is involved.

The self-configuring aspect of AppleTalk is made possible by the Apple Name Binding Protocol (NBP), which allows for dynamic establishment of node names and addresses. AppleTalk also includes a protocol, Apple Filing Protocol (AFP), for establishing access to and resolving conflicts in the remote shared file subsystem. To support remote printing, the AppleTalk system uses Printer Access Protocol (PAP).

One of the most seductive aspects of Macintosh networking is that the Macintosh comes with a built-in network port. This port connects to a network of dual twisted-pair cabling running at 230.4 Kbits/sec. The system, called LocalTalk, can support up to 32 users in its basic configuration, with up to 1000 feet between nodes. The major drawback is the low transmission speed, which means that file access, as well as most network functions, is slow.

Many alternatives to the LocalTalk connections are now available, alternatives that include EtherNet support for Macintosh IIs. The EtherNet connection, called EtherTalk by Apple, allows for connection to standard IEEE 802.3 systems. Macintoshes also have been successfully networked over RS232 links and fiber-optic systems.

The server for an AppleTalk supporting system can be one of several systems, including Apple's own Appleshare, Novell NetWare for Macintosh, and Sun's TOPS. These systems all implement support for AFP directly. TOPS and NetWare for Macintosh allow for the integration of PCs and Macs.

The connection to a server from a workstation is established by a desk accessory called the Chooser. This DA enables you to select a server, register your name and password, and specify which volume on the server to open. The same method of establishing access applies to printers; you select them through the Chooser.

Networking with the Macintosh is straightforward. Although many vendors offer a large range of connectivity products, however, few Macintosh applications really use the network in a multiuser manner. The major exception might be in the area of groupware, where electronic mail systems are becoming extremely sophisticated.

The Macintosh, despite its built-in networking support and highly sophisticated operating system, is still a new player in local area networking, but the Macintosh may become a major player as the applications become available.

Chapter Summary

The choice of workstation is the single most important aspect of system functionality. In the past, such decisions were based on network compatibility more than any other criteria, and often the list of compatible machines was severely limited. Today, however, many types of workstations can be placed on the same network and can communicate and share resources.

General compatibility and the capability to integrate dissimilar machines moves the selection process back to looking at the workstation itself: what jobs the machine must perform and what software the machine must run, as well as size, cost, and management issues.

DOS workstations are viable for the foreseeable future and are satisfactory for many applications. When multitasking workstations are required, the OS/2, Unix, and Macintosh machines with their respective operating systems all offer unique advantages.

8

LAN Evaluation

The previous chapters had one goal: to build a foundation for evaluating and selecting a local area network. The LAN market offers shoppers many choices in networks, features, components, and prices. This variety tends to complicate the selection process, but a wide variety of choices also enables users to design systems especially suited to their particular needs.

Long before the network is actually up and running, many components must be evaluated: applications, software, peripherals, workstations, servers, and LAN hardware. The consideration of applications software and peripherals can wait for the moment; this section concentrates on the components of the basic system.

Determining the Applications and Environment

In most cases, the selection process should be based on the intended applications and on the environment in which the network is used. The first stage in the evaluation process, therefore, should be a careful description of the LAN functions and the physical site.

The answers to the following questions about the physical site and the needed functions will help you develop a careful description:

Physical Site

Workstation locations

What is the maximum distance between workstations?
Are workstations clustered or distributed?
Is the site a multifloor facility?

Existing cable

Is there any existing cable?
Is the cable telephone wire (twisted pair)?
Is the cable host-to-terminal cable such as RG-62?
Is the cable some other type (specify)?

Functions Workstation activity

How many workstations?

What types of workstations will be used (brand and model)?

How many hours will each workstation be in use?

What are each workstation's applications (word processing, data entry, and so on)?

What percentage of each workday is devoted to each application?

Performance

What is the desired response time? (Select comparable.)
8088 floppy drive
8088 hard disk drive   80286 hard disk drive

Which is the primary consideration?
Cost?
Performance?

Answers to these questions help determine the right LAN system for a particular site. Following are some examples of how the site definition is used.

Examining the Physical Site Requirements

Physical site requirements help determine what network cable and equipment arrangements are best. Each type of cable has built-in distance limitations. The four relevant types of cable are twisted pair, baseband coaxial, broadband coaxial, and fiber optics. Twisted pair supports short runs. Baseband coax supports longer runs. Broadband coax and fiber optics support extremely long runs. Transmission speed is limited by cable, too, with fiber optics being the fastest, followed by baseband coax, broadband coax, and twisted pair.

In addition to general cable characteristics, you should consider the types of available cable. You may be able to use already installed cable on the LAN. Twisted-pair and 3270 cabling (RG-62) often are available and can be used for LANs, provided that the cable is in satisfactory condition for high speed transmissions.

Twisted Pair

Before you decide to use installed telephone wire (twisted pair) for a LAN, you should test carefully its condition and suitability. Voice transmissions are much more tolerant of media imperfections than are data transmissions. Barely audible noise on the line that is only annoying during a telephone conversation often prevents successful data communications.

Telephone systems often are a collection of old and new wiring and switches, and this media frequently fails during high-speed data communications. Higher data transmission rates (in excess of 1M/sec) and longer distances between communicating devices increase the likelihood of data communications failure.

Telephone-wire systems, however, are being used successfully for LANs in many buildings—and with a considerable savings in cabling costs. Do not reject the idea without testing its feasibility.

Broadband Coaxial

Existing broadband cable systems can be used for new LAN installations, provided that the existing installation supports two-way communications. Many corporations and campuses have a broadband cable system that was installed for cable TV transmissions. Converting a cable TV system to support broadband data transmissions is seldom practical because the initial cable TV installation was designed for one-way communications. LANs are two-way communications systems. Installing new broadband cable usually is cheaper than converting the existing system. Due to the large potential savings of using an existing cable system, its feasibility for a particular site always should be analyzed by an expert.

Understanding Long-Term Implications of Cable Selection

Cable selection has long-term implications that are especially significant in large installations. If properly chosen and installed, LAN cable can give satisfactory service for 10, 15, or more years before the cable has to be replaced or upgraded. Because the cable and cable installation costs typically are 50 percent of the cost of the entire installation, careful planning is well worth the effort.

Matching Network Topology to the Site Layout

Network topology should be matched to the site layout. The arrangement affects the amount of cable that must be purchased and installed. Even the cable bulk should be considered. Some cable trays may not have room for three or four more wires that may be required by some arrangements. If workstations are clustered, a star topology is ideal. If workstations are distributed through individual offices, a linear bus topology is good. The distributed star topology is a natural choice when connection must be made to small clusters of workstations distributed through several offices. Premises wiring schemes, such as the AT&T Premises Distribution System and the IBM Cabling System, were designed as wiring schemes for large buildings. These schemes use a star topology for individual floors and connect the floors with riser cables—a good strategy for high-rise installations.

Determining Network Functions

Network functions and performance are closely related. Looking at the checklist, you may realize that the proposed network has a current need for eight workstations. If three workstations will be added within a few months, also include those as current workstations. As the function (including number of users, applications, and volume of traffic) increases, performance will degrade. Advance planning can prevent the problem.

Long-range growth should be considered and included in your overall network strategy. Because of the flexible architecture of networks, however, you usually do not need to install a high-performance system in anticipation of a future need. The subject of network growth is covered in detail in Chapter 19.

The number of workday hours a workstation is in use is a factor in determining the station's impact on the network. For example, a workstation may be used by outside salespeople for an average of three hours a day, or the workstation may be used a full eight hours a day. The types of applications and their percentage of the day's activity also affects the network. Word processing is a light user of a network because most processing is done locally. Database work is a heavy user of a network because data must be sent back continually to the network to update the shared hard disk.

Evaluating NICs

All the components in a LAN have the potential to affect the LAN's performance, yet no classification scheme commonly is available to rate LAN component performance. Because performance ratings are not available, you have to use what statistics are available to estimate performance.

The network interface card (NIC) has four characteristics that typically are used to predict NIC performance:

- ❑ Bit rate
- ❑ Access method
- ❑ Onboard processor
- ❑ NIC-to-host transfer features

Considering Bit Rate

The bit rate often is referred to as the speed of the LAN. LANs are rated according to the speed of data crossing a clear piece of cable. Most of today's LANs have bit rates from 1 Mbit/sec up to 16 Mbits/sec delivered by the NIC. Actual throughput is never 100 percent of the bit rate because of other LAN performance factors; because of individual NIC design factors, one 10 Mbits/sec NIC may have very high throughput, whereas another 10 Mbits/sec NIC may have very low throughput. Therefore, bit rate is a poor way to compare LANs, especially when the bit rates of the systems being compared are close.

Bit rate, however, should be considered in the selection process. Although a high bit rate does not guarantee high throughput, a low bit rate does guarantee low throughput. A 1 Mbit/sec LAN might get a high 80 percent of the bit rate as throughput. That amount, however, is only 0.8 Mbit/sec or 100 kilobytes per second throughput. A 10 Mbits/sec LAN might be much less efficient, getting perhaps 40 percent of the bit rate as throughput. Yet 40 percent would amount to 4 Mbits/sec throughput.

Choosing a Cable Access Scheme

The cable access scheme of a NIC tells virtually nothing about its actual performance. A token-passing access scheme is slightly more efficient in high-traffic situations than a contention scheme (CSMA-CD); however, the difference would not be significant for most installations.

Evaluating the Onboard Processor

The onboard processor also is a poor way to judge NICs. Logically, an onboard processor should provide a faster, more efficient NIC. In practice, though, the firmware used to control the onboard processor often is inefficient, and that factor increases system overhead.

Comparing NIC-to-Host Transfer Features

NIC-to-host transfer features—the fourth of the NIC evaluation features—are the most valuable for making comparisons. The width of a current transfer bus is 8, 16, or 32 bits. A NIC with a 16-bit-wide bus interface transfers data twice as fast as an 8-bit-wide interface. A 32-bit-wide bus is, likewise, twice as fast as a 16-bit interface.

Three methods are used to cross the bus and transfer data: shared memory, I/O port, and direct memory access (DMA). Shared memory is the fastest because it involves no data transfers. DMA is the slowest because all data must be transferred into a contiguous area of memory to be read.

Considering the Types of Workstations Supported by NICs

One other criterion that should be considered when evaluating NICs is the types of workstations the NICs support. The IBM PC bus is a standard and all the NICs discussed in this book can be plugged into PC or PC-compatible buses. The IBM micro-channel bus also is supported widely. Additionally, many LAN companies make NICs that also support other buses. If your company wants to network different types of PCs, bus compatibility becomes an important issue.

Today, much of the decision for network interface cards is dominated by cost in smaller LANs and by overall requirements and cost for larger LANs. NICs with transmission rates of 1 Mbit/sec should be used only on smaller LANs. Where high speed is required, a 16-bit or 32-bit NIC-to-host transfer is desirable.

Evaluating Servers

Many computers can act as network servers. Most are PC-compatible machines; however, several machines have been designed especially for use as network servers. The features used to describe network servers in Chapter 4 are the primary ones used in evaluation. These features are as follows:

- ❑ Processor
- ❑ Clock cycle speed
- ❑ Wait states
- ❑ Memory (max)
- ❑ Expansion bus
- ❑ Bus width

Understanding the Processor

The processor is the most commonly understood performance factor. Anybody who has ever used an 8088 workstation and then switched to an 80286 workstation knows the effect of faster processors.

Processor speed is rated according to how much data a processor can process and transfer in a single block. The Intel 8088 processor, which is used in PC- and XT-compatible machines, processes data 16 bits at a time and transfers data 8 bits at a time. The Intel 80186 processes and transfers data in 16-bit blocks. Intel's 80286, used in AT-compatible machines, also is a 16/16 processor. The Intel 80386 and the Motorola MC68030 process data 32 bits at a time and transfer 32 bits at a time. Faster machines like the 80386 also offer slower bus slots in addition to the 32-bit slots.

Evaluating the Clock Cycle Speed

The processor is driven at a set speed by a component called a clock crystal. Faster clock cycle speeds result in faster performance. An 80286 machine with a 6 MHz crystal, for example, might be able to perform a task in one second, but, with an 8 MHz crystal, the machine could do the same task in 0.6 seconds.

Understanding Wait States

In computers, circuitry performance and processor/clock crystal performance must be balanced. A processor that runs faster than the circuits can support must be slowed down. You can slow down a processor by placing wait states between the processor and the circuitry. One wait state is a period of time equal to one cycle of the clock crystal. Because wait states cause a delay in the delivery of data to the circuitry, the flow of data matches the capability of the circuitry. A machine with one wait state is slower than a machine with zero wait states, all other things being equal.

Evaluating the Maximum Memory Available

Memory maximum refers to the total amount of random-access memory (RAM) supported in the machine. Available RAM can be used in a server to store data temporarily in electronic memory. Because accesses to electronic memory are much faster than accesses to a physical disk, available RAM does affect performance.

Understanding the Expansion Bus

Expansion buses, which enable computers to adapt to changing technology, affect performance and adaptability. Machines with industry-standard expansion buses, such as PC-compatible machines, generally transfer data slower than machines that use proprietary buses. However, expansion buses often are desirable. For example, new generations of NICs generally perform better than old NICs. The old NICs can be replaced, provided that the machine has an expansion bus. Moreover, an expansion bus permits the machine to serve multiple networks when that capability is supported by the network operating system.

Evaluating the Bus Width

The bus width involves the same issue as the NIC-to-host transfer width discussed under network interface cards. A 32-bit-wide bus transfers data twice as fast as an 16-bit-wide bus.

Evaluating Operating Systems

The choice of network operating system, perhaps more than any other LAN component, determines the success of the LAN (see Chapter 6, "Network Operating Systems"). Traditionally, the criteria used to evaluate network operating systems include the following:

- ❑ Performance
- ❑ Functionality
- ❑ Compatible applications
- ❑ Extras (bells and whistles)
- ❑ Cost

These criteria are very oriented to end-user demands. A manager in a workgroup or department has some PC users and wants to network them. The decision is essentially a short-term tactical one. When LANs have no place in the company's long-term strategic data communications system, these criteria may suffice.

Evaluating Performance

The tactical issues, of course, are still relevant. Performance of the operating system is still important to individual users, some of whose applications may require specific performance levels. Performance also is a factor in the total number of workstations that can be placed under one operating system; a high performance operating system can support more workstations. Therefore, when a network is growing, performance of the operating system is another factor in assessing the real cost of the system, because a low performance operating system might require more file servers and operating systems to support a given number of workstations.

Evaluating Functionality

Functionality is an issue related to each site's requirements. Most network operating systems can perform similar basic functions, but they do vary in the user and management interface for these functions, as well as in some special functions.

As LANs are integrated into strategic networks and begin supporting activities that are critical to the organization, new criteria become important in operating system selection. The end-user's criteria do not go away; strategic criteria are added. The strategic criteria include the following:

- ❑ Reliability
- ❑ Manageability
- ❑ Migration path
- ❑ Standards compliance
- ❑ Cost

Evaluating Reliability and Manageability

These criteria might be divided into two groups: how the system functions today, and how easily the system will adapt to tomorrow's changes. Reliability and manageability are necessary characteristics of any system that is critical to the organization. These characteristics are system issues that managers of information systems in multiuser environments are familiar with, but which have not been of much concern on smaller, tactical LANs.

Planning a Migration Path and Standards Compliance

Migration path and standards compliance are interrelated issues that determine how well a technology will merge into new technologies. Standards compliance is increasingly meaningful as network technologies mature and real standards, such as the OSI protocols, emerge. However, vendors need to do more than just agree to support new standards. Because tracking standards can be very costly for an organization, an orderly migration plan for moving to those standards must be formed.

Evaluating Cost

Cost appears in both lists; however, cost is measured differently for tactical and strategic systems. In a tactical system, for example, the cost is measured against specific tasks and short-term goals. In a strategic system, costs are measured against corporate, long-term goals and the evaluators are typically upper-level management. Cost for strategic LANs should certainly be estimated as an annual amount, spread across a long period of time. If a particular network operating system does not appear to be a long-term product—lacking the ability to integrate into existing or planned networks, lacking a strategy for supporting standards, or lacking a clear product migration path—the operating system probably should be avoided. Histories of past performance on these issues, statements of direction, and analysis of the operating system's fundamental architecture should provide good clues for the evaluation.

Estimating Hardware Performance

Hardware performance should be measured as a separate issue from network operating system performance. In general, performance on a network is best expressed as throughput: how long does a request take to make its way from the workstation through the network to its destination? The two key hardware elements in that throughput are the NIC and the server. Utilities, such as the Novell Perform utility, can measure throughput. A less precise, though useful, measurement can be made by using a watch to time standard operations such as file transfer or program loading on perspective systems.

Understanding the NIC

A particular NIC-server combination can develop a maximum amount of throughput for a LAN. If that throughput is expressed in kilobytes per second, the NIC-server combination can put only a certain amount of kilobytes per second on the network.

Understanding the Server

Each network user shares that network throughput. If your NIC-server combination can deliver 300K per second throughput, and you are the only active user on the network, then your potential for receiving data is at 300K per second. If two other people are using the network at the same time, the total throughput now is divided among three users. Each could get a maximum of 100K per second.

Evaluating a NIC-Server Combination

One other factor is significant: how much throughput a single workstation actually can handle under a particular NIC-server combination. Because of workstation limitations, that figure usually is going to be less than maximum NIC-server throughput. To calculate the probable throughput available to each workstation for a given NIC/server combination, therefore, you need to know the following three items:

- ❑ The maximum throughput
- ❑ The single-station throughput
- ❑ The number of users

Of these variables, determining the number of users is the most difficult. The type of application and the number of hours per day devoted to that application decide the actual load on the network. For example, you might have a ten-station network, but one workstation is in the boss's office and is never used. Obviously, when you are calculating the number of people that divide up the available NIC-server throughput, you divide by nine workstations, not ten, even though the network actually is connected to ten workstations.

That example, however, is rudimentary. The number of users needs to be defined much more carefully. For an estimate of user activity, categorize users into five groups. (The site questionnaire at the beginning of this chapter will help in user definition.)

Type 1—A Very Light User

A type 1 user uses the network very lightly, mostly for local processing applications—that is, word processing and spreadsheets. This person is classed as a 1 to 5 percent user of the network, depending on how many hours a day the user spends utilizing the network.

Type 2—An Active User

A type 2 user is more active, using applications that require more disk access. This type of work includes light database activity or mail merge. This person is a 5 to 10 percent network user.

Type 3—A Shared Disk User

A type 3 user must frequently access the shared disk for such applications as heavy database or mail-merge work. As a general rule, applications for this type of user spend about the same amount of time accessing the shared disk as they do manipulating the data at the workstation. This person is a 10 to 20 percent user of the network, again depending on the number of hours spent using the application.

Type 4—A Very Heavy User

A type 4 user is a very heavy user of the network, doing applications that require a great deal of disk access. Such applications include reservation systems. The type 4 user is a 20 to 40 percent user.

Type 5—A Constant User

A type 5 user is someone who constantly demands as much throughput as the station can deliver. Continuously copying files from the shared hard disk, as in a backup operation, or performing compiles in a program development environment are examples of this type of user's applications. A type 5 user is a 40 to 100 percent user.

Using the Performance Formula

The formula for estimating system throughput is

T = M / U

T stands for available-per-workstation throughput; *M* stands for maximum network throughput, and *U* stands for 100 percent users. A 100 percent user is a person running an application that uses the network to the maximum possible from a single workstation. The figure for 100 percent users is developed by adding the percentages together for all users on the system. A sample site might have the following users:

5 Type 1 users each with a weight of 0.04 = 0.20

10 Type 2 users each with a weight of 0.10 = 1.00

1 Type 3 user with a weight of 0.20 = 0.20

Total: 1.40

For the example, the NIC-server combination is an ARCnet network with an IBM AT server. Table 8.1 shows the maximum NIC-server throughput: 104.54 K/sec for the ARCnet-AT combination.

The formula using the site load and throughput figures from table 8.1 is the following:

74.6714 = 104.54 / 1.40

That formula indicates that the available per station throughput is approximately 75 K/sec (74.6714).

Now compare that figure with the data in table 8.2. A single workstation can support a limited amount of throughput, which is considerably less than the maximum throughput that can be generated by an entire network. The actual throughput that a workstation delivers will be the available per-station throughput or the maximum single-station throughput, whichever is lower.

In this case, the maximum single-station throughput for the ARCnet AT combination is 64.41 K/sec. Because that number is lower than the available per-station throughput derived from the formula, 64.41 K/sec is the actual throughput of each workstation on the network.

Table 8.1
Maximum Network Throughput

	Server Type				
Network Type	286A	AT	XT	S-Net	3Server
E	235.15	167.40	81.61		155.90
E+	410.11	278.30	125.65		
G	48.62	46.38	41.25		
O	0.00	57.01	48.12		
P	374.05	228.71	95.35		
PCN	147.75	116.19	110.86		
A	115.31	104.54	76.34		
Star					267.28
StarLan	99.35	105.24	88.06		

Network Type

E	3Com EtherLink
E+	3Com EtherLink Plus
G	Gateway Communications G-Net
O	Corvus Omninet
P	Proteon ProNet
PCN	IBM PC Network
A	ARCnet
Star	Novell Star
StarLan	AT&T StarLan

Server Type

286A	Novell 286A
AT	IBM Personal Computer AT (6 MHz)
XT	IBM PC XT
S-Net	Novell S-Net
3Server	3Com 3SErver

Note: Figures for table 8.1 were developed using six AT workstations and performing continuous read operations. All figures are in kilobytes per second. Novell Advanced NetWare was used as the operating system on all the tests except those run on the 3Com 3Server, which were run with 3+.

Table 8.2
Maximum Single-Station Throughput

	Server Type				
	286A	AT	XT	S-Net	3Server
Network Type					
E	174.93	144.40	77.52		
E+	140.06	116.85	71.64		73.53
G	32.52	31.27	25.54		
O	0.00	32.65	26.58		
P	104.85	88.69	57.80		
PCN	45.51	40.69	38.54		
A	70.67	64.41	44.40		
Star				14.39	
StarLan	53.55	48.84	37.14		

Note: Figures in table 8.2 are based on the specified network interface cards and servers connected to a single PC/AT workstation.

The final step is to compare the actual throughput with the performance of a known system. Most people compare throughput according to an 8088 or 80286 stand-alone workstation. This comparison is shown in table 8.3.

Table 8.3
Comparison of Throughput with Known System

	AT	XT
Floppy	21.61	16.04
Hard Disk	119.40	58.22

The performance of the sample system is 64.41 K/sec or approximately the same as an XT hard disk.

Evaluating New Products

Vendors will continue to improve their products to deliver greater performance, and throughput will change with the introduction of these products. New performance data can be calculated by using the data in tables 8.1 and 8.2 with the NIC and server evaluation criteria discussed earlier. A faster server processor or clock cycle speed or an improved NIC-to-host interface produces higher performance than that shown in these models.

Chapter Summary

This evaluation system illustrates how individual workstation performance changes as the amount of network traffic changes. Network traffic, as you have seen, is a function of the number of users, the types of applications, and the hours per day of actual workstation operation. Workstation performance on the network also changes according to the type of server, NIC, and workstation.

Another important factor in network performance is the configuration and use of the system. This factor is the topic of Chapter 12.

III

Applications on the Network

Includes

Applications Software

Applications Programming Interfaces

Electronic Mail

Groupware

Distributed Data Services and SQL

9

Applications Software

The availability of excellent applications software is a major reason for the appeal of personal computers. More than 40,000 software packages have been written for DOS-compatible PCs. The large amount of software available is not all that is important; the unique nature of the software also is significant. The development of PC-based software marks the first time that a library of full-functioned computer programs has been written specifically for a nontechnical user community.

When people consider attaching their PCs to a LAN, the first question they want answered is whether they can still use PC-based software. The answer to this question is almost invariably yes. Of the tens of thousands of DOS-compatible software applications, all but a small handful of programs can be used on a PC LAN. What is often misunderstood, however, is that software applications differ widely in how they run on the network. Furthermore, specific incompatibilities may occur—for example, between a memory-resident LAN operating system and other memory-resident programs, or between a LAN operating system that expects to control a particular interrupt (PC-control mechanism) and another program that expects to control the same interrupt.

Determining Hard Disk Compatibility

New LAN users often encounter some surprises in running their single-user applications. Usually, the first thing a new LAN user wants to do is put a favorite application program on the hard disk, then share the program. The user assumes that because the software works on a floppy, the software ought to work on a network hard disk. This assumption may be wrong if the program comes on a copy-protected disk.

Networking enables businesses to store on a network hard disk a single copy of a software application that several users can share. Centralized distribution, from the server to multiple users, is a convenient way to manage software. This distribution ensures that everybody uses the same version of the software and makes the software application easier to support. Unfortunately, some packages use a copy-protection scheme that prevents the package from being loaded onto a hard disk. Such packages cannot be copied onto the network's hard disk. Instead, they must be loaded into the PC workstation's floppy disk drive to run the application.

The packages still run on the network; most program files and all the spreadsheet data can be stored on the shared hard disk. You also can create and store templates for the application on the hard disk and share the templates and the data among other network users. The only limitation is that while running these applications, every PC workstation must load the program initially from a protected copy in drive A. Most of the benefits of networking still are available to users, although part of the program must be loaded locally.

Site Licensing

The reason behind copy-protection is easy to understand. Without some kind of protection, people could buy one $500 single-user package, load the package onto the network, and share it with everybody in the office. From the user's perspective, however, a different consideration exists: single copies of application programs become very expensive when the single-copy price is multiplied by a department or company of users.

Site licensing is a compromise. Many software companies now offer a discount for multiuser installations. Pricing may be by the company, in which case, after the license is purchased, any employee of the company can legally use the software. The pricing also may be by the site, the network, or a certain number of users. These schemes all are similar in that the software price per user is less than the single-user price.

Single-User Applications

A LAN is a multiuser environment because workstations attached to the LAN can share its resources. Applications software is one of those resources. Enabling network users to share one copy of an application is convenient. With the exception of some copy-protected software discussed previously, most applications software can be stored on the LAN and shared among the networked users (see fig. 9.1).

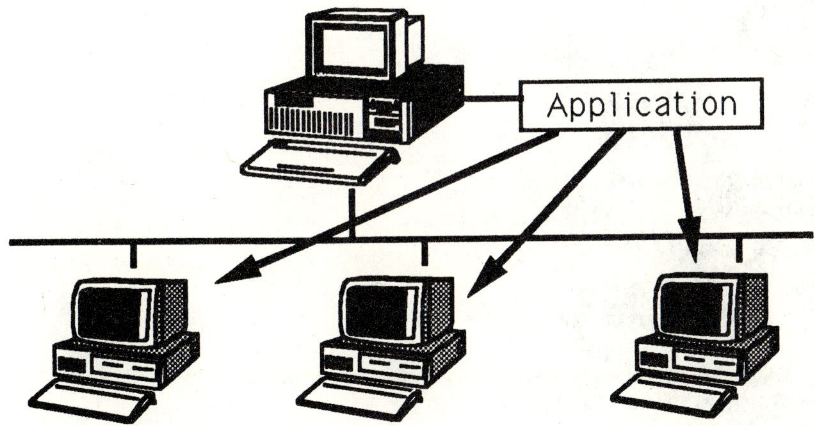

Fig. 9.1. On a LAN, applications usually are stored at the file server and downloaded to workstations.

The data created by those applications also is shareable—but with limitations. The difference is that applications usually are read-only files, but data files often must be modifiable (read/write). When two or more people modify data at the same time, the data can be corrupted. Software that is written to protect data in a multiuser environment is called multiuser software.

Not all software has to be multiuser, however, to perform adequately on the LAN. Some applications are primarily single user. They work correctly whether they run on a single PC or a LAN. The following categories of software commonly are used on the PC:

1. Word processing
2. Spreadsheet
3. Database
4. Communications
5. Graphics

Word-processing, spreadsheet, communications, and graphics software are single-user applications. Ordinarily, you should not let someone else modify a spreadsheet while you are modifying the same spreadsheet. Communications refers to the modem-based, 300- to 2400-baud applications, not high-speed networking communications. Conferencing will make communications a shareable, multiuser application, but the communications software available today still is single-user.

Most problems of concurrent access involve databases and database management systems (DBMS). A database is any compilation of information, usually including lists, records, and short amounts of text. Most companies have only one database for a category of information. Only one database should exist so that everyone updates and uses the same information.

A DBMS is applications software that enables users to manipulate and perform many useful operations with the database. As a common resource, the database should be fully available to everyone who needs to use the database. The networked DBMS is responsible for making the database available simultaneously to multiple users while protecting the data from the problems that may result from multiple access. Single-user DBMS software can be run on a network but may invite disaster.

A multiuser approach file locking can protect single-user applications. If one user opens a file and a second user tries to open the same file, the network can automatically deny file access to the second user. In a sense, this approach is multiuser. When applications require that several people open and access the same file, however, file locking is inadequate. In the example that follows, consider what happens on a typical network if the DBMS has not been written to handle multiuser access.

Two users each load a copy of the database management application. One common characteristic of the DBMS is to make as few writes as possible because disk access slows the system down. When loaded, the DBMS is held in memory. If user A wants to retrieve a record, the information on where that record is and how to retrieve the record is found in the memory of user A's PC, not in the disk server. Because the two PCs are not sharing each other's memory, they do not share the data—only copies of the data.

As long as the data on the disk remains unchanged, no problem occurs. But, suppose that user A deletes a record from a database which user B also is using. User B should somehow be informed of the change; otherwise, both users could destroy one another's work.

A network operating system can provide locking down to the record level. But locking, deleting, and unlocking the record does not solve the problem outlined here. The information in the memory of one PC does not match the information in the memory of the other PC. Somehow, user B must be told to reread the data, and user A must be told to write the update so that when user B reads the record, the data will be accurate. A single-user DBMS does not perform this task.

Multiuser Applications

How then is the problem solved? The only solution is to use a multiuser approach so that the multiuser software writes the file to disk and updates the file correctly. With this procedure, user B knows when a change has been made and when to reread the data. In this way, multiuser DBMSs manage multiple writes to disk. When a record is marked as modified, the multiuser DBMS informs the file on the disk. User B looks at the file on the disk and sees that the file has been modified. This procedure lets user B know that the information and index are invalid and that the file must be reread.

When user A opens a data file, deletes a record, or modifies a record, a bit is set on the file on disk. This bit indicates that the file has been modified. Before user B does anything with that data, the application checks the bit and sees that the file has been modified. The program rereads the data out of the index file, then retrieves the data and performs an update on the file in the PC's memory. These two users appear to be sharing memory, but they really are sharing the disk and synchronizing its use.

Selecting Single-User Software

Certain applications have been identified as essentially single user. A word-processing package, for example, is classed as single user because, typically, two or more people do not need to work on the same file at the same time.

Single-user software, however, can be enhanced to be more functional and take advantage of the features offered by a LAN. One such enhancement is the support of multiple output devices. Most single PC workstations have one output device, usually a small dot-matrix printer. Most single-user software reflects this situation: during configuration you select one output device—the only device you can use without entering the configuration program and reconfiguring the software.

On LANs, however, two or more output devices usually are shared on the network. They may include a laser printer and several dot-matrix printers loaded with special forms or paper (printout paper, invoices, shipping labels, and so on). Applications software packages that allow easy output device selection from within the program are desirable in a LAN environment.

Some single-user applications now are equipped with their own locking capability to lock data files and password schemes to prevent unauthorized access. These features already may be available through the network operating system, but by providing them through the application, the software developer makes these features easier to use in some circumstances.

Efficiency is another consideration. Some software programs are better suited to networking than comparable programs. For example, a program that runs mostly in memory is more efficient than one that accesses the disk frequently. Even in a single-user environment, frequent disk accesses slow down response time. On a LAN, disk-access requests must contend with requests from other users; therefore, a high number of requests may reduce system performance.

Older software programs often are guilty of a flagrantly wasteful number of disk accesses, at least from a LAN perspective. These programs were written when 64K of RAM was considered standard. To deliver functionality but stay within the memory constraints, programmers left much of the application on disk, to be picked up as needed.

Programming on the Network

This chapter has given you the tools to select appropriate software products. You, however, may want to do some programming and to design your own software. In this section, you look at applications from that perspective.

LAN programmers are faced with several issues unique to a LAN's multiuser environment. Foremost among these issues is the impact of PCs on the network. A LAN is not a single-processor system. On the LAN, processor and memory in each PC are autonomous for every user. Because the LAN comprises intelligent PC workstations, the LAN application actually is residing in a multiprocessing environment.

In this multiprocessing environment, duplicate data may be stored in several workstations. A lock/write/unlock update sequence can be executed by one PC to the hard disk, but if the old data in other machines is subsequently restored to the hard disk, these later disk writes may destroy the original update.

Programmers writing for multiuser host-to-terminal systems do not have this problem because all the processing and memory reside in the host machine. This potential problem is fundamental in LAN multiuser systems, however, and must be solved by the programmer.

To synchronize updates and provide data integrity, the programmer can use any of several tools. These tools include file locking, record locking, field locking, and transaction processing. (Transaction processing means clearing local memory and locking and rereading the data before modification.)

File Locking

Each option has advantages and disadvantages. To decide which option is best for a particular situation, the programmer must judge each multiuser problem separately. File locking, for example, limits the accessibility of the entire database to other users—often an unacceptable requirement. To a much lesser extent, record locking also limits data accessibility and is sometimes inappropriate for large, multiuser systems. Field locking adds processing overhead and may reduce application performance, and field locking places the smallest possible restriction on data accessibility.

Selecting the Language

The next issue facing the programmer is language selection. To write applications for LANs, you can use the same language packages you have used for stand-alone (non-networked) PC applications. If several users share your applications, however, you may want to switch to a language available in a network version. Typically, a network version of a language includes locking routines. These features simplify application programming, because to give the application basic multiuser functionality, all you have to do is use these built-in lock and unlock calls.

Unfortunately, most network versions offer no multiuser features beyond basic locking. Management of printers and other shared resources on the LAN usually is not supported, and you must write the appropriate subroutines to handle these devices.

If you are an active multiuser programmer, you should develop and maintain your own library of multiuser subroutines. This process starts with an assessment of your programming language. You must learn what functions the language provides and what other functions are up to the programmer to create. After you know the language's limitations, you can begin to build your library with subroutines that are appropriate for your particular applications.

The preceding paragraphs on LAN multiuser programming hardly scratch the surface of this complex topic. Multiuser programming for a LAN is certainly one of the most difficult areas in computer programming and, potentially, one of the most rewarding. The growth of local area networking is closely tied to the quality of application programs that are developed.

Chapter Summary

LAN technology has just begun to explore the potential of distributed processing. LAN hardware and operating systems are now mature enough to support sophisticated, innovative applications that create new environments and do not merely mimic traditional host-to-terminal environments.

Even IBM, that staunch proponent of host-type networks, has acknowledged the significance of distributed intelligent networks. Systems Network Architecture (SNA) is IBM's overall plan for office communications. An increasingly important component of SNA is defined in Logical Unit (LU) 6.2 and the Advanced Program-to-Program Communication (APPC) implementation.

APPC enables application programs to communicate with each other across LANs and host (mainframe/mini) systems without having these communications routed through the host computer. Such program-to-program communication makes data accessible from a variety of systems without the intervention of the end user. For example, you could be creating a database report and ask for data that is not on your system to include in your report. With APPC, the application could go out and get that data from another system without your having to tell the application what to do or how to do it. You do not even have to be aware that the other system was contacted.

Distributed processing applications soon will play a major role in data processing. Programmers who understand LANs and internetwork communications among intelligent systems are in great demand.

10

Applications Programming Interfaces

The application programming interface (API) provides a channel, or linkage point, between the application and the underlying software. That software might be an operating system or communications software, such as LU6.2, depending on the needs of the application. APIs are used by programmers but also directly impact the end user. IBM focused on APIs in its System Application Architecture (SAA) as strategic components of the product range. Standards organizations are promoting APIs as the most strategic route to portability and compatibility.

Some vendors have proprietary APIs promoted as providing significant benefits over other vendors' or standards organizations' offerings. The trend in network computing, however, is to support multiple APIs simultaneously. If you decide on this type of system, you have more options from which to choose, and these systems are less expensive. When you choose a system that supports multiple APIs and has the capacity to incorporate new APIs, you have a good migration path to new technology.

Understanding API Basics

The purpose of an operating system is to supply services to application programs. These services cover a wide range of needs:

File input/output
Printer output

Communications
Device handling
Date and time measurement
Operator input
Display output

In all cases, you need a mechanism through which the programmer can inform the operating system that a service is required. The protocol used to do this is an Applications Programming Interface or API. The means by which the operating system is accessed depends on the architecture of that system.

The distinction between an API and the service that the API provides access to is a subtle one. The service may be used frequently without an actual API. The service is, in effect, a monolithic application that provides a certain functionality that cannot be controlled by a programmer. The API extends the versatility of the service by enabling applications to integrate with that service and enhance its functionality.

The program or process requesting an API service has a relationship to the service routine much like the client/server model. The program or process (client) requests a function to be performed by the service routine (server) that returns the results. The API accesses the service routine through a call/return feature or through interrupts (a signal that temporarily stops a process, usually so that another process can be executed), using registers, stacks, and parameter blocks.

Call/returns jump to the service routine section of code. The call results in the service routine being entered and executed, the function being performed, and control being passed back to the calling routine. *Interrupts* rely on a processing feature that signals an event. Interrupts often can be serviced faster than call/returns.

How data is passed from the calling process to the called process is important in understanding the wide range of methods used in making the connection. The processor's *internal registers* are a common way of passing data, but the amount of information you can pass usually is fairly small. For example, the Intel 8086 processor has 13 16-bit registers, of which only 12 can be used for passing data. This processor, therefore, enables a maximum of 24 bytes of data to be passed.

Another processor feature, the *stack*, allocates an area of random-access memory (RAM) as a scratch pad of information about processes and their status. When a call is made, the address of the memory location to which the routine is to return when the application is completed is kept on the stack. Most processors enable the programmer to manipulate the stack so that information to be passed to or from the service routine can be held temporarily.

Parameter blocks are another method of communication between a service routine and the caller. The parameter block contains information laid out in a standard format compatible with the service routine. The address of this parameter block usually is passed to the service routine in a processor register or on the stack.

A detailed analysis of the processes involved when working with parameter blocks is beyond the scope of this book. The procedure depends on the design of the processor and the architecture of the operating system. Most manuals on assembler programming for a specific operating system cover the mechanisms involved.

Examining Specific Network APIs

The key APIs with respect to PC networking are the DOS 3.1 network services and the Network Basic Input/Output System (NetBIOS). For OS/2, networking is achieved by extensions to the basic operating system and includes NetBIOS, Named Pipes, and many other communications services. Literally dozens of APIs are relevant to networking and are supported by operating systems including Unix and Macintosh.

Some of these APIs are more correctly referred to as interprocess communications (IPCs), as discussed in Chapter 4, "Application Processing." To show some of the common features of network-related APIs, this chapter reviews the functions supported by the DOS 3.1 network, NetBIOS, and OS/2 Named Pipes.

DOS 3.1 Network Functions

The DOS 3.1 network functions are accessed when the application issues an interrupt 21h (21 in the hexadecimal counting system). The actual function required is specified by setting a register (the AX register) to the function value. New to this version of DOS, these functions offer operations that provide basic network support in conjunction with the IBM PC Network Program and NetBIOS.

The DOS 3.1 functions cover multiuser file access, workstation identification, and input/output redirection. The key functions related to networking are the following:

Function: Extended Open File

Purpose: To enable a file to be opened with access and sharing modes specified

Detail: This call enables the conditions on multiuser access to be specified. The access mode defines the way the file is to be used, enabling Read Access (no write to the file is allowed), Write Access (only writing to the file occurs), and Read/Write Access (read and write occur). Sharing mode defines what can and cannot be done when you open the file in a specific access mode.

Function: Lock Unlock File Access

Purpose: To lock or unlock an area in a file to ensure that only one user at a time has access to that area

Detail: A file first must be opened with the Open a File function in a mode appropriate for the type of access required. The calling program uses this function to define a range of bytes by an offset, and a length by the contents of four registers. Another register is set to 0 if a lock is requested and to 1 if an unlock is requested. If another program has opened the file in a mode that denies the program access, DOS retries the operation three times before returning an error message. The file is locked for less than 10 seconds. Using Lock Unlock File Access is, however, good practice for multiuser programming.

Function: Redirect Device

Purpose: To connect network directories and print devices for local logical drives and printers

Detail: This interface defines the network directory and the local logical drive to which the call should be redirected. A subdirectory on a remote server, therefore, can be accessed as if the subdirectory were a local resource. The same applies for the redirection of local printer output to a network printer. If the remote device is password protected, the password must be given when the call is made.

The Network Basic Input/Output System

The Network Basic Input/Output System, NetBIOS, was a revolutionary service that supported a connection between nodes on the same network. Today, the NetBIOS features seem limited because the system has no implicit support for internetworking. NetBIOS addresses only a small range of the functionality required by sophisticated applications.

When using NetBIOS, you communicate with the NetBIOS code by performing an interrupt 5Ch under PC DOS, and the required function is passed through the AX register. The functions can be divided into four groups: general purpose, name support, session support, and datagram support.

General-purpose commands are not involved with communication; they deal with initialization (establishing the link) and setting parameters. The association of names with resources and services is controlled by the name-support function. The establishment of a link between two names to enable communications is controlled by the session-support function. Datagram support enables messages to be sent as unacknowledged transmissions to a specific name or as a general broadcast. The following are general-purpose commands:

Command: Add Name

Purpose: To add a unique name to the list of names

Detail: Add Name takes a maximum 16-byte name and checks to see that the name is unique on the network. If the name is unique, it is added to the name table. Each node has a default, permanent node name set when NetBIOS is initialized. This feature enables specific services, applications, users, and so on to be identified by name rather than address.

Command: Call

Purpose: To request that a session be established with another node

Detail: Call initiates a connection to another name on the network or within the local system. In the past, up to 32 sessions could exist on a network (a limit of 32 conversations between named entities on the network), but several manufacturers have extended the limit.

Command: Send

Purpose: To send data to another entity, using an established session

Detail: This API call enables up to 65,535 bytes of data to be sent to a receiving name. The command also allows for several sends to be queued, a useful technique for large data transfers.

Command: Listen

Purpose: To enable a session to be established with another node

Detail: Listen is the complement of Call. This function specifies a name as acceptable for a session to be established. If you specify a wild card, this function identifies a session with *any* calling name. Unless a Listen is issued, no call can be accepted.

These NetBIOS API calls are a small selection from a large command set. NetBIOS, however, is a low-performance service for the needs of sophisticated applications.

OS/2 Named Pipes

OS/2 is the first multitasking operating system from Microsoft and IBM for the PC. OS/2 follows the trend first set by Unix and then by Apple with the multitasking Macintosh operating system. The other critical aspect of OS/2's similarity to the Macintosh is that the system can be extended to have a mouse, an icon, and a windows-based front-end presentation system. In a network, the multitasking capability combined with advanced presentation technology enables you to develop new application areas. Named Pipes is one of the many interprocess communications APIs available with OS/2.

Named Pipes is a system device with the properties of a file. This type of device is referred to as a *pseudo-file*. The purpose of the Named Pipes API is to enable intercommunication between applications. In networking, the locations of the applications are irrelevant. Although a pipe acts like a file, a pipe uses no disk space—it is a memory structure that holds the data carried from one application to another. The following is a description of the pipe command:

Command: DosMakePipe

Purpose: To create an interprocess communications pipe

Detail: A call to the DosMakePipe command is required before a pipe can be used. To set up a pipe, you must give the size of the pipe and identification details for input and output purposes. The maximum size of a pipe is 64K.

This call is the only one that directly relates to the Named Pipes API. The actual access to the pipe is achieved through standard file read and write calls. Data is read from the pipe on a first in/first out (FIFO) basis. The flow of data, therefore is always in the same sequence in transmit and receipt.

The Named Pipes technique is simple and flexible, but the 64K pipe-size limitation makes transferring large volumes of data impractical. In a network environment, the error conditions that may interfere with the successful operation of a pipe are interpreted as a file access failure. This confusion may lead to additional complexity if the application design requires guaranteed and verifiable delivery of data.

Understanding the Functions of Network APIs

The network APIs existing today cover a wide range of functions that can be split into five main areas:

- Systems services
- File services
- Communications
- Interprocess communications
- Store-and-forward services

Systems Services

Under *systems services*, the APIs enable you to account for resources, an important feature in an era when your business edge is honed by networking computing systems. In a large network system, this capability is vital because it enables you to analyze costs and system usage.

Other systems services are the more technical aspects of using and maintaining the network. Network access usually is controlled by an API that enables you to specify name and password and sometimes to pass parameters. This feature is important for applications that have embedded knowledge of how to use the system. For example, an accounting application that knows how to log into a server and request specific services available to only that log-in account provides a new dimension to system security.

Network maintenance covers configuration and diagnostic APIs. Some of these APIs fall into the network-management area, although for many of today's networks, the integration of network management tools with the key configuration and diagnostic APIs is minimal. One of the broadest approaches to using the network maintenance APIs can be seen with IBM's Netview product—applicable across IBM's mainframe, mini, and LAN offerings.

Configuration APIs usually are available only to users with the highest level privileges, because these APIs enable the creation and manipulation of accounts, reconfiguration of operational parameters, and control of the availability of services.

Diagnostic APIs are targeted at preventive as well as corrective maintenance. The range of functions provided by a particular manufacturer's diagnostic API depends on the following three factors:

- How open the system is for developers
- The richness of the functionality of the network subsystems
- The degree of integration of network subsystems

The usual services available for testing purposes enable you to determine the quality of connection between nodes and to gather error-condition statistics for all computers connected to the network.

File Services

File-service APIs on network computing systems have to support a wide range of client operating systems. This need can lead to some interesting compromises in service supply and to some network management problems. The best-known APIs cover support for DOS and OS/2, Macintosh, and Unix workstations, and, in several network operating systems in which the client OS is not network-aware, have a one-to-one correspondence with the stand-alone APIs.

Database APIs often are included with file service APIs because they are closely related services. Structured Query Language (SQL), for example, offers standardized access of databases. SQL is an API supported by many vendors. SQL, consequently, has many variants (see Chapter 13, "Distributed Data Services and SQL"). Although the American National Standards Institute (ANSI) has defined a standard for SQL, the standard lacks some of the more advanced facilities found in commercial products. This fact has led to a low level of acceptance, but the proposed revision of this standard should go a long way to ensuring that SQL is adopted as a fully accepted standard.

Communications

Communications APIs, particularly for access to mainframes and the transport of data between nodes, are numerous. Many of the critical communications APIs are de facto standards, although the decade of the 1990s will see the Open Systems Interconnection (OSI) standards defining the direction of the market. Some of the key communications APIs have been developed by IBM and include High Level Language API (HLLAPI) and LU6.2, which may be considered the successor to NetBIOS.

By supporting transactional-based communications, LU6.2 extends the session services provided by NetBIOS. This facility is a fundamental requirement for integrating business-critical applications that span the levels of computing.

Interprocess Communications

Interprocess communications (IPCs) also is an area rich in APIs. OS/2 Named Pipes, an IPC, already has been mentioned. Some communications APIs also can act as IPCs when used to communicate between processes in the same workstation. Many IPCs, however, are not supported or offer inadequate performance when implemented across network connections (see Chapter 4, "Application Processing").

Store-and-Forward Services

Store-and-forward APIs are relatively rare at present, although store-and-forward technology is well established in subsystems. For example, many implementations of the ISO X.400 specification are available, but no single API exists for gaining access to X.400 services (see Chapter 11, "Electronic Mail").

Chapter Summary

The range of applications programming interfaces (APIs) available on network systems covers a large variety of services. For the applications developer, the biggest difficulty is identifying standard APIs instead of transient APIs.

Open Systems Interconnection (OSI) standards will produce truly portable and broadly accepted specifications. Alternatively, technologies such as remote procedure calls (RPCs) that enable an application to call a subroutine located on another computer will simplify some of these API issues for transport protocols.

To network users, APIs may appear to be of little relevance because they are technical and apparently only a developer's issue. An awareness of APIs and their strategic importance, however, can help you make decisions when you need to evaluate new technologies. The key to this evaluation is to weigh any decision in favor of a product that supports multiple APIs and is designed to migrate to new technologies as they appear.

11

Electronic Mail

User-to-user communications is one of the services made possible by a LAN. Many local area networks have built-in utilities that enable a user to send one-line messages to other network users. Although this facility is occasionally useful, true communication among PC users on a network requires a special application software package called electronic mail.

Electronic mail, or *E-mail*, is an extremely powerful office automation tool. E-mail is faster and cheaper than traditional, paper-based message or memo systems. Most large corporations use E-mail applications because of these advantages. The trend is to migrate these applications off the mainframe or other host-based system and run them as distributed applications on local area networks.

The reason for this migration of E-mail applications to LANs is the same as with many other applications. When all E-mail activity is centralized and run on a single machine, the processing and storage requirements can be extensive (even on a 10- to 20-user system). Because E-mail activity comprises many small tasks, however, electronic mail is well-suited to a LAN, where most of the processing is distributed to intelligent workstations.

Although E-mail applications are widely used in smaller organizations, the adoption in that environment has been slower. The emergence of groupware and office productivity packages is accelerating adoption. Groupware typically includes E-mail functionality in addition to other capabilities, such as scheduling and project management, that also enhance office productivity. (For more information, see Chapter 12, "Groupware.") By the mid-1990s, few offices will be without a LAN-based, E-mail system.

Defining E-Mail

E-mail is a message encoded as electronic impulses and passed over transmission lines (see fig. 11.1). The message may be a memo, letter, file, graph, digitized image, or any combination.

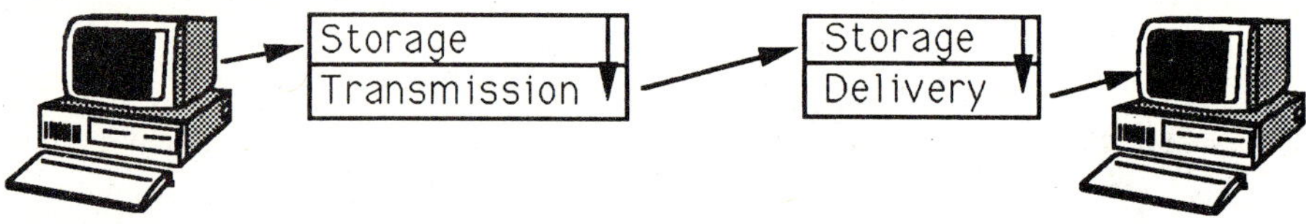

Fig. 11.1. Electronic mail enables users to send almost any type of information from one workstation to another.

Electronic mail eliminates most of the problems and delays involved in getting a physical document from one person to another. In a well-designed system, the message becomes available to the addressee almost as soon as the message is sent. Unlike a telephone call, however, both parties need not be available simultaneously for communication to succeed. E-mail effectively eliminates "telephone tag" when two parties want to communicate but are never available at the same time.

The technology that gives E-mail this flexible communication capability is called *store-and-forward technology*. Store-and-forward works exactly as the name implies. A message is created and stored until the sender is ready to forward, or transmit, the message. When the message is received, it is stored until the addressee is ready to pick it up.

Store-and-forward communications are the opposite of real-time communications. Real-time communications, such as a telephone conversation or a face-to-face discussion, occur without any delay. Another example of real-time communications is the simple messaging system included in most LAN operating systems, which enables you to send a one-line message to a particular address or to broadcast the message on the network. These messages are sent in real-time and received in real-time, if the addressee is sitting at his or her workstation.

Store-and-forward has advantages for the users and the communication system. In a store-and-forward system, people send messages and receive them at their convenience. A user does not have to interrupt some other activity to have a conversation. Busy people who are normally difficult to reach become accessible.

The processing and communication system benefits in much the same way. Most processing in a store-and-forward system can take place when the CPUs are not being heavily used. Communication can occur when line costs are lowest or when private systems are least used. Store-and-forward enables you to balance the load among system resources.

Using E-Mail

The main component of the electronic mail system is a "post office," an area on a networked hard disk reserved for mail. This post office serves as the central message holder and has "in" and "out" baskets for each user (see fig. 11.2). When a message is sent, a link is established between the sender's "out" basket and the addressee's "in" basket.

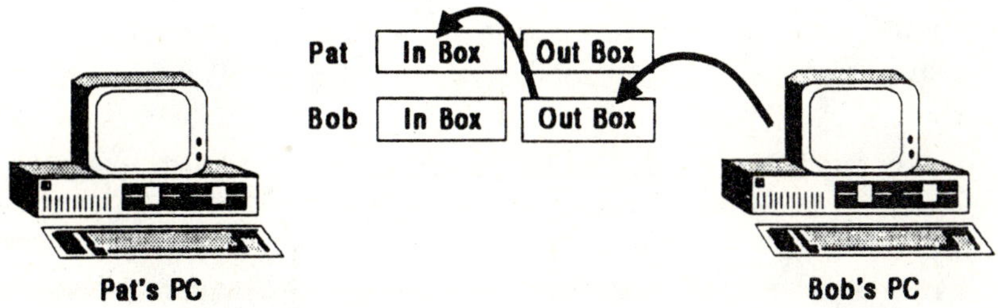

Fig. 11.2. Sending mail.

After the message has been sent, the addressee is informed that mail is in the addressee's "in" basket. Some mail packages require that the user query the system to find out whether mail is waiting. Other packages send notification to the addressee's status line as soon as the mail is posted or whenever the addressee logs onto the network. When the addressee calls for the mail, the sender is informed of successful delivery. Any user can put mail into a personal "in" box at the post office. Other users can open an "in" box and read or delete its contents without knowing the "in" box owner's name and password.

Most E-mail packages include an editor for memo writing. The more popular E-mail packages have full-featured word processors built in. In either case, users have the option of writing messages on their own word processing software if that method is more convenient.

The efficient operation of the mail system depends, in part, on how the system is used. For example, when several users are sent a document, a new copy of that document typically is made for each user. With large documents, you can save disk space by sending a message to read a document with a particular file name in a public area of the shared disk, instead of copying and placing the file into the mail system.

Mail programs usually permit you to scan the contents of the mailbox (your mail directory). A display will show the date, source, and title of each message so that you can read important messages first. For labeling messages, users should decide on a common system. You or any other user then can tell quickly what kinds of messages are in the mailbox. A message title may be prefixed with a label, such as RPRT, DOC, MEMO, PERSONAL, or GRAPH. As an added refinement, some mail systems let you search for mail. For example, a menu might list all the mail sent by John or all messages labeled RPRT.

Because mail may be retained in mailboxes, you need a method for determining the current status of each piece of mail. Mail can be flagged as "already read," "awaiting reply," "save until a certain date," and so on.

This chapter describes how basic E-mail is used. Often E-mail applications are integrated with other office automation applications. The combined office automation package still can perform E-mail functions, but may be able to handle project management, conversation management, scheduling, and conferencing (non real-time). Project management enables you to track activities and commitments of any group activity. Conversation management is the process of monitoring communications and the status of requests, replies, and general discussions. All these automation functions permit users to communicate, cooperate on projects, and coordinate activities without ever having to alter personal schedules to have a meeting or make a telephone call.

Selecting an E-Mail System

E-mail should be considered a strategic resource to the organization. The first step in choosing a system is to make some realistic projections about how the E-mail package will be used. E-mail packages offer a variety of features. If planning indicates that a certain kind of functionality might be needed, you are better off getting a package designed to support that feature, instead of getting a package *not* designed for that use and having people use the package for that purpose anyway.

The following paragraphs contain some guidelines for choosing an E-mail system.

The E-mail package should be easy to use. Generally, people dislike and avoid a system that they cannot use intuitively. This tendency is especially true if they are using the E-mail package all the time.

The E-mail package should be convenient. Many E-mail packages are terminate-and-stay resident programs that operate in the background and are instantly available. You do not have to exit the application in which you are working before you can use E-mail. This kind of convenience is important. Adding to the convenience is the trend to incorporate E-mail into other applications. Groupware and other office automation applications are examples.

Another area that directly affects convenience is the user interface. Several different types of interfaces are available. These interfaces include menus and/or command-line control, graphical interfaces, and simple E-mail handling commands on up to elaborate communications structures. The interface selection is an important issue with long-term ramifications.

E-mail should be portable. When employees are on the road any significant amount of time, they must not be completely out of touch. The ease with which a particular E-mail package can be transported is an important factor to consider. You should consider what the E-mail package requires (hardware, software, and connection media) to go on the road. For example, is a hard disk required? Of course, laptop PCs have all the power of desktop PCs, with fast processors, plenty of RAM, and hard disks. In many instances, though, a floppy disk-based system is preferable to a hard disk system in a portable machine. Floppy disk systems are cheaper, often run longer on battery power, and tend to be more reliable in mobile systems.

E-mail should be powerful. A powerful E-mail package enables you to send transmissions across many different communications systems. You can send multiple messages or single messages to multiple addressees all with ease and efficiency. (Multiple addressing is convenient but also can cause problems. When a message is sent to multiple people, as on a CC list, any response by any recipient normally is sent to every person on the CC list. This situation contributes to the "junk mail" problem found on some E-mail systems.)

E-mail should be flexible or connectible. Depending on your environment, E-mail should have gateway support so that you can send and receive messages among different systems. FAX and Telex gateways also are becoming extremely important.

E-mail should support efficient archiving. Although most systems have an archive capability, the features are not all equally easy to use. Archiving is the storage of files or messages for later reference. To work efficiently, archiving should be convenient. Retrieval should be possible with many different parameters, including date, sender, topic, and group (conversation or project).

The E-mail package should be acceptable to the users who will work with the package. The technical issues of E-mail system design are important, but they are not the only considerations. The needs and capabilities of the people using the system also must be considered.

User acceptance of an E-mail system cannot be taken for granted. Systems fail if they are not appropriate for the people who will be using them. If the system is not selected carefully, people may refuse to use the system, or they may misuse or underuse the system.

A Standard Mail System: X.400

The incapability of one application to talk to another application is a continual problem in computing. E-mail packages may be especially limited if they cannot communicate with other E-mail packages, because the effectiveness and reach of the system is reduced.

One solution to the problem for E-mail systems is the E-mail *gateway*. Many vendors have gateways that convert messages from one format to another so that two or more systems can be interconnected. Gateways, however, are not the complete solution. A big problem is the number of gateways that may be required to enable an organization to communicate wherever necessary. That requirement likely would include gateways from a LAN-based E-mail system to one or more other LAN-based systems. Then, the organization needs a gateway to interconnect the LAN-based system with a mainframe-based system, and gateways to interconnect one or more minicomputer-based systems. Users probably also want to connect to one or more public E-mail systems, such as MCI Mail.

One way to reduce the number of gateways and simplify the system is to move toward an E-mail standard. For years, a standard E-mail system has been discussed and promoted. Now, finally, that standard is a reality. The standard for E-mail systems is defined by the International Standards Organization (ISO) and the CCITT (the international telephone and telegraph standards group). This standard is known as X.400. The X.400 definition was published in 1984. Although the X.400 continues to be enhanced, and more work is needed in the area of a standard application interface, X.400 is a functional standard.

Most E-mail systems currently offer an X.400 connection or have committed to offering one in the near future. Offices that use E-mail simply for interoffice communications do not need to go out and purchase X.400 capability. X.400 will soon become an important component of most wide-area E-mail communications, and anyone planning an E-mail system should be aware of what X.400 covers and when its use is appropriate.

The CCITT X.400 standard is a messaging system well on its way to becoming a worldwide standard. X.400 enables user facilities to send messages back and forth, using store-and-forward technology. X.400 is part of the Open Systems Interconnection (OSI) movement. The concept of OSI is that any computer system, of any model and from any vendor, should be able to communicate with any other system.

CCITT's Recommendations for Message Transfer

X.400 is a collection of eight CCITT recommendations for message transfer.

X.400 describes the general architecture as composed of four entities:

- User agents
- Message transfer agents
- Message transfer
- Interpersonal messaging services

A *user agent* (UA) is the user interface to X.400. A user agent accepts a message from a user and sends the message to a message transfer agent. User agents may support local editing, message storage, and archiving. In X.400 terms, a user is not necessarily a real person but is any person or process that creates and sends messages on X.400.

A *message transfer agent* (MTA) receives messages from the originating UAs and delivers those messages to the UA addressees. In essence, MTAs handle the routing and management of the messaging system. An MTA provides the store-and-forward facility that is independent of specific applications. Messages can contain any collection of binary encoded information, such as text, graphics, facsimile, and so forth. A group of MTAs are referred to collectively as the Message Transfer Service (MTS).

In large systems, multiple MTAs accept messages and move them around. Each MTA has multiple UAs, and the job of the UAs is to get messages from users and hand them to MTAs.

Message transfer includes the definition of messaging services, such as delivery, notification, forwarding, redirection, time-stamping, and conversion (to match requirements of dissimilar hardware). Nearly any data communications network can support X.400 message transfer.

Interpersonal messaging services supports the submission and delivery of messages primarily destined for human beings rather than machines. The messages, therefore, also include control information that human users can read.

X.401 specifies the requirements for the message handling system.

X.408 specifies how one character set can be converted to another.

X.409 specifies presentation transfer rules and the standard notation for describing data structures.

X.410 specifies a standard for invoking processes on remote networks.

X.411 specifies the message transfer sublayer protocols within the Application Layer of the OSI model.

X.420 specifies the message content architecture, including memo headers and multipart body types.

X.430 specifies the rules for accessing teletex terminals.

These rules define an X.400 architecture. Vendors use all these rules to build X.400-compliant systems. By definition, any system that follows the rules can communicate and pass information back and forth to and from any other system that also follows the X.400 rules.

In the 1988 X.400 revision, the user agent was broken into two parts. One part is still called the user agent. That part basically defines how messages are composed and displayed.

The other part is called the *message store*, which is exactly what you would guess, a place where messages can be stored. The message store is especially helpful for PC users, because storing messages on the PC is not always possible. The X.400 architecture assumes that the user agent will always be there to accept messages. That situation may not be the case with a PC. PCs get turned off. Often they are unavailable to do message reception because they support only single tasking.

A central message store now handles the reception of messages from the MTA and the storage of messages from the UAs. The machine running the MTA software should always be turned on and ready to receive messages. The message store, therefore, serves as a mail hub.

Disadvantages of Using X.400

Although X.400 offers many benefits, X.400 also has some significant disadvantages. One of these disadvantages is the expense. X.400 was designed by committees as a general solution. The committees included anything that anybody wanted, which has caused X.400 to be large and costly to implement. For example, the first X.400 gateways are estimated to cost in the $2,000 range. Because that price is close to the typical cost of an entire E-mail system for one LAN, adding X.400 support doubles the cost.

Another significant problem is that X.400 does not have as yet a defined and standardized application programming interface (API). Each X.400 vendor has developed its own API, and of course an application written to one X.400 API does not work on the X.400 system of another vendor. Moreover, the APIs that have been developed are extremely complex and require thousands of hours for the completion of an application. Although standards and vendor committees are working to solve the X.400 API problem, no standard API is available. Few X.400 applications are likely to emerge before the mid-1990s.

Finally, X.400 is a limited solution. X.400 is based on an OSI-compliant set of protocols. Systems that do not adhere to the full OSI set for internetworking are not OSI-compliant. For example, OSI specifies X.25 or X.32 connections at the Transport Layer. Low to moderate traffic networks will find X.25/X.32 much more expensive and complex than an asynchronous connection.

For all these reasons, the adoption of X.400 during the early 1990s probably will be limited to large wide-area networks, especially those networks used by governments that require OSI compliance within their own systems.

NetWare MHS

The problems associated with X.400 are contrary to three important goals of standardization: reduced system costs, simplified development, and increased application availability. These problems will limit the use of X.400 at the local level, even while X.400 is increasingly implemented in large wide-area systems.

The many benefits of a general-purpose store-and-forward system, however, are still desirable on local area networks. To meet this need, Novell has promoted a system called NetWare Message Handling System (MHS). Not a product in the traditional sense, the MTA (mail engine) for NetWare MHS is available free of cost from Novell. Novell's purpose in promoting MHS is to provide store-and-forward capability to LAN users and to encourage applications developers to use this capability as a platform for new LAN applications.

NetWare MHS is the only messaging platform, other than X.400 implementations, that is used by multiple vendors. Like X.400 implementations, NetWare MHS handles all the communications issues, including modem handling, message receipt and delivery, acknowledgments, and so forth. Literally any application might become the front end (user interface) of a NetWare MHS system, including an E-mail application, a database application, a spreadsheet, or a graphics program. Any of these applications could use NetWare MHS to send their output to another person using a compatible application.

Currently, NetWare MHS is supported by applications developers on such products as Framework III (Ashton-Tate), DeskView E-Mail Companion (Quarterdeck), DaVinci eMAIL, ParaMail (Paradox), Coordinator (Action Technologies), and WordPerfect Office (WordPerfect).

NetWare MHS is similar to X.400 and is designed as a complementary service aimed at LANs. The API for NetWare MHS is extremely simple, enabling the porting of applications to MHS with minimal programming effort.

NetWare MHS has an engine (MTA) that accepts messages. When the MTA is contacted, it does some handshaking and finds out who is calling. Then MTA adapts itself to accept whatever is being transmitted in any of several formats that the sender can use (currently four formats are supported). NetWare MHS produces and supports multiple outputs, including X.25 and asynchronous transmissions.

Electronic Data Interchange

Organizations that have several E-mail systems (mainframe, mini, PC, public, and so on) are plagued with the problem of how to pass information from one system to another. X.400 is one solution, although it focuses primarily on the underlying store-and-forward mechanism. A solution operating at a higher level is Electronic Data Interchange (EDI). X.400 and EDI have considerable overlap in their definitions; however, EDI focuses primarily on defining the nature of the information transferred.

E-mail is an extremely efficient way to transfer formal business communications. Unfortunately, however, E-mail has no generally accepted content definitions that would support such business communications among dissimilar E-mail systems.

Hard copy delivery systems offer one solution. AT&T Mail has hard copy delivery; EZLink has a Mailgram; MCI Mail has MCI Custom Mail; the Source has Mailgram; CompuServe can get you into MCI so that you can use MCI Custom Mail; Telemail has Telemail Xpress; and Quickcom (GE) has a Quikgram.

Facsimile (FAX) is an alternative to these systems. FAX enables the user to send a message as a graphic (unstructured) picture to a recipient. With over four million FAX machines in use today, and the number growing rapidly, FAX comes close to being an instant general mail system.

All sorts of business-oriented documents such as invoices, bills-of-lading, receipts, and so forth can be transmitted through FAX. FAX also has several disadvantages. One disadvantage is that you have no record of the communication. Even as immediate as FAX delivery is, people may not pick up the message—and you have no way to verify delivery. FAX messages are not easily manipulated in a computer. They permit a hard copy printout, or they can be stored electronically. To manipulate the information, however, you must rekey that information, a process that often leads to data-integrity problems.

These limitations are pushing the industry toward a standard for the transfer of structured, machine-readable information. That standard is provided in Electronic Data Interchange.

EDI is aimed at defining and communicating among a diverse range of information categories. The following are the four most prominent areas:

- ❏ Trade data (purchase orders and invoices)
- ❏ Electronic funds transfer
- ❏ Interactive applications (reservations systems)
- ❏ Graphics (CAD drawings and electronic publishing)

The business orientation of EDI is clear from these categories. An important part of EDI that makes EDI well-suited to business communications is an emerging definition of process-to-process communications—one computer talking to another without human intervention. X.400 definitions are limited to human communications—person-to-person.

In process-to-process communications, an application can contact another application and request that the receiving application perform some task (see fig. 11.3.). This type of communication can handle such things as routine database updates without the expense of a person typing the information. A process may be programmed, for example, to transfer information from one location to many or from a remote location to a central one. This update can occur regularly, possibly at night when communication costs are reduced, and probably more reliably than if a person is required to input the information.

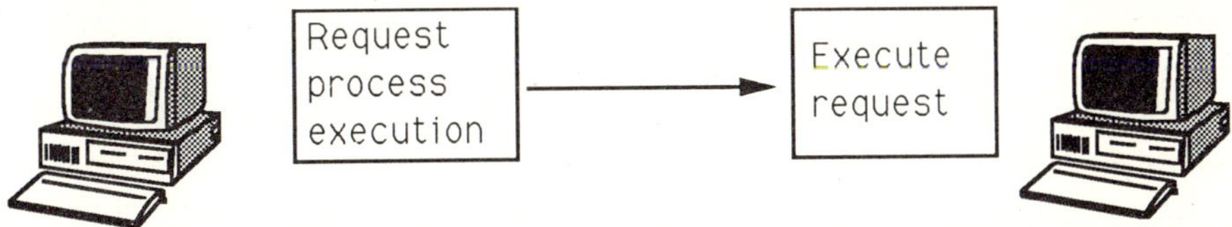

Fig. 11.3. Process-to-process communications.

EDI is defining how these types of communication can take place. Most of the mechanisms that use process-to-process communications are store-and-forward, because of the cost advantage of store-and-forward and because real-time communications are seldom a true requirement for business communications. Interactive, or real-time, communications links are not viewed by EDI committees as a critical need at present.

Setting Up an E-Mail System

Most PC-based E-mail systems have similar components. The primary components are the workstations, hubs, and hosts. A *workstation* is a computer where the user sits and runs the user software (called a user agent or UA) to compose and read messages. A *host* is a machine that connects to other machines to transfer messages. Hosts also are called message transfer agents (MTAs). A *hub* is a type of host that other hosts call to leave off messages and pick them up.

Choosing the Configuration

The simplest configuration is a stand-alone workstation; the user agent and the host are integrated into one machine. The next simplest configuration is multiple UAs connected on a LAN, in which all UAs talk to a single host. This host acts as a router to transfer messages, but not as a hub; users do not call into the host.

The next step in system size is a LAN with multiple host machines. In this environment, one host typically is set up as a router to enable the host to dial out and send messages outside the LAN. That approach usually is more efficient than enabling every host to have dial-out capability.

The concept of workgroups is one of the primary aspects of E-mail system design. A *workgroup* defines a group of people. Most of the communication performed by these people is confined to the workgroup, thereby defining the limits of the workgroup. The people in your company with whom you communicate most often probably are within your workgroup. Most people do more intra-workgroup communicating than inter-workgroup communicating.

People in the workgroup can be on single-server LANs, multiple-server LANs, or larger networks.

When people in the workgroup are addressed, they are addressed as a particular user name at a particular workgroup. A workgroup-wide router (part of the MTA) maintains a table of the physical location (workstation) of each person in the workgroup. As the system grows to encompass an entire organization, then multiple organizations, a third name normally is added to the addressing. In this three-part naming system, the convention followed is typically company name at workgroup name at user name.

Setting Up the Workgroups

Workgroups can be single- or multiple-tiered. In a single-tiered network, everybody in the workgroup can connect to the workgroup-wide router directly. The workgroup-wide router is named as the preferred hub of all hosts other than the workgroup-wide router itself.

In the multiple-tiered network, hubs are set up between the host and the UA/workstation. Each UA/workstation has a designated hub where the workstation sends and receives messages. The multiple-tiered network often is selected when the telecommunications link between hubs is not expensive, but the link between the hubs and the network router is more costly. A large, multiple-tiered network is easier to maintain than a large single-tiered network. The reason is that maintenance tasks such as installing and removing users can be done closer to the local level, often by network administrators.

If a U.S. company has offices throughout Europe, having each European office call the U.S. headquarters every day is costly. A more cost-effective approach may be for the offices to call a single European office and for that office to call the U.S. headquarters and transfer all the messages at one time. This type of design is a multiple-tiered system.

One tradeoff is a loss of immediacy, because some time is required for those messages to filter back to the host where they are going to be used. Reliability also is threatened in that two links must function for the system to function. If the low-to-mid-tier link or the mid-tier-to-host link fails, the system fails. A single-tiered system has only a single link and is more reliable because the system has less components that can fail.

Planning the Workgroup Structure

Another option in network design is the structure, which can be a tree-structured workgroup or a ring-structured workgroup. In a tree-structured group, a single workgroup-wide router provides all the routing services for the whole group (see fig. 11.4). In a ring-structured workgroup, all hosts in the group perform routing functions (see fig. 11.5). No single host provides those routing services for the whole group.

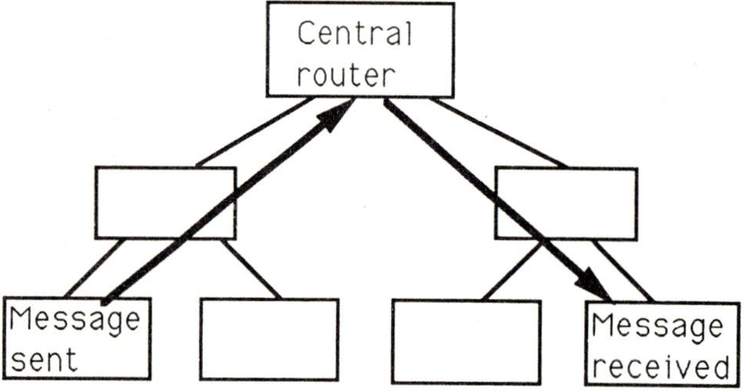

Fig. 11.4. A tree-structured network is hierarchical with a central router.

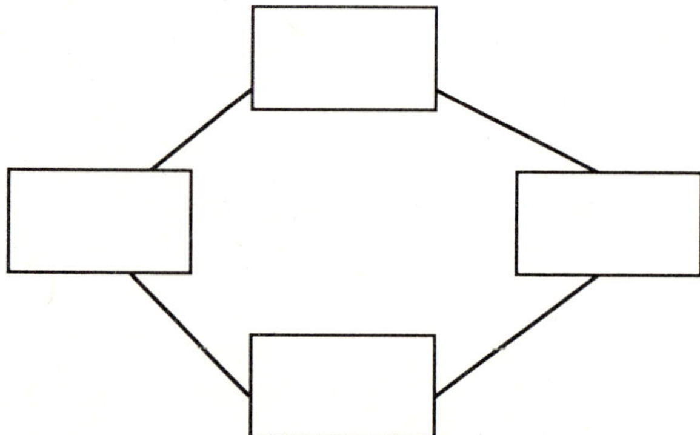

Fig. 11.5. In a ring-structured network, the routing function is distributed among all hosts on the network.

Nearly all E-mail installations use the tree-structured design. In the ring-structured workgroup, the administrator at each host has to set up the system so that it knows where to look for all other hosts. The tree-structured workgroup requires fewer technical users and reduces the amount of work for administration.

A disadvantage of the tree-structured design may be inefficient use of communications resources. Going from UA/workstation to hub, to host, back to another hub, and finally to the addressee is not the most direct route. To optimize the system, some routing functions can be placed in local hubs or host machines. When one of these machines gets a message for an unknown addressee, the machine routes the message through normal channels up to the central host. When the machine knows the addressee, however, the workstation can route the message directly to the addressee or through a shorter connection. This type of optimization usually is arranged only for heavily used connections. Otherwise, the basic tree structure is maintained (see fig. 11.6).

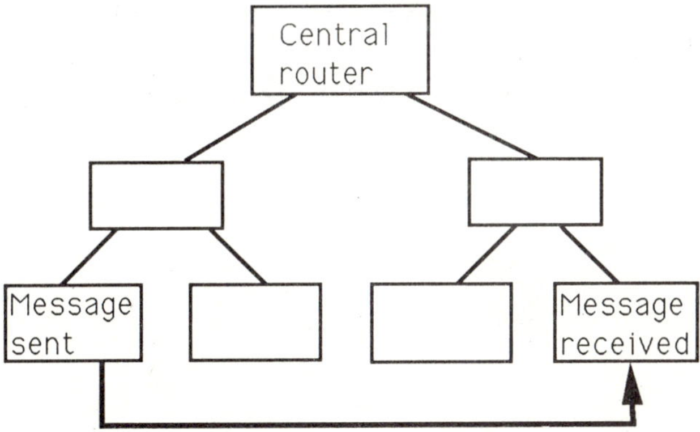

Fig. 11.6. A tree-structured network can be optimized to enable some routing functions in local hubs or machines.

Speaking of Communication . . .

One final thing to consider about building a successful E-mail system is E-mail jargon. Communicating regularly, perhaps exclusively, with another person through E-mail can create some surprising problems.

One person, for example, notified another person that a message had been forwarded. The message was written, "I resent your message." Of course, the person who got this message wondered why the other person was angry. This misunderstanding was cleared up when the sender explained that the message was supposed to be "I re-sent your message."

E-mail communication lacks the clues, such as tone of voice, on which people rely in normal conversation. Using E-mail, people need to be especially clear, perhaps even redundant, to make sure that they are understood.

Chapter Summary

Electronic mail, E-mail, is a powerful office automation tool, enabling users to send and receive memos, documents, and other graphic and text communications efficiently. Handling these communications via electronic means offers advantages in speed and retrieval over conventional paper-based communications.

E-mail's store-and-forward mode of operation enables people to have a conversation even though both parties are not available at the same time—an advantage over telephone systems.

12

Groupware

The last few years have seen the term groupware applied to a variety of applications. In many cases, the group orientation of the software only prevents conflicts during data access. Although this capability is a prerequisite for groupware, it hardly differs from the old concept of multiuser software. Real groupware, however, is available and offers improvements in office automation.

Groupware is software designed to be used by a group of people where interaction and coordination are needed. Groupware is characterized by the following features:

- ❑ Coordinates data access
- ❑ Coordinates group activities
- ❑ Focuses on group tasks and/or group communications

Groupware is not just a marketing strategy to make multiuser software sound interesting. Multiuser data access is very different from workgroup support. Multiuser software addresses a coordination problem at a fundamental level, as the following example shows:

> *Problem:* I want to review the text you are creating.
>
> *Solution:* If you are editing the text, I must wait until you finish, then edit my comments into the text or into a separate document. You review my comments by the same method.

By comparison, groupware uses multiuser access support, but structures the access. Groupware knows the meaning of the data and the way that the data is to be used. The coordination problem at the multiuser level is the same, but at a groupware level, the problem becomes one of coordinating activities. Groupware facilitates and, to an extent, automates management of group activity. See the following solution that groupware provides for the same problem as the preceding example:

> *Problem*: I want to review the text you are creating.
>
> *Solution:* If you are editing the text, I must wait until you finish (same as the multiuser example). Without changing your text, I tag the areas that I want to comment on and make my comments. These comments are available when you access the document and request to see the comments. You then can edit and merge the comments into the text.

Groupware has some hidden problems that go with the advantages. The first problem is how to get all participants to use the keyboard. The technical staff and managers probably are comfortable with keyboards, but the president may delegate the task to a secretary. If a substantial number of executives refuse to use the groupware, its effectiveness is reduced drastically.

The second problem is politics. The introduction of a new methodology often is greeted with suspicion. Habits are hard to change—what worked in the past is good enough. This inertia can mean that organizations that truly need groupware to improve communications or business find excuses to stay with the tried and tested, even if the old method is not as effective. Introduce groupware systems, or for that matter any systems, carefully and induce as little shock as possible.

Why Use Groupware?

Organizations change for many reasons: business pressures, social pressures, technology pressures. The one certain thing in this evolution is that the current structure of most companies has to change.

The paper "The Coming of the New Organization," by Peter Drucker (*Harvard Business Review*, January-February, 1988) discusses this issue in detail. Drucker characterizes the management structure of most corporations as command-and-control-based. In this strategy, commands to and responses from the work forces are passed up and down chains of control (management hierarchy). The military discovered this system centuries ago. Companies that developed from the pressure of the industrial revolution, provide a model that meets the current management needs.

Today, technological and business pressures are decreasing the value of the command-and-control management system. Social pressures reinforce this trend. Technology evolution enabled businesses to adopt strategies that reduced the need for manual labor and caused a shift to increasing levels of clerical labor. The clerical work force, supported by new technologies, is tending to become an expert work force that resists the command-and-control model.

According to Drucker, "The typical large business 20 years hence will have fewer than half the levels of management of its counterpart today, and not more than a third of the managers . . . the typical business will be knowledge-based, an organization composed largely of specialists who direct and discipline their own performance through organized feedback from colleagues, customers, and headquarters. For this reason, it will be what I call an information-based organization."

The information-based organization that Drucker speaks of is possible only with the support of information technology. Information technology is in many respects an organizational and management strategy; information technology is concerned with how the information is used in a group, or team, environment. Groupware is directed at providing this organization and management.

The most important aspects of groupware in the new organizations will be the coordination of experts' activities and improving the quality and efficiency of communications among the experts.

Groupware Development Issues

Current examples of network and host-centric groupware applications are electronic mail, group scheduling, and calendaring. A major advantage of these groupware applications is the capability to integrate the activities of multiple users. Workgroups distributed in space, time, and processing location require groupware that understands the network environment and uses that knowledge to support the users and their activities.

For software vendors, the hard part is deciding to what extent a particular application should take advantage of its environment. For example, the more an OS/2 application pursues features unique to OS/2, the less similar that same version is to its Macintosh implementation. The provision of unique features in an application also can mean more work for software manufacturers and distributors. Special features can mean different documentation, added technical support, and more difficult maintenance and enhancements.

A number of major manufacturers, therefore, are choosing to develop to the lowest common denominator. This decision usually makes development and support much easier, but something is sacrificed in the process. After all, the user buys a Macintosh instead of a workstation running Unix with applications using X-Windows for a reason. Writing to the lowest common denominator has to reduce the worth of that software on the Macintosh or the Unix machine.

The problem that groupware is facing today is that the existing standards are mostly hardware or communications standards and do not truly integrate the processing functions. IBM's Systems Application Architecture (SAA) with the promised portability across the IBM product range and its Common User Interface (CUI) may be a step in the right direction, but SAA will require a much broader base of manufacturer and developer support to ensure industry-wide commonalty at a basic level of presentation and communication.

Electronic Mail Groupware

The most common example of groupware is *electronic mail*—a system for sending and receiving messages and data on a store-and-forward basis. *Store-and-forward* means that the recipient of the communication need not be on the system when the message is sent. The system stores the messages and forwards them on request.

The current offerings in this technology range from the most basic, proprietary schemes to standards-based implementations. Proprietary systems usually have the advantage of speed and simplicity but often are poor in offering interfaces that permit third-party developers to integrate other applications. Proprietary systems also tend to be implemented on a limited range of computing platforms.

The standards-based systems excel in the capability to span a wide range of platforms and offer a rich set of applications programming interfaces (see Chapter 10, "Applications Programming Interfaces"). To explicitly support group activities is outside the bounds of the standards, because group activities are not defined concepts. Groupware, therefore, mainly is found within proprietary systems, although standards-based services and systems may support groupware and permit some communications outside the proprietary environment.

The aspect that distinguishes groupware electronic mail from the generalized kind is the addition of functionality to the process of communication. The generalized package acts as a sender and receiver of lumps of text with or without attached files.

The groupware systems enable a message to be sent, with a request for an answer, by a certain date. This request is noted by the receiving system that builds a schedule of requested responses for the user to act on. Classification by the sender of a message as urgent can make that message appear before all others. (The sophisticated groupware system enables the receiver to tell his system that messages from a particular user are never to be considered urgent if that user is known to classify everything as urgent.)

Electronic mail groupware also can be an integrator for the company. If all employees have access to a terminal, electronic mail can become part of the corporate culture by providing an internal-communications medium.

Contrary to expectation, most companies which have tried to switch to electronic mail find that the volume of paper used in the organization does not decrease, and in fact, the company suffers a paper explosion. People print out all of the messages to read them. Persuading employees to change the way they deal with messages requires rigorous training and internal promotion of the system.

Some groupware electronic mail systems attempt to impose a structure on communications by requiring that you define the mode of the conversation ("this is a request," "this is a promise," and so forth). This strategy is doomed to failure, however, unless the participants in the message exchange are performing a function that makes this structure natural. Modeless messages are what the general-purpose user wants, even though the mode of the message may be obvious.

Future electronic mail groupware probably will accommodate a degree of group integration across different vendors' software. This integration will require that the actual intention of messages be better understood and defined. The application of knowledge-based technology to the purpose of messages will be the key to making integration possible so that the necessity to state the mode of a message (promise, request, acceptance) is eliminated.

The expertise of the system will infer the intention of the message and flag the status of a conversation appropriately—like having a personal assistant read your mail and categorize what responses are outstanding and what action is required. The system, however, will not understand the contents of the message. The system understands only the state of the message within the conversation and how the message relates to the activities of the group.

Document-Handling Groupware

The major uses of computer systems are document generation, storage, and retrieval. Networks often are used to provide central storage, output resources, and centralized control.

Document-handling groupware structures these tasks to improve the efficiency of the activities and to provide organizational control. The basic activity of text generation on a network requires that the user's access to text files be coordinated.

Document-handling groupware enables users to take documents out of the common storage areas like checking a book out of a library. Other users can see who has that document and when the document was taken.

The ability to control the version number is another group support feature. This feature can be a vital control in environments where you have sequential construction of material, such as in contract writing.

The ability to create documents as templates for a group is important, particularly in legal and government enterprises. Sophisticated document-handling groupware systems also support document routing that enables a document to be created, possibly as a form (containing predefined fields with controlled value ranges and so forth) and passed on to another user who adds data or performs another function. This revised document then is passed to another user, possibly based on what information has been entered, and so on.

This aspect of document-handling groupware is similar to electronic mail groupware but is differentiated by the focus on a document of a defined type. The document-handling groupware may, in fact, be built to work with an electronic mail system or subsystem.

Group Scheduling and Calendaring

The task of scheduling for a group of people is one that has driven many secretaries to distraction. The problem of reconciling the attendees' available time with facilities' availability can, in large organizations, be a time-consuming activity.

The use of groupware to perform this function can make the task simple. The basic coordination of people and resources can be handled by simple algorithms, although more complex methods enable issues such as alternatives to be generated and rated for viability. Where groupware comes into this picture is in enabling the various components of the task to be distributed across time and space.

The problem with some calendaring systems is that they make the decision for you. The groupware approach is to poll participants and the staff who manage resources and establish the time and place cooperatively.

Sophisticated scheduling systems also generate agendas and coordinate the distribution of minutes. The groupware approach is to abstract the agenda from the interaction of the group as part of the procedure of scheduling. When the scheduling system is integrated with electronic mail, the system can distribute the agenda and documents for the meeting and the minutes after the meeting has occurred.

Conferencing

Meetings require face-to-face contact, but sometimes all the necessary participant are not available at the same time or in the same place. The alternative approach is to use conferencing. This groupware system enables a sequence of messages to be generated by a group and structured. The structure often is in the form of an initial statement, linked to comments that are linked to comments.

Conferencing is differentiated from electronic mail in that electronic mail is essentially one-to-one or one-to-many. After you attempt to perform a many-to-many conversation, the sequence of statement-then-comment disappears, and the flow of exchanges remains one-to-one. Conferencing provides the many-to-many structure while maintaining the sequencing.

The two modes of conferencing are real time and store-and-forward. A real-time conference requires all participants to be on-line at the same time. This type of conference really is a groupware-mediated meeting and, unlike a face-to-face meeting, does not require the participants to be in the same country, or even the same room. The other advantage over a meeting is that the meeting room and other facilities of typical conferences are no longer needed. The disadvantage is that unless the system supports graphics and, in some cases, sound, the conferencing system may not be adequate for certain types of meetings.

Store-and-forward conferencing does not require all participants to be simultaneously available. This type of conference is potentially implementable through an electronic mail system or subsystem but requires a radical reorganization of the way that messages are handled. The system stores messages for retrieval when required.

Selecting Groupware

Selecting groupware is complex. The wrong choice may cause serious disruption of current work or make no contribution to the organization. Worse still, the wrong selection may cost the company time and money.

Consider the following key factors when assessing groupware:

- ❑ Standards conformance
- ❑ Ease of integration with the organization
- ❑ Ease of integration with existing systems
- ❑ Effectiveness gain
- ❑ Efficiency gain
- ❑ User-interface presentation
- ❑ User tailoring
- ❑ User skill allowance

The standards your organization has adopted, or expects to adopt, must be compatible with the implementation of a groupware system. You may be able to use the groupware in an isolated way—as a separate system from other applications. This isolated usage can work but may create a problem in the future, particularly if working practices change.

How easily the groupware system integrates with the structure of your company is important. The organizational and management aspects of groupware can be met with resistance when users are not given a role in its selection. Although this resistance is a problem in the introduction of any new technology, groupware highlights the problems because the new system changes working practices for a large number of people simultaneously.

The ease of integration with existing systems is a potential problem because groupware design often is very different from the design of conventional software. Better and more sophisticated groupware systems support input and export services for data in industry standard formats so that integration is easier.

The twin issues of gain in effectiveness and efficiency are important in justifying the adoption of groupware systems. Effectiveness is not the same as efficiency, although the concepts often are used interchangeably. Efficiency relates to the speed and ease with which a job is done. Effectiveness is concerned with the usefulness of the job. Groupware impacts both areas. Groupware, for example, may improve the efficiency of a person scheduling meetings. Groupware also may improve the effectiveness of those meetings if, for example, a structure for responses is established and more people can offer their ideas.

If not implementing a groupware package is going to make you lose the competitive edge over your competition, cost justification is not necessary. Maintaining a competitive edge often relates to the survival of the company.

The final aspects are user-interface presentation, tailorability, and user skill allowance. How well the groupware presents itself and the process the groupware embodies is vital for gaining user acceptance. How much the interface and process can be tailored to meet the users' needs determines how easily the system integrates into current working practices. To ensure that the system can accommodate increasing user skill, the groupware must have variable levels of assistance and direction that match the proficiency of the user.

Many of the criteria for selecting groupware are not vastly different from the criteria used for selecting a word processing system. The criteria are more subtle, however, and reflect the need for matching corporate cultural, management, and task needs to the services provided by the groupware.

The Future of Groupware

Groupware will evolve as companies, management, and networks evolve, and the future of groupware will involve expert and knowledge-based systems. Future groupware will offer improved interfaces between the user and the computer and between the computer and the rest of the network system.

The user-computer interface will be based on natural language (plain English) input and will adapt to the needs of the user. The users' characteristics will be part of the support embedded in the groupware. Functions, such as the capability for the groupware system to "know" what topics in a conferencing system are of particular interest to a user or group of users, is an example of future groupware capabilities. If the conferencing system is to be of general use, all text will be plain English, which requires that the system "understands" the text and the groups' needs.

The short-term promise of groupware is to support functions within an endeavor (intra- or inter-company) more efficiently than is achieved today. The long-term promise will see entire companies integrated by groupware that will be as fundamental to conducting business as the staff.

Chapter Summary

Groupware is applications software that provides a set of traditional functions, such as electronic mail, appointment calendars, project management, and so forth. Virtually any office function may be supported by a groupware application. The integration of the activities of all users on the system is a key feature of groupware. The system also may integrate several functions, enabling project management information, for example, to be communicated by electronic mail.

As part of the integration of activities and functions within the office, groupware packages have the goal of improving organization and management among members of a workgroup. These packages often include structures for communications, organization, and management, and if these structures are used, the result often is improved efficiency and effectiveness of the workgroup. When workgroup members are separated by time and space, groupware often is the only practical solution for organizing and managing the group.

13

Distributed Data Services and SQL

The first step in the evolution of networking was resource sharing. Resource sharing enabled multiple clients to access a set of centralized resources. Resource sharing increased the cost effectiveness of what were at the time extremely expensive resources.

The next step in the evolution of networking was workgroup computing. The revolutionary feature of this phase was that multiuser applications supported a group of users carrying out a common set of tasks. The task might be word processing, for example, where the group activity was the creation and modification of documents. Because the users could share a common set of files, new ways of working were enabled.

The key area that recent evolutions in networking focus on is the issue of transparency. Local applications, therefore, should be able to access network facilities and function consistently within the local system. Compatibility with the local system is of vital importance as networks grow.

The opposite of a transparent service is a nontransparent service. Nontransparent services are not consistent with local service access, and the access of nontransparent services often requires special commands and routines. Every time you need access to a nontransparent service, you have a consequent learning curve and functional gap. If you are a word processing operator, for example, and you want a template document from a network service, you do not want to have to exit the word processor and run a file transfer utility. The ideal method is to use a file retrieve function that the word processor supports.

Enterprise networking was the successor of workgroup computing. Enterprise networking extended network services throughout an organization, and, in some cases, to external networks. This type of network system connected broadly compatible networks. Enterprise networking tended to integrate systems similar by either vendor type. The focus on similarity in networking may have been because a single supplier provided all the core technology, or because the workstations on the network were all PC DOS based.

Enterprise networking does not disallow or prevent links to alternative suppliers or systems. The connections, however, are non-transparent and sometimes very complicated to implement. The lack of transparency of these connections makes them poorly integrated with the rest of the network.

Network computing is the current level of evolution. Network computing differs from previous network philosophies in several important aspects. First, network computing simultaneously supports multivendor workstations, server platforms, and operating systems. The network, therefore, can be built using the workstation technology (workstation hardware and software) appropriate for the task.

Second, the network computing system also integrates multiple standards to enable different workstations and servers to share databases and resources transparently. All the network computing workstations and servers use and provide services consistent with their own standards.

Third, the network computing system supports distributed services and processing that enable the entire network to be seen as a single computing system. On most large networks today, databases, communications gateways, high-speed processors, and many other resources and services are distributed—meaning that they are not all on the same network or even operating under the same operating system. Networks are multivendor and multilevel (for example, mainframes, minicomputers, and PCs). Network computing is aimed at integrating these systems and providing transparent access to them. The integration of these facilities enables the network computing system to be as flexible and cost-effective as possible.

Distributed Data Services

To support network computing technology, a new area of network services is required. Distributed Data Services (DDS) fulfill the needs of network computing. Distributed Data Services are addressed by many vendors under a variety of names. The intent of all of these vendors is to control and deliver services to users, regardless of the physical location of those services.

Distributed Data Services address the following issues:

1. Transparency of data location
2. Transparency of data format
3. Standard access methods

The transparency of the location is crucial to the support of network computing. Applications need to access data from a wide variety of sources; in many cases, however, the data is spread across several other databases. Transparent data location support enables the application to perform input/output operations on *logical databases*, that is, on databases presented in a different format from what actually exists. The actual data presented by the logical database can be derived from several other databases.

A database, for example, might be stored on the mainframe. An application on the PC needs to use this database, but cannot access the database directly because of the differences in format between the mainframe environment and that of the PC. DDS technology solves the problem by setting up a logical database that the PC can access. In fact, the mainframe database is not changed, but its data is made accessible from PC commands; therefore, the PC is accessing a logical database consistent with PC formats.

DDS techniques use a data dictionary to define the mapping of the logical database structure onto the real database structures. When an I/O request is made, the DDS processes use the definitions in the data dictionary to access the physical files and construct the data records. The records are in the format of the logical database.

A logical database for current orders, for example, may access selected fields from the customer database, the accounts database, and the products database. The data dictionary can specify the fields in the physical files to be translated into the required field format for the current orders file of the logical database. The data dictionary specifies how the DDS processes resolve the problem created by the customer database being on one file server and the other two databases being on another server.

The transparency of the format is important if the databases are resident on systems with different operating systems and processors. Format transparency may be as simple as one processor storing the data in reverse order. Ensuring transparency may be complex if the record types used by the logical and physical databases have incompatible formats and require significant amounts of processing for translation between the two formats.

The third issue that Distributed Data Services address is the key technology to DDS support. Structured Query Language (SQL) provides a generic access method for databases. SQL also limits physical location as a design issue for network applications. Understanding what SQL is and how SQL can be used in a network environment requires some basic knowledge of database technology. This knowledge is provided in the following section.

Understanding Database Basics

A *database* is simply a file in which you store pieces of interesting data. Databases get complicated in two basic areas: how the database is structured and how you access that data. The structure of a database can range from the simple to the extremely complex. A simple database consists of a set of records in a "flat" file—a simple list of data. This structure differs from hierarchical files that are tree-structured with categories and subcategories. *Record* is the term applied to an entry in the database. A record in a flat file may be of fixed or variable length. A *field* is a range of data describing a particular characteristic of a record.

For variable-length records, each record is delimited (defined) by a standard separator. Separators may be carriage returns, line feeds, or both. Although you can open the file at any point and find a record, you first must search for a delimiter before you can establish the extent of the record.

The advantage of a flat file in database applications is its simplicity. Unless complex delimiters are used, a flat database file can be accessed by many different types of software, including word processors. In fact, the text you are reading now has its origins as a database of sentences.

The problem with a flat file of variable-length records is that replacing a record of one length with a longer record is difficult. One way around this problem is to use a fixed-length record; obviously, this solution requires that you know the maximum length of a record before you define the database. Such an approach also requires that you actually use as much of each record as possible (see fig. 13.1).

```
ThisΔisΔdataΔinΔ      Mr.ΔJonesΔ0198ΔΔΔΔ
aΔflatΔfile.¬•Re      Mrs.ΔSmithΔ12768ΔΔ
cordsΔareΔofΔvar      Mr.ΔBrownΔ165788ΔΔ      Δ = space
iableΔlength¬•Ea      Miss.ΔGreenΔ789066      ° = null
chΔrecordΔisΔdel      Mrs.ΔLewisΔ6678ΔΔΔ      ¬ = carriage return
imitedΔbyΔaΔpair      ~°°°°°°°°°°°°°°°°°      • = line feed
ΔofΔcarriageΔret      °°°°°°°°°°°°°°°°°°      ~ = end-of-line
urn/lineΔfeedΔch      °°°°°°°°°°°°°°°°°°
aracters.¬•~°°°°      °°°°°°°°°°°°°°°°°°
```

Fig. 13.1. The contents of a flat file with variable-length records on the left and fixed-length records on the right.

If you use a maximum record length of 256 bytes (characters), for example, but 95 percent of your records are 4 characters long, you are wasting disk space. Although the wasted space for a thousand records may not be significant, wasted space can be significant when dealing with a million records. For a million records, 256 million bytes (characters) would be allocated in the database; slightly more than 239 million bytes would be wasted if you used only 4 of the allotted 256 bytes per record. Such an organization is an unacceptable use of space.

The major problem with a flat file structure, particularly when thousands of records are involved, is how to find a specific data item or set of data items rapidly. With a flat file, you must scan the file from beginning to end, comparing the data in each record against a template. Such a search involves reading every record. If the result of a database search indicates that you must search for records of a different type, you must read the entire database over again.

You can structure records to provide more information about the data that each record holds. You could ensure that the records for a name-and-address database always start with the surname, for example. Whenever you add a record to the database, you insert the record in alphabetical order. To add a record, read the current database and write each record to another file until you find a record that should come *after* the record to be inserted. Then, write the new record to the work file and continue copying records from the old file until all the records are in the work file. Erase the old file and rename the work file using the old file name.

This procedure works adequately for databases of a few hundred records. The update process has an acceptable overhead and you can use search methods such as the binary chop to find needed data. The *binary chop* is a simple method for reducing the search time in a database sorted in some order. The binary chop operates by reading the middle record in the database (if 1,000 records exist, the binary chop reads record 500). Then, the chop compares that record to the record being sought. If, for example, you are searching a 1,000-record database for all the records containing the name *SMITH*, the 500th record may be *MITCHELL*. MITCHELL comes before SMITH in an *ascending sort* (a sort starting with low values and going to high values).

Now you know that the SMITH records come between record 500 and record 1000. The next step is to read the record halfway between these limits. Suppose that this record contains *THOMPSON*; you now must chop in half the range in which you are likely to find the SMITH record. This range is now 500 to 750. You determine the halfway point as record 625. Record 625 is *SMITH*.

If you were trying to retrieve multiple SMITH records, all you know at this point is that you have found one of the records. The other SMITH records may be before or after the record found. Search forward and backward from the current record until you run out of SMITHs.

The binary chop is certainly a more efficient search method, but is inadequate if you need to search more than the surname field. You may want to search the name-and-address database for all people using the 213 telephone area code. To do this search, you have to go back to reading each record in the database because the only order imposed on the database was based on the surname field. You could re-sort the database based on the area code field and then use the binary chop search method to retrieve data, but continual re-sorting is very inefficient.

The solution to the inefficiencies associated with flat files is to provide an index to the data in the file. An index is a separate file that contains information about specific fields sorted into ascending or descending order. For the name-and-address database, an index file would contain an entry, by field, for each record; the entry acts as a pointer to each record in the database.

Consider a very small database for fruit, suppliers, and costs:

Record number	*Database record*
1	Chilies,Mexico,$5
2	Apples,England,$10
3	Eggplants,America,$8
4	Bananas,Jamaica,$12
5	Apples,Argentina,$20

The fields you want to access are fruit type and country of supply.

The index file for the fruit type field would look like the following, sorted and alphabetized by fruit type:

Fruit Type	*Record Number*
Apples	5
Apples	2
Bananas	4
Chilies	1
Eggplants	3

This index file enables you to search for a fruit type by reading down the list of fruit types (if the list is not long) or by using a binary chop until you find the type you want. Suppose that you wanted to buy 10 boxes of apples and wanted the best price. Look in the index to find *apples*, read the record number of the first *apples* entry, and go straight to the specified record in the database to get the price (in this case, record 5).

In the fruit example, you discover that a box of Argentinean apples is $20. Check the index to see whether any other entries for apples exist. Because another *apples* entry exists, read record 2 from the database to discover that English apples are only $10.

If instead of 5 records, 5,000 records were in the database, you can see how an index significantly reduces the search time.

On a network, such optimizations as indexes are vitally important to ensure that data traffic across the network is minimized. When data must cross a network, the difference between reading all the records in a database and reading a much smaller index file to find the record that you actually want can mean the difference between poor and acceptable performance.

The efficiencies produced by indexing, however, may not be adequate to maintain performance. In many applications, the database may be indexed on a large number of fields. Corporate databases may have several database files totaling several gigabytes; the associated index files may occupy megabytes of disk space.

Structured Query Language

The solution to the large-index/slow-access problem is to have a database engine, or server. A server handles the accessing of data when given a description of the data required. The Structured Query Language (SQL) server uses this principle.

SQL is a language for accessing data. SQL enables you to describe the relationship between fields that may be in multiple databases so that you can specify the records you want to access. SQL has a place in stand-alone systems as a method of isolating the front-end application (the user interface and querying procedures) from the access method that often deals with complex communication and system design issues. This isolation can be beneficial to individuals developing an application. During development, a simple database access method is adequate, but the option of moving to a networking platform at a later date is attractive.

In a networked SQL environment, the standard client-server network defines the relationship between the SQL client and the SQL server. A client makes requests and a server answers those requests. The client formulates an SQL request that is transmitted to the SQL server through a network transport mechanism. LU6.2 or NetBIOS, for example, are transport mechanisms that can be used to link an application requiring SQL service to the SQL server.

The SQL server receives the request, performs the various database accesses, field comparisons, and calculations, and returns the result of the operations to the client. This arrangement enables client workstations with relatively low processing capacity to use a high-performance SQL server platform instead of their own limited processing resources. Additional benefits are that network traffic is reduced and databases are isolated from direct access by client workstations.

Isolating databases from client workstations can be a critical design factor where security is an issue. The SQL server effectively places a barrier between the client and the data that cannot be circumvented. In a well-organized and well-managed network, only the SQL server has direct access to corporate databases.

The mechanisms used by the SQL server to access data are much more advanced forms of indexing than those discussed previously. The basic principles of indexing still apply, but incorporate refinements that improve performance, integrity, and flexibility. A key strategic enhancement is embedding transaction-processing support in the SQL server. *Transaction processing* ensures the integrity of the database in case of a failure at a client site, during transmission of a request or reply across the network, or failure of the SQL server itself (see Chapter 22, "Risk Analysis and Reliability").

The SQL server can implement a process that resides in the file server. The NetWare SQL server, for example, is a process loaded into the server environment to become part of a multitasking operating system. Although running the SQL server and the file server in one computer has obvious advantages of maximizing the investment made in the server system, the combination potentially degrades the performance of the SQL server and the file server (see Chapter 4, "Application Processing").

An alternative strategy to the SQL engine residing in the file server system is to dedicate a node on the network to running the SQL engine. The SQL engine may be resident under a standard workstation operating system (Unix, OS/2, or DOS) or be an added component to a network bridge.

SQL is actually an impressive technology. Mainframes and minicomputers have used SQL technology for many years to increase the portability of applications and simplify the construction of multiuser database systems. Portability increases when a generic language like SQL is used. Construction simplicity comes about because the SQL commands have a much higher-level definition of relationships between data than is enabled by direct access to the database. SQL commands request a service (a high-level request) while direct database requests are by name and location (a low-level request).

In the mainframe and minicomputer world, three of the best-known SQL databases are DB2, Oracle, and Ingress. Many of these big-system products recently have migrated into the LAN environment. This evolution is important because it enables a consistent approach to data access across the spectrum of business computing technology. The introduction by IBM of Systems Application Architecture (SAA) and the common user interface have great significance for SQL technology.

SAA can make possible the portability of applications across the IBM-compatible world. This potential portability ensures that SQL applications can use any resource with standard SQL server capability. SAA and SQL will be of vital importance in the design and construction of corporate-wide networks, leading to the further improvement of network computing.

The role of SQL in network computing is to provide a standard database access method for a wide range of computing systems. In this sense, SQL is so critical that it becomes a basic requirement for all network computing systems.

Chapter Summary

The evolution of computing has moved from isolated computers to workgroup computing, enterprise computing, and network computing. Workgroup computing connects the workgroup. Enterprise computing connects the entire organization, but is limited to single-vendor solutions. Network computing, the most recent evolution, is designed to integrate distributed services and resources.

A key to the success of network computing is Distributed Data Services (DDS). Distributed Data Services permit the transparent access of data through standard access methods, regardless of the location or format of the data. Structured Query Language (SQL) is a standard access method that permits the realization of DDS. SQL has achieved wide support and appears destined to be an integral part of DDS in the foreseeable future.

IV

Communications

Includes

Internetworking

The Host Connection

14

Internetworking

The backbone-and-cluster design is the most popular for large networks. The backbone often is a high-speed LAN capable of handling all internetwork traffic. The emerging technologies for high-speed backbone networks are impressive, such as the 100 Mbits/sec FDDI (Fiber Distributed Data Interface) cable specification. The clusters are local networks, with one cluster typically supporting the users on one floor of a multistoried building or one workgroup within the organization. Cluster networks usually are 1 Mbit/sec up to 16 Mbits/sec.

The backbone-and-cluster design may be the result of planning, or this design may evolve as the use of LANs grows in the organization. For example, a department manager buys three or four PCs, then gets a LAN to connect them. At the same time, other managers are going through the same growth process and purchasing LANs independently.

Many departments eventually are networked and want to communicate with this system on an interdepartmental basis. A backbone network usually is the best way of connecting these clusters, although the clusters also can be linked together in a daisy chain (one connected to the next, which is connected to the next, and so on). The backbone-and-cluster network is illustrated in figure 14.1.

The key to making this kind of arrangement work is internetworking. Also called internetting, internetworking is the process of connecting networks, permitting data to move freely

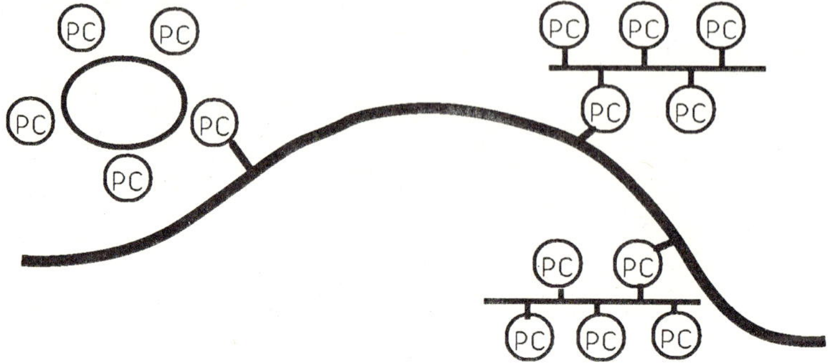

Fig. 14.1. The backbone-and-cluster network consists of small networks (clusters) attached to a central network (backbone).

among large numbers of networks and populations. Through internetworking technology, LANs are attached to other LANs, other communications networks, remote sites, individual stations, and wide-area networks.

Internetwork Hardware

The devices used for internetworking depend on the degree of compatibility between the networks. The OSI Model, introduced in Chapter 2, helps to illustrate how connections are made.

When two networks are being connected, the connections are made at the first identical OSI layer. For example, if layers 1 and 2 of the OSI model on the networks are different, but layers 3 and up are the same, the connection is made at layer 3 by having identical layers talk to each other within the connecting device.

Devices called *repeaters* achieve the lowest level of interconnection. Signal-regenerating hardware devices, repeaters make a cable interconnection at layer 2 (Data-Link Layer)—actually a layer-1-to-layer-1 connection that is implemented in layer 2 (see fig. 14.2).

Because repeaters extend the distance of a network, if you are using an EtherNet LAN but need to go farther than you usually can, you can install a repeater to achieve the added distance. When a repeater is installed, it creates a physical break in the cable. The

Fig. 14.2. The repeater connects two cables by making a connection at the Data-Link Layer of the OSI Model.

signal is received on one side of the repeater, regenerated, and passed on to the next section of cable.

A repeater does not stop the flow of network traffic, but takes everything from one side and passes it out the other side. The purpose is to compensate for any degradation in signal quality that may have occurred prior to the repeater being used.

The next level of interconnection is called a bridge. A *bridge* connects two fundamentally identical networks with a different physical element at the bottom (see fig. 14.3). For example, a bridge can connect two networks with different bottom layers at layer 3 of the OSI model (the Network Layer); everything from layer 3 up must be the same. The best example of a bridge in current use is between a broadband token network and a baseband token network. Everything on these networks is identical except the hardware systems.

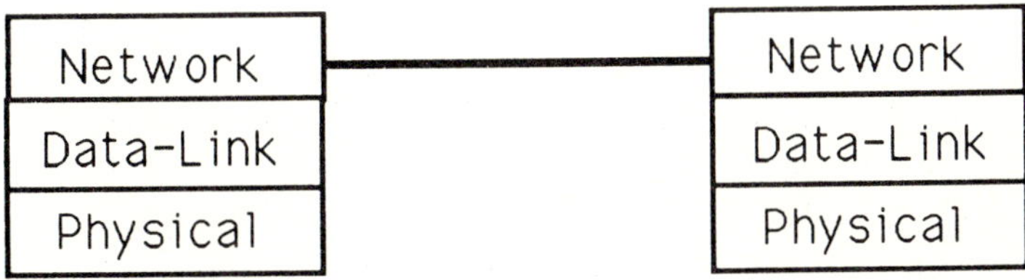

Fig. 14.3. A bridge makes a connection at a higher level than a repeater.

A device that interconnects the bottom three layers, making the connection at identical Transport Layers (layer 4), is called a *router*. (The router frequently also is referred to as a bridge.) Routers provide a sophisticated level of services. For example, routers can bridge an EtherNet contention network and an ARCnet token network; the connections are made in the access method and in the physical hardware. For communication to occur through a router, the upper layers of the network (layers 5, 6, and 7) must be the same (see fig. 14.4).

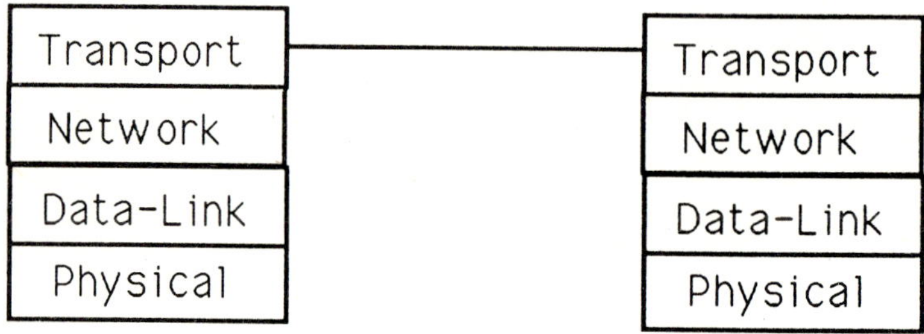

Fig. 14.4. A router connects networks at the Transport Layer.

A router has two sections, each of which has transmitting, receiving, and processing capabilities. When a signal arrives at a router, the signal is buffered (stored), and some protocol conversion is performed to make the signal compatible with the other side. The message then is passed to the other side and transmitted onto that network.

Networks may have several bridges that provide links to as many networks as needed. A router can receive a message addressed to another network and, in this case, is "smart" enough to know the best way to transfer the message so that it moves on to the correct destination. If a link in an internet becomes inoperative, a router can retransmit messages through another route. To avoid a bad link, a router also can reroute a message a longer distance. Rerouting provides redundancy (a backup scheme) in the system.

Some routers also can handle load balancing. If, for some reason, the traffic load on one link becomes too heavy, routers may be able to shift some of the load to other routers and links to balance the message load going across them.

To connect totally dissimilar networks, a gateway is used. *Gateways* perform protocol conversion for all seven layers of the OSI Model. A common use for a gateway is to connect a LAN and an SNA mainframe computer, changing protocols and retransmitting packets between two entirely different systems.

Routers and gateways can manipulate the packets being sent. With routers, that manipulation may be some determination of where the packet comes from (Net A) and where the packet is going (Net C).

In a gateway, that decision may be more complex, because a gateway can perform more functions. A gateway not only performs the router's function (determines where the packet is going) but converts the message from one packet format to another or from one data code system to another.

As interconnection takes place at higher levels of the OSI Model (for example, a router compared to a bridge, or a gateway compared to a router), the task of interconnection becomes more complicated, and more processing power is needed to perform that task. All things being equal, a gateway is slower than a router, which is slower than a bridge, unless the processing capability is raised proportionally. A good strategy always is to use the lowest-level connection possible. Use a repeater instead of a router, therefore, if either device can do the job.

Routers actually regulate a network's traffic flow, reading every packet on the network and passing internetwork traffic onto another network. Routers do not necessarily alter the form of the packet. They may just retransmit each internetwork packet in its original form.

A repeater or bridge regenerates and repeats a signal, usually after the signal has traversed a long cable section and suffered attenuation and distortion. A router performs store-and-forward services in addition to retransmitting signals.

Frequently, routers are used to interconnect identical networks and to interconnect networks with different types of hardware. Compared to one giant LAN, a series of smaller LANs internetted through routers has some highly desirable benefits. The foremost of these benefits is security. LANs operate in a broadcast mode: information retrieved or transmitted goes onto the network and traverses the entire cable system. Only the station specifically addressed reads the data, but the data physically is presented to each station. A person who wants to thwart the addressing scheme and receive unauthorized transmissions has an open invitation to do so and can modify a PC to read all transmissions.

Partitioning the data system into small self-contained networks reduces this vulnerability. Although the networks are interconnected by routers to permit internet communications, ordinary network traffic remains local. If an accounting system is on a separate network, accounting data is not transmitted beyond that network unless the data specifically is sent to another network. Files can be downloaded and uploaded all day to the accounting system's hard disk without the data traversing other network cables.

Another benefit of routers is reliability. If one network goes down because the server stopped functioning or because of a fault in the cable, other networks and the departments they serve are not affected. Because the internetworking routers isolate such problems, the functioning networks, although connected, experience no downtime or data loss.

A third benefit of using routers is performance enhancement within the individual network. Suppose that a network has 12 workstations, each of which generates approximately the same amount of traffic. In a single-network environment, all the traffic for those 12 workstations goes on the same cable. If the network is split into 2 networks of 6 workstations each, however, the traffic load is cut in half. Because each network has its own server and hard disk and is largely self-contained, fewer PCs make demands on the network cabling system.

A final benefit of routers is greater networking range. In some networks, for instance, cable length cannot exceed 1,000 meters. A router effectively nullifies this limitation by performing the function of a repeater and reconstituting the signal. Physical range can be whatever is required by the particular installation, provided that a router is installed before the maximum cable range is exceeded. (All networks have some upper limitations on the number of routers supported, but using routers can create networks that cover extremely long distances.)

Remote Interconnection

Until now, this chapter has discussed the options for hard-wired interconnections. These interconnections between local communications systems run on a dedicated cable system. Hard-wired systems, however, are only part of the communications needs of many companies. These companies also need to connect remote PCs, LANs, and other communications systems and services into the network.

A remote connection often is achieved through the attachment of a modem to any PC workstation that needs to communicate outside the LAN. By converting between a computer digital signal and a telephone-type analog signal, modems enable computers to send and receive across standard telephone lines. The modem makes the connection from the LAN workstation to the outside but makes no direct use of the LAN.

Two software options permit LAN-to-remote interconnection; these options are classified as remote log-in and screen transfer. With remote log-in, you dial into the LAN through a PC acting as a bridge. (You log into the LAN as if your PC is physically attached to the network.) The only limitation is that the response across the telephone line—usually 1200 to 2400 baud (bits per second)—is very slow compared to local response times on a LAN.

Using screen transfer, a remote PC is connected to a PC attached to a LAN. The remote PC takes control of the local PC, issuing keyboard commands and receiving the display output.

The choice between these two interconnection options is strictly a transactional issue. If you can run the bulk of your application locally, and all you want to do is perform some transactional access onto a file server, logging into the network with your own PC through a remote connection is a good way to accomplish that task. The remote connection is not practical for moving large files and applications back and forth, because of the slow speed of the telephone line connection. If you need to load an application stored on the network that is not in your local PC, you are better off executing on the network by using a screen-transfer program (see fig. 14.5).

Remote execution is ideal when the application program is stored on the LAN. This method reduces the amount of traffic sent across relatively slow telephone lines. Only commands and display screens must be passed between the remote PC and the network.

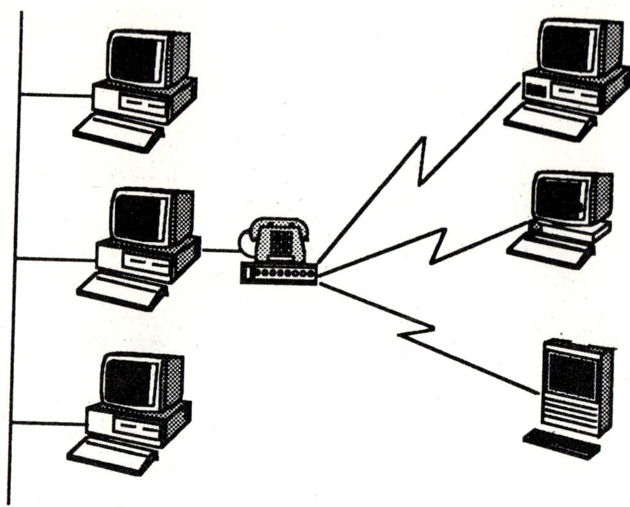

Fig. 14.5. Screen transfer applications enable workstations to send screens of information via telephone lines and modems back and forth to a networked PC.

Remote execution also is excellent for remote PC support services. An analyst can replicate a situation at a remote LAN and solve problems at the remote site.

Asynchronous Gateways and Modem Pools

The cost of a telephone line, modem, and communications software package can be expensive if several PC workstations need this equipment. With a LAN, these communications resources can be shared, resulting in significant cost savings.

When attached to the LAN, the asynchronous gateway, with its software, manages the asynchronous communications resources for the network. From one to a dozen modems, each with its own telephone line, can be attached to the gateway. A gateway attached to multiple modems is called a modem pool. Users request an asynchronous connection, and the gateway assigns an available modem and phone line.

In addition to the direct cost savings for modem pooling, the asynchronous gateway approach offers a major indirect savings. Instead of inexpensive 1200- or 2400-baud modems, high-speed modems in the 4800- to 9600-baud range can be used. Such modems are expensive (although prices are dropping rapidly), but when several users share the modems, the per-user cost drops. The communications cost drops because each communication takes less time.

X.25 for Wide Areas

Beyond the local site, public X.25 networks are becoming very popular. The need arose in the early 1970s for a common protocol that would make public data networks compatible. In 1976, the Consultative Committee for International Telegraph and Telephone (CCITT) adopted Recommendation X.25 that has become the most widely used interface to public networks.

In the United States, three different kinds of X.25 networks are available to the public on a leased basis: Tymnet, Telenet, and AT&T. These public X.25 networks usually provide less expensive X.25 services than available on a private basis.

For major data communications services, such as business support systems and information databases, X.25 is an excellent communications protocol, and these services are proliferating rapidly. The capability to gateway into X.25 networks, therefore, is an important network feature that greatly expands the range of network applications (see fig. 14.6).

X.25 networks can be used in many ways. A business may use an X.25 network to integrate dispersed branches or to access remote on-line databases. One tax accounting company has put together a huge computer network to service some 7,000 clients located around the country. The company furnishes PCs to big and small accounting firms and gateways the firms into an X.25 network. This arrangement enables everyone to communicate. If one center is busy processing tax returns, a request for processing can be relayed to another center. In this way, the processing load is balanced.

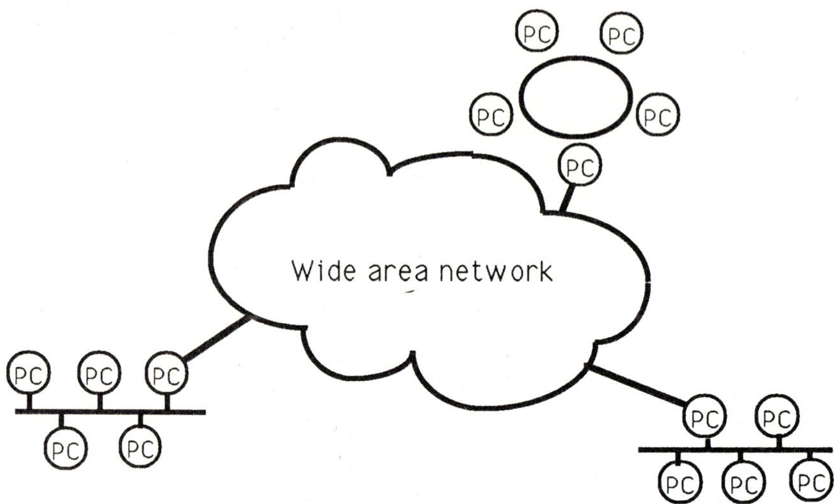

Fig. 14.6. Wide-area networks can extend beyond the local cabling system.

X.25 Options

When planning to install a wide-area network gateway, you must consider the amount of traffic that will go through the gateway. A public network may be justified if the connection is solely for some low-volume administrative function. You can access public networks in two ways. You can install a gateway that is public-network-interface-compatible, enabling you to use the X.25 protocol, or you can use a modem to connect to the public network, with your system appearing as an asynchronous terminal.

An asynchronous modem and dial-up line are appropriate for very low traffic loads. To access the network, you turn on your modem, load your communications software, and dial the number. This inexpensive method enables many remote sites to access the LAN or the mainframe center. The method even works with an electronic mail system, in which the mail is collected at some regional point and remote users dial in to pick up and send mail.

With heavier traffic, this method is slow and inefficient. The solution is higher-speed lines that send messages quickly and cost less per mile than voice-grade lines. You can choose between a dedicated leased line or a public data network. Public data networks, such as

Tymnet and Telenet, are more economical unless you have extremely high traffic, in which case the dedicated leased line may be the best choice. The cost of using an X.25 link on a public data network is inexpensive compared to paying the telephone bill for six or more PCs communicating with X.25 over voice-grade lines.

Chapter Summary

Today's internetworking technology provides excellent connections at the middle and lower layers of the OSI Model. This technology, however, still is rudimentary when used to connect two entirely dissimilar systems and to convert all seven layers from one system to another.

For example, when a middle-level connection such as a router is used, the resulting internetwork can be transparent to the end user and to applications software. You can communicate and use resources physically located beyond your local network environment with the same ease that you use the local system.

On the other hand, when communication occurs through a gateway to a dissimilar system, some functionality usually is lost. File transfer between systems or terminal emulation at the PC currently are the extent of connection functionality.

You cannot access another dissimilar computer system with a PC operating in "intelligent mode"; the PC must emulate a dumb terminal. You generally cannot pass formatted documents from one application to another without losing the formatting codes and perhaps some accuracy, due to translation limitations. Electronic mail messages cannot be passed from one mail system to another.

These limitations are the last major obstacles to the powerful PC-based communications system that is emerging. The local area network is the first step in this system; the eventual goal is global internetworks.

15

The Host Connection

As you have already seen, a major benefit of networking is that microcomputers and the work performed on them no longer are isolated. Information can be passed from one computer to another and read and updated as needed. The process of linking PCs and combining their capabilities creates a flexible new computing resource. In the corporate environment, the next step is to link this new resource with an established one: the mainframe computer.

This step is still evolving, a process that no doubt will continue during the early 1990s. The primary reason for the slow integration is that mainframes and PCs represent two different technologies and two different management cultures. The mainframe is a host computer by tradition if not by necessity; the PC is today's foundation for distributed processing. The mainframe is a central resource managed and protected by professional data processors; the PC is a tool of end-user computing.

Gradually, these two different worlds are being brought together. Both environments have established functions and large installed bases. More importantly, perhaps, each environment has its own unique capabilities that complement each other and add power and efficiency to data processing.

The PC began its entrance into corporate computing through first-rate, PC-based applications programs, such as word processing and spreadsheets. These early PC programs were easy to learn and use. Often, they were a distinct improvement over comparable mainframe programs. However, the PC remained isolated from the mainframe and was unable to access corporations' primary data banks.

Then devices began to appear that enabled the PC to communicate with the mainframe and manipulate mainframe data. PC-to-mainframe communications was a prerequisite to making the PC part of large-system computing. Now that the PC is established, the door is open to explore fully the other applications of an intelligent desktop workstation in a mainframe world.

Examining the Hardware Connection

The hardware connection is the fundamental, physical connection between the PC and the mainframe. In the past, the typical hardware connection went directly from the PC to one of the controllers on the mainframe network. The PC, therefore, took the physical place of a terminal. The connection today usually is through a local area network. Using the LAN as part of the hardware connection lowers the per-node connection cost, improves system manageability, and can reduce the overhead on mainframe processing and communications resources. (These advantages are covered in the "Selecting the Gateway" section of this chapter.)

When considering connecting a LAN to a mainframe, you should follow three simple goals that can offer some guidance in your selection and configuration decisions and also help define the function of the hardware connection. The first goal is to provide data paths among all environments. This rule differs from most implementations in the past in which environments were separated by the level of computing and by the vendor—the IBM mainframe network, the DEC minicomputer network, the PC network, and so forth—as isolated systems. Logically, the hardware design should provide the foundation for network computing, the system of distributed resources in a heterogeneous environment.

The second goal is to provide support for remote systems and users. One of the ways that computing has changed is in the requirement to integrate remote facilities. Companies want to tie all their computing and information resources in a single system. This design enables you to base your decisions about whether to centralize or distribute resources and management functions on effectiveness and cost.

The third goal is to control costs through selection of hardware technology. The hardware connection is the most expensive component in the network. Selecting hardware is a process of determining the amount and type of traffic along various links and then choosing the hardware that supports the bandwidth requirements in the most cost-effective manner.

Choosing the Type of Connection

The choices for hardware connection range from low performance/ low cost to high performance/high cost. The following four hardware options are in current use:

- ❑ Asynchronous dial-up
- ❑ Synchronous dial-up/leased line
- ❑ Coaxial cable
- ❑ Token-ring network

(Although mainframe examples are used here, nearly all the connections have identical counterparts for LAN-to-minicomputer connections.)

Asynchronous, or *async*, connections are communications that send messages at irregular intervals (asynchronously). The asynchronous connection typically uses standard telephone lines and connects the computers at either end through low-cost, asynchronous modems (see fig. 15.1). The benefits of this approach are that the technology is widely available and mature and can be implemented at a relatively low cost.

The disadvantages of async connection are limited speed and reliability. Async protocols offer poor error-detection and recovery capabilities. This fact plus the low-grade communications lines typically used force users to keep transmission speeds low—normally 2400 or 4800 bits/sec, possibly up to 9600 bits/sec. In high-traffic environments, the slow speed and poor error handling (increased retransmissions) raise the cost of data communications

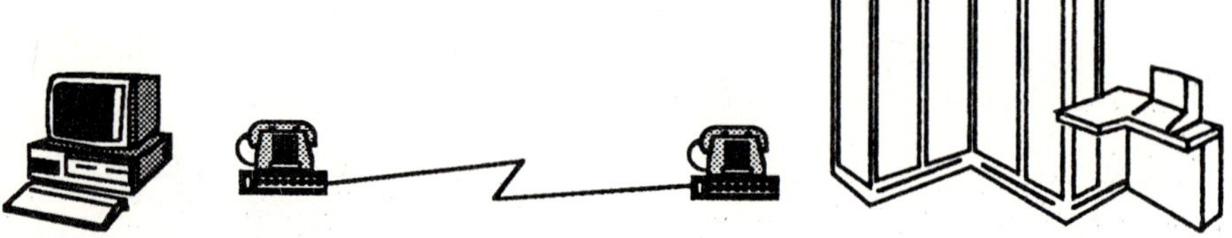

Fig. 15.1. An asynchronous connection links the mainframe and the LAN through telephone lines and low-cost asynchronous modems.

services to the point that higher quality hardware connections become more cost-effective. For low-volume communications between the LAN and the mainframe, however, asynchronous communications are often the best choice.

Synchronous, or *sync*, connections use a communications protocol that sends messages regularly according to a precisely timed clock pulse. Sync connections have one advantage in common with async: the capability to use standard telephone lines and widely available technology. Additionally, the synchronous protocols provide improved error handling and recovery that accommodates an increase in transmission speeds, usually up to 19.2 Kbits/sec (see fig. 15.2). Although synchronous hardware (modems and so forth) is more expensive than async hardware, it still is relatively inexpensive.

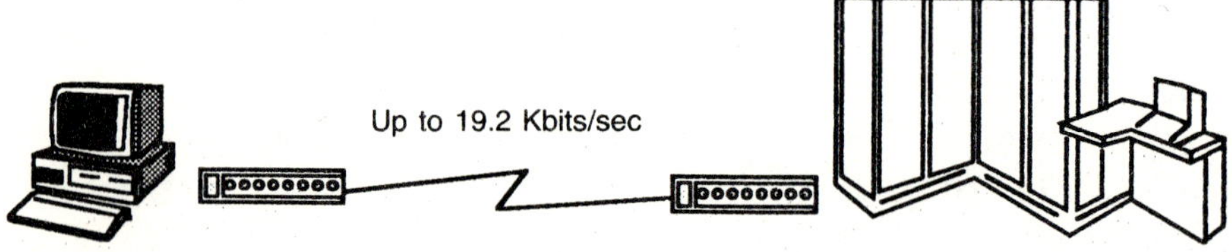

Fig. 15.2. Synchronous connections can support faster data transfer rates than async because of improved error detection and recovery.

Coaxial cable is the third hardware connection choice. Coax uses a dedicated coaxial cable from the LAN to a 3299 multiplexer (see fig. 15.3). Then, the cable is connected to a 37X5 communications controller at the mainframe. The benefit of the coax connection is speed: the coax link from the LAN to the 3299 operates at 2.3 Mbits/sec. The coax connection can be expensive if you use the connection in a new installation. If supporting equipment such as 3299s are already installed, however, the coax connection is relatively inexpensive and provides a definite improvement in performance.

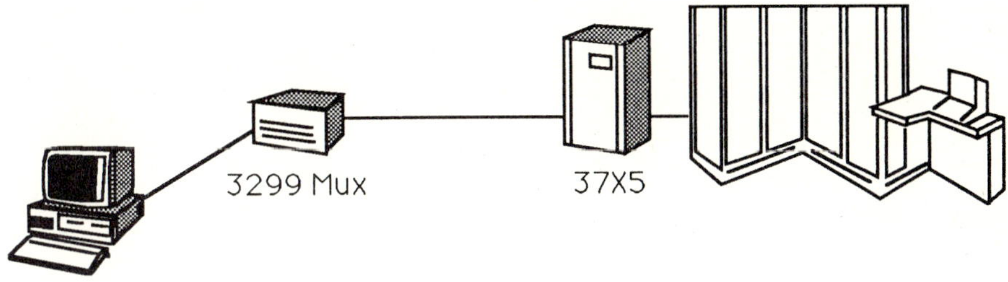

Fig. 15.3. Coax connections attach to the mainframe via a 3299 multiplexer and support speeds up to 2.3 Mbits/sec.

The newest hardware connection method is a *token-ring network*. A token-ring interface card is installed in a 3174 cluster controller or a 3725 or 3745 communications front-end controller (see fig. 15.4). The token-ring connection is the most expensive method of connecting LANs to mainframes when an existing terminal network is already in place. This type of connection offers distinct advantages, however, including even cost advantages in a new installation, depending on how the system is designed.

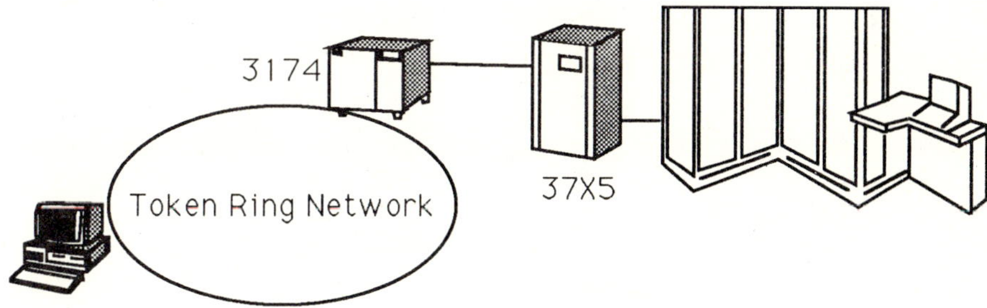

Fig. 15.4. The IBM 3174 cluster controller can be attached directly to the token-ring network.

Token ring operates at 4 Mbits/sec or 16 Mbits/sec, giving token-ring performance superior to any of the other connection alternatives. Because of this speed, many more mainframe sessions can be supported with adequate performance. The 37X5 connection further simplifies the network and reduces the required hardware, thereby reducing management and support costs (see fig. 15.5).

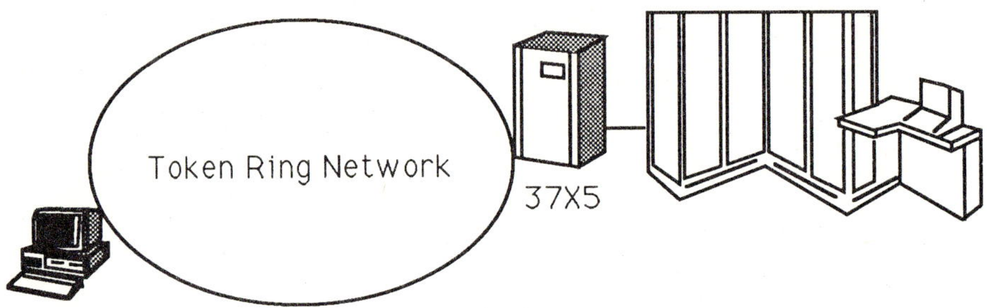

Fig. 15.5. Connecting the token-ring network to an IBM 37X5 reduces hardware and management overhead.

Also important in network planning is the long-term position of token-ring technology. Token ring is a strategic direction for IBM and has become a recognized standard. More development will occur for token-ring technology than for any of the other hardware connection methods. The performance of token ring also will become a more critical advantage—even a requirement—as distributed applications and process-to-process communications become widespread.

For remote hardware connections, asynchronous or synchronous communications using dial-up or leased lines usually are the only choices. Standard telephone lines offer significantly lower cost but are less reliable and slower. Leased lines are higher in cost with commensurate increases in reliability and speed. The choice normally is based on an analysis of traffic flow. High volumes of traffic from remote facilities usually warrant the use of leased lines.

Selecting the Gateway

All the hardware connections require a *gateway*: a hardware and software system that handles protocol conversion between the mainframe and the PC environment. In the connection between a stand-alone PC and a mainframe, the gateway function is provided in the emulation circuit board and software that runs on the PC.

Although gateways that support such protocols as X.25 and asynchronous communications are available, the SNA gateway is becoming the primary LAN-to-mainframe link (see fig. 15.6). In most configurations, the gateway emulates a 3274 cluster controller. PCs attached to the LAN can initiate a 3270 session with the mainframe through the gateway. To start the session, the PC must load an emulation program; the PC requires no special emulation hardware.

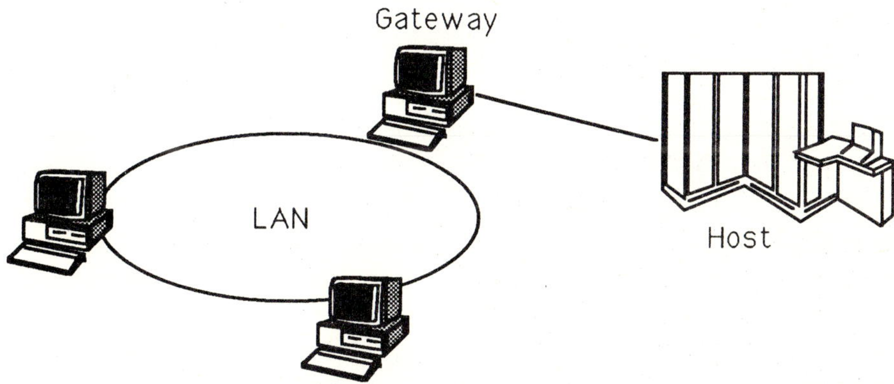

Fig. 15.6. A gateway accommodates mainframe access from any workstation on the network.

Gateways have a fixed number of ports, each of which supports a mainframe session. Gateways come in 8-, 16-, 24-, 32-, and 64-port versions. The gateway usually supports as many as five or six simultaneous mainframe sessions on a single PC. Each session takes up the entire screen, and users can switch from one session to another.

Functionally, the gateway and the emulation board solutions are basically the same. Both enable the PC to function alternately as a

3278 terminal and a microcomputer. The primary reason for opting for the gateway-type link is a significant savings in cost.

A port for a PC on an SNA gateway costs between $175 and $400. Providing the same connectivity with an emulation board costs approximately $1,000 for the emulation board and another $500 for a port on the 3274 cluster controller. Additionally, the gateway approach requires only one connection between the LAN and mainframe. With emulation boards, each emulator-equipped PC must be furnished with its own dedicated 3270 cable, usually at a cost of several hundred dollars each. The resulting cost difference between the two solutions is considerable. Compared to the emulation board solution, the gateway method saves well over $1,000 per PC workstation.

The greatest savings through LAN gateways stems from the fact that many people use the mainframe connection only 10 or 20 percent of the time. One gateway that supports 30 sessions may satisfy the needs of 100 users on the LAN. The same connectivity with traditional 3274 cluster controllers would require three or four controllers and sessions dedicated to the workstations. The dynamic support of the LAN makes the LAN gateway approach much less expensive.

This cost savings through dynamic allocation of limited communication ports has another important advantage in that it permits better management of communications and mainframe processing resources. Emulator-equipped PCs can place a heavy burden on a mainframe communications system because of their capability to download large files, run multiple sessions, and use mainframe storage areas through virtual host storage (VHS). A gateway also enables many users to access the mainframe. You can limit the number of simultaneous sessions from the LAN to the mainframe by restricting the total number of gateway ports available. A 15-workstation departmental LAN, for example, may have an 8-port gateway that reduces the potential load on the mainframe system. As the network grows and needs additional mainframe ports, you can add more gateways.

Several processing options must occur to link the PC to the mainframe, and some of these processes can be taken care of at the gateway computer or at the PC. For efficiency, controller emulation should be done on a coprocessor board within the gateway computer. Modem and line control, line management, session control, and session/data distribution also are run best at the gateway PC and preferably on a coprocessor board. The PC workstation should handle terminal and printer emulation and format translation. Most gateway systems follow these guidelines for distribution of functions.

The gateway can be run as a dedicated or a nondedicated machine. The nondedicated gateway has a lower entry cost, and most vendors enable nondedicated gateway software to run on a file server or a workstation platform. The disadvantages of a nondedicated gateway are reduced reliability and performance. Some gateway coprocessors are so powerful that performance is almost unaffected by using the gateway platform for some additional function, but reduced reliability usually is a serious limitation of the nondedicated gateway and is almost unavoidable.

The network interface card (NIC) that attaches the gateway to the LAN is a critical component of the system. In a standard file server, the NIC handles single requests from each workstation. Although this load is higher than the load for a NIC in a workstation, the workload is still relatively small. In a gateway server, the NIC must handle multiple requests from each workstation because of the requirements of the session protocol. These multiple requests place a heavy load on the NIC in the gateway, and its selection criteria must be more stringent as a result.

In essence, the gateway NIC must be a high-performance card with a coprocessor and onboard memory. The software used to drive the NIC also must be of high performance. In a system in which the driver or the NIC is inadequate, periodic failures of the system will occur under load. When you have this problem, you should probably replace the gateway NIC and its driver. This problem is less common with newer high-performance NICs and drivers because vendors have begun to address the increased needs of high-performance connections.

Selecting Software

After the hardware choices have been made, the next major decision is the choice of software. *Software* defines the environment of the system and delivers the functionality. Four fundamental goals in software selection are

- ❑ Supporting productivity
- ❑ Accessing host data
- ❑ Using host applications
- ❑ Delivering transparent access

Productivity relates to the tasks people must perform and the available technology. When system planners make their decisions based on these two issues, the result is optimized productivity. The alternative, and one common in PC-to-mainframe connectivity, is to look at how tasks have been performed in the past and emulate those procedures as closely as possible with new products. This style of planning results in inefficient use of the new technology and in productivity that is far below the potential.

Host data and host applications are valuable resources that should be accessible to the PC user. Some software enables the PC to use mainframe processing and communications links, but ignores or provides poor links to mainframe data and applications. Real connectivity requires total integration of the environments, and you should keep this need in mind when selecting software for the LAN-to-mainframe connection.

Transparent access is the highest level of connectivity and one that is only beginning to be possible. In a gateway environment, protocol conversions and emulation techniques inevitably mean that something is lost. The loss may be functionality, performance, ease of use, or all three. One strategy for reducing the problem is to design the application so that the PC and mainframe environments provide complementary services (see "The Advantages of Using PCs as Mainframe Workstations," later in this chapter). Another strategy is to run client-server protocols at the mainframe and completely merge the systems; the PC remains a PC and does not emulate a terminal. This latter strategy is becoming more prevalent, but because of the large installed base of host applications, this strategy cannot be a total solution at present. Terminal emulation will probably be required for decades.

Two general types of software are used in the LAN-to-mainframe connection: interactive, session-oriented software and file transfer, batch-oriented software.

Choosing Interactive Software

Interactive software is used to enable the PC, acting as a terminal, to manipulate mainframe data. This mode is a requirement for accessing host applications designed only for terminal communications.

Types of Emulators

The most primitive of the terminal types is the teletype, or TTY, terminal. TTY terminals transmit and receive data line-by-line. Software written for TTY terminals tends to be basic and to use few, if any, higher-level display or keyboard features available in some terminals.

The next evolution in terminals was the intelligent terminal. This machine has a limited capability to process information and is a major improvement over the TTY terminal. An intelligent terminal transmits and receives in block mode, usually screen-by-screen. This method accommodates useful capabilities such as full-screen editing and windowing.

One of the most widely used systems of intelligent terminals is IBM's 3270 series. The 3270 terminals are used in on-line (interactive) sessions with an IBM host computer. These highly functional terminals support such features as text insertion and deletion and automatic cursor movement.

Through emulation hardware and software, the PC workstation can perform the same functions as the 3270 terminal. In addition, the PC can receive and store data from the host computer, modify or reformat display data, and run local applications programs that analyze the data. The host can be an IBM System/370, IBM 308X, or 43XX processor. The PC can be connected with coaxial cable to a channel-attached IBM 3274 or 3276 cluster controller or connected remotely to a bisynchronous or SNA/SDLC 3274 cluster controller.

A 3270 emulator is a type of gateway. Through this gateway, virtual circuits are established between host and terminal devices and go to a bisynchronous or SNA network and the IBM host. The emulation package includes a circuit board that supports the physical connection between the PC and mainframe system. Also included is software that runs on the PC and provides 3270 functionality.

The 3279 is a color text device. The 3B and 2B models are graphics models, but limited applications have reduced their acceptance. Even though the 3278 is a monochrome device and the 3279 is a color device, most users choose to emulate a 3278 with a color PC and create a color display. A PC with a color monitor can take all the special screen attributes such as reverse, blink, and highlight and use them with color. On the PC, you can define a different color for each attribute.

Emulators are available to make the PC look like the 3278 or 3279 terminal, although accommodations are required for some models. The 3278 Model 2 display is PC compatible, with 24 lines plus a status line. Model 3 has a 32-line display plus a status line; Model 4 has a 43-line display plus status line. Because you cannot put more than the standard 24 lines on the PC screen, when handling large displays, the emulators enable you to use the PC's PgUp and PgDn keys to scroll the screen. Because of the widespread use of PCs with their 24-line display, the 24-line format has become the de facto standard. The 32-line and 43-line displays are less popular because most new applications support only the 24-line devices.

The IBM PC keyboard provides all the special functions of the 3270 series keyboard, although some adaptation is needed because the numbers and positions of the keys differ. Many companies, including IBM, DCA, Novell, and Pathway Design, provide 3270 emulation packages.

Evaluating Emulators

The first step in evaluating a 3270 emulator is to check that the emulator is hardware- and feature-compatible with your system, beginning with the PC. All emulators do not work with all IBM PC compatibles. The emulator board should fit any slot and be used like any other circuit board. Other parts of your existing system, such as cluster controllers, may be "IBM compatible" but not compatible enough to support a particular emulator without some modification.

After you check compatibility, the next step is to look at emulation quality and how that quality is achieved. All emulator designers make accommodations for the screen and the keyboard, but these designers tend to follow their own rules. Which designer's scheme is best is a matter of personal preference. As you evaluate the emulator, test each key of the emulator-equipped PC. You may notice considerable variation in what a key actually does, what the documentation says the key does, and what the comparable key on a 3270 does. You often have a real advantage if the emulation software enables you to map the keyboard to your own preferences. Some users find that changing keyboard layouts when moving from one emulator to another is difficult; setting up a personal profile largely eliminates the problem.

A third step is to evaluate the emulator software. This software must perform a number of functions, the first of which is to enable you to enter the emulation mode. From there, many of the emulators enable you to run concurrent PC and 3270 modes, controlled through a toggle switch. One key shifts the PC environment back and forth between PC and 3270 modes.

The emulator software has an important feature, the *transfer utility set*, that appears with varying degrees of success on early emulators. An emulator should be able to bring files down from the host to the PC and return them to the host when processing is completed. The transfer utilities should support whatever environment is necessary. This point is critical: you must make certain that the software supports not only the two-way transfer but also the mainframe environment—TSO, VM/CMS, or both.

How the information is displayed also should be taken into account. Compare the emulated display with the 3270 to see whether status lines or comments are the same and whether all the characters are compatible. Because some differences can occur in the character sets, designers must choose representative characters.

The emulator should be totally compatible with your present system. You should be able to disconnect the coax and connector from the 3270 terminal and plug the cable directly into the emulator board on the PC. Then, when you turn on the system and start the emulator software, you are connected to the mainframe.

As part of a LAN, a terminal-emulation package can serve individual users who need to access the mainframe. The only concern is that the emulator settings must not conflict with any other devices within the PC workstation. For example, if you have a modem in a PC, a 3270 emulation board, and a network interface card, you must know the interrupts and all the I/O channels being used by each. If some of the interrupt settings are identical for two or more boards, the system does not function properly.

Most emulators permit the concurrent use of other communications software, including networking software, as long as the interrupts and channels are not duplicated. The emulator software should permit the changing of channels so that conflicts can be avoided. If a specific address is already used for communications, you should be able to reset the emulator address so that the communications programs do not "collide" with each other.

The network sets up its own communications system, managed by the network interface card and network software. The network does not affect the PC's three parallel ports (LPT1, LPT2, and LPT3) and two serial ports (COM1 and COM2). Other devices, such as printers, modems, and emulators, however, use these ports and must be directed properly.

Choosing File-Transfer Software

The other type of PC-to-mainframe software is file-transfer software. *File transfer* is the mode used to bring mainframe data down to the PC for processing. File transfer offers some advantages over interactive sessions. For example, files can be transferred at times when the mainframe and communications network are least used, such as just before the normal business day begins. Batch transfers do not necessarily require a user to monitor the transfer, which frees personnel. The main value of these transfers, however, is that they enable mainframe data to be analyzed and processed with PC software.

For file-transfer software, the first criteria to investigate is the operating systems supported, such as VM and MVS. Within these systems are several specific environments, such as CICS, TSO, and CMS. Different file-transfer software typically is required for each environment.

File-transfer software should be able to handle the transfer of text and binary files. The software also should be compatible with standard file-transfer commands, especially those supported by IBM (assuming that you have an IBM-compatible environment). IBM has a highly functional set of management functions in the 3270 environment, and you probably should evaluate software as to how well it supports these functions and commands.

You can accomplish file transfer with some PC-based software simply by tricking the host 3270 software into "printing" to a disk at the PC. Better performance, however, is available through special file-transfer software with components on the mainframe and the PC. One function of this software is to compress the data before transfer, thereby shortening the transmission time.

The Advantages of Using PCs as Mainframe Workstations

For an analyst, or for anyone else whose position requires that many jobs be done concurrently, the terminal-emulating PC can be effective. Perhaps an analyst works on the mainframe, writing and maintaining programs. In addition, the analyst may need to support local PC users and their applications software. With a LAN-attached PC that can emulate a mainframe terminal, the analyst can work in the PC and mainframe environments and reach out to many physical locations—all from a single workstation. Suppose that the analyst is working on a project on the mainframe in a 3270 mode, and somebody comes in with a question about a spreadsheet. The analyst presses a couple of keys and brings up the application. After assisting the spreadsheet user, the analyst returns the mainframe to 3270 mode.

With electronic mail, this process is even better. A question can be asked through a PC-conveyed memo. The sender references the appropriate files that the analyst can call up from the central hard disk. The analyst then can send back a response. Although the two users may be miles apart, the interaction is the same as if they were sitting next to one another.

Another interesting feature of the PC and terminal emulator is that you can capture a complete session, saving all the data to disk on the PC or LAN. At the end of a session on a dumb terminal, the session is gone. If you want to know what you did or want to remember a particular piece of information, you have to run the session again from the start. With the PC, you capture and review the session at your convenience. You then can store the whole session for later viewing or analysis.

Many terminal operators—the people in planning, finance, accounting, and inventory—extract bits and pieces from large files. Typically, these operators look through thousands of pages of output but manipulate just a few pages. With a 3270 emulator, the operators can extract and manipulate information locally on their PCs. PC software programs usually are much easier to use than comparable mainframe programs—and often more powerful. Mainframe programs often lack the sophistication of the smaller programs written for the PC.

You help the host system when you download menial tasks that do not require mainframe power. This setup reduces the work load on the mainframe, which then can support more operators and be more accessible to them. The mainframe is best used to store extremely large files and databases and to run large programs and handle extensive computational tasks, such as executing large compiles. All other work should be run on the PC, if possible (see fig. 15.7).

Another advantage in downloading to the PC is cost. For example, an engineer can bring down subroutines from files and manipulate these subroutines on the text editor, and maybe even run a compatible compiler on the PC level. When a subroutine checks out, the engineer can put the subroutine into the mainframe and do the final run, which costs many hundreds of dollars per hour of computation time. The engineer saves time in manipulating the program, which, of course, saves dollars.

Frequently, part of the processing is done on the host mainframe, and another part is downloaded to the PC for processing. For example, suppose that a mainframe system produces an analysis in metric values. An engineer downloads the analysis into the PC, extracts and places the data into a spreadsheet. The spreadsheet

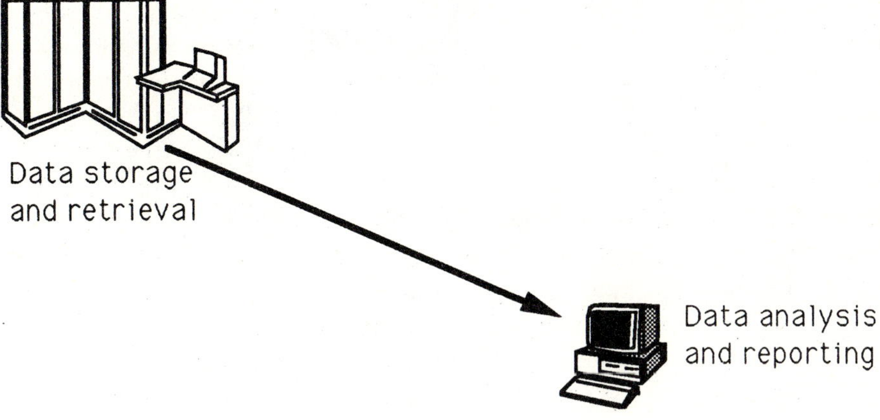

Fig. 15.7. One of the most productive ways to use the LAN-to-mainframe connection is downloading and processing host data with PC-based application software.

converts from metric to English, performs the financial analysis, and uses PC applications to produce a portfolio of graphics showing the financial or engineering aspects of the analysis. Then, the new analysis is integrated into all the word processing documentation, packaged into a proposal, and printed in the LAN environment. The graphics also are put into a slide format for multimedia presentations.

This example points out the added value of the PC environment. The PC can take the basic data held by the mainframe and augment the information in many ways, performing tasks in a more cost-effective manner and with better output than the mainframe can. Word processing, graphics, and analysis are all areas in which PC software has gained superiority over mainframe software.

Comparing Mainframe and PC Applications

Understanding the relationship between the mainframe and the PC is still a matter of applications. Mainframe applications are good, but for the most part they do not employ the rich assortment of user interfaces available on the PC. When creating mainframe applications, developers usually make the applications device-independent. This approach forces the developers to go to the lowest common denominator of keyboard entry and screen presentations. Typically, they do not employ color, special highlighting, sound, or other features available on PCs and even some terminals.

The philosophy for application development on the PC is that a good set of user-interface features exists and should be used. PC applications began at a level that was much richer than the mainframe application because of the quality of the user interface. In more recent years, with the PC becoming a workstation platform, the power of the applications has increased significantly, giving PC applications even greater advantage over their mainframe counterparts.

Graphics applications, in particular, now favor the PC. At one time, mainframe graphics packages were definitely superior, and the mainframe still has some easy-to-use, powerful packages. Comparatively, however, these packages now are more costly than PC-based applications that also have expanded in power. The original PC products that drew pie charts and bar charts could not handle free-form images and special annotations, boxed annotations, and so forth. Now numerous PC packages perform full composition work—not just producing a simple chart, but creating total images.

This comparison of application features, however, is not meant to suggest that the mainframe has no purpose. When large-scale processing is necessary, the mainframe usually is the appropriate platform.

A more common need for a mainframe is to use the mainframe as the central database for the corporation. Even with the best current micro technology, planning connections of thousands of locations, thousands of miles apart, is not feasible. Although microcomputers can handle a database through database server technology, only the mainframe presently can handle an extensive number of distributed databases. The mainframe is well suited to manage many different databases and interconnected applications.

Finally, companies with mainframes typically have large amounts of money invested in the hardware and software and in the communications networks to service the system. Companies often view the mainframe environment as THE computing environment. They look for ways to enhance the environment through such technology as client-server networks, PC applications, and PC processing power. You can argue that the relationships of these systems will change—indeed that is the position of this book. Today, however, the acceptance and growth of PCs and distributed networks depend on their capability to integrate satisfactorily into the established mainframe environment. The most common way to enable integration is through terminal emulation.

Cooperative Processing

In IBM environments, 3278 emulation is a standard mode of PC-to-mainframe integration. With 3278 emulation, the data often stays on the mainframe, and the PC augments or uses the data as a standard 3278 terminal. Optionally, the data can be downloaded into the PC for manipulation and enhancement. When the PC with 3278 emulation downloads a file, the PC is still emulating a 3278 because of the protocols in use. To make the system transfer data, two new programs are called: one on the mainframe, and one on the PC. These programs are designed to work together, and use the normal path of a 3278 data stream to accomplish the transfer.

Such coordination among two programs running on different machines is an early form of cooperative processing. *Cooperative processing* is a mode of operation in which two or more machines run pieces of the same application. This mode is particularly useful in maximizing the capabilities and synergies that are available in the PC-to-mainframe environment. One method of enabling PCs to work on mainframe data is file downloading from the mainframe to a 3278-emulating PC. Other, more powerful methods also have been developed, however.

One of the newest and most far-reaching schemes for cooperative processing is built into IBM's Systems Application Architecture (SAA). SAA is designed to enable distributed processing, but with the mainframe maintaining its host personality. SAA includes protocols that permit PC-to-mainframe communications and support the concept of specialized processing functions occurring at any appropriate level within the computing environment. The Communications Manager, part of IBM OS/2 Extended Edition, provides a set of functions that includes terminal emulation, file transfer, client-server relationships, and peer-to-peer program communications. Although these functions have been available under DOS, in the OS/2 Extended Edition, they are more powerful and easier to use.

Additionally, SAA is beginning to solve one of the biggest problems in cooperative processing: the standard development interface. Writing software for an application that moves between the mainframe and the PC is difficult because both environments must be supported. The best way to accommodate this situation is through an architecture that both sides can follow for application development so that the application does not have to become overly complex. This issue is one of standardization in SAA.

For example, applications at one time had to be printer dependent, including enabling all the different escape sequences to perform special tasks on the printer. As time went on, device drivers began to appear. A *device driver* is a program that has a standard application interface for input and a device-specific interface for output. Different drivers are written for different devices. The application makes high-level requests for a particular printer function. The device driver then knows exactly how to make this function happen. In this way, one application can drive many dissimilar types of printers.

SAA provides this common standard interface for cooperative processing in a distributed environment, reducing the cost of application development and encouraging full use of the facilities of the PC environment in PC-mainframe integration.

Chapter Summary

The primary goal of the PC-to-mainframe link is to enable distributed resources to be accessed from any point on the network, regardless of vendor environment or machine type (mainframe, minicomputer, or PC).

The PC-to-mainframe link is fundamental to the integration of PCs into large organizations. This integration involves a hardware link and a choice of software types. Hardware links can be asynchronous, synchronous, coaxial cable, or token ring. Your choice should be determined by an analysis of the amount of traffic and the cost of the various options. High-speed links may be more expensive to install, yet because of their greater capacity, may reduce actual costs.

The local area network with a gateway is an efficient way to link populations of PCs into a mainframe environment. The LAN lowers the per-node connection cost, improves the manageability of the system, and can reduce the impact of PC workstations on the mainframe system.

The choice of software is basically a choice between interactive software, such as IBM's 3270 series, and file-transfer software. Interactive software for terminal emulation is needed to access mainframe applications from the PC. File-transfer software enables mainframe data to be downloaded for analysis and processing at the PC.

V

Network Management

Includes

Management Strategy and Practice

Batch Processing

Installation

Performance

Maintenance and Diagnostics

16

Management Strategy and Practice

Personal computers encourage individual ways of doing things. If an office has six PCs, the six users may have six ways to do everything: six formats for correspondence, six modifications of every application program, maybe even six totally different programs for the same application. When several marketing personnel are doing marketing analysis, you hope that they are all using the same basic data, but they probably are not. After the marketing database is put on a local floppy disk, the database often is changed, and the resulting analyses often is based on somewhat different data.

Managers often deal with the problem of PC-changed data in one of two ways. They ban PCs and use a host-based terminal network, or they use PCs to generate batch files, collect them at the end of the day, and merge them into a central database.

Other problems are more subtle and difficult to control. For example, one employee may be creating and using excellent applications for the PC, but may not give other employees access to the applications. While the employee stays with the company, all this creative potential is lost to other employees; when the employee leaves, the applications frequently are lost.

Problems like these illustrate that every office that uses PCs needs a system to handle information flow. Networking PCs is a big step toward improving the organization and manageability of the PCs, but networking is only a first step. An organized plan for how data is stored and controlled must be part of the network from the start.

Choosing the Network Supervisor

The most practical approach to organizing the network is to appoint a manager. Essentially, the network supervisor's duties are to make sure that the network functions at its best and that data on the network is protected from loss or misuse. Much can be done in software to organize a network and protect networked data. For a business to derive the most benefit from a network, however, a human being must supervise network operations.

Deciding who should be the network supervisor and what jobs that person will handle depends on many factors. The problem most companies face is that no one in the company knows much about local area networks. A mainframe-oriented data processing professional will find a LAN to be a management challenge very different from host-to-terminal systems. Frequently, the LAN dealer is the first to play the role of network supervisor. Dealers often install and configure the LAN and train the people who will be using the LAN. This practice enables the system to be functional and productive while the supervisor-to-be is learning the job.

The job of network management can evolve into one of two kinds of managers: a supervisor or an administrator. The administrator's job is to add users and applications to the network and to monitor network security. The supervisor performs these jobs too, but is more technically knowledgeable. The supervisor plays an active role in configuring the system and customizing network applications and routines. Companies with large networks and multiple communications systems often need to develop this level of expertise for network management. Smaller companies frequently can give the responsibility of network management to a less technical network administrator.

Mapping Out the Network: The Initial Planning

All local area networks have a central storage device containing one or more hard disks. The first thing to do is to decide how best to use that storage. To make this decision, you need to map out the areas connected by the network. For example, the typical small sales company shown in figure 16.1 has the the following departments:

1. Administration
2. Accounting
3. Sales
4. Shipping and Receiving

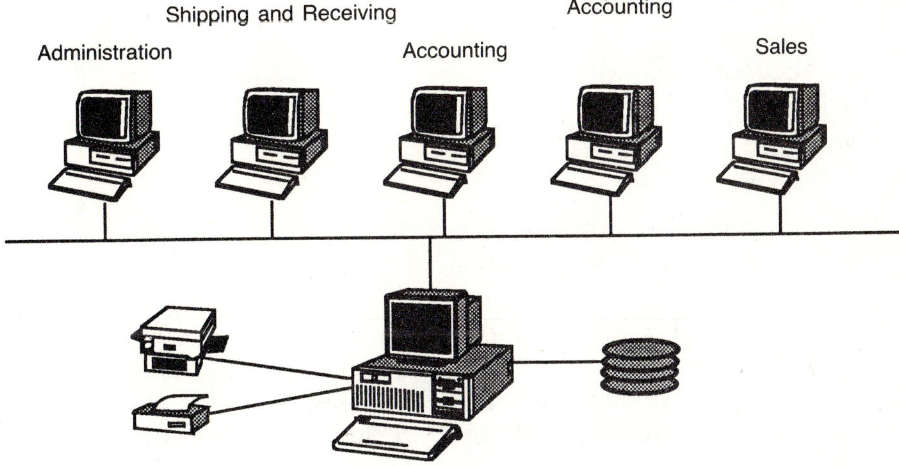

Fig. 16.1. A typical small office network includes several departments.

On this sample network, one network supervisor has been appointed. Administration has three users: the owner, the manager, and the secretary. Accounting has two users: the accountant and the bookkeeper. Shipping and Receiving has one network user: a clerk. Sales is the largest department with six salespersons and two secretaries, all of whom are given user status on the network. Each of these users is given a name and password and, in network jargon, is made a user on the network. In addition, a group user has been designated with access to public (nonrestricted) data files. This group user is named Everybody.

Included in the company's shared data files are the following:

1. System programs
2. Applications
3. A database with customer records
4. A database with sales orders
5. Contracts and proposals
6. Correspondence
7. Sales objectives
8. Individual sales records
9. Personnel records
10. Purchasing
11. Inventory
12. Accounts receivable
13. Insurance records
14. Tax records
15. Electronic mail

After the departments, the users, and the files are listed, the next element in planning the network involves hardware. This hypothetical sales company has one dedicated network server, one PC per user, one high-speed dot-matrix printer, and one laser printer. Accounting, Sales, and Shipping and Receiving each have a dot-matrix printer loaded with frequently used forms. Company data storage is on a single hard disk. Each PC has one floppy disk drive as well.

Organizing Files

The next task is to group the identified files (admittedly an abbreviated list) according to the department that usually manages and creates the data in each file.

System programs and application programs are installed and managed by the network supervisor and are labeled *NS* in the list. Personnel records, insurance records, and correspondence will come from Administration. Individual sales records also are maintained there. Therefore, you should label these files in your list as *Admin*.

Accounting will create the accounts receivable and tax records. Label these files as *Acc't*.

Shipping and Receiving creates records of shipments to and from the company. This department also controls the stock, develops purchasing orders, and keeps inventory records. Label these files *SR*.

Sales is responsible for creating and maintaining customer records, sales orders, contracts and proposals, and sales objectives. Electronic mail (the stored messages, not the application) is labeled *E* for everybody—the group user name. Label these files *Sales*.

The list of files and their "owners" now looks like the following:

Files	*Owners*
System programs	NS
Application programs	NS
Customer database	Sales
Sales orders	Sales
Contracts and proposals	Sales
Correspondence	Admin
Sales objectives	Sales
Individual sales records	Admin
Personnel records	Admin
Purchasing	SR
Inventory	SR
Shipments	SR
Accounts receivable	Acc't
Insurance records	Admin
Tax records	Acc't
Electronic mail	Everybody

Assigning Users

The next step is to identify who uses certain files and what type of use the files require. Such decisions will differ from company to company. The reason for setting up this exercise is to illustrate the options. For the sake of brevity, only six users will be studied.

1. Business manager (M)
2. Accountant (A)
3. Shipping and receiving clerk (Clerk)
4. Sales secretary (Sec)

5. Everybody (E)
6. Network supervisor (NS)

The files that these users need to access probably would be the following:

File	*Owner*	*Users*
System programs	NS	NS
Application programs	NS	E
Customer database	Sales	M, Sec
Sales orders	Sales	M, Sec
Contracts and proposals	Sales	M, Sec
Correspondence	Admin	M
Sales objectives	Sales	M, Sec
Individual sales records	Admin	M, Sec
Personnel records	Admin	M
Purchasing	SR	M, Clerk, A
Inventory	SR	M, Clerk, Sec, A
Shipments	SR	M, Clerk
Accounts receivable	Acc't	M, A
Insurance records	Admin	M
Tax records	Acc't	M, A
Electronic mail	NS	E

The users, of course, have different uses for the files. One user may need to see a file but may not be involved in updating the information that file contains. This user would be given Read-Only (R-O) privileges. A user who actively updates the same file would require Read/Write (R/W) privileges. Although some network operating systems offer many more privilege levels, these two should suffice for this illustration. The network supervisor has all rights to system files, but in the list, only the files the supervisor actively controls are noted as used by the supervisor. Everybody is given Read-Only privileges to application programs, which enables them to load and execute the programs, but not modify them. Many network operating systems have an access privilege called Execute (or some similar name) designed for application users. If that privilege is available for application users, it should be assigned in place of Read-Only.

Files	*Owners*	*Users, Privileges*
Systems program	NS	NS (R/W), E (R-O)
Application programs	NS	NS (R/W), E (R-O)
Customer database	Sales	M (R-O), Sec (R/W)
Sales orders	Sales	M (R-O), Sec (R/W)
Contracts and proposals	Sales	M (R-O), Sec (R/W)
Correspondence	Admin	M (R/W)
Sales objectives	Sales	M (R-O), Sec (R/W)
Individual sales records	Admin	M (R/W), Sec (R-O)
Personnel records	Admin	M (R/W)
Purchasing	SR	M (R-O), Clerk (R/W), A (R-O)
Inventory	SR	M (R-O), Clerk (R/W), Sec (R-O) A (R-O)
Shipments	SR	M (R-O), Clerk (R/W)
Accounts receivable	Acc't	M (R-O), A (R/W)
Insurance records	Admin	M (R/W)
Tax records	Acc't	M (R-O), A (R/W)
Electronic mail	NS	NS (R/W), E (R/W)

Setting Up Directories

Each user has a set of individualized directory rights. Usually, each set is different, but in larger organizations users may be placed in groups with identical directories and access privileges.

The supervisor has the most extensive directory. The supervisor's main directory would include the following subdirectories: SUPERVISOR, SYSTEM, ADMINISTRATION, ACCOUNTING, SHIPPING AND RECEIVING, and SALES. In each of these directories, the supervisor would have full access privileges.

The business manager needs to be able to read all of the user data on the system, but will require Read/Write access to only Correspondence, Personnel Records, and Insurance Records. The manager's subdirectories will include SYSTEM, ADMINISTRATION, ACCOUNTING, SHIPPING AND RECEIVING, and SALES.

The accountant needs the following subdirectories: SYSTEM, ACCOUNTING, and SHIPPING AND RECEIVING. Because the accountant does not need to modify or see most of the files in the

SHIPPING AND RECEIVING subdirectory, that subdirectory will include listings for only Purchasing and Inventory.

The remaining directories for all the network users would be set up in a similar manner. Each user is given a directory that reflects that user's particular needs and functions within the company.

One important point should be made about directory privileges. Although a great deal of data may be stored on the network in potentially shareable form, opening up all the data files to every user is not necessary or even desirable. A good network operating system provides considerable flexibility in structuring a user-access scheme. The network is much easier to use when the clutter that each user must deal with is reduced. In addition, this kind of system improves data integrity and the security of the data.

The objective in organizing the network is to give each user only as much authority as is needed to fulfill a particular job. For example, the user in Shipping and Receiving does not use the accounting files, the sales report, or even operating system utilities. These programs and data should not be available, even to the level of being able to list the names, to the clerk in Shipping and Receiving.

Determining What Files Go on the Network

To illustrate the organization of a typical system, some general assumptions have been made about the data that will go into the central storage. Actually, *what* goes on the central disk is as important as *how* that data is arranged—perhaps even more important.

In general, all application programs should be stored on the network. Even if users have PCs with local hard disks, users should be encouraged to move their applications to the network where the applications can be most easily supported. Data files, too, should be stored on the network where they can be shared with other users. Even if the data files are not going to be shared, the advantage of network storage is that the supervisor regularly backs up the files. Users have a tendency to omit this precaution. Users may prefer to have some data files stored locally. Local storage should be limited to personal files, calendars, and other data that supports the user's activities.

If the software comes in a multiuser version, it can be stored on the hard disk and shared by anyone on the network. (Some multiuser packages restrict the number of users and, of course, these restrictions should be followed.) The software should be listed in the directory of every user who may need that program. In most cases, access to the software will be restricted to Read-Only, or Execute-Only if that privilege is supported by the network operating system. In this way the program can be used, but not modified or deleted. The supervisor, of course, will have full privileges to perform whatever tasks are necessary to maintain the program. The supervisor also can add utilities and define access rights as needed.

Single-user software packages also can be stored on the network, provided that a separate software package is purchased for each PC that will run the software. Single-user software often is satisfactory even in a multiuser, network environment (see Chapter 9, "Application Software"). Of course, if the software is copy-protected, network storage may be impossible.

Copy protection, which typically prevents a program from being copied from floppy disks onto a hard disk, is especially prevalent in older versions of software but exists on some current packages as well. When your favorite software is copy-protected and not available in a multiuser version, your options are more limited. In this case, the applications software stays at the individual workstations. Only the data files, the end products of those applications, will be stored on the network hard disk.

In moving software to the network, the important thing to note is that the supervisor ensures that only one version of the software and related utilities is available to the users. Users will not be using different versions. That ensures that all files created with this particular application will be compatible. User training and support are simplified because they need to cover only one version of the software.

Decisions concerning file-access privileges should be determined at the time the file is approved for storage, as discussed in the preceding section.

Using Descriptive Names To Identify Files

A data file can be something of an enigma to everyone but its creator. One of the easiest ways around this problem is to adopt common naming conventions for your files. If names are well chosen, a quick look at a directory can provide considerable information.

You can use up to eight characters in a file name in DOS, followed by a three-character extension separated from the file name by a period. DOS reserves specific characters and extensions for its own use, but, essentially, you can use a wide variety of characters. Apple's operating system permits names up to 31 characters in length in which a DOS-type extension can be created (periods are accepted characters names). If your network includes more than one type of workstation, standardizing naming conventions will simplify file management. The extension is particularly useful as explained in the following discussion.

You can start your naming scheme with the kind of information that helps identify the type of file. You can adopt some of the familiar file-name extensions for this purpose and add extensions particular to your own office. For example, BAK can indicate a backup file, DOC a document, TBL a table, and so on.

In many cases, you will want to know who last updated a file. You can use three of the eight file name characters to make this identification: two characters for the initials, preceded by an underline. Then, five characters are left for the particular file name. If five characters are not enough, consider assigning an available character such as a percent (%) or ampersand (&) to each file user with Read/Write privileges. In this way you increase to seven the characters available for the file name.

The file names should be standardized for quick recognition. For example, a typical file in the Sales Department may be a record of all the sales for a specific month. The file name might be SALEJAN%.DOC, indicating that the sales file for January was updated last by Fred (indicated by the percent sign) and that the file is the primary document. If this data is saved in graph form, the file name might be SALEJAN%.GRF.

The time and date of the last update often are significant, and you have the option of trying to squeeze this information into the file name. Most networks, however, have a clock that labels the time and date of each write. This label becomes a useful adjunct to each file name, no matter what workstation operating system is in use.

Regardless of the naming conventions involved, each user should be required to get information on the file before updating the data. As part of the procedure for updating a spreadsheet, for example, the user should find out who updated the spreadsheet most recently and when the update was performed. Then, the user has some basic information about how to proceed.

Controlling the User Interface

A good network is a powerful, and therefore complex, system. One of the responsibilities of the network supervisor is to tailor the network for every user's needs and capabilities. Each user should "see" only as much of the network as is necessary.

Frequently, the strategy used to simplify networks for the user is to install a front-end menu utility. When you log onto the network, the first thing you see is the main menu listing several options. A message at the bottom of the screen states that you should type a specific letter to select an option. The options might be the following:

A Word Processing
B Spreadsheet
C Database
D DOS
E LOGOUT

If you type *A*, a word-processing submenu pops up so that you can select a data subdirectory and an output device. You make this choice by pressing the appropriate key. As soon as you press the key, the application loads; the system is pathed to the chosen data directory, and when you are ready to print, the output goes to the chosen printer. When you exit from the chosen application, a well-designed menu system will take control of your machine again and display the Main menu.

Virtually all network supervisors in large companies use the menu approach. This approach relieves them of teaching users about paths and directories. In fact, because of the front-end menu, users are not required to know anything at all about the network.

Menus can be as simple as a text file that displays the options and several batch files that execute the instructions. For example, you might create a batch file named A.BAT. When the user types *A*, the batch file takes over, creates the necessary paths, and loads the application. All that processing occurs automatically without the user seeing anything more than the options and results (see Chapter 17, "Batch Processing").

Commercially available menu programs offer much more advanced facilities than batch-file menu systems can. Some of the features include a variety of menu screens, submenus, and other menu services.

For the single-application user, even a menu program can be avoided. An autoexecute (AUTOEXEC.BAT) file can be activated at log-in or by the user typing some key word such as *START*. That autoexecute file makes the paths and loads the application without the user ever having to insert floppy disks, consider options, or create paths to data. Therefore, the network user actually can see a simpler computing environment than a stand-alone computer user.

Chapter Summary

PCs must be managed. Otherwise, PCs present enormous support problems and may reduce data integrity to the point that no PC-originated document can be trusted for the accuracy of its data. Networking the PCs is one of the most practical steps to management, but networking is only a first step.

Management involves storing files on the network and ensuring that users have appropriate rights to use those files. All program files (applications) should be stored on the network hard disk where they are most easily controlled and supported. Except for personal files, most data files should be stored on the network so that they can be shared with other users and protected with regular backups.

Access to network files should be authorized according to specific user requirements. Users should not be given access to any files they do not need to use; similarly, if users do not need to modify a file, they should be given Read-Only access, which prevents them from making modifications or deleting the file. Such steps simplify the environment for users and increase the manageability and security of the network and the reliability of the data.

17

Batch Processing

This chapter deals with batch-file concepts and batch-file designs for some specific network needs. For a complete listing of commands and descriptions of their syntax, refer to the workstation operating system documentation. The explanations and examples in this chapter are for DOS 4.0 and OS/2. Earlier versions of DOS support most, but not all of the features and commands discussed.

No single tool is more important to the network user and supervisor than the batch file. Batch files can simplify access to an incredible array of interrelated resources, and can enhance the information/communication function of the LAN far beyond the basics. Batch files run on stand-alone and networked PCs but become crucial in managing and simplifying the LAN environment. Without exception, every successful LAN installation makes use of batch files.

What Is a Batch File?

A batch file is a text file containing a series of operating system commands. The commands in the file execute sequentially after you enter the name of the batch file at the operating system command line. You can invoke several—perhaps hundreds—of instructions by simply starting the batch file with a one-word command.

Batch files do not have to be complex chunks of programming. Most batch files are short lists of operating system commands. A typical batch file is no more than half a dozen lines of instruction. Yet batch files can be extensive, sophisticated instruction sets.

Using Batch Files To Simplify Procedures

Batch files are versatile and can simplify even the most complicated procedures. For example, if you frequently issue the same five commands when you start your system, you can put those commands in a batch file and name the batch file STARTUP.BAT. When you enter the command STARTUP, the file with those five commands runs, and the commands are executed. Batch files can be invoked from the console or from other batch files (see fig. 17.1).

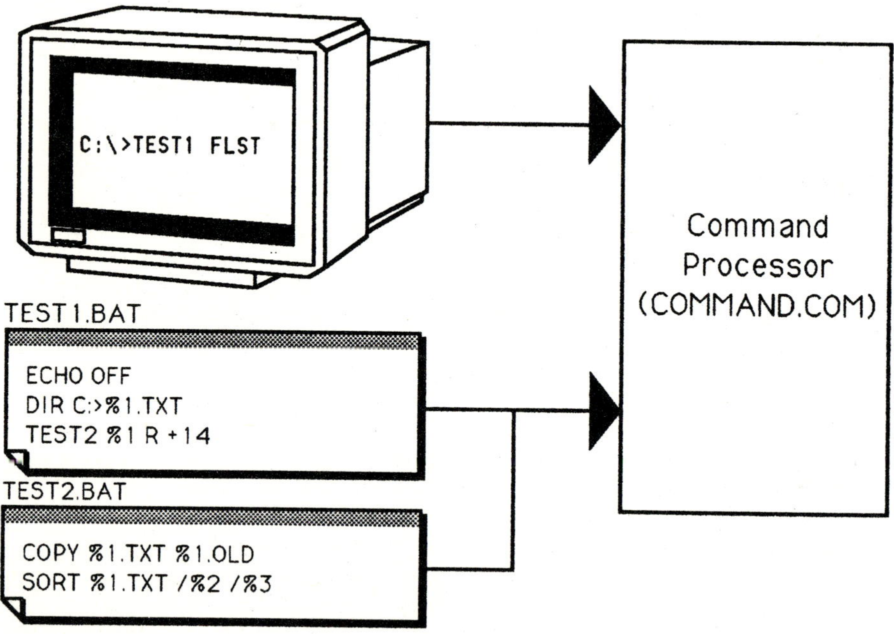

Fig. 17.1. Batch file operation.

Besides reducing the amount of necessary typing, batch files also supplement fallible, human memories. Batch files often are used to find data files tucked away in some obscure corner of the disk. You locate the file once and then write a batch file that leads the system to the file. For example, a report on the sale of brass thimbles might be nested under a subdirectory for household items nested under a subdirectory for brass items. You may forget how you set up this hierarchy, but if you entered the correct path in a batch file named BTHIMBLE.BAT, you can find the report easily by typing the command *BTHIMBLE*.

The structure of the PC DOS file system is described as hierarchical. Each data storage area, or directory, is logically "below" another directory. The directory that all directories are below is called the *root* directory, represented with a backslash character (\). A directory below another directory is called a *subdirectory*.

Your default directory is called your current directory. Any non-specific references to files or other directories are defined relative to the current directory. For example, a request to open the file FRED.TXT assumes that the file is in the current directory. A request to open FRED.TXT in the root directory would describe the file as /FRED.TXT from anywhere in the directory system, or *tree*.

You use the CD command to change the current directory to another directory. The argument is the specification of the directory to become the current directory. For example, if you have two directories, BIN and DATA, branching out from the root directory, and your current directory is data, the full description of this directory, is C:\DATA. The backslash (\) after the drive identification, *C:*, indicates that the description, or path, is from the root directory of the drive.

To change to a subdirectory of BIN, called USR, use the CD command. The full command line is CD \BIN\USR. The CD command also can be used in batch files to change to a subdirectory containing programs or data to be used.

The root directory of a the boot drive (the drive PC DOS booted off) contains a special batch file: AUTOEXEC.BAT. This batch file is executed automatically as soon as the operating system is loaded. This system facility is useful when a program such as a menuing system is to be the first thing that a user sees. Loading the network interface also is a function for which the AUTOEXEC batch file is used.

Of course, the next question is, how do you remember to ask for BTHIMBLE when you are looking for brass thimbles? The answer is to create a menu file that lists resources and tells you what to type (the batch file name) to call up each resource. This menu can even be part of a batch file. You enter the command *MENU* (assuming that your menu file is called MENU.BAT), which starts a batch file that takes you to the menu and then prints the menu on-screen. You then can scan the menu to find the needed resource and the command to access that resource. This system of a menu and batch files is used on hundreds of thousands of LANs to make finding remote resources easy.

Using the PATH Command in a Batch File

The workstation operating system normally is placed in its own directory, which is not the root directory. For your system to use DOS or OS/2 commands from any directory on the system, you need to issue the PATH command to tell the system where to find DOS or OS/2. The PATH command you use might be something like the following example:

```
A>PATH C:;C:\DOS40
```

You can enter the command manually when you start your system. Remembering even this relatively simple DOS command syntax, however, is an unwanted challenge for most of us. And you have to remember to enter the command every time you start your system. Otherwise, you cannot use operating system commands when you need them.

Adding the PATH instruction to a start-up batch file, however, is much more practical. This approach ensures that the system can always locate DOS or OS/2 when needed.

How Commands Are Executed

The batch file executes instructions sequentially. The batch file, therefore, is like an errand list: go to one place and do something, then go to another place and do something else, and so forth. When an instruction is issued by the batch file, none of the remaining instructions execute until after that first instruction is completed.

A common network manager's batch file illustrates how this process works. Managers often want to get users into an application without the user having to issue any commands, and they want to prevent the user from exiting the application and going back to the operating system level. The manager can install a batch file that starts the application as soon as the user logs onto the network. The user can work with the application and is completely free to use any of its features. While the application is running, however, the batch file still controls the system. The application is running as a batch file instruction. Other instructions are waiting to take over when the application "instruction" is completed.

In writing this batch file, the network manager can make the next instruction (the one that follows the application instruction) a command to log off the network. Then, if the user exits the application and tries to get to the operating system, the user is logged off. With a batch file consisting of as few as three or four lines, the network manager has simplified the user's job and improved network security at the same time.

Understanding the Operating System Environment

To create effective batch file systems, you need to understand the elements of the operating system environment that can be used by or can affect the operation of batch files. These elements are the rules of batch-file creation, priority of execution, and, finally, how to create a batch file.

The Rules of Batch-File Creation

When you begin to make a batch file, the rules you need to follow are highly dependent on the operating system for which the batch file is written. The following set of rules and commands refer to batch files used in DOS 4.0 and OS/2 environments. Other environments, such as earlier versions of DOS, support batch processing with slightly modified rules.

- You must construct a batch file as a plain text file. If you unintentionally include any control characters in a batch file, the batch file may run but not as expected.
- Lines in batch files may be a maximum of 127 characters.
- A batch file name follows standard naming conventions. The file-name extension, however, for DOS and OS\2 must be BAT for real-mode batch files, and the extension for OS\2 must be CMD for protected-mode batch files.
- You can use in a batch file any command available through the operating system (including files with the extension COM and EXE). In addition, several special operating system commands are designed particularly for batch processing.
- You can chain batch files by invoking the name of a new batch file at the end of a series of instructions in a batch file. The new batch file then begins to run when the name is encountered. Any instructions in the original batch file that follow the starting of the new batch file are ignored.
- Batch files can be nested. During the execution of a batch file, control can be temporarily passed to another batch file. The new file then runs, but when its execution is completed, control returns to the first batch file that continues to completion.
- To run a batch file, you merely enter the name of the batch file. The extension is not required to start the processing (see the following discussion of priority of execution).
- You can stop a batch process by pressing Ctrl-Break or Ctrl-C, although this ability may be disabled by various available utilities. The commands BREAK=ON and BREAK=OFF do not affect batch-file processing; BREAK=OFF does not prevent the termination of a batch file with Ctrl-Break or Ctrl-C. The BREAK command affects only the ability to terminate programs.

Priority of Execution

In general, using unique file names within a system is a good practice. The DOS and OS/2 operating systems, however, do not require unique file names, as long as each identical file name has a different extension (or type). When a batch file and a program file have the same file name, the operating system has to resolve which file to execute. The basis for this decision is which file type is found first.

Batch-file types may be BAT and CMD, depending on the environment in which they are intended to operate. Program files may be COM or EXE, depending on how the programmer has constructed the application. If you intend to run the batch file EXAMPLE.BAT or EXAMPLE.CMD, and an executable file of the COM or EXE type exists, the operating system finds and runs the executable file rather than the batch file. Files with the COM extension are executed before files with the EXE extension.

If you have batch files called EXAMPLE.BAT and EXAMPLE.CMD, and you enter the command *EXAMPLE*, DOS ignores EXAMPLE.CMD and executes the instructions in EXAMPLE.BAT. OS/2 has to decide which batch file to search for first. To maintain a degree of compatibility between DOS and OS/2, Microsoft decided that OS/2 should search for BAT files first. In this example, the batch file EXAMPLE.BAT is found and executed before EXAMPLE.CMD. This fact may cause unexpected results in a multitasking environment, because the batch file may contain commands not appropriate for an unprotected environment. You can avoid this problem by entering the entire file name.

In networks, the problems of different operating systems using incorrect batch files can present major headaches for system administrators if the proliferation of batch files is not controlled.

How To Construct Batch Files

The last of the basic elements is batch-file creation. You can use any of three different methods to construct a batch file:

- ❑ *The COPY command.* The COPY command is quick and easy to use but is unsuitable for lengthy batch files because the command does not enable you to make corrections without completely re-creating the file.
- ❑ *The EDLIN program.* This DOS utility supports the creation and modification of batch files. This method is always

available. (EDLIN is on every system because it is shipped with DOS and OS/2.)

- *The word processor.* This highly flexible method is ideal for creating long batch files. You must have a word processor that provides direct creation of plain text files (files that do not contain control characters). Some word processors can convert their files to plain text; others offer what is called a "nondocument" or "programmer's" mode for the creation of plain text files.

The simplest method to learn but the least flexible is the COPY command. You can use COPY to copy keyboard input into a file. You must ensure, however, that the file name you specify does not exist already. Otherwise, the old file is overwritten and lost, without you receiving a warning or a chance to select which file you want to save.

The following example uses the COPY command to create a demonstration batch file. (In all the examples in this chapter, the text appearing in the `special typeface` is generated by your computer and appears on-screen. The text appearing in regular typeface is what you type.)

```
A:\>COPY CON DEMO-01.BAT
MD DEMODIR
CD DEMODIR
COPY \*.BAT
CD ..
DIR DEMODIR
DEL DEMODIR\*.BAT
RD DEMODIR
^Z
  1 File(s) copied

A:\>
```

Note that sometimes you need to enter two returns after the ^Z before the `1 File(s) copied` message appears.

This demonstration batch file performs some basic directory and file functions and then removes all the directories and files that were created, just to ensure that you have enough space on disk to run the rest of the examples in this chapter.

One disadvantage in using the COPY method to create a batch file is that you cannot edit the lines. After you press Enter on a line, that line is permanent. You have to retype the entire batch file to change one line.

Another way to create a batch file is to use EDLIN, the line editor included on your DOS disk. For example, at the DOS prompt, type the following:

```
EDLIN BATCH.BAT
```

If the BATCH.BAT file does not exist already, you see on the next line the message `New file`. Then EDLIN displays an asterisk, which is the EDLIN prompt. At that prompt, you tell EDLIN the mode you are going to use. You type an *I* to indicate that you are going to insert lines. EDLIN then displays the number `1` (the number of the first line), followed by a colon and an asterisk:

```
1:*
```

Type the first line of your batch file and press Enter. A new prompt with a different number appears each time you press Enter. When you have finished entering the lines of the batch file, start a new line by pressing Enter. Press Ctrl-C to leave insert mode; then type an *E* and press Enter to end the EDLIN session and close the file. The file is saved and stored on disk. To create the same batch file that COPY constructed in the preceding example, use the following procedure:

```
A:\>EDLIN DEMO-01.BAT
New file
*I
        1:*MD DEMODIR
        2:*CD DEMODIR
        3:*COPY \*.BAT
        4:*CD ..
        5:*DIR DEMODIR
        6:*DEL DEMODIR\*.BAT
        7:*RD DEMODIR
        8:*^C
*E

A:\>
```

Although EDLIN is cumbersome to use, you can go back and correct mistakes. You also can add to or change previously created batch files. (Consult your DOS manual for complete instructions on the use of EDLIN.)

The third way to create a batch file is with a word processor. To use this method, load your word processor and open a document. Type each command at the left margin on a separate line. When you are finished, save the file as an ASCII file. (This process is covered in more detail in the text discussion of individual word processing programs.) When you save the file, use any file name you want, but be sure to use the BAT or CMD extension required for all batch files.

Storing Batch Files

On a network or a stand-alone system, the best place to store a batch file often is in a directory mapped to a search drive or subdirectory. Storing the batch file there enables you to call and let the file start doing its job, no matter where you are in the system. On a stand-alone machine, you define search subdirectories by using the PATH command (see your DOS or OS/2 manual for details).

You can place batch files in an established search directory, such as the PUBLIC directory, if you are using Novell NetWare. If you want a more organized approach, you can set up a new directory called BATCH (or something similar) and use that directory for all your batch files. Care must be taken to ensure that the commands and files used by the batch file are available from whatever drive is in use when the batch file is started.

For example, the SET PATH command enables you to specify which drives and directories should be searched to find commands if they are not on the default drive. If you set up your network so that the batch files are on a network drive—drive Z, for example—in a subdirectory called NETBATCH under the PUBLIC subdirectory in the root, then, using DOS 4.0, you would use the SET PATH command as follows:

```
C>SET
COMSPEC=C:\COMMAND.COM
PROMPT=$p$g
PATH=Z:.;Y:.

C>SET PATH=%PATH%;Z:\PUBLIC\NETBATCH

C>SET
COMSPEC=C:\COMMAND.COM
PROMPT=$p$g
PATH=Z:.;Y:.;Z:\PUBLIC\NETBATCH
```

Using the SET command by itself shows the current environment strings. The second use of SET in the preceding example modifies the PATH variable that tells PC DOS the search path to use. The argument %NAME% is a new feature in PC DOS 4.0 that enables you to use the value of an environment variable, *NAME*, as a replaceable command line parameter. In this example, NAME is used to get the current value of the PATH variable so that the value can be added; without it, the current PATH setting would be overwritten.

Using Batch-File Commands

Most operating-system commands can be invoked in batch files. Some commands, however, are designed specifically for batch processing. For nonprogrammers, many batch commands may be difficult to understand, at least initially. If you are administering a network, spending a little time studying these commands is worth the effort. Their value will become even clearer when you see how they are used in the sample batch files at the end of this chapter.

Clearing the Screen: CLS

You often may want to clear the screen as part of a batch process. You can use the command CLS anywhere in the batch file, and all data displayed on-screen will be erased. The following example demonstrates the CLS command:

```
A:\>COPY CON DEMO-02.BAT
CLS
^Z
   1 File(s) copied

A:\>DEMO-02
```

(Screen clears, and cursor is positioned at top of screen.)

```
A:\>
```

Displaying Messages: ECHO

The ECHO command is a frequently used command that controls the display of information on-screen. This command causes any string of characters written after the command (on the same line) to be displayed. The command ECHO OFF suppresses echoing of the command lines:

```
C>COPY CON ECHOTEST.BAT
ECHO This is line 1
ECHO OFF
ECHO This is line 3
ECHO ON
ECHO This is line 5
^Z

    1 File(s) copied

C>ECHOTEST

C>ECHO This is line 1
This is line 1

C>ECHO OFF
This is line 3

C>ECHO
This is line 5
```

ECHO also is useful for preventing or enabling the display of batch instructions. The command ECHO ON causes the machine to display the batch commands as they are processed. ECHO OFF is the opposite, causing the machine to suppress the display commands. The commands are executed but the command line is not displayed. ECHO OFF does not prevent the screen output from displaying the command.

When batch files are written for nontechnical users, as is often the case on a network, running the commands without showing them to the user usually is preferable. If you start the batch file with the ECHO OFF command, nothing shows on the user's screen. If during the batch processing some message needs to be passed to the user, you can insert the ECHO command. Everything that follows ECHO—on the same line as the command—is then displayed. ECHO OFF is still in control of the display, however, and succeeding lines continue to be suppressed from the display. Look at the following example:

```
A:\>COPY CON DEMO-03.BAT
ECHO OFF
COPY DEMO.BAT DEMO.TXT

ECHO Good Morning, Mark.
DEL DEMO.TXT
^Z
   1 File(s) copied

A:\>DEMO

A:\>ECHO OFF
   1 File(s) copied
Good morning, Mark.

A:\>
```

In this example, the instructions issued after the ECHO OFF line are suppressed, and only the screen output is displayed. The message `Good Morning, Mark.` is displayed, after which the remaining instructions are again suppressed.

Note in the example that the command ECHO OFF is displayed. Normally, you will want to suppress that command as well. To do so, use the @ symbol. When you insert @ in front of any line, that line is suppressed. For example, @ECHO OFF prevents the display of ECHO OFF, as in the following example:

```
A:\>COPY CON DEMO-04.BAT
@ECHO OFF
COPY DEMO.BAT DEMO.TXT
ECHO Good Morning, Mark.
DEL DEMO.TXT
^Z
   1 File(s) copied

A:\>DEMO

   1 File(s) copied
Good morning, Mark.

A:\>
```

Using Command-Line Parameters

When you start a program or a batch file, you may prefer to pass information to the process as part of the command line rather than wait until you are asked to provide input. Information that you give immediately following the path and name of the program or batch file is called the *command tail.* In the following command line, therefore, the command tail is *A B C D.*

```
A:\>DEMO A B C D
```

The command tail is split into command-line parameters defined by spaces. In the preceding example, *A*, *B*, *C*, and *D* are the command-line parameters of the command tail.

Ten command-line parameters are directly available to batch files under DOS and OS/2 and are identified as %0 through %9. To use them in a batch file, put %0 or another parameter wherever you want to access that parameter. The technical name for a parameter, when referred to in a batch file as %0, %1, and so on, is a *dummy parameter*, *replaceable parameter*, or *variable*. Dummy parameters represent a value or text string not known at the time that the batch file is created and enable you to use the batch file for more than one specific function.

%0 is reserved for the path and name of the batch file. You can use this parameter in a batch file to check the path and name of the batch file. For example,

```
A:\>COPY CON DEMO-05.BAT
@ECHO OFF
ECHO The %%0 command line parameter is %0
^Z
   1 File(s) copied

A:\>C:

C:\>A:\DEMO

The %0 command line parameter is A:\DEMO

C:\>
```

Note: You must use %% in the ECHO message line to display a single percent symbol (%). A single percent sign (%) indicates that the next character is the number of the parameter.

%1 through %9 are available in the same way as %0 but can be used to pass any information needed to the commands in the batch file. Using the same batch file as in the preceding example, the next example demonstrates how to access the other command-line variables:

```
A:\>COPY CON DEMO-06.BAT
@ECHO OFF
ECHO The parameters are %0, %1, %2, %3, %4, %5, %6, %7, %8, %9
^Z

   1 File(s) copied

A:\>C:

C:\>A:\DEMO A B C D E F G H J
```

```
The parameters are A:\DEMO, A, B, C, D, E, F, G, H, J

C:\>
```

Shifting Parameter Values: SHIFT

In some instances, the 10 command-line parameters (%0 through %9) are not enough. If you need to access more than 10 parameters in a single batch file, the SHIFT command is the solution. This command moves, or shifts, the value of each of the given parameters to the next higher parameter. The value of the %0 parameter becomes the value of the %1 parameter, %1 becomes %2, and so forth. For example,

```
A:\>COPY CON DEMO-07.BAT
@ECHO OFF
ECHO First 10 parameters : %0, %1, %2, %3, %4, %5, %6, %7, %8, %9
SHIFT
ECHO Parameters shifted : %0, %1, %2, %3, %4, %5, %6, %7, %8, %9
SHIFT
ECHO Parameters shifted : %0, %1, %2, %3, %4, %5, %6, %7, %8, %9
^Z

   1 File(s) copied

A:\>DEMO P1 P2 P3 P4 P5 P6 P7 P8 P9 P10 P11

First 10 parameters : DEMO, P1, P2, P3, P4, P5, P6, P7, P8, P9

Parameters shifted  : P1, P2, P3, P4, P5, P6, P7, P8, P9, P10

Parameters shifted  : P2, P3, P4, P5, P6, P7, P8, P9, P10, P11

A:\>
```

The SHIFT command used this way enables you to access as many command line parameters in a program as you need. This example demonstrates a fundamental use of the SHIFT command, but in practice, most people seldom need more than nine command-line parameters. SHIFT, however, does have another extremely powerful use. See this chapter's section on "Conditional Looping" for more information.

Testing for a Certain Condition: IF

Often, you want to do something only if a certain condition is met. The command IF enables you to do just that. The condition to test for follows the IF statement and may be one of the following:

==	To test for text equality, as in IF %1 == FRED
ERRORLEVEL	To test whether the last command executed resulted in a specific exit code (see your DOS or OS/2 manual for more information), as in IF ERRORLEVEL==2
EXIST	To test whether a file exists as specified, as in IF EXIST FRED.TXT

The command following the test is executed only if the test is true. In the following example, the command to be executed after the test is to echo a message:

```
A:\>COPY CON DEMO-08.BAT
@ECHO OFF
IF %1 == FRED ECHO FRED was found.
^Z
   1 File(s) copied

A:\>DEMO-08 FRED

FRED was found.

A:\>
```

You also can test whether the condition is *not* true by putting NOT before the test:

```
A:\>COPY CON DEMO-09.BAT
@ECHO OFF
IF %1 == FRED ECHO FRED was found.
IF NOT %1 == FRED ECHO FRED wasn't found.
```

```
^Z
   1 File(s) copied

A:\>DEMO-09 fred

FRED wasn't found.

A:\>DEMO-09 FRED

FRED was found.

A:\>
```

Changing the Sequence of Commands: GOTO

At any point in a batch file you can jump to another part of the file by using the GOTO command followed by a label name. The *label* marks the place from which execution should continue. You signify a label by preceding the label with a colon (:). The only restriction on label names is that they cannot use periods (.). In the following batch file, the first ECHO command is executed, the second skipped, and the third executed:

```
A:\>COPY CON DEMO-10.BAT
@ECHO OFF
ECHO One.
GOTO SKIP
ECHO Two.
:SKIP
ECHO Three.
^Z
   1 File(s) copied

A:\>DEMO-10

One.
Three.

A:\>
```

Conditional Looping

Often, you want to have one operation or a set of operations performed in an identical manner several times. You can accomplish this task by writing a batch file with the same code repeated multiple times, but the batch file would lack flexibility. You can achieve the same result with a much shorter batch file by using the SHIFT, IF, and GOTO commands or the FOR command.

With the SHIFT, IF, and GOTO commands, you can design your batch file to execute the appropriate operations on a particular parameter, such as %1. At that point, you insert the SHIFT command, which makes the next parameter, %2, become %1. IF and GOTO are used to loop the processing back to the beginning of the batch file by testing whether the parameter has been set. If the parameter is set, the process starts over, but this time the process operates on the next specified parameter. For example, to make specified copies of a file, use this batch file:

```
A:\>COPY CON DEMO-11.BAT
@ECHO OFF
COPY DEMO-11.BAT DEMO.BAT
:LOOP
IF %1. == . GOTO EXIT
COPY DEMO.BAT DEMO.%1
SHIFT
GOTO LOOP
:EXIT
ECHO Finished - no more parameters in command line.
DIR DEMO.*
DEL DEMO.*
ECHO Cleaned up - demo finished.
^Z
   1 File(s) copied

A:\>DEMO-11 TXT DOC ASC
   1 File(s) copied
   1 File(s) copied
   1 File(s) copied
   1 File(s) copied
Finished - no more parameters in command line.
```

```
Volume in drive A has no label
Directory of   A:\

DEMO     BAT      229   2-21-89  10:49p
DEMO     TXT      229   2-21-89  10:49p
DEMO     DOC      229   2-21-89  10:49p
DEMO     ASC      229   2-21-89  10:49p
        4 File(s)    763648 bytes free
Cleaned up - demo finished.

A:\>
```

Alternatively, the FOR command enables you to loop on a list of parameters or predefined values. The preceding example also can be achieved as follows:

```
A:\>COPY CON DEMO-12.BAT
@ECHO OFF
COPY DEMO-12.BAT DEMO.BAT
FOR %%A IN (%1 %2 %3 %4 %5 %6 %7 %8 %9) DO COPY
DEMO.BAT DEMO.%%A
ECHO Finished - no more parameters in command line.
DIR DEMO.*
DEL DEMO.*
ECHO Cleaned up - demo finished.
^Z
   1 File(s) copied
```

The loop in the preceding example is controlled by the variable %%A. The command FOR %%A IN (list) DO takes the next item in (list) and puts that item in the variable; then, the command removes the item from the list. The command after DO then is executed (optionally using the variable), and the whole line is restarted. The looping terminates when (list) is empty. Variables can be any single letter preceded be %%. In the example batch file, all the command-line parameters may not be given; the example has three parameters only, and up to nine may be given. In that case, the value in the (list) is blank, and no action occurs.

```
A:\>DEMO-12 TXT DOC ASC
   1 File(s) copied
   1 File(s) copied
```

```
   1 File(s) copied
   1 File(s) copied
Finished - no more parameters in command line.

Volume in drive A has no label
Directory of   A:\

DEMO     BAT       229    2-21-89   10:49p
DEMO     TXT       229    2-21-89   10:49p
DEMO     DOC       229    2-21-89   10:49p
DEMO     ASC       229    2-21-89   10:49p
        4 File(s)     763648 bytes free
Cleaned up - demo finished.

A:\>
```

The looping process is controlled by the variable (defined in this example by %%A) taking the values in the list given in parentheses following IN and substituting them in the command following DO where the variable is reused. You can define the variable as any single alphabetic letter following the %% symbols. If any parameters are missing in the command line, the values placed in the list are blank, and no action is taken.

The disadvantage of using the FOR command is that you are limited to a maximum of nine parameters in the list following IN. If the items in the list can be predefined, however, any number of parameters may be explicitly stated, providing the total line length is less than 127 characters. For example,

```
A:\>COPY CON DEMO-13.BAT
@ECHO OFF
COPY DEMO-13.BAT DEMO.BAT
FOR %%A IN (TXT DOC ASC) DO COPY DEMO.BAT
DEMO.%%A
ECHO Finished - no more parameters in command line.
DIR DEMO.*
DEL DEMO.*
ECHO Cleaned up - demo finished.
^Z
    1 File(s) copied
```

```
A:\>DEMO-13
   1 File(s) copied
   1 File(s) copied
   1 File(s) copied
   1 File(s) copied
Finished - no more parameters in command line.

Volume in drive A has no label
Directory of   A:\

DEMO     BAT      229   2-21-89  10:49p
DEMO     TXT      229   2-21-89  10:49p
DEMO     DOC      229   2-21-89  10:49p
DEMO     ASC      229   2-21-89  10:49p
        4 File(s)    763648 bytes free
Cleaned up - demo finished.

A:\>
```

Using Other Batch Files: CALL

You can start a new batch file from within an operating batch file. This arrangement is called *nesting*. The first batch file starts, and at some point, a second batch file is started. The second batch file runs to completion, after which control reverts to the first batch file, and that file is completed.

Under DOS version 3.0+, it is necessary to start another command interpreter to execute a nested batch file, as in the following example:

```
C>COPY CON DEMO-900.BAT
ECHO This is the first batch file.
COMMAND /C DEMO-901
ECHO Back to the first batch file.
^Z

     1 File(s) copied

C>COPY CON DEMO-901.BAT
ECHO This is the nested batch file.
^Z
```

```
     1 File(s) copied

C>DEMO-900
C>ECHO OFF
1

C>ECHO OFF
2
1

C>
```

DOS version 4.0 supports the CALL command to execute nested batch files.

The command to invoke a nested batch file is the CALL command. For example, CALL WORDPROC calls a file called WORDPROC.BAT. WORDPROC.BAT might load a word processor application and path to specific data-file directories. When the user finally finishes using the word processor and exits the application, the original batch file resumes control and completes its series of instructions.

In general, you should avoid nesting, because the resulting batch files are complex and inflexible. Running single-function batch files, perhaps from a menu screen, usually is preferable. Nonetheless, network administrators may encounter situations where nesting is desirable, especially with nontechnical users who need a single application only. To demonstrate the use of CALL, the following example simply displays messages indicating which batch file is being processed;

```
A:\>COPY CON DEMO-14A.BAT
@ECHO OFF
ECHO This is DEMO-14A.
CALL DEMO-14B
ECHO This is DEMO-14A.
CALL DEMO-14C
ECHO This is DEMO-14A.
^Z
   1 File(s) copied

A:\>COPY CON DEMO-14B.BAT
```

```
ECHO This is DEMO-14B.
^Z
   1 File(s) copied

A:\>COPY CON DEMO-14C.BAT
ECHO This is DEMO-14C.
^Z
   1 File(s) copied

A:\>DEMO-14A
This is DEMO-14A.
This is DEMO-14B.
This is DEMO-14A.
This is DEMO-14C.
This is DEMO-14A.
A:\>
```

Temporarily Halting Processing: PAUSE

The PAUSE command normally is used to provide a temporary break in processing so that a user can perform some task. In operation, PAUSE suspends processing and displays the message `Press any key to continue ...`. Typically, PAUSE is used with the ECHO command. ECHO enables you to tell the user what action is needed (for example, `Insert the key disk`). When the action is completed, the user can press any key to resume batch execution.

Another use of the PAUSE command is to control the number of instructions processed in a batch file. In long batch files, you can insert PAUSE commands at appropriate break points throughout the file. When each PAUSE command is reached, the user can choose to continue or end processing by pressing Ctrl-C or Ctrl-Break. For example,

```
A:\>COPY CON DEMO-15A.BAT
@ECHO OFF
ECHO This is DEMO-15A.
PAUSE
CALL DEMO-15B
ECHO This is DEMO-15A.
^Z
```

```
   1 File(s) copied

A:\>COPY CON DEMO-15B.BAT
ECHO This is DEMO-15B.
PAUSE
^Z
   1 File(s) copied

A:\>DEMO-15A
This is DEMO-15A.
Press any key to continue ...
This is DEMO-15B.
Press any key to continue ...
This is DEMO-15A.
A:\>
```

Inserting Remarks in a Batch File: REM

You can use the REM command to insert an explanatory comment in a batch file. Comments inserted with the REM command are displayed unless you use the ECHO OFF command to suppress the display of the line. A comment used with the REM command can be any string of characters up to 123 bytes long.

REM command statements (usually referred to as *remarks*) are helpful if you need to explain long or complex batch files within the text of the file. If you or another person needs to evaluate or modify a batch file, remarks can—and should—be included in the file to explain clearly the file's purpose and how it works.

In large network environments that have many batch files, proper use of remarks makes system maintenance much easier.

```
A:\>COPY CON DEMO-16A.BAT
@ECHO OFF
REM
REM Announce the name of this batch file.
REM
ECHO This is DEMO-16A.
REM
REM Wait for user input before continuing.
```

```
REM
PAUSE
REM
REM Now 'CALL' the next batch file
REM
CALL DEMO-16B
REM
REM We're back ! Announce batch file name again.
REM
ECHO This is DEMO-16A.
^Z
   1 File(s) copied

A:\>COPY CON DEMO-16B.BAT
REM
REM Announce the name of this batch file.
REM
ECHO This is DEMO-16B.
REM
REM Wait for user input before continuing.
REM
PAUSE
^Z
   1 File(s) copied

A:\>DEMO-16A
This is DEMO-16A.
Press any key to continue ...
This is DEMO-16B.
Press any key to continue ...
This is DEMO-16A.
A:\>
```

Managing Input/Output

DOS and OS/2 enable you to take input from and send output to various sources and destinations that you specify. This capability can be convenient in batch-file processing. You use the greater-than (>) and less-than (<) symbols to redirect output and input. The following example sends the results of a directory listing to a file called HISTORY.LOG:

```
A:\>DIR

Volume in drive A has no label
Directory of    A:\

COMMAND   COM     25307    03-17-87    12:00p
DEMO           <DIR>       01-12-89     7:43a
DEMO2     TXT      1350    02-01-89     1:23p
TEST           <DIR>       02-04-89    11:17a
DEMO3     TXT       346    02-01-89     1:47p
          5 File(s)    7567360 bytes free

A:\>DIR > HISTORY.LOG

A:\>TYPE HISTORY.LOG

Volume in drive A has no label
Directory of    A:\

COMMAND   COM     25307    03-17-87    12:00p
DEMO           <DIR>       01-12-89     7:43a
DEMO2     TXT      1350    02-01-89     1:23p
TEST           <DIR>       02-04-89    11:17a
DEMO3     TXT       346    02-01-89     1:47p
HISTORY   LOG         0    02-08-89     2:45p
          6 File(s)    7567360 bytes free

A:\>
```

In this example, you write the results of the directory command that normally would appear on-screen to a file called HISTORY.LOG. If the file already exists, the old information is overwritten; if the file does not exist, the file is created automatically. If you use two greater-than symbols (>>), the results are appended to an existing file. Again, if no file exists, a new file is created. As you can see from the example, if the file is created in the directory you are listing, the output file is opened and has a size of 0 bytes; the directory listing is displayed, and the listing is written to the file.

When you use the less-than symbol (<), you designate that input should be received from a new source, such as a data file, rather than the keyboard. You might use the following example to connect to a network and log in, using a name and password stored in a file called MYLOGIN.INF:

```
A:\>COPY CON MYLOGIN.INF
MDURR
SECRET
^Z
   1 File(s) copied

A:\>LOGIN < MYLOGIN.INF

Good afternoon, Mike. You are attached to server AURORA.

A:\>
```

Another use of redirection is to suppress output from a program that you do not want a user to see for some reason. In the following example, the screen output from the log-in program is sent to a file called JUNK.TXT, and the log-in message does not appear:

```
A:\>COPY CON MYLOGIN.INF
MDURR
SECRET
^Z
   1 File(s) copied

A:\>LOGIN < MYLOGIN.INF > JUNK.TXT

A:\>
```

Additionally, you can send data to the null device (NUL) that throws the data away, the console device (CON), a printer port (LPT1, LPT2, and so on), or any other device available in your system. Consult your computer's user manual and DOS or OS/2 manuals for more information on devices available in your system.

Piping

In batch-file systems, you often want to send the screen output from one program to another program as the input to the second program, a process called *piping*. You can use this procedure for a wide range of purposes, from sending a name and password to a network log-in program, to searching the screen output from a program for specific text.

To instruct the operating system to divert the screen data created by a program to the next process, you put the vertical bar character (|) between the text that specifies the first command and its arguments and the text specifying the second command. For example, to send to the FIND command the output of the TYPE FRED.TXT command, so that you show lines only in FRED.TXT containing the word "DEMO," use these commands:

```
A:\>TYPE FRED.TXT
LINE 1 - DEMO
LINE 2 - TEST
LINE 3 - DEMO
LINE 4 - TEST

A:\>TYPE FRED.TXT | FIND "DEMO"
LINE 1 - DEMO
LINE 3 - DEMO

A:\>
```

Using Filters

Filtering is the process of managing input data according to a set of rules into a required output format. This process can be as simple as pausing after displaying 23 lines of data on-screen or as complex as finding or sorting text. The standard filters offered by DOS and OS/2 are FIND, MORE, and SORT.

The FIND Command

The FIND command enables data from the input device to be searched line-by-line for specific text strings. The command sends any appropriate lines to the output device. This command is useful, for example, if you need to edit a list of file names to retain only those files that match certain naming criteria.

The first part of the next example shows the directory listing for drive A. By using the FIND command, you can display only the lines containing the text string <DIR>—the lines that list the directories on the disk.

```
A:\>DIR

Volume in drive A has no label
Directory of    A:\

COMMAND  COM     25307    03-17-87    12:00p
DEMO          <DIR>       01-12-89     7:43a
DEMO2    TXT      1350    02-01-89     1:23p
TEST          <DIR>       02-04-89    11:17a
DEMO3    TXT       346    02-01-89     1:47p
        5 File(s)    7567360 bytes free

A:\>DIR | FIND "<DIR>"
DEMO          <DIR>       01-12-89     7:43a
TEST          <DIR>       02-04-89    11:17a

A:\>
```

The MORE Command

The MORE command is used to control the display of data on-screen. The input data stream is echoed to the screen and paused when the screen is full. The message -More- appears on-screen. By pressing Enter, you can display the next screenful of data. If the input data stream is anything but plain text, which uses only the carriage return/line feed pair to delimit lines and no other control characters, the display may not be easily readable. The following is an example of the syntax of the MORE command:

```
A:\>TYPE FRED.TXT | MORE
```

The SORT Command

The SORT command is used to rearrange a file's contents in ascending or descending alphabetic or numeric order. The command takes data redirected from a source and outputs data by redirection to a destination. The source and destination may be a device, such as COM1 or AUX, or a file. If not specified, the input is taken from and output sent to the console. The largest file that can be sorted is 64512 bytes. For example,

```
C>COPY CON TEST.TXT
Z
P
T
A
^Z

        1 File(s) copied

C>SORT <TEST.TXT >TEST.SRT

C>TYPE SORT.SRT
A
P
T
Z

C>
```

Using AUTOEXEC.BAT on a Network

The AUTOEXEC.BAT file is an optional facility of DOS and OS/2 that, if located on the boot drive, automatically runs after the operating system has been loaded and initialized. In the AUTOEXEC.BAT file, you may want to set up paths to local drives. You also may load any terminate-and-stay resident programs compatible with your network software.

The AUTOEXEC:BAT file is a special type of batch file in DOS and OS/2. If AUTOEXEC:BAT has been created on the boot drive, the file is run after the operating system is loaded and initialized. In the AUTOEXEC.BAT file, you may want to set up paths to local drives. You also may load any terminate-and-stay resident programs compatible with your network software.

A typical AUTOEXEC.BAT file might be:

```
C:>TYPE AUTOEXEC.BAT
SET PATH=C:\PROGS,C:\SYS
SET PROMPT=$p$g
SK
MENU
```

This AUTOEXEC file would first set the PATH to be used and then define that the prompt should show the path to the current directory. Sidekick would be executed and then, finally, a menu program would start.

After you initiate the connection to a network file server, you may find that control is passed from the local AUTOEXEC.BAT file to a network log-in batch process. Any commands that exist in the original AUTOEXEC file may not get executed after the network connection has been established. If these unexecuted commands are intended to provide configuration or service specifications relating to the workstation, unexpected effects may occur.

After you have initiated the connection to a network file server, an attempt to log in may transfer control to a network defined log-in procedure. If this occurs before all the commands in the original batch file are executed, the remaining commands are ignored, which can cause problems if the commands were intended to configure the workstation for the network environment.

As a general rule, you should limit the AUTOEXEC.BAT process to setting up the minimal environment necessary before joining the network. The last commands in the AUTOEXEC.BAT process should be related only to establishing the network connection. Any commands after the network connection commands should relate to error recovery in the event that the network log-on fails, such as displaying an error message to the user or retrying the connection.

Using Batch Files on a Network

Batch files on networks can, if used in shared directories, gain a new dimension of complexity. When used in nonshared directories, if you have adequate access rights, batch files act as they would in a stand-alone system.

If batch files, piping, and redirection are used in shared directories, the problem of two or more users creating the same file can cause error conditions that effectively abort the batch process. This situation is particularly dangerous when the objective of the batch-file system is to insulate the user from direct access to the operating system.

If you have a batch file on a network drive, and you log out or use a network command to remap your drive to a different subdirectory, the batch file is no longer visible to the operating system, and an error message is generated. You can work around this problem by keeping the batch file in a RAM disk or ensuring that the file is always on an available drive.

The following examples feature typical network batch files. The examples are as generalized as possible, but are based on a Novell NetWare environment.

Example 1, the file LGIN.BAT, logs a user into the network. This batch file is quite complex and is designed to be as general as possible. The batch file, however, contains a few assumptions about where various files are located.

Example 1

```
@ECHO OFF
CLS
REM
REM ================================
REM                          LGIN.BAT
REM ================================
REM
REM A batch file to log in or re-log in a user to a network.
REM
REM
REM Check if we're already logged in, using an environment
REM variable that will exist if we logged in using this file.
```

```
REM If the variable doesn't exist, then we'll join the network
REM and the variable will be set ...
REM
IF NOT %ONNET%. == YES. GOTO NEXT1
REM
REM We're not attached to the network, so execute the network
REM software with another batch file. If we can't join the
REM network the error condition will either be handled by the
REM called batch file or this batch process will be aborted by
REM the called batch file.
REM
CALL A:NETSW
REM
REM Set up the environment variable to show if we're on the
REM network ...
REM
SET ONNET=YES
REM
REM --------------------------------------------------------------
REM
:NEXT1
REM
REM Now clear the screen and display a welcome message ...
REM
CLS
TYPE F:MSG01.TXT
REM
REM --------------------------------------------------------------
REM
:NEXT2
REM
REM We'll pause to let them read the message, and then clear
REM the screen and run the login program ...
REM
PAUSE
CLS
LOGIN
REM
REM Check if we logged in successfully ...
REM
```

```
IF ERRORLEVEL == 0 GOTO NEXT3
REM
REM The ERRORLEVEL returned wasn't 0 (a successful login),
REM so we'll loop back again after displaying a message ...
REM
TYPE F:MSG02.TXT
GOTO NEXT2
REM
REM -------------------------------------------------------------------
REM
:NEXT3
REM
REM If the user's login script doesn't take over from this
REM batch file, we'll continue here ... so now we display
REM the supervisor's welcome message ...
REM
CLS
TYPE Z:\PUBLIC\SYSMSG.TXT
PAUSE
CLS
REM
REM And finally we'll run the system menu ...
REM
MENU SYSMENU
```

Example 1A shows the file MSG01.TXT, the first message file to accompany the batch file LGIN.BAT. The second message file, MSG02.TXT, is in Example 1B.

Example 1A

```
==========================================
           Welcome to the corporate network system.
==========================================
Please stand by to log in ... if you don't have a network identity
please contact the System Administrator on extension 3142 between
the hours of 09:00 and 17:30, to get registered.
You can also log in as the guest user with the name "Guest" and
leave a message for the Administrator.
==========================================
```

Example 1B

```
==========================================================
            An error has occurred during your login.
==========================================================
Either you made a mistake in typing your name and/or password, or
the name you are trying to use is not valid. You may try again or
abort this login process by typing ^C ...
If you need help, please contact the System Administrator on
extension 3142 between the hours of 09:00 and 17:30.
You can also log in as the guest user with the name "Guest" and
leave a message for the Administrator.
==========================================================
```

Example 2 is the batch file, SYSMSG.BAT, that sets up the system administrator's message.

Example 2

```
@ECHO OFF
CLS
REM
REM ======================================================
REM                        SYSMSG.BAT
REM ======================================================
REM
REM This batch file sets up the system administrator's message
REM SYSMSG.TXT and sets the file access flags that are needed
REM to make the file accessible in a multiuser environment.
REM
REM Move to the Z: drive & change to the PUBLIC subdirectory ...
REM
Z:
CD \PUBLIC
REM
TYPE MSG03.TXT
PAUSE
CLS
REM
REM Make a copy of the message template and throw away the
REM "1 File(s) copied" message ...
REM
COPY TEMPLATE.MSG SYSMSG.TMP>NUL
```

```
REM
REM Edit the template file ...
REM
REM First is there no editor specified ? If not use EDLIN.
REM
IF NOT %1. == . GOTO NEXT1
EDLIN SYSMSG.TMP
GOTO EXIT
REM -----------------------------------------------------------
:NEXT1
REM
REM If there is an editor specified, then check if it exists ...
REM
IF NOT EXIST %1 GOTO ERROR
REM
%1 SYSMSG.TMP
GOTO EXIT
REM -----------------------------------------------------------
:ERROR
REM
REM The editor specified didn't exist. Display a message and
REM quit ...
REM
TYPE MSG04.TXT
PAUSE
CLS
GOTO THEEND
REM -----------------------------------------------------------
:EXIT
REM
REM Ok ! We've edited the file; now finish up and go home ...
REM ... reflag the old message file as read/write, ...
REM
FLAG SYSMSG.TXT RW
REM
REM ... and delete it ...
REM
DEL SYSMSG.TXT
REM
REM ... and replace it with the new one ...
```

```
REM
REN SYSMSG.TMP SYSMSG.TXT
REM
REM ... then flag the file as shareable and read only.
REM
FLAG SYSMSG.TXT SRO
CLS
ECHO Finished.
REM ------------------------------------------------------------
:THEEND
```

In Example 2A, you can examine MSG03.TXT, the first message file to accompany the batch file SYSMSG.BAT. Example 2B shows MSG04.TXT, the second message file to accompany SYSMSG.BAT.

Example 2A

```
========================================
             SYSMSG - Set up the system message.
========================================

This batch file allows you to set up the system message that is
viewed by users logging in with the LGIN batch file.

You may enter the path and name of an editor to use; if none is
given, the EDLIN editor will be called.

If you want to abort this file, enter ^C now ...

========================================
```

Example 2B

```
========================================
                     SYSMSG - Error !
========================================

The path and/or name of the editor you gave in the command line
was either incorrect or the file doesn't exist there ...

========================================
```

18

Installation

Personal computer users tend to be blasé about PC installation and maintenance. This attitude may be justified because of the ease with which PCs can be repaired. When you install a network, however, the situation changes drastically.

A network is inherently more complex than a stand-alone computer. Unlike a single PC, a network is not movable. Many of its problems may be difficult to diagnose. Moreover, whereas downtime of a single PC will not seriously damage company operations, downtime of a network can bring business to a halt. How you handle the installation phase of networking will have an effect on the network's initial cost, reliability, maintenance, expansion, and reconfiguration.

As part of any network plan, you must know the building and electrical codes. You must assess the data security measures required by your company, and you must know whether certain elements of the network, such as the cable, will be subjected to high temperatures, moisture, caustic fumes, or other conditions that might require special installation. Because no building layout remains static indefinitely, you should try to estimate probable changes. With this basic knowledge, you can begin installation planning.

Maintaining an Installation Log

As you install your network, you should maintain a record of the system. This record should include full details about the kinds of cable and connectors used, the way in which the connectors are installed, and the name of the cable supplier.

In the installation log, describe the network's limits, including the number of nodes, as well as the maximum length of cables and the minimum distance permitted between nodes. You also should describe the various kinds of hardware used in expanding the network, such as taps, repeaters, and passive or active HUBs. Much of this information is already in the user's manual or the technical manual supplied by the network vendor. Repeating the information in your log ensures that these descriptions are readily available when work is done on the installation.

A schematic diagram of the cable system is essential, of course. Each PC, hard disk, printer, and any other device on the network must be physically numbered, with the corresponding number also marked on the diagram. Network addresses should be noted, too, especially if they differ from your equipment numbering system. If dedicated cables are used for any devices, tape an identification label to the end of each cable and indicate in the diagram each cable's use.

Be sure to update your diagram if the cables or nodes are moved or the system is expanded. If you list and date every service/maintenance job in the log, each entry serves as a reminder to update the diagram. The network supervisor should keep a hard copy of the installation log. If you want the information stored on-line, this record should be kept in addition to the hard copy log.

Mark faceplates and patch panels with a cable number and the location of the other end of the cable. The easiest way to mark a faceplate is to write the information directly on the back of the faceplate.

Installing Cable

Cable installation for a local area network is often just an afterthought. If you ask many network users about their cable, they will point to some exposed, stapled coax high on the wall, snaking in and out of offices.

This simple method of installation has several advantages. This method is inexpensive, fast, and easy to maintain and modify.

Rearranging furniture and workstations poses little problem; just pull down the cable, and then tack it up to conform to the new layout.

This open, informal cable installation may not conform to some of the local building and fire codes. The exposed cables also are more likely to be subjected to physical abuse that could produce an intermittent short in the network. Another obvious disadvantage is the unsightliness of the exposed cables. Coax on the walls may be appropriate for a factory but not for many office decors. The trick is to install the cable so that the cable is hidden and protected, meets local codes, yet is accessible and easily adapted to new office arrangements.

In the most commonly used methods of cable distribution, cables are routed through one of the following:

1. Surface raceway
2. Conduit
3. Over-ceiling cable tray
4. Under-floor duct

Often you will have to use several of these methods to complete one network system.

Surface raceways are covered metal channels that can be attached to walls and routed wherever necessary. This method of installation is simple, protects the cable, and is easy to maintain and modify. By using surface raceways, you avoid the expense of going inside existing walls, ceilings, or floors.

Conduit is a metal pipe used to shield cable. Many local codes permit conduit-shielded cable to be run on the surface, as with surface raceways or through walls and ceilings.

An under-floor cable installation is the most secure from tampering but may be impractical unless the cable has been installed during building construction. Relocation of workstations, however, can be difficult with under-floor cables.

Use of over-ceiling cable trays is ideal, provided that the over-ceiling space is accessible. Offices with drop ceilings frequently use this method of cable distribution. Cables are brought down to PC level through the wall partitions. Depending on the code, you may be able to omit the cable tray and simply route the cable through the ceiling. New kinds of cable meet fire safety codes by requiring the use of trays and other metal armor. Over-ceiling routing of nonconduit cable runs is often the most practical and inexpensive solution, particularly in small installations.

Planning Ahead

Before you begin a network installation, you should plan for future modifications, growth, and periodic repair. This planning is especially important for the cable distribution phase of installation.

Unless you use surface raceways, some cables will be buried in floors, ceilings, and walls. The less burying of cables, the better, but even the cables in buried systems can be made accessible. Use conduit and raceways that are somewhat roomy and be sure that no sharp bends are in the route. Then, if cables prove defective or must be changed for some reason, they can be pulled out from a convenient access point. Using larger-than-required conduit and raceways also accommodates future expansion of the system, especially with Star topologies in which each PC has its own dedicated cable.

Cable Handling

Before you buy a network, be sure to request information about cable characteristics from the network vendor or cable supplier. You have no control over the cable's electrical properties, but you may have three or four choices of cable that meet electrical specifications and offer additional features. Any cable supplier should be able to show you the options.

A standard coaxial cable has a center conductor and a shield. Cable with a second shield is called *triax*. *Twinax* is cable with two conductors and a shield. Generally, you cannot substitute cables, such as using triax for coax, without making modifications. If the manufacturer puts a coaxial cable connector on the network interface card, you should connect coax to that card. However, adapters are available that let you connect twinax to a coaxial cable connector. Then, if your installation is subjected to high levels of interference, twinax enables both signals to be carried on inner conductors protected by the outer shield. You should check with a cable supplier for the feasibility of such an arrangement for your particular network.

Cable information from a vendor or supplier includes handling procedures for the cable. Improper cable handling can cause intermittent transmission problems that plague the network and may force you to rewire the entire network. Severe damage can result from seemingly harmless actions, such as pulling the cable with excessive force or pulling the cable around a tight radius. Small amounts of damage are magnified in longer runs of cable. The longer the run, therefore, the more care you should exercise in cable handling.

If you kink cable, especially coax, you are inviting problems (see fig. 18.1). Twisted-pair cable is less susceptible to kinking-related damage as long as the kinking does not physically cut through the cable. Coax cable is different. *Coax* is a tube with a helical spiral that holds the tube around the center conductor. If you kink a coax cable, you change the distance between the center conductor and shield, altering the impedance and capacitance at that point. The result of a kink, therefore, is a damaged spot on the cable that can block transmission.

Do not kink cable with sharp right-angle bends.
Do make rounded bends.

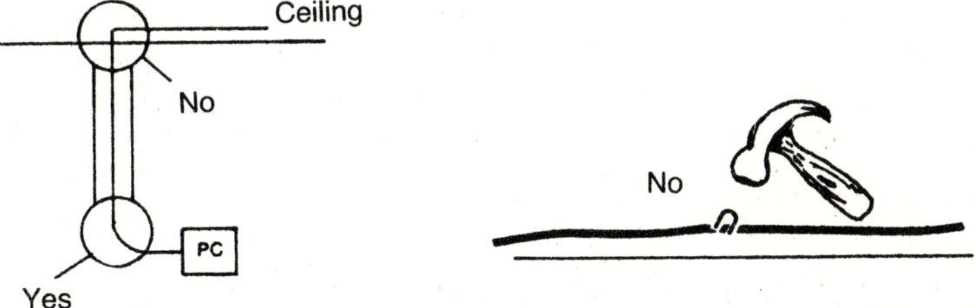

Do not compress cable when attaching to structure.

Fig. 18.1. Cables should be pulled carefully to avoid damaging the protective sheathing or flattening and compressing the cable.

The difference between kinking and bending is a matter of degree. Cables are meant to be flexible, up to a point. If a flexible cable is to be installed in a fixed, bent configuration, the minimum bend radius recommended is five times the cable's diameter. (This general rule should be checked for each cable.) A greater bend creates a kink.

A cable is not designed to support weight, not even its own. If you run a cable in the open instead of through conduit or trays, attach the cable with proper cable clamps at least every 10 to 15 feet. Attach transceivers, line interface devices, and other cable hardware to solid supports: part of the building or specially constructed additions.

If you attach a cable to a wall improperly, you can produce a problem like kinking. If you put a metal staple over the cable and pound the staple into the wall, the staple can crimp the cable just as if the cable were kinked. Therefore, the cable should be attached with special cable mounts with a metal or plastic band that snugly fits the cable's circumference and a tab that extends from the band and may be nailed into the wall.

In most installations, at some point you will have to pull the cable through a narrow opening. Too much force will stretch the braid and crimp the dielectric. Severe pulling can stretch or break the center conductor.

Moisture also can create problems for a network. If moisture gets into the end of coax cable, for example, the moisture changes the cable's electrical characteristics and eventually causes corrosion and signal degradation. The best protection from moisture is to keep the cable capped; if the cable is going to be in a wet location or shipped to a wet climate, your cable definitely should be capped. When cable is stored inside a building in a dry climate, the cable does not need to be capped. Generally, water is a problem, but humidity is not. Of course, in very adverse conditions, such as 100 percent humidity, corrosion of uncapped cable is likely.

Underground installations usually have moisture problems. Moisture may enter flexible cables through pinholes in the jacket or through the ends of the cable. The combination of moisture and large fluctuations in temperature can cause condensation in the cables. At low spots in a cable length, the moisture will collect and may cause corrosion or shorting of a connector. In addition, underground moisture has a rapid corrosive effect on buried cables. Special cables that are highly impervious to moisture are available for underground use. Underground cable also should be encased in a metal sheathing to protect against damage caused by rodents (see fig. 18.2).

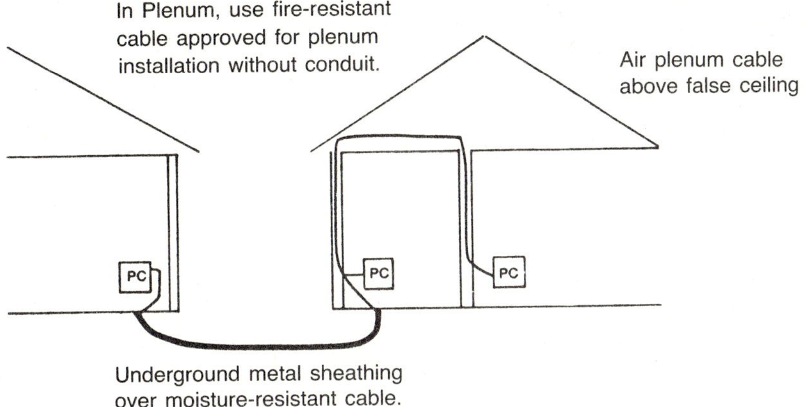

Fig. 18.2. When cable is run through any hostile environment, it should be protected by outer casings.

Using Cable Connectors

You can purchase cables already assembled to your specifications, or you can make up your own cables from bulk cable and connectors. BNC connectors with two-lug bayonet attachments commonly are used on local area networks. These quick-disconnect devices add very little resistance to the line. No special training is needed to learn how to install them.

Two basic types of connectors are available for building cables. One is the wrench-crimp type, and the other is the tool-crimp type. The *wrench crimp* is reusable and has a connection that must be soldered. Care must be taken to heat the connector and the cable wire to avoid a cold solder joint. The *tool-crimp* connector needs no soldering but does require a special crimping tool. This tool must be properly adjusted to make a good connection.

These two types of connectors are identical in performance and strength. Installing the wrench-crimp connector, however, takes longer. For a person installing not more than 20 or 30 connectors, the wrench-crimp connector is the better choice because the tool-crimp connector requires the purchase of a crimping tool.

Cable hardware is being improved. One innovation is a single-piece BNC connector for RG-62, a cable type used for terminal networks, such as 3270 networks, and for many ARCnet networks. Because the connector is a single piece, the connector terminates more reliably and is mechanically stronger and simpler. Using just a stripper, you can install this connector in almost one-third the time that it takes to install other connectors. Installation takes about 30 seconds per connection and requires no soldering or crimping.

Wall plates that fit on a standard electrical box are available from any electrical supply house. These plates are drilled with one, two, or four holes to hold BNC bulkhead connectors. The cable can be brought through the wall; then, the BNC connector can be installed. Twisted-pair cable can be terminated with a modular phone jack for which a variety of wall plates and other accessories are available. Phone lines and network cables can be run conveniently to the same wall plate. This task can be accomplished with appropriate plates, and no interference should be experienced.

A tremendous amount of new hardware is designed for twisted pair telephone use. Most of this hardware works fine for data network applications. You can get modular panels that support the little square, clear plastic connectors you see on telephone cords. Six- and eight-position modular jacks are available for use with data. Some of these jacks are shielded.

Using Fire-Retardant Cable

The plastic jacket on cables burns much like a fuse. A flame starts at one end of the cable and moves quickly down its length. This spreading of fire commonly is referred to as the *wicking effect*. When the jacket burns, it produces a very toxic gas. Fire codes increasingly reflect this danger, making some type of fire shield or other safety device mandatory for new installations.

Often, the best way to meet the fire codes is to use plenum cable. Plenum cable versions of coaxial cable are fire retardant. The jacket of plenum cable is made with fluorocarbon insulations and will burn, but with low smoke and low flame. Plenum cable can be installed in false ceilings without conduit (see fig. 18.2).

Plenum cable is more expensive than standard cable but less expensive than standard cable with code-required conduit. Plenum cable also is stiffer than RG cable and more difficult to manipulate. However, because plenum cable does not require conduit, the installation is easier.

Cable Testing

Before you install the cable, be sure to inspect the cable visually for any obvious cuts or damage to the jacket. Look for kinks, too. Then, test the electrical soundness of the cable and connections.

Cable testing can be an expensive process. In most cases, however, you can run a DC test on the cable and connectors. Use an ohmmeter to check for a certain number of ohms resistance in the line. Do not confuse the ohms of impedance, a cable specification, with the ohms of resistance, for a given length of cable. A DC test is based on the ohms of resistance, documented for every type of cable at specified lengths. If you have made a good connection and the cable is in good condition, the DC resistance should be very close to the resistance specified by the cable manufacturer for the length of cable.

To check resistance, place the ohm meter probes on the center conductor at each end of the cable. Then, test the shield by holding the probes on the outer shells of the connectors. Finally, place a probe at one end of the cable on the center conductor and the probe at the other end of the cable on the shield. The resistance should be infinite, indicating that the conductor and shield are properly isolated from each other.

Fault Tolerance

As you plan for network installation, you should consider *fault tolerance*, a design concept that reduces the likelihood of system failure. Ideally, any network component that constitutes a single point of failure should be duplicated. Then if the component fails, its redundant counterpart can fill in while the repair is being made.

Obviously, fault tolerance can be very expensive insurance. The single points of failure on a local area network are a dedicated disk server, a hard disk, a printer, and the network cable. Duplicating each of these points, just for the sake of protection, might be unjustified on a typical network. On the other hand, you have already seen that the performance of multiple small hard disks may be preferable to that of a single large hard disk, and on most networks you usually can justify at least two printers for normal operations.

Depending on the network's architecture, the server may be any PC designated as a server by application. If you have more than one PC on the network, redundancy is built in. If the network requires a special computer dedicated to server duties, however, the redundancy will require a significant cost. If the dedicated device is an IBM PC AT, you can use a second PC AT in the network as a workstation. Then, if the server PC AT fails, the workstation PC AT is available to act as the server.

If your network uses a dedicated 68000-based server or a larger machine, you may not want to buy a second redundant server. Most network companies offer a 24-hour turnaround on repairs. Two days in downtime may be a reasonable risk compared to the cost of another server, especially if your backup tapes can be off-loaded to an available hard disk and files can be processed in stand-alone mode.

The final single point of failure is the cable. Ideally, you should have another cable that enables you to jump across a link if it fails. If your system is reasonably accessible, you might accomplish this new link by having a couple of cables made up and stored, ready to use as jumpers. If your system runs underground or is difficult to access, however, you should run two cables for each link and use one as a standby.

In the purest sense, fault tolerance means that the system continues uninterrupted if one component fails. The solutions suggested here will involve some downtime. With current technology, true fault tolerance is prohibitively expensive, except on very large networks.

Reducing Interference

As you plan your network, one of your goals is to reduce electrical interference in the system. Interference is generated internally and externally. Longer cable runs and higher data rates result in increased interference. This kind of interference is difficult to regulate. Some interference, however, is caused by the radiated fields of nearby electrical equipment; this interference can be reduced or eliminated by avoiding the source.

A signal in one system can produce electrical interference in an adjacent system; even circuits within the same system can cause interference among its circuits. Network cables can radiate, or *cross talk*, a signal into nearby cables. Cross talk is the passage of two signals through the same circuit. One signal is the intended signal, and the other is an unwanted signal that may be caused by outside sources or by the cable itself.

The ***shield***, or ***braid***, in coax carries the modulated signal (see fig. 18.1). Because the shield is on the outer edge of the cable and largely unprotected, outside signals can mix into the desired signal carried on the shield. This mixing causes cross-modulation, or cross talk, creating noise and interference. The amount of potential cross talk on two parallel runs of cable depends on the relative spacing of the cable and on the grounding systems used.

Using a good quality of cable and having tight connections properly affixed to the cable will reduce the likelihood of interference that corrupts data. No transmission cable—shielded twisted pair or baseband coax—should be routed next to power cables. If possible, anything electrical should be avoided, such as an electrical motor. An elevator switch room almost always generates interference. Fluorescent lights and air conditioners generate interference because they are high-voltage transformers.

Any of these sources of interference can create problems. Unfortunately, no hard and fast guidelines exists to tell you what you can or cannot do. Appropriate measures vary from cable to cable and from installation to installation. The measures you select also depend on the type of cable and its use. Sources of interference may be impossible to avoid without considerable effort and expense.

Sometimes cables can be laid directly on top of fluorescent light fixtures with no problem. If you have only one conduit, and your cable must go under a runway, or if you must place your cable under a street and you have to put your signal cable with electrical cables, try the arrangement; you have no other choice. Anytime you can avoid getting near a power cable, you are better off to do so.

If the cable is well-shielded and the demands on your signal cable are low, outside interference probably will not affect network operation—especially if you are making short runs of 50 feet or less. If you are not using the network for anything especially data-intensive, such as CAD/CAM requiring heavy data rates, you are less likely to have trouble. Simple order entry traffic with low data rates may be fine, even in close proximity to a source of interference. High data rates tend to intensify an existing interference problem.

Sometimes an interference problem is intermittent. The problem may appear only when an air conditioner motor starts up, for example. The motor throws a large pulse down the ground wire, and somehow the pulse is picked up on the ground of the network. You can solve this problem best by putting a bypass or filter directly on the motor, instead of altering the network wiring. You probably should filter the line where it plugs into the wall.

When you are forced to run data cables through fields of interference, such as in a cable tray with high-voltage power lines, you can use fiber-optic cable. This kind of cable is completely immune to electromagnetic interference.

Grounding

Grounding is another important element in proper network installation but may create more problems than it solves. A ground can be a source of interference, for example.

A *ground* is a path that lets an electrical system dump high voltages that may damage the system and its components. With coaxial cable, that path usually is a connection to the shield routed to an earth ground. A spike of high-voltage electricity is shunted off onto this ground system and dispersed into the earth.

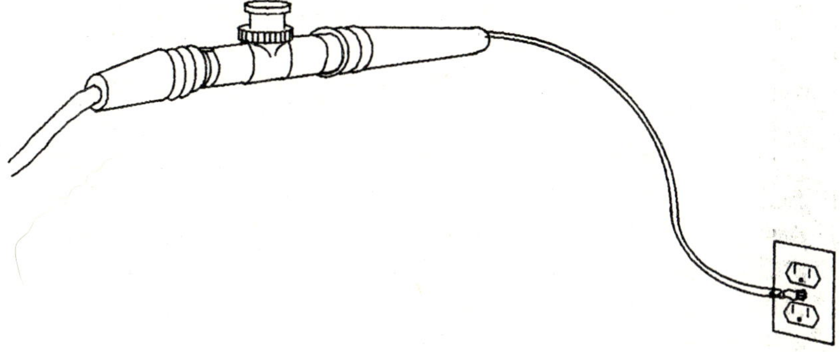

Fig. 18.3. Proper grounding of cables and equipment reduces interference and improves the reliability of the network.

Problems arise when the ground system is attached in more than one place. A *ground loop* may develop. A ground loop occurs when external interference rides the ground and stays on the shield without being shunted off. This ground loop can damage the desired signal. Unfortunately, ground loops cannot be avoided in any practical way because a network usually has many grounding points. Adding another ground increases the number of possible ground loops.

Most small local area networks have sufficient grounding in their hardware design. The shield is connected to the chassis of each device connected to a ground wire on the AC plug. Usually, you can install the network with no additional ground, and you can depend on the chassis to provide the ground. If a problem develops, such as noise on the network cable or a large number of message retransmissions, the system ground is not functioning properly. In this case, you should ask for some advice on additional grounds from your network vendor.

Some larger installations, however, definitely will need special grounding. Ground electrical potential in the same building can vary. One circuit in a lab may have its own transformer, for example, while a circuit in accounting also may have its own transformer. The result is a sizable difference in potential at the two grounding points; you can get many hundreds of volts of static discharge on the cable.

Every AC circuit that network devices are plugged into should be on the same transformer. If these circuits are on different transformers, you should ground the cable. Otherwise, you should not have to worry about the circuits because they ground through the connector, back through the AC line into the outlet. On a long cable run, however, you do not want the cable to ground through the chassis; you want the cable quickly grounded to earth. As a general rule, if the network cable has a span of 200 feet or more, without any PC or peripheral device connected to the cable, an extra ground connection is necessary.

Chapter Summary

Cable installation—planning, documentation, and installation—is critical to system reliability. Poor installation can cause data transmission errors that will plague a system until the problem is corrected.

Of all the problems discussed in this chapter, the most common are cable kinking and stretching. Cable must be handled carefully during installation and protected properly to prevent damage after installation. If you follow these basic procedures, you can rest assured about your cable system; the system will continue to provide dependable service for decades.

19

Performance

In previous chapters, LAN flexibility has been discussed often, and nowhere is that flexibility more apparent than in the area of performance. A LAN is a dynamic modular system; its performance changes as new users and applications are installed and components are shifted and added to the system.

Performance strategies can be divided into two areas. The first area is physical: how you *configure* a LAN for maximum performance. The second area is operational: how you *use* a LAN for maximum performance. This chapter examines both areas in two situations: setting up a LAN, and identifying and curing performance bottlenecks in an operational LAN.

The Data Path

Data on a LAN moves through a series of processes and transfer points. A request, such as "Give me file X," begins at the PC workstation. The network software intercepts and routes the request to the network interface card (NIC). The NIC divides the request into message units (packets) and sends the requests onto the LAN cable (see fig. 19.1).

The cable carries the packets to a NIC resident in the network server. When the NIC receives the packets, it must break up the packets and reassemble and deliver the request to the server. The server analyzes the request and decides whether the request is executable. If the request is approved, it is routed through the disk channel to the hard disk that reads the requested data. The response

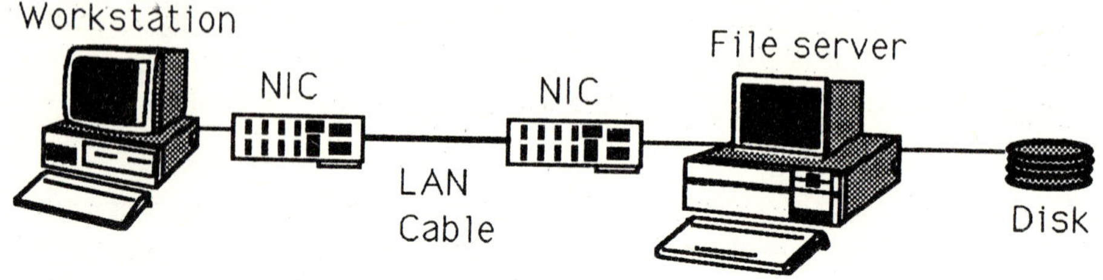

Fig. 19.1. On a LAN, data moves through a series of process-and-transfer points.

now must make its way back to the requesting PC workstation, going through the same processes and transfer points as the request, only this time in reverse order.

Each process and transfer point in the system is a potential bottleneck—a place where overall system throughput is reduced. On a LAN, system throughput is no faster than the system's slowest component. Suppose, for example, that the entire system can support a throughput of 300 kilobytes per second, except for the disk, which can read or write data at a maximum of 100 kilobytes per second. The disk's speed controls and limits the whole system's throughput.

Using Disk Caching To Speed Up Network Operation

The amount of data moved is less a performance factor than the number of times the data is moved; data is accessed in blocks. Moving several blocks at one time is more efficient than moving one block at a time. A series of transfers can be a major cause of poor performance.

One way to speed up network operation is to eliminate as many data transfers as possible. Data transfers can be eliminated by disk caching.

Most network operating systems support some form of *disk cache*, or electronic memory storage system. With caching, information is retrieved from the disk and stored in random-access memory (RAM) until needed by the application. Data requests from the application are answered in RAM and do not have to go to the disk. This process speeds up the response time because electronic RAM is much faster than the hard disk.

Caching also reduces the number of transfers needed, because larger blocks of data are moved in a single response. Information usually comes off the disk in 512-byte sectors. If the cache can hold 2,000 bytes, one transfer can grab two extra sectors in addition to the one requested. When the next sector is called for, that sector already may be in the cache, speeding up delivery.

The simplest caching is a read-ahead scheme. When a program requests data from a disk, the cache system picks up the requested data and any additional data that follows. For many types of applications, the next read request to disk may be for that additional data, which already is in electronic memory when the second request comes. If the next batch of information is already in the cache, the operating system does not have to go to disk, and valuable time is saved.

When four or five people are working on a hard disk, disk accesses may run at about the same speed as floppies when you use your computer, depending on the application. If each user can get a large block of data each time a transfer is made, however, the network can deliver data to the workstation at speeds approaching the speed of a dedicated hard disk. By having the cache memory in the system, the number of *seeks* is reduced. A random seek from one region of the disk to another may average from 30 to 100 milliseconds.

Systems that cache disk directories and file allocation tables (management and organization tools used in all random-access storage systems) deliver significantly better performance than systems that do not cache. Through caching, you can eliminate all the directory and file allocation seeks beyond the initial acquisition. Caching in the server also is a primary factor in the maximum size of the network. The more RAM available at the server for caching, therefore, the more users and open files the system can support.

Caching does not always improve application performance. A database application, for example, usually uses random records in scattered locations on the disk. In such a situation, the cache scheme grabs extra blocks that follow the requested data, but those extra blocks probably are not the ones designated in a subsequent request.

Two types of caching are done on LANs: server caching and workstation caching. Because of the multiple tasks and the different needs of applications, server caching always is used.

Workstation caching is useful only during non-multiuser operations, when the data is not being shared with anybody else. The workstation caches data locally and reads the data out of workstation memory rather than going back to the server. If the file is opened under multiuser file and record locking, the workstation must go back to the server to get new data to make sure that the data is current. In a multiuser application, therefore, the data in a workstation cache cannot be used. When running multiuser applications, workstation caching should be turned off because caching adds to the overhead without providing a useful function.

File caching is one of the big users of RAM. No simple formula can determine how much RAM is needed by the cache. The other system activities may require a little over 1M of RAM in the server; the server, therefore, probably should start with 2M of RAM.

The next step is to estimate how much of the time users are doing redundant reads. Would file caching be a benefit? You can put 6M of extra RAM in the file server to do file caching, but if the data one user reads is not likely to be read later on, that caching is not going to be of much value.

Some network operating systems contain diagnostic utilities that indicate cache utilization, such as the number of disk requests serviced from cache. A good indication that caching is effective and that increasing the cache size will improve system throughput is if 80 to 90 percent of the requests are from cache memory.

Sometimes bringing an entire database into RAM is worthwhile. For example, on a multiuser database, much of the disk activity involves synchronizing access to the data. The file server handles the synchronization itself, but heavy disk I/O is required. Being able to access the data from memory speeds up the throughput significantly. At the start of each business day, you can run a program that reads the entire database and brings the database into RAM. Every time the data is needed, such as when a customer calls in with an order, the information is already in RAM and quickly available.

Besides common databases, the biggest benefit for server caching is when the system is working with executable files. Typically, employees come in at about the same time and load their electronic mail application. The first time the application is read, it is cached in RAM. From then on, everybody else loads the application from the server cache.

Improving Access Time by Organizing Files

Access time also can be improved through file organization. With a network, many people use the mass-storage hard disk and create files on the disk. If users organize the file structure to the best advantage, they can reduce access times.

With early versions of DOS, files were kept in a *flat* directory. After the introduction of DOS Version 2.0, root-structured, or hierarchical, directories came into common use on PC LANs. This kind of structure nests, or subordinates, directories so that they appear as branches of the top, or root, directory. Every directory in the main directory can contain many subdirectories, each of which, in turn, can have many subdirectories, and so on (see fig. 19.2).

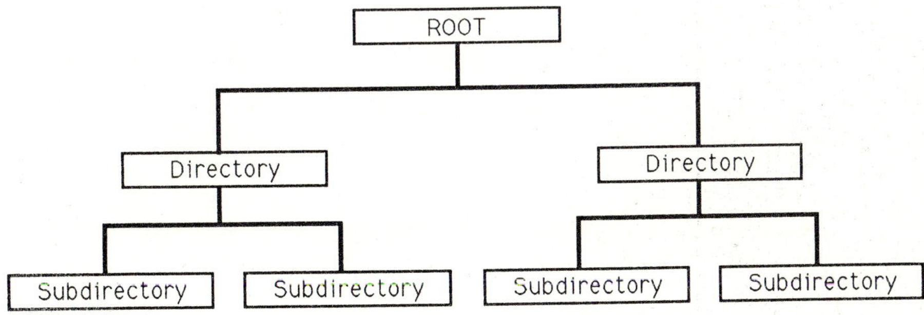

Fig. 19.2. Hierarchical directories.

A person who has not used hierarchical directories may be inclined to create elaborate paths and structures, and this complexity often results in files being periodically lost in the labyrinth.

Another more serious problem with hierarchies is that they degrade performance. As a rule, try to limit the number of levels you create.

To retrieve a file, the system must move through the root structure in the same way that you would if you were searching manually. Nearer files take less time to retrieve than more distant ones do. If you are working 20 levels down from the root directory, you can retrieve and store files without noticing a loss in speed. If you are 20 levels down on one path and want to get information from a subdirectory on a different path, however, you sacrifice considerable speed because the operating system must look into each subdirectory, following the path that you have specified. The operating system looks at the first directory you specify in the path, then moves the pointers to the next directory, and so on, through the path.

To achieve the best organization, make directories horizontal. The root directory is at the base and, in addition to the common information that everyone uses, may contain a subdirectory for each user. In that subdirectory, each user can have one or two subdirectories. You rarely need to go more than two or three levels deep in hierarchical directories.

If you think that you need more levels, you can better maintain network access speed by opening another directory from the root directory. This approach makes files easier to find. Files nested very deep have a tendency to get lost.

Network Servers: How Many To Use?

The initial choice of a network server is based on current users and applications, but as the LAN gains acceptance, more workstations and applications will be added. Eventually, the server will not be able to handle the workload, and performance will begin to decline.

A typical LAN of four or five workstations might start off with an IBM PC XT server (see fig. 19.3). The PC XT probably can be used in concurrent mode so that the computer also can be used as a workstation. With the addition of another workstation or two and a rise in traffic, the concurrent PC XT server quickly becomes a bottleneck.

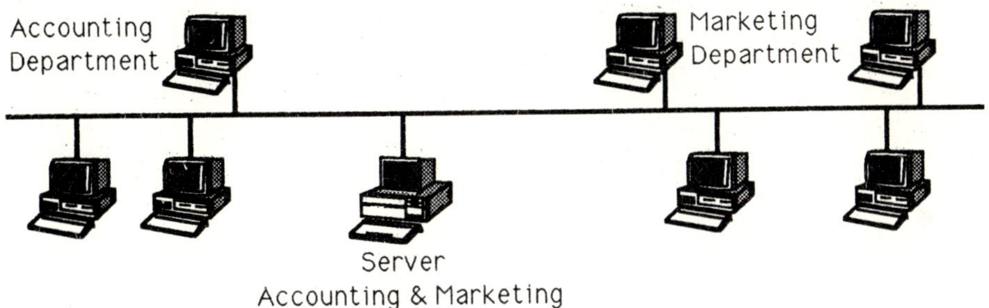

Fig. 19.3. Small networks often start out with one server and hard disk providing data storage for the entire network.

One advantage of LAN architecture is that performance upgrades do not necessitate replacing the entire system. The first step should be to dedicate the PC XT server; then, all the PC XT's processing power goes to serving the network.

If a dedicated PC XT server does not improve performance sufficiently, or if the system's performance is satisfactory but degrades later, the next step would be to purchase a faster server. A faster server has a wider processing and data-path bandwidth, a higher clock cycle speed (expressed in megahertz), and a lower number of wait states. In the example, an IBM PC AT might be installed as a server and the PC XT placed out on the network as a workstation.

When performance becomes inadequate, several upgrades are possible. A faster server can be installed and the PC AT reconfigured as a workstation. A second server also can be installed; two servers have the effect of doubling the network's server power (see fig. 19.4). Another option is to upgrade the operating system to one that supports the PC AT in protected mode. (An 80286, such as that on the PC AT, can operate in PC mode with a maximum of 640K of

RAM or in protected mode with as much as 16M of RAM for caching.) If you have more than one disk on your server, a disk coprocessor board can be an effective and relatively inexpensive way of improving performance (see "Solving Disk Channel Problems").

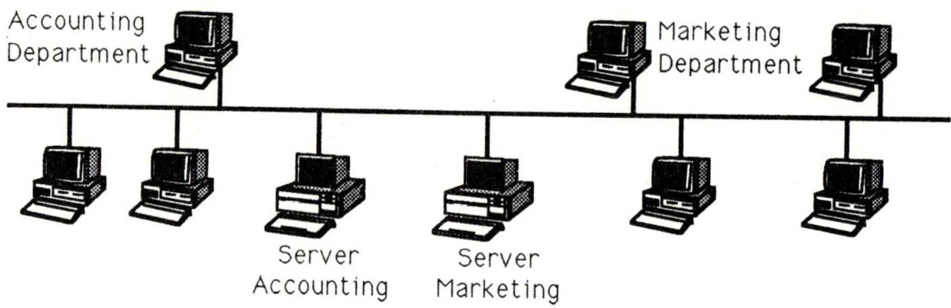

Fig. 19.4. Adding a second server with its own disk subsystem.

In LANs that have been upgraded to this point or that started in this configuration, further server upgrades are accomplished with the addition of more servers. Every time a server is added, the users and applications should be distributed evenly among the servers so that the loads are balanced. One LAN can support several dozen servers, representing a huge amount of power for disk and network management. Before you add more servers, however, you should consider other performance bottlenecks.

Upgrading the server may seem futile if you recall that the system's slowest component regulates throughput. Disk channels are limited to reading data at 160K per second and writing data at 100K per second. Most medium servers can surpass that throughput; therefore, a faster server seems to be a waste of power.

The disk channel, however, does not entirely determine system performance, even though that channel is slow. The server performs many tasks in addition to disk I/O. If only 15 percent of a server's processing capability is used while reading 160K in one second, the remaining 85 percent of that second can be devoted to those additional tasks. Overall throughput, therefore, is speeded up.

Solving Disk Channel Problems

Nevertheless, the disk channel often is the cause of a LAN's performance problems. As a general rule, if the red light on the hard disk flashes most of the time, that flashing indicates a disk channel bottleneck.

Suppose that you want a LAN to provide throughput equal to that of a local PC XT hard disk. A PC XT hard disk has a throughput of 58K per second, or about half the throughput of a disk channel. Calculate how much a given application does disk I/O. If the application does disk I/O 20 percent of the time, 10 workstations can use up the disk channel's throughput. If all the workstations request disk I/O simultaneously, only 2 stations can get hard disk performance. If 10 workstations are on the network, simultaneous disk I/O requests from all stations results in the per-station throughput dropping to about 15K per second—approximately the speed of a floppy disk drive.

The disk channel is composed of three basic parts: disk controller, connecting cable, and disk drive. When evaluating disk subsystems, remember that a 16-bit-wide controller bus (in which the controller plugs into the server bus) is twice as fast as an 8-bit-wide bus.

The number of disk interleaves is another performance indicator. If a disk channel is slow, data is spaced at intervals of one every two or three sectors on the disk rather than in contiguous sectors. A two-to-one interleave occurs when sequential blocks of data are separated by one sector. A slower disk requires a higher number of interleaves. A disk subsystem with a two-to-one interleave, therefore, probably is faster than a disk subsystem with a five-to-one interleave.

Disk drives differ in their capability to move the disk's read/write heads across the disk, a process called seek-access time. Drive specifications include a figure called average-access time. A low average-access time indicates a fast drive.

In addition to installing faster disk subsystems, you can improve disk channel performance by adding multiple disk channels. Some network operating systems support up to five disk channels in one server. Operating systems usually support several disk drives per channel, but adding disk drives to only one channel increases storage space and does not improve performance. To improve performance, you must add a separate channel—another disk subsystem complete with controller, cable, and disk.

Even adding more disk channels does not guarantee improved throughput, unless the disk I/O is balanced evenly between the two channels. If most people on the network use a big database in daily activities, and that database is on one disk channel, adding any number of disk subsystems does not alter performance. Everyone still contends for the one channel. One disk cannot have multiple channels.

In a network with multiple disk subsystems, many storage strategies are possible. Applications can be stored on one disk, and user directories can be stored on another. Half the user directories and applications also can be stored on one disk and the other half on the other disk. The alternatives are endless. What is important is that approximately the same number of disk requests go to each disk channel.

A second server adds at least one more disk channel. When the disk channel and server are suspected bottlenecks, this solution is probably the best.

Avoiding Cable Bottlenecks

The cable is another potential bottleneck, especially on LANs with multiple servers. The cable can become a bottleneck if a dozen people start accessing several servers simultaneously. A cable bottleneck should show up as a high number of collision and retry statistics for the network.

One way to open up a cable bottleneck is to replace the cable and network interface cards with a faster system. This solution is very expensive.

Another way to open up the cable bottleneck without replacing the cable and NIC hardware is to use multiple servers and bridge between them. You first should examine the network applications and files. Intradepartmental file sharing and communications usually are heavy, and interdepartmental traffic is minimal. Therefore, you can break the network connection between one department or cluster of departments and another department or cluster. The cable on each side of the break needs its own server and shared hard disk to become a self-sufficient network.

Before the cable is divided, every transmission sent by any device traverses the full length of the cable. By dividing the cable, you reduce the traffic load to whatever transmissions are sent by the devices remaining on each network. The result is fewer transmission errors and retries and faster response times.

By breaking the network in this way, however, you isolate two sections of the company and prevent those divisions from sharing data and communicating over data lines. Remember that these activities are two of the reasons for networking in the first place. To solve this problem, you can install a bridge that connects networks and permits internetwork traffic (see fig. 19.5). A bridge between two networks enables users to pass data back and forth and work as if there were only one network. ("Bridge" is used here to refer to several types of connection devices, including bridges, routers, and gateways.)

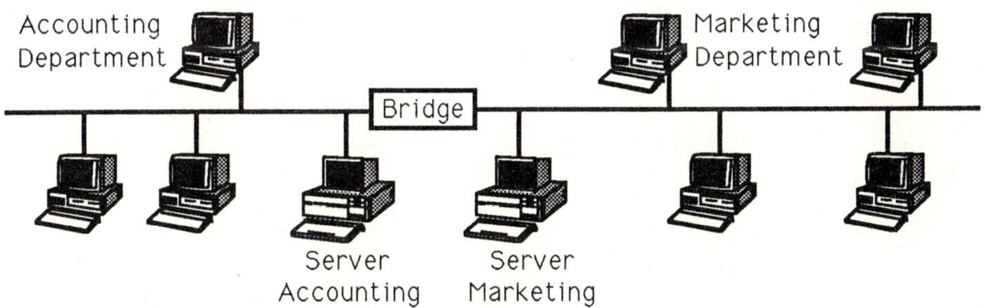

Fig. 19.5. When the network is divided by a bridge, messages remain on one network unless addressed to cross the bridge.

The main difference between an internet and a single network is that on an internet, intranetwork traffic does not cross the bridge. Only data specifically addressed to some person or device on the other network passes through the bridge and runs on the other network. Bridges have several useful features, as discussed in Chapter 14.

An alternative to this remove-and-replace strategy is to place the server in the logical center of the network and install one NIC in the server for each half. The server, therefore, has two NICs on its bus. The network operating system bridges the two NICs together so that they look like one network to users, sharing resources and communicating as usual. The cable is divided physically so that it is carrying half as much traffic. (Novell Advanced NetWare supports this kind of internal bridging with as many as four identical or different NICs in the same server.)

Chapter Summary

The key to maintaining desirable LAN performance is an understanding of the LAN's modular design. Performance, or throughput, is determined by the system's slowest component. If LAN performance degrades below an acceptable level, you can remedy the problem by identifying the bottleneck and taking appropriate steps: adding a disk channel, upgrading the server or adding a second server, or upgrading the operating system.

Visual clues often identify bottlenecks. For example, if the red light on the hard disk is on continuously, a bottleneck probably is occurring. An 8088-based server can support only a few users and easily becomes a bottleneck as the system grows.

Another way to identify bottlenecks is to use hardware specifications and published benchmarks. You also can perform your own benchmarks to measure throughput of a specific component, although this procedure takes time and requires advanced technical expertise.

In a worst-case scenario, you may have to upgrade two or perhaps three components before obtaining satisfactory performance. Unlike upgrades of shared processing systems, however, a LAN performance upgrade never requires the replacement of the entire LAN.

20

Maintenance and Diagnostics

Two aspects of networking usually are low on the list of interesting issues where small networks are concerned. The first is maintenance; the second is diagnostics. Both of these issues are critical in any component of a company's business. Maintenance is not just about fixing things when they break. Maintenance also concerns issues such as support downtime and cost effectiveness. Comprehensive and useful diagnostics are a prerequisite for reliable maintenance.

Together maintenance and diagnostics provide the tools to ensure that your network can continue to provide a level of service that meets your company's needs.

Using Network Diagnostics

On small networks, with a couple of PCs sharing a hard disk and a printer, diagnostics can be an unnecessary complication. As a network grows, so does the need for monitoring the network and diagnosing its problems. Diagnostics are thus a mandatory component of large networks.

The presentation of data to help users maximize the usefulness of the network diagnostics is an important issue. Utilities that reveal reams of data but do not assist in the interpretation are useless except to the experienced technicians.

User diagnostics should be chosen with great care. If they are too complex, users will avoid them. If the diagnostics do not provide a useful and informative analysis of the data, no matter how simple that data is, the same problems will arise.

Running Self-Tests

Most networks have low-level, self-test procedures that run automatically when the network is powered up. These tests usually cover the cable and hardware configuration and, if nothing else, test the network interface card. This testing is the most basic level of diagnostics and acts as an extension of the host workstation's Power On Self-Test (POST). A failure occurring at this level usually is internal to the board (such as a component failure or configuration error) or related to a cabling fault (such as not being attached to the network cable.)

If a new PC has just been added to the network, the self-test may show that the network interface card and another subsystem in the PC are using the same set of interrupts or memory addresses. This problem is a common fault that requires you to go back to the documentation and make the appropriate changes.

Some self-tests perform loop-backs by electrically isolating the network interface card from the rest of the network. A signal is transmitted and "looped back" to the same card. This procedure enables the card to verify that a signal is being sent and received. Another self-test may be used for specific links within the network to verify that attached devices can communicate with each other. This communication often is part of the low-level functioning of the network and enables the configuration to be established before any data traffic begins.

After a power-on self-test, any discovered problem usually is indicated by an error code displayed on the monitor. The intention is that the user will call the network user-support center or system vendor/installer and report the error condition. The user then is told which part is malfunctioning or is talked through more advanced diagnostics.

Collecting Network Information

Beyond the initial check-out of the self-test, a great variety of network diagnostic support is available. Maintaining performance and managing and expanding a network system require information. Network performance monitoring and diagnostics systems can provide much of the necessary supporting information that is not supplied by the system itself.

Generally, the needed information covers three major groups:

- Status
- Utilization
- Performance data

Status concerns the information that summarizes the operation of the network. These parameters essentially are collected over time and tell you how the network has performed historically. Three of the major status parameters are error rates, time-outs, and connection quality.

- The *error rate* is the number of failures or corrupted data packet receipts that have occurred in the course of operation of a particular function.
- *Time-outs*—when an expected event does not occur within the expected time—are an important measurement. They often indicate that a configuration is marginally coping with the imposed load or that hardware is failing.
- *Connection quality*, the quality of the link between two nodes, is directly related to the functional viability of that connection. By testing the quality of the connection, you can assess whether an apparently poor performance is due to heavy traffic or whether the number of retries due to faulty connections is wasting bandwidth. The connection quality obviously is related to error rates, but because connection quality is such a vital metric of performance, it should be seen as a unique network measurement.

Utilization is a measure of the peak loading (regular periods of highest activity) and the level of service that can be delivered. A utilization measurement often indicates that a redistribution of existing resources can satisfy an expansion need. The two major areas of measurement are the following:

- *Configuration efficiency:* A frequent cause of poor performance is an inadequately set up system. Poor allocation of RAM to support cache buffering can lead to disk thrashing and poor response. Other causes and their solutions are discussed in Chapter 19, "Performance."
- *Equipment availability:* Units on a network that have a poor duty cycle (the ratio of being operational to being out of service) can indicate that the unit is not up to the dependable performance required for that service. The availability records for that equipment can show where the problem lies.

Performance data reveals the capability of the system to perform its functions. Because raw performance data often is massive and indigestible, the way in which the measurements are presented is crucial to revealing the "hidden" information.

Some networks support centralized or distributed statistics gathering. This feature may be intrinsic to the network or may be an add-on package by a third-party supplier. The openness of the architecture of a specific network is often the key to the range of network diagnostics available. The problem is that vendors are unlikely to meet the entire range of user needs. The ability to extend a system by using add-on products from a third party is vital to building sophisticated networks.

The *response time* of the system, particularly as perceived by the user, is one of the critical issues. Possibly more than anything else, response time defines whether the network is a success. The measurement you are interested in is not the average response but the maximum (worst-case) response.

Traffic volumes reveal how the tasks on the network are being used. You might expect a word processing package to be a relatively low-traffic volume generator. If the type of activities for which the word processor is used range from short memos and letters to electronic mail, however, the loading will be quite different. Traffic monitoring enables you to detect and evaluate these kinds of factors.

One version of traffic monitoring is transaction counting. A transaction can be defined in many ways, but the common events that are used are input/output requests and disk accesses. True transactions are file updates that are identifiable as atomic (singular) events. Many networks provide a primitive method of load measurement by displaying the number of transactions per second. Although software for compiling and saving this information may not be included, simply noting the reading at various times during the day can be useful for predicting when you need a second disk server.

An *audit trail* is a record of who used the network, how long the network was used, and what file was accessed. This information can be used to provide billing information and network security. Audit trails presently are implemented in one of four ways: in the network operating system, using existing hardware, in a special device attached to the network, or in the applications software.

When audit trails are tied to transaction processing, the ability to keep a trail of the actual transactions may be provided. If such a trail is kept on a Write Once Read Many (WORM) drive, the WORM drive acts as a highly secure archive. In the case of catastrophic failure, you can use the audit trail to reconstruct an entire database, regardless of whether the audit trail is on a WORM drive or other media. Manual reconstruction uses a backup copy of the database and adds the transactions in sequence. This process solves a problem that is difficult to correct by normal means but straightforward by audit trail reconstruction.

Recognizing the Importance of Status Information

Network status information is probably the most necessary of the diagnostics services. A status report from the disk server should include a list of files currently being accessed, the file user's location, and whether a file is locked or available to others. Other useful information includes the user's current error status, charge information, and input/output rate. The last item, input/output rate, is a useful measure and can lead to some valuable insights into the loading characteristics of users and the software they access. The rate also may indicate attempted security violations.

A common method of cracking the security of a network relies on the idea that by logging in under a real account name and randomly trying passwords, you can successfully log in. Published lists are available that contain the 1,000 most popular user's passwords. By using this list, a hacker has a head start in breaking the security of a network. Monitoring the input/output rates for log-in requests detects such programmatic security breaking if a log-in failure limit is not set. (Log-in failure limit is an important security mechanism. Some network operating systems enable you to limit the number of failed log-ins so that someone with access to the system and knowledge of a user name cannot try numerous passwords in a break-in attempt. After the limit is reached, the user name is denied access until reset by the supervisor.)

If the network operating system permits queuing for files, the network manager should be able to get status information about the queue. The manager should be able not only to check the queue, but also to alter the order of entries in the queue. Most print servers permit queuing. Access also should be available for operators of the queue—users who have a subset of the manager's rights—so that they can, for example, modify only their own jobs or the jobs for the group to which they belong.

Some networks keep a status list of every device that is connected and logged on. Then, if the device fails, goes off line, or runs out of paper, the failure is posted in the list. Usually, every PC has immediate access to the status list, or the network operating system may have an alert generator. An *alert generator* warns one or more users that an exception condition has occurred. In some cases, the alert informs the network manager. In other cases, the alert is a general one, targeted, for example, to all users of a particular printer. Alerts are a powerful facility that is a fundamental requirement in large networks.

A failure may go unnoticed. If a network node never transmits, you discover that the node has failed only when the node does not respond to a message. An extension of the diagnostics service is the periodic sending of status-checking messages by nodes. These messages immediately detect any failed node, but they also place additional overhead on the network. In many cases, such "Are you alive?" messages are unnecessary for workstations. For gateways and device servers (print servers, modem servers, and so on), check messages may be highly desirable.

Status checking also helps in planning the network. For instance, 200 devices may be on the cable, but the manager plans for only 10 to be active at any given time. Periodically, the manager does a status check to see how many devices are active. The manager may be surprised to find 20 or 30 active devices, in which case another server or a redesigned cabling system may be needed.

An alternative to having the node generate a periodic status message is using a status interrogation that is externally initiated. The program could be automatic or require human intervention. The problem of network message overhead is reduced, and you can watch the critical nodes rather than the entire system.

Using Third-Party Diagnostics

If a network itself does not support adequate diagnostics, you can attach a third-party product. For instance, a bit error rate tester makes test transmissions and loops them back, calculating the number of bits transmitted and the number of bits in error.

Low-level diagnostics involves two basic approaches. The hardware approach relies on adding monitor systems that trap network traffic and analyze its structure and content. These systems usually require highly trained technicians to interpret the data, but are excellent in identifying complex or obscure problems.

The software approach requires that the network has diagnostic and status interfaces available. The diagnostics software intercepts and analyzes network input/output for error conditions, quality, and performance data. You then can output the analyzed data in standard formats to allow for analyses that the diagnostics software cannot perform. For example, the Macintosh has several packages that gather network statistics, and you present the data by using a separate spreadsheet package.

The software approach usually is much less expensive (typically 10 times cheaper) than hardware diagnostics and presents the collected data much better. The software approach, however, relies on the system having the diagnostic interfaces available and usually is incapable of capturing the fine detail of network traffic.

NetWare: An Example of Built-in Network Diagnostics

One of the more advanced built-in network diagnostics monitor facilities is an intrinsic function of Novell NetWare. A NetWare file server usually is an 80286- or 80386-based computer with a keyboard and display. A user can call up the monitor display by typing the command *monitor*.

The network monitor displays a grid with six cells, one for each workstation on the network. As more workstations are added, the screen can be scrolled to show additional cells. The station number displays in the upper left corner of each cell. The principal function of the cells is to indicate the activity of a group of workstations. The name of the last five files opened and still in use by the station is shown, along with the type of access (such as shareable or locked).

Another information item provided by the monitor display is percentages of server utilization. This value, updated once each second, shows the amount of file-server processor time used by network requests during the previous second. With this figure, you can determine how close the file server is to being fully loaded. If, for example, the file server is 70 to 80 percent utilized, the file server may be causing a performance bottleneck. To remedy the situation, you can replace the file server with a more powerful machine or add a second server to the system and share the load between the two machines.

NetWare uses cache buffering to improve disk throughput and make the network operate more efficiently. Cache buffering is a method of improving performance that works for reading and writing to the disk subsystem. When a disk read request occurs, the request is for a specific sector. Because read requests usually are for sequential sectors, the system can service subsequent reads from the buffer by reading the required sector plus the next one or more sectors (held in RAM). The sectors in the buffer are delivered much faster in answer to a request than sectors stored on a hard disk.

When a write request occurs, the data is written to a new sector in the cache buffer, where the data is held until the system has time to write the data to disk. If the sector to be written to is already in the cache buffer, the system uses the existing sector to ensure that the cache is holding only a single copy of the data.

Whenever the network is operating, therefore, some data usually is in a buffer. Modified disk buffers are written to disk during processor idle time or when more buffer space is required. If the network is shut down at one of these times, data is lost, and the entire file might be destroyed. To prevent this problem, you must write all the buffered data to disk before shutting down the network, using specific commands to clear buffers.

The upper right corner of the monitor display shows disk I/O pending. The value of this message is the number of cache buffers that have been changed in the server's memory but have not yet been written to disk. This figure reveals the amount of work that the server is doing.

The 82586 Chip: An Example of Diagnostics in Hardware

Efficient coprocessors that incorporate diagnostics are starting to appear in network hardware. The Intel 82586 chip, designed for contention (Carrier Sense Multiple Access with Collision Detection, or CSMA-CD) networks, such as EtherNet, has built-in diagnostics and management functions. This controller chip sends back to the CPU status information on every message handled. The number of collisions and message errors is collected and reported. Such information is a good indicator of the overall condition of the network. For example, a high percentage of CRC (message error) messages suggests a hardware problem or continual interference, such as radio frequency or electrical interference.

The 82586 chip can implement systematic diagnostics for the individual workstation and for the rest of the network. A network user can put the chip in a loop-back mode in which a send-and-receive cycle is implemented within the single workstation. When a check shows that messages are properly transmitted and received at the workstation, the problem usually is outside the workstation. The chip also has external loop-back capability for isolating problems between PCs.

You can find a break, or short, in the network by using the 82586. The chip not only diagnoses that a short exists but also estimates the distance of the short from the workstation in a process called *time domain reflectometry* (TDR). A diagnose command in the 82586 chip is available to perform a self-test routine for checking the main CPU.

The 82586 supplies the software with routing information about the network's health, including how many collisions are experienced before the message gets through and how many packets are received with errors. Statistics are kept on individual packets, and the chip keeps in memory a running tally of three or four key parameters. Statistically, these parameters represent the health of the network.

Looking to the Future

Network diagnostics for network systems are still primitive. Managers who gain experience with networks are going to want more sophisticated diagnostics, however, and managers' needs are likely to be answered by the network industry.

Increasingly, office automation equipment is aimed at being compatible with networking. Networks are growing rapidly in numbers of users, applications, and attached devices, and all this growth will necessitate accurate monitoring systems.

The latest wave of diagnostics systems tends to use icons, windowed environments, and graphic displays to portray the state of the system. Future network diagnostics will undoubtedly draw on expert systems to assist in the interpretation of network diagnostic data. The benefit of this approach will be enormous, because this approach enables relatively untrained users and junior technicians to diagnose and correct major network problems with little or no assistance.

Analyzing the Network Manager's Role in Diagnostics

A network system comes with the tools to tailor each user's environment to particular capabilities and needs. Stations can be set up to run a single application; this kind of structure requires the user to know little about the network. Or stations can be set up to give the user considerable flexibility and power over the network's resources.

Each network should have at least one knowledgeable user, designated as manager, to manipulate these setup options. For most networks and most applications, the manager does not need to be a programmer. The manager, however, should be familiar with the network, the operating system, and the utilities.

The manager is responsible for setting up workstations, maintaining network applications, backing up files, and performing other administrative chores. Network security, which includes assigning passwords and access privileges, also is the manager's responsibility.

An astute manager is an integral part of network diagnostics. This manager develops a feel for the way the network should function and usually is quick to note slower response times and higher error rates. The less sophisticated the built-in diagnostics, the more important becomes the manager's intuitive understanding of the network.

Part of the manager's job is to monitor the network periodically (including examining the percent of utilization, number of retries, and so on) to see how efficiently and reliably the network is working. One helpful figure is the number of transactions completed over a period of time. Records should be kept by hour, day, and month. Such records show peak hours, days, and months when the network is heavily used. With this data, the manager can manage these peak times more efficiently, conceivably enabling a system to last another year without additional hardware simply by shifting use and distributing the work load.

Utilization figures also help to determine exactly where a bottleneck is developing: in the cable, the disk drive, the printer, or the server. Typically, these devices can slow down or bottleneck a network when you are trying to share central resources and manage peripherals in a multiuser environment.

Some good visual signals can suggest areas of bottlenecking. If the red light on the hard disk is on most or all of the time, the hard disk is being overused. The system needs a faster hard disk, a second hard disk, or both.

Networks are seldom static. They grow, and planning for that growth is mandatory. Performance measurement helps with this planning, ideally with diagnostics that show the pattern of performance degradation. A manager should be able to anticipate a need for expansion based on the network's usage profile so that the next phase of growth can be planned.

Good performance usually is defined as fast response and ready availability. Response time data should be maintained for each networked PC and for the network as a whole. The manager can use such data to indicate the performance of network configuration and software. The most useful response data is a measurement of the performance of the software actually in use. Although benchmarking software can show performance and response, the tendency is for the results to be an idealized picture of the real system. If the testing is carefully planned, the actual applications will reveal far more about what the users see and whether the system meets their needs and expectations.

Performance information can be used in cost control. One of the problems with networks—and with computing in general—is that use is not evenly distributed. Overall use of the network may be well within the range that permits good performance. If 80 percent of the network use occurs during 10 percent of the workday, however, the network may need more equipment.

Applications monitoring, as distinct from response evaluation, can play a special role in evaluating services and planning improvements. Basic performance indicators show how well the network is working. Applications monitoring indicates how well the network handles each separate application, how each application affects response time, and how each one ties up the server. This monitoring also provides detailed productivity analysis of each workstation by showing exactly how much of each kind of work has been done at each station.

Using Maintenance Services

The setup of maintenance service arrangements is often planned as an afterthought. Even when a major system failure has occurred, the performance of the maintenance services is rarely evaluated. The justification of maintenance is a cost-effectiveness issue. If you can quantify the cost of downtime for each function of your network and relate that to the cost of prevention and cure, you have a basis on which to judge need and cost.

The two services of maintenance are support and repair/ maintenance services. *Support services* include network systems support and applications support. *Repair/maintenance services* include off-site repair services, on-site repair services, and preventive maintenance services.

Support Services

Support services are available from a variety of sources: manufacturer, vendor, installer, or other third parties. The original manufacturer usually is considered the best choice for support of its own products.

In some cases, however, a manufacturer or vendor who is supplying a nonintegrating product disclaims responsibility for supplying support. (*Nonintegrating* describes a product that does not create or enable a system directly but is a component of a system.) This disclaimer is not unreasonable, because the environment may well be outside the supplier's experience. A PC manufacturer may not warrant its PC when used as a network server, for example, or an application software publisher may not warrant the application in a network environment.

Similarly, the integrating supplier (the network operating system manufacturer or vendor) can offer support only to generic (of a type) components. When you use nongeneric components, the possibility of unknown features or incompatible functions prevents the vendor from being able to perform a quick diagnosis. For example, a hard disk that conforms only to the manufacturer's proprietary design may not function on the network.

In practice, you should determine compatibility before installation and assess the support that the manufacturer might offer. In many cases, manufacturers do not offer free support. They expect that the organization that sells the equipment to you also supplies the technical advice. The best advice usually is advice you pay for. If a manufacturer has a support service, you should review and compare that service to other third-party offerings. Always try to get references on the quality and timeliness of any support supplier from existing clients.

After you have arranged the support service, keeping notes on all contacts with the service supplier is important. You need a record of problems and actions to reference in case of disagreement.

A formal procedure for solving problems is worth developing. This type of procedure ensures that the staff knows who is knowledgeable in the organization. The designated staff members follow an established procedure and contact the support services with the right information. This procedure speeds up the process of fault diagnosis and builds a positive and cooperative relationship within organizations. Documentation methods should be developed to record the progress of the problem. In addition, the internal staff members should have access to a workstation that is near a phone or, even better, to a cordless phone that lets them move freely around the network.

Applications support is much the same as network systems support. Applications developers frequently warrant the operation of a package under PC DOS but not under a network operating system. You need to get assurances before implementation that the package and the network are compatible. Because few companies provide support for applications software, the services available from the developer or vendor may have to suffice.

Repair Services

Repair and maintenance services are sometimes coupled with the support services through one company or as a collaborative venture between a manufacturer and a maintenance service company.

Repair service may be off-site, and the user (as the equipment owner) bears the cost of shipping. Off-site repairs can be cost effective if downtime is not a problem. The turnaround time, however, can be significant—and much longer than for on-site repairs. On-site repairs usually are more expensive and, if not contracted, involve a call-out charge as well as the cost of the work.

Preventive maintenance usually is associated only with printers, plotters, and other electromechanical systems. Some maintenance companies, however, run routine cable tests, visual inspections, and general health checks on floppy drives and other components. For the larger networks, this maintenance can show significant benefits because the complexity of the system tends to ensure that a problem always is happening somewhere.

Evaluating Charge Methods

All these services—support, repair, and preventive maintenance—usually are charged on a time-and-materials (T&M), fixed-cost (or per-call), or contract basis. Each charging method has its own advantages, and, again, you return to assessing the cost effectiveness of each choice.

For T&M work, you are charged for the amount of time spent on the problem and for the cost of parts. For fixed-cost repairs, you pay a known price for a specific repair or call out. Fixed cost for support can be effective if you have internal technicians who can evaluate a problem and determine when outside support is cost-effective.

The only way to evaluate which option is the best is to have an accurate picture of the expected failure rates of your system components and then work out the costs over a time period. In practice, this information is rarely available, and most decisions are based on other factors, such as the nearness of the service supplier.

Contracted services are preferable in many cases, because agreed response times and escalation procedures are established. The more sophisticated service companies offer schemes that provide replacement hardware if a problem cannot be resolved within a certain period of time. Contracts can cover T&M work and fixed-cost work on an as-needed basis or may be a global charge that covers the cost of repair of any defect in a specified range of equipment on the network.

Knowing the Value of Maintenance

Attempting to build a network system of any size without designing maintenance into the plan is a recipe for disaster. The lack of a preventive maintenance plan is frequently the cause of avoidable problems.

You should consider carefully the cost of each form of maintenance and evaluate the options in relationship to the benefit gained. To skimp on maintenance is a false economy, because high-reliability and high-integrity systems depend not only on good design and implementation but also on good servicing.

Chapter Summary

Maintenance and diagnostics capabilities often are overlooked during system selection and set up. Properly implemented, maintenance and diagnostics improve the reliability and performance of the system as well as its cost-effective operation.

Diagnostics include self-tests to check hardware components, activity monitors, error logs, and other history information that enable a supervisor or maintenance specialist to evaluate the system and its components. Network supervisors should familiarize themselves with the diagnostic processes on their networks so that they can identify and solve a problem before the problem causes a complete failure.

Maintenance typically is supplied by specialists within the company or from outside sources. Maintenance may include periodic tuning, cleaning, and on-site monitoring of the system. The most common type of maintenance agreement, however, is for service calls after a problem develops. Regardless of the specific nature of the maintenance agreement or procedure, network supervisors must be familiar with its terms. This maintenance information includes a list of appropriate people to call with increasing levels of technical expertise as required.

VI

Security and Reliability

Includes

Security

Risk Analysis and Reliability

Data Protection

Viruses and Inoculations

Disaster Recovery

21

Security

Security for microcomputer LANs has increased in importance, and more vendors are supplying LAN security systems. As end users become more aware of the value of the vast amounts of data being accumulated and of the need to protect that data, more users adopt such systems.

Newspapers carry stories almost every week about some computer network being penetrated, for financial gain or as a prank. Most of these break-ins involve large corporate networks and wide area networks. As local area networks proliferate and tap into national and international data communications systems, these local networks also will become targets.

Companies that do sensitive work, such as those with defense contracts, are often heavily involved in data security. Other companies may be aware only of the threat but not of their own vulnerability. Most analysts agree that businesses and institutions, such as schools, will have to suffer loss through theft or vandalism before they establish measures to protect their data.

Understanding the Need for Network Security

All the features of electromagnetic media desirable to a user also make this media vulnerable to theft and damage. Information stored on disk is easily copied, easily altered, and easily erased. As larger amounts of critical data are stored in this way, the significance of the problem grows.

A stand-alone personal computer is easy to secure. You simply put your disks in a safe, and store your computer in a locked closet. When you attach that computer to a network of computers, however, security becomes more complicated. Even a "local" network probably spreads through several offices, with connecting cables running in ceilings and floors and in halls and basements.

A thief or vandal can tap into any one of a dozen or more spots on the network, many of which are secluded from normal observation. Tapping into the network from some hidden spot on the cable, however, usually is not necessary. A person can simply log onto a convenient PC and steal or damage data at will. Unfortunately, the easier a system is to use, the easier the system is to misuse.

Like any other kind of insurance, data security involves trade-offs. You must weigh the cost of the potential loss against the cost of protection as well as any inconvenience the security measures may cause.

Quantifying the Risk

Before you can realistically decide how much time and money to invest in data security, you must analyze and quantify the risk. Risk analysis has been elevated to a precise discipline. For the purposes of this book, however, you do not need to examine formulas or other exact methods of quantifying every risk associated with networked data. You can look briefly at some of the elements of risk analysis. Risk analysis can help you to develop a preliminary description of your data's value and potential for loss.

The first thing to do in planning your data security program is to put a value on the data you are going to protect. You need to determine two values, in dollars, for the information stored in your data system. One value is the cost of re-creating the data; the other is the value of lost business if a competitor should gain access to your data. These two figures should be easy to obtain or at least to estimate. Many smaller companies have never considered the potential loss of their stored data. If nothing else, such an appraisal should encourage the use of data backup and the insistence on serious password-security procedures.

Next, you should identify any possible threats to your data. If your data has little or no monetary value to a competitor, then you probably have little risk of theft. On the other hand, the value of your data to a competitor may be great, with the risk of theft proportionally high.

The physical volume of valuable data is another element to consider. If the volume and diversity of the data are extensive, the chance of a total loss by theft is reduced. A related calculation is the frequency of potential thefts. This figure can be difficult to predict unless you have compiled a history of losses over some period of time. Law enforcement agencies and some trade associations keep extensive records of thefts, defined by type of business, kind of penetration, and value of loss. Contacting these groups may turn up sufficient data to enable you to make an intelligent prediction of risk. In addition, you should make a detailed study of any active attacks on your data so that you can estimate the cost of countering a similar attack.

Vandalism is another threat, possibly more serious than theft because of the greater frequency of vandalism. A discontented employee may decide to "get even" by destroying or altering important files, or an act of vandalism may be done as a prank or game, just to see whether it is possible.

After you calculate the value of your data and the types of risks, the final element in risk analysis is the data's vulnerability. Remote access is one factor that causes data to become more available and more vulnerable. When people can access your network remotely, the potential for loss increases.

Locally, the risk to data goes up when the network's contents are generally known. The capability to see those contents (for example, files, servers, and other resources) is controlled partially by the operating system and partially by the site administration. Using the user-profile system, the administrator limits the user's view of the network so that the user sees only resources he is authorized to use. The other resources are hidden to preclude intentional or unintentional tampering.

Making a risk analysis enables you to answer many questions about where risks are greatest and how much money and procedural inconveniences are necessary to thwart these threats. You then should consider steps to building a secure data network.

Establishing Levels of Security

You cannot have 100 percent security. With enough skill and enough time to complete the job, a perpetrator can defeat any security measure. You cannot do much about the skill of a would-be thief, but you can make time work for you. If you can make certain that a break-in will be a time-consuming project for a thief, you have gone a long way in protecting your data. Therefore, all serious security systems are layered with not one but several security measures. For a local area network, the following strategies should be considered:

1. Physical security
2. User identification
3. Encryption
4. The diskless PC
5. Protection against cable radiation
6. Call-back security

Ensuring Physical Security

Data security can take many forms. The simplest is physical security, which may be a lock on the computer or a guard at the door. With physical security, a would-be thief must attack and defeat your security measures before becoming a threat to the data.

Locks can set up barriers anywhere from the back door to the office to the computer itself. Key locks now are provided for IBM PC ATs and most compatibles. The lock interrupts the power to the display and keyboard but enables the terminal to remain on-line. Turning the key powers up the user interfaces; the key cannot be removed while the system is on. This kind of physical security soon will be available for personal computers, especially networked PCs.

An alarm system works in partnership with your physical security measures. Locking devices are designed to increase the time needed for penetration. Alarms put an effective limit on the amount of time available. Professional criminals do not run just because they hear an alarm or think that they have tripped a silent alarm. Most know precisely how much time they have before the police arrive. If a thief cannot get through the security system's physical barriers in the time available, then the criminal will abandon the effort.

Locks and alarms can be part of effective security and provide excellent protection against outsiders, but these protections may be of little value against employees.

Requiring User Identification

Several techniques can be used to restrict access to authorized users. All these techniques are based on some kind of identification: personal, such as ID badge; key word, such as a log-in name and password; or key number.

Personal Identification

On most networks the first line of security is personal identification. You physically recognize people who are authorized to be in your office, sitting at a PC. A local area network presents some additional security problems because of its dispersed nature and because many people have access to the network. Remote access through modems and telephone lines is used widely on LANs, which makes dispersion essentially infinite, and dispersion thwarts personal identification, one of the best types of security systems. With remote access this kind of identification is impossible.

Badges and personal recognition, therefore, may not be successful in large companies where everyone is not personally known. In a company with many employees, a counterfeit badge may in fact be all that is necessary to penetrate a security system based solely on identification. Companies must rely on passwords and classified access schemes to protect data.

Passwords

Password security adds no cost to the network and is potentially a useful security measure. After logging onto the network, the user must type a password. Theoretically, unauthorized access is prevented, but the password system often is misused and ineffective.

Passwords usually are chosen because they are easily remembered. This fact also makes them easily guessed. Common assignments include first name for the log-in name, and last name or title for password. The value of passwords is further diluted when employees give their passwords to others in the organization. A password often is given out because another employee needs to read a particular file or to perform some task for an absent employee.

You can improve password protection through systematized procedures and more sophisticated operating system password utilities. Passwords should be assigned by a network manager, not by the individual. This assignment method reduces the likelihood that someone will identify the password in half a dozen guesses. Many network operating systems have a password utility that enables authorized users to change their own passwords. Such a utility should be deleted from all users' directories and given only to the network supervisor.

Over time, passwords will become generally known, particularly within a small office or department. This decaying security can be stopped by periodically issuing new passwords, for example, every month. One additional advantage of changing passwords regularly is that employees will take more seriously the password system and the subject of security.

Log-In Security

The network operating system should be designed to thwart attempts to break into the system. For one thing, the password should not be "echoed" back to the screen when the user types the password during log-in. The system should enable a user to attempt a log-in no more than three times. After that, the system should temporarily invalidate the log-in name and notify the network supervisor of a failed log-in. An audit trail also can be provided to record the number of password attempts from a given user or station. The presence of the audit trail utility that monitors the password system is a deterrent in itself, especially to malicious or casual vandals.

A sophisticated thief, however, can collect log-in routines and passwords as they are entered, often simply by tapping into the network. The network operating system can be enhanced to make this activity more difficult for the thief. Passwords can be encrypted at the workstation and decrypted at the central processor so that the data on the cable is unusable through a tap.

Encrypting Data

Encryption is the process of changing intelligible data into unintelligible data; *decryption* reverses the process. For most local area networks, data encryption is used only when the security threat is substantial.

Ensuring that data is secure in a network environment is more difficult than ensuring the security of physical documents. Typically, data in a network is held in a common storage facility, and anyone authorized to use the central storage has the potential to access classified files. The best solution to this potential problem is to store the data in an encrypted form. Then, any unauthorized person accessing the file cannot read its contents.

Encryption techniques cover a broad range, from simple encryption that guards against accidental disclosure, to sophisticated methods that protect against all but the highly trained criminal who has an in-depth knowledge of cryptanalysis and considerable deciphering equipment. Most encryption schemes are based on mathematical operations that are "computationally unfeasible." These schemes are based on prime numbers which are so large that even the computational power of a mainframe computer cannot break the code within a practical time period. Implementing encryption protection usually means that you purchase an encryption software and/or hardware package and process your data through the package to encrypt and decrypt.

Two primary types of encryption exist: link and end-to-end. *Link encryption* is used to make data unreadable while on a point-to-point link, such as between two PCs. Link encryption prevents the casual reading of data.

End-to-end encryption protects data anywhere on the system. This type of encryption corresponds to Layer 4 (the Transport Layer) in the OSI Reference Model. Because Layer 4 is end-to-end, encryption here can provide protection to any number of communications links or intermediate networks.

Encryption Keys

Encryption key systems commonly are found on dial-up networks but also are available on LANs. A *key* is essentially a formula for coding and decoding a message. Keys are carefully distributed to authorized users. In fact, the security of the distribution channel for keys often establishes the security level of a system.

Such a system of secret keys is difficult and expensive to maintain, especially as the number of participants increases. To overcome these disadvantages, a new key called a "public key" was devised. This technology now is available from many sources. Public keys may be published openly, and they permit almost any individual to use a public key to code and send a message to another person. To decode the message, however, the receiver must use a secret key. A secret key consists of two prime numbers that are not published.

One other application of public keys is to authenticate messages. You can use your secret key to encrypt and send a message to a second person. That person then uses your public key to decode the message. If your public key decodes an encoded message sent by you, then proof has been provided that you did send the message. In other words, the public key is an electronic signature.

All keys are factorable and therefore limited in their level of security. Over the last few years, a debate has been going on about how complex a key should be. Generally, any encryption system provides file privacy against casual perusal. Encryption systems, however, can go far beyond providing file privacy. The Data Encryption Standard (DES) is an encryption system designed by IBM and adopted by the National Bureau of Standards in 1977. Using an encryption system that conforms to the DES standard generally is considered sufficient protection against unauthorized access. Most criminals and vandals are unable to break into a communications system and steal or alter data that has been encrypted according to the DES standard. With the largest and fastest computers available today, however, DES encryption schemes probably are breakable.

On-Line Coders

The easiest measure to take for LAN security is to attach an encryption device at either end of a communications link. Several companies make such devices and can modify them for specific applications. After the devices are installed, the system is fully transparent to the user. With each person using an encryption box, the message sent between parties is encrypted while on the line.

Another way to set up a system is to place an encryption box between each PC and the network. Then, all the data that goes out on the network and all data stored on the hard disk is encrypted. Ideally, the device can be modified and tuned to provide the speed and security needed. If necessary, a public key system also can be built in.

To get an idea of how such a security system might work, suppose that you have three groups on a network: administration, accounting, and sales. All the data on the network can be encrypted. The administrator can read everything, but accounting and sales can read only their respective files. Each user can optionally encrypt the data. With each transmission, the encryption device asks the user whether to transmit in the clear or with encryption. The administrator's device also asks of the administrator, `Which key do you want: admin, accounting, or sales?`

Using a Diskless PC

The power of the PC itself is a potential security threat that you should consider. One of the advantages that the personal computer has over dumb terminals is the PC's local storage capability. Information can be locally manipulated and stored on a PC's floppy disks and then transferred to central storage. From central storage the information can be made available to other users and maintained and backed up properly.

With local storage devices, users can maintain their own backup system, independent of the central system. The degree of autonomy associated with a personal set of data disks is appealing to many users. At the same time, such autonomy creates two threats to data security.

One threat is unintentional. Because two copies of data exist, one on the central disk and one locally, the copies may be updated independently. Eventually, unique data on one version may be lost when the two "copies" are merged.

The other threat is that a local disk drive permits data theft. A person with access to the network and with a local disk drive can copy large amounts of data onto floppy disks in just minutes. The data then can be easily hidden and removed from even reasonably secure buildings.

Most network vendors now provide the capability of booting a local PC workstation from a central server so that diskless PCs can be used on the network. Such machines require full-time networking and permit no local storage. A common reason for using diskless PCs is cost. Because diskless PCs require no local floppy controller or disk drive, the cost of a workstation is reduced. Equally important, however, is the increased security offered by a diskless PC.

Take away the disk drive and you take away the means for stealing the data, but you also reduce the power of the PC. In many instances local storage is preferable so that the PC can be used as a stand-alone workstation in case of a network failure. One answer is to exchange a local floppy drive for a local hard disk. Then, not only does the user have all the benefits of local storage, but local speed and efficiency also improve. No ready way, however, is available to copy or remove data.

Diskless PCs have been hampered by software problems. Many applications programs are designed to run only from a local floppy disk drive. Diagnostics and the operating system itself usually require at least one local drive. Increasingly, however, software vendors are providing some mechanism for their applications packages to be stored on a hard disk and used in a multiuser environment. A company then can make its own decisions about how to configure PCs. Probably the answer will be a variety of configurations to fit particular circumstances.

Protecting against Cable Radiation

Whenever information is transmitted, even through cable, unauthorized persons can potentially intercept that information. The possibility also exists that a vandal can tamper with data or destroy data files.

Several methods are available for protecting data on the cable. The first thing to do is to put the cable out of sight. You should take this step anyway, to prevent damage to the cable and to meet building codes. Security is a secondary benefit. Install cables in protective raceways in areas where penetration is less likely.

A second technique is designed to protect against data interception. A radio signal that is broadcast onto the air waves can easily be intercepted and the information stolen. Such emissions, however, are not limited to broadcasted radio signals. A data cable radiates intelligible signals just as a transmitting antenna does. Simple intercept equipment located near the cable can pick up and record these transmissions. More sophisticated devices can intercept the signals a considerable distance from the cable.

You can eliminate the likelihood of signal interception by using a ***shielded cable***, a cylinder of braided copper wire that encases the intelligence-carrying wires. If one shield does not reduce emissions to satisfactory levels, more shields can be added. Frequently, cable with the necessary electrical characteristics is available in only one version. If additional shielding is needed, special shielding conduit is available that meets government security standards.

Another way to eliminate the cable radiation problem entirely is by using fiber-optic cable. Fiber optics technology uses a glass fiber to carry a beam of light. Information is passed when the light is modulated. With fiber optics, no signal is emitted outside the cable; therefore, data cannot be intercepted. Because fiber-optic cable also is extremely difficult to tap into physically, fiber-optic is ideal for security purposes.

Using Call-Back Security

Throughout this chapter, remote access has been mentioned as a significant threat to data security. Remote workstations are part of many LAN environments, enabling a user to access the network remotely, log into the network, and use the system as if the user were local. Securing this type of access requires special measures.

Call-back security and user management are part of dial-up systems and can be used with remote PC-to-network traffic. With call-back security, when you want to access a computer, you can call into a different number rather than call in directly. You indicate that you want to access the network, and the security device arranges for a call-back to your location. In other words, the system has embedded within battery-supported memory a complete listing for every allowed user. Included in this file is a seven-digit ID number that you must punch in when you want to access the file, a telephone number at which you can be reached, and the host systems to which you are allowed access.

This security device also keeps track of user priorities. If all available lines are busy, the device sets up a queue based on the priority of the user. The device informs the caller regarding queue position. When a line becomes available, the device contacts the user. Therefore, the user never has to get busy signals. The device also keeps accounting information for traffic statistics and bill-backs.

Chapter Summary

Security is needed on most networks. As companies increase their dependency on the network, the need for security also increases. You do not, however, want to make your network as secure as possible, because that level of security also makes it difficult for authorized users to gain access. The best plan is to determine the risk through risk analysis and to implement appropriate security measures.

22

Risk Analysis and Reliability

A user unintentionally reformats a shared disk. A hard disk crashes, destroying the data of eight users. A computer virus attacks a company's data processing system and causes almost total system failure for three days; over 400 employees are effectively out of work while the system is repaired.

These problems and hundreds of other similar problems occur every day among the million-plus LANs in use. The downtime and loss of data that results—even the occurrence itself—could be prevented or minimized in nearly all these cases. The answers are found in the study of network reliability.

Computer use is changing rapidly. In the past, with central computing facilities and host-based systems, the majority of the work done by computers was batch-oriented information storage and retrieval. If an organization's computer was unavailable for 30 minutes a day, the firm usually found the periodic loss an acceptable inconvenience.

Personal computers and LANs are bringing about a revolutionary change in how people use computers. These systems provide uniquely accessible computing resources. The software is easy to use, the PCs provide fast response, and the data is readily available to the user. Because of this accessibility, the systems are increasingly integrated into the operational activity of organizations. People use computers in the minute-by-minute business of doing their jobs, as true extensions of themselves. Reliability is even more critical than in the past and should be built in and maintained on every LAN.

Using Reliability Guidelines

In 1988, more than 60 computer vendors developed and endorsed a set of guidelines for distributed system reliability. These guidelines follow:

Analysis and Planning. Every successful distributed system installation requires site and risk analysis, and creation of a plan for disaster recovery. Analysis and plans must be reviewed periodically.

System Administration. Every reliable distributed system should have an assigned administrator. The training needed by that administrator depends on the unique requirements of the distributed system and on the available resources.

There is a growing need for personnel trained in distributed systems and reliability. Vendors and users must support development of effective training programs to increase the number of trained personnel available in the future.

Power Quality Assurance. Many reliability problems stem from poor electrical power quality. Most of these problems can be prevented easily and economically. Distributed computer systems require clean, computer-grade power, free from the transients, spikes, brownouts, and blackouts typical of commercial-grade power.

Servers, communications components, and critical workstations should have battery backup power, and may benefit from intelligent power protection. All network components need conditioned power. The level of protection to be implemented depends on each organization's software and hardware reliability requirements.

Data Disaster Recovery Planning. Data backup and off-site storage should be an assigned task with continuing management supervision. Backup copies of all applications programs should be stored off-site, in their original and user-configured versions. At a minimum, you should conduct incremental daily backups of system data, with complete backups of system disks performed at a frequency determined by the criticality of the data and applications.

The convenience of automated backup can pay off in added reliability. Established procedures for test and verification of backup data also are necessary.

Redundancy. All hardware and software components are subject to periodic failure. These failures can be the result of component deterioration, environmental conditions, or misuse. Some components are not critical to system operations and some can be easily replaced. However, if a component's failure will cause unacceptable downtime, then an identical, redundant component should be integrated into the system. That redundant component provides a system feature known as fault tolerance, taking over and continuing normal operations in the event of a primary component failure.

Risk analysis will help determine the need for fault tolerance. Risk analysis also permits identification of particular system components where fault tolerance is a cost-effective reliability strategy.

For systems where downtime is not a critical issue, a policy for purchase and inventory of redundant components can provide cost-effective system reliability. Redundancy can be as simple as having tested spare cables available to be used in case of a wiring defect, or having a spare workstation, disk drive, or memory card available for installation in case of a component failure.

Management Tools. Reliable hardware components alone do not guarantee a reliable system. Equally necessary are software utilities to manage the hardware. Easy-to-use software tools for system management make local management easier for administrators, and are absolutely necessary for remote management. These utilities monitor system health, provide warnings of potential problems, and help managers locate problems quickly.

Systems that grow to require large subnetworks, or systems that are geographically dispersed, cannot be economically staffed with specialists at every site. Many important network management functions can be accomplished remotely with hardware and software tools. A systems approach to using tools such as these can greatly enhance reliability.

Distributed System Management. The ease of installation and usability of distributed systems have been responsible for the rise of the myth that these dispersed systems, especially systems of PCs, do not need management. In fact, every system with resources shared by multiple users requires management. Computing is changing from several professionals managing a single computer to single professionals managing multiple computers in distributed environments. In these new environments, innovative management is essential.

A focus on system reliability is mandatory in today's computing environments. Reliable systems pay off in more effective use of resources, more efficient business operation, and more satisfied customers. System reliability in distributed environments requires a combination of hardware, software, and management commitment.

Table 22.1 lists the corporations who have endorsed the 1988 guidelines.

Table 22.1
Corporate Endorsements for the 1988 Guidelines

Advanced Digital Corp.	Expandable Software
Advanced Digital Information Corp.	Gateway Communications
Aldridge Co.	Gazelle Systems
Alloy	Harris Lanier
Alpha Technologies	Integrity Software
Alywa Computer Corp.	LAN Group International
American Power Conversion	LANDA
Archive	Localnet Communications
Artisoft	Macola
Banyan	Microsoft
Best Power Technology	NetLine
BIIC Data Networks	Network Compatibility Group
Blue Lance	

Brightwork Development
Business Works
California Software Products
Citizen America
Conetic Systems
Connect Computer
Construction Data Control
Convergent Technology
Core International
Corvus International
Datapoint
DCA/10 Net
Delta Technology International
DNA Networks
DSC-Nestar Systems
Easynet
Elgar
Everex Systems
Exebyte
Network General
Northern Telecom
Novell, Inc.
Ontrack Computer Systems
Orchid Technology
Precision Standard Time
Progress Software
Proteon
Quadram
Quarterdeck
Racet Computers
Salemaker Software
Standard Microsystems
SynOptics Communications
TDT Group
Torus Systems Limited
Unisys
Univation
WordPerfect

Endorse with Additions for Consideration

3Com

IIT Research Institute

Endorse with Recommendations for Future Enhancement

Thomas Conrad

These guidelines provide a good foundation for system reliability. Among the important concepts in the guidelines is, first, that reliability is best achieved through the system approach. Individual strategies, such as tape backup systems and fault tolerant disks, are only partial solutions. A complete set of reliability enhancements is needed. The reliable system includes power conditioning, a backup device with removable media, redundant systems as required, system management utilities, and a system administrator to monitor the health of the network.

A second concept presented by the guidelines is that distributed system reliability is characterized by issues other than shared reliability. Different, often new, sets of reliable solutions are needed for distributed processing.

A third concept is that, although not every system has the same degree of need for reliability, system planning should always consider reliability. This idea has led to the recommendation that risk analysis, like site analysis, is a necessary part of designing LANs.

Performing Risk Analysis

Risk analysis is discussed in Chapter 21, "Security." For this discussion, risk analysis is used to examine risks associated with *unintentional* threats to the system.

Determining the Effects of Component Failures

When a failure occurs on the network, the results vary, depending on the type of application and the component that fails. The initial phase of risk analysis requires a definition of the application to determine the effect of an individual component failure.

A file server failure is one of the most serious types of network failures. The system, the whole network, ceases to function until the server can be restarted. Downtime is always a consequence of server failure. The seriousness of that downtime depends on the type of application. Frequently a server failure also causes loss of data. Again, the probability and severity of data loss depends on the application.

Failures of the shared hard disk are a catastrophe for nearly all networks and applications. Data stored on the disk is lost and must be rebuilt with a backup copy previously made. In the worst case, where a backup does not exist, the data must be rebuilt from the ground up—one keystroke at a time.

A workstation failure is often an isolated problem affecting only the user. The user may be able to reboot the system and continue with no more than the loss of memory-resident data entered since the last time the user saved to disk. The failure becomes more serious if the user is working under a time constraint and is finishing work for others to use.

If the workstation failure is so severe that the workstation needs repair, the user may be able to move to another workstation temporarily. The broken workstation, however, may have special characteristics, such as high-resolution graphics. If no other machine with similar characteristics is available, not only the workstation, but its user, may be "down" while the workstation is repaired.

The failure of peripherals and other network resources each have their own degree of seriousness. As a first step in risk analysis, each component on the network should be listed with a notation as to the probable impact of its failure and the plan of action should that failure occur. Some typical components and the impact of their failure are listed in table 22.2.

Table 22.2
Impact of Component Failure

Component	*Impact of Component Failure on System*
Server	Severe; downtime and possible loss of data
Disk subsystem	Severe; downtime and probable loss of data
Workstation (standard)	Minimal; no system downtime or data loss
Workstation (with special features)	Serious; downtime for application
Printer (dot-matrix)	Minimal; not required for application
Printer (laser)	Serious; downtime for application
Network cable system	Severe; system downtime

This list is based on an application that requires one special workstation (graphics capability) and a laser printer. If either of these machines fails, the application cannot continue until the fault is repaired. This example illustrates an important step in reliability planning.

Estimating the Cost of a System Failure

The next step in risk analysis is estimation of the cost of a single system failure. For this phase, a *system failure* is one that causes downtime and data loss. A system failure can be caused by a hardware failure, such as a disk crash. An application failure can have similar results. A user error that corrupts a shared database or reformats the shared disk is another example.

For this phase, you can use the Novell Risk Worksheet, shown in table 22.3. The worksheet has four major sections. The first three sections deal with establishing the cost of a single failure. In the fourth section, you calculate the anticipated number of failures for a given configuration, computing the failure-associated cost of the specified configuration. Using this worksheet, you can decide whether new reliability enhancements are cost-justified.

Cost of Lost Data

The first cost figure to calculate is the cost of the data lost because of the failure. This figure is not an estimate of the cost to develop the data, but an estimate of the value of the data to the business—specifically, how much revenue the data was expected to produce. You need to determine the amount of lost data and the recoverability of that data.

As with all other areas, the potential for loss should be minimized as part of the planning process. The daily use of a backup device can limit your loss to material entered since the last time the data was copied and stored in the removable backup system.

Research indicates that nearly 50 percent of all backup device users back up daily. Slightly less than 50 percent back up weekly. The remainder of backup users back up infrequently, and an estimated 70 percent of all network users have no backup device at all. These statistics suggest that the majority of systems users are vulnerable to nearly open-ended financial loss due to a system failure. As part of risk analysis, a daily, automated backup system should be instituted,

Table 22.3
Novell Risk Worksheet

Lost data		$______
Factors:	Frequency of backup Number of users Recoverability Type of application	
Personnel downtime		$______
Factors:	Type of failure Number of users Mean time to repair	
Company image		$______
Factors:	Alternate suppliers Number of failures (yearly) Length of downtime	
Anticipated losses (3 years)		$______
Factors:	Components Size of system Applications/end-users	
Total anticipated loss (3 years)		$______

complete with "grandfathered" storage. (For more information, see Chapter 23, "Data Protection.") Otherwise, the full impact of a system failure is difficult—or maybe impossible—to estimate.

Because the recoverability of data is dependent on the type of application, you need to note the specific application on the risk analysis worksheet. Data in an inventory system, for example, is 100 percent recoverable. You can always go back to the physical inventory and count items. On the other hand, data in an order-entry system may be only partially recoverable. For example, if the application receives telephone orders from a consumer customer base, many lost orders cannot be replaced. The owner or manager of the system should be able to estimate the percentage of recoverability of these orders. As the percentage declines, the value of the lost data increases proportionately.

The type of application also can determine the importance of the data to the business. If the application is a strategic one on which the entire business depends, then the value is greater than if the application were a support application that might perform administrative or organizational functions. The loss of such a support application and its data for a day or two usually does not hinder operations severely.

Suppose that a certain accounting firm with a gross income of $3 million a year has 25 employees, each working an eight-hour day. Because a daily backup is performed, eight hours worth of data is potentially at risk. The type of application is an accounting application. Because the application uses data stored in various other databases, the data in the accounting application is 100 percent recoverable.

After this information has been determined, you can calculate the cost of lost data. Divide the gross revenue by the number of employees to determine how much each employee is expected to produce for the company annually. In this case $3 million divided by 25 is $120,000. Then divide $120,000 by 2,000 hours (8 hours multiplied by 25 employees) to determine the hourly production. The result is $60 per hour.

Suppose that 14 people are using the accounting application. Multiply $60 by 14, and multiply the result ($840) by 8 hours. The result is $6,720. This figure says that the lost data had a specific value. Yes, the data can be recovered, but that 8 hours of production was lost, and its value was $6,720.

Cost of Personnel Downtime

The next section in the risk worksheet is personnel downtime. This cost figure is the hourly wage of the people who must wait while the system is repaired. The factors in this calculation are the type of failure, the number of users, the hourly wage of those users, and the mean time to repair (MTTR).

Suppose that the type of failure is a disk crash. The number of users is 14, each of whom earn $15 an hour. The MTTR is one day; in other words, getting the system back on-line after a disk crash requires one full workday. You calculate the cost of personnel downtime by multiplying the hourly wage by the number of hours and multiplying that figure by the number of employees using the application: $15 × 8 = $120; $120 × 14 = $1,680. The cost of personnel downtime for this failure is therefore $1,680.

Cost of Lost Image

Company imagc, the third section in the risk worksheet, is often one of the most difficult items to quantify. Defined as the willingness of customers to deal with a particular company, *company image* has a direct impact on anticipated gross receipts. Most people agree that reliability affects people's willingness to deal with a company; the less reliable a company is, the less customers the company has. How do you determine the cost to image (and reduced future revenue) that results from a lack of reliability?

The factors that relate to reliability and company image are alternate suppliers, number of failures (per year), and length of downtime.

If a company has one or more aggressive competitors who can provide similar products or services, then poor reliability probably will persuade many customers to go to a competitor. If a company's products and services are unique, customers may have to remain with the company even though the company is unreliable.

The number of failures within a given time (such as a year) and the length of downtime obviously also affect the image. For example, if you are a regular customer of a company, and that company loses your records or cannot deliver as promised, your opinion of the company is altered by how often the problem occurs and how long you must wait for the problem to be fixed.

The owner or manager of a company may have a good idea of just what effect a day's downtime has on company image, and certainly should be able to determine the stability of the company's customer base. One way to begin to estimate the cost of a failure (one day's downtime) to company image is by multiplying the gross expected annual revenue by .1 percent. In the previous accounting firm example, the calculation is $3 million multiplied by 0.001, which equals $3,000.

Using the .1 percent figure as a baseline estimate means, in essence, that when a one-day failure occurs, one customer in a thousand decides to go to a competitor. If you order a product from a mail order house and they lose the order, will you continue to patronize that company? If you go to your bank's automatic teller machine (ATM) two or three times in a row and find the ATM out of order, will you think about changing banks? A conservative estimate says that one person in a thousand will decide to change to a competitor when the present company cannot deliver services.

So far, using the example of the $3 million accounting firm, you have estimated the following costs for a one-day failure:

Lost data	$6,720
Personnel downtime	$1,680
Company image	$3,000
Total	$11,400

Several variables contribute to these figures and to the total, but assume that $11,400 is the average cost of a system failure. To be sure that this assumption is correct, after estimating one possible type of failure, go back and estimate the cost of other types of failures, such as a server failure, an application software failure, or a network hardware failure. In general, most of the data remains constant if you are assuming that the failure results in downtime for a specified length, such as a single day, and if you are considering a single network. Other networks almost certainly produce different cost estimates depending on the number of users and the type of application.

Note: The cost of repair is not considered here. Obviously, some failures are more costly to repair than others. In most cases, however, the primary costs in system failure are the impact of that failure on the business.

Number of Anticipated Losses

The last section on the risk worksheet involves computing the number of anticipated losses. The factors that affect this calculation are the types of components in a system, the size of the system, the physical environment, and the users.

Calculating the reliability and predicting the number of failures for a distributed processing network is an emerging capability. Until the late 1980s, most reliability models had focused on single components or perhaps on hardware or software systems independently. Little work had been done on modeling the reliability of a complete system of hardware and software, and almost no formulas existed for modeling the reliability of a network of distributed intelligent machines. This lack was a significant roadblock in the growth of strategic distributed systems. Professional data processors needed such modeling tools to choose and configure systems properly.

To address this need, the Illinois Institute of Technology Research Institute (IITRI) in Rome, New York, was commissioned by Novell to develop a reliability model for distributed systems. IITRI has pioneered in the development of standards in reliability since its founding in 1936. Among its many activities, IITRI operates the Reliability Analysis Center, a designated U.S. Department of Defense Information Analysis Center. IITRI's research facilities and information data bank are available to government, military, and civilian analysts.

The model that IITRI produced has two basic functions. The IITRI model enables the estimation of failures for a given period of time and provides a means of comparing the reliability of one configuration with an alternative configuration.

A common feature of failure prediction and reliability modeling is a calculation known as the time between failure, usually expressed as a mean (mean time between failure, or MTBF). An MTBF number is an estimate of how long an item may be expected to function properly. (Specifically, MTBF predicts the point in time at which most failures will occur for a large population of like items.) Many manufacturers provide MTBF data on their products, but some do not. If you cannot find the MTBF of a particular product, estimate MTBF based on table 22.4 and your experience or that of your systems integrator or other knowledgeable source.

Table 22.4
Network Component MTBF

Component	*MTBF*
Network server	30,000 hours
Workstation	30,000 hours
Hard disk	20,000 hours
Disk controller	40,000 hours
Cable system	80,000 hours
Network interface card	40,000 hours

Failure estimation is developed by inverting the MTBF. To invert the MTBF, divide the number 1 by the MTBF. Assuming that MTBF is calculated in hours, the inverted MTBF tells you how many failures will occur in one hour. That number usually is a small, not too informative fraction. To make the number more understandable, the failure-per-hour figure usually is multiplied by a suitable number of hours.

For example, suppose that the MTBF for an item is 10,000 hours, and you are interested in estimating how many failures might occur in three years of continuous operation (26,280 hours). To calculate this figure, divide 1 by 10,000. The answer is 0.0001. Then multiply 0.0001 by 26,280 hours. This result is 2.628. In other words, in three years of continuous operation, this item is predicted to fail 2.6 times.

To calculate the number of failures for a set of items (in the case of a network, components in a system), you can add the numbers of failures for all the components. Suppose that one component of a two-component system has an MTBF of 20,000, and the other component has an MTBF of 30,000. To predict total system failures, you must invert the MTBFs, add them, and then multiply the result by a period of time (such as 26,280 hours):

$$[(1/20{,}000) + (1/30{,}000)] \times 26{,}280 =$$
$$[0.00005 + 0.0000333] \times 26{,}280 =$$
$$0.0000833 \times 26{,}280 =$$
2.19 failures

This two-component system is estimated to have 2.19 failures in three years of operation.

You can apply this formula to a typical LAN configuration having a file server, a hard disk system, a network cable system, network adapters, and workstations. The formula for estimating the numbers of failures per hour (FPH) for this system is

F = Sf + HDf + NCf + NAf(n) + Wf(n)

where

F = system FPH
Sf = file server FPH
HDf = hard disk subsystem FPH
NCf = network cable system FPH
NAf(n) = network adapter FPH (times the number of adapters)
Wf(n) = workstation FPH (times the number of workstations)

To use this formula, calculate each FPH individually and then sum them. If the MTBF for a file server is 30,000 hours, you determine the FPH for the server (Sf) by dividing 1 by 30,000. The result is 0.0000333.

A disk subsystem is composed of a hard disk and a disk controller. You must determine the FPH for each component and add the results to find out the FPH of the subsystem. If the MTBF for the hard disk is 20,000 hours and the MTBF for the controller is 40,000 hours, the FPH for the hard disk subsystem (HDf) is determined as follows:

(1/20,000) + (1/40,000) =
0.00005 + 0.000025 =
0.000075

The network cable system might have an MTBF of 80,000 hours. Its FPH (NCf) is calculated by dividing 1 by 80,000, resulting in an answer of 0.0000125.

To find the FPH of the network adapters on the network, first determine the FPH for one adapter and then multiply by the total number of adapters. Suppose that this example network has 14 workstations and 1 file server, each of which has a network adapter. If the MTBF for the adapter is 40,000 hours, the calculation for the FPH of the adapter [NAf(n)] is

(1/40,000)(15) =
(0.000025)(15) =
0.000375

With 14 workstations on the network and each workstation having an MTBF of 30,000 hours, the calculation for Wf(n) is

(1/30,000)(14) =
(0.0000333)(14) =
0.0004666

Now you can add these calculated FPHs to determine the system FPH (F):

0.0000333 + 0.000075 + 0.0000125 + 0.000375 + 0.0004666 =
0.0009624

If you want to find out how many failures to expect from this system in three years of continuous operation (26,280 hours), multiply the system FPH by 26,280. The result is 25 failures, or a failure for every 1,000 hours of operation.

These calculations provide several useful pieces of information. You know approximately how many hardware-related service calls the system will need. You also can take each component and estimate how often that component will fail during the three-year period. For example, the file server with a 0.0000333 FPH will have 0.875 failures in three years. The hard disk subsystem with a 0.000075 FPH will fail 1.971 times in three years. For your 15 network adapters, with a combined FPH of 0.000375, expect 9.855 failures in the 26,280-hour period. Your 14 workstations, with combined FPH of 0.0004666, will fail an estimated 12 times; you might expect one of your 14 workstations to fail about every 2,000 hours of operation.

You can use this information to decide what spare parts might be appropriate. A spare network adapter that costs $200 or $300 probably is a justified purchase, for example. If the success of the application requires that all 14 workstations be on-line, then buying a spare workstation might be a logical decision.

Deciding whether all 14 workstations must function all the time brings up an important issue in risk analysis. The goal of the risk worksheet is to estimate costs related to system downtime and loss of data. For most local area networks, the failure of a single workstation probably does not cause system downtime or data loss. In risk analysis, you should not simply list all the components on the network. Instead, list only those components that will cause system downtime and data loss in the event of a failure.

For many networks, the file server, the hard disk subsystem, the network adapter on the file server, and the cable system are the critical components. If any of them fails, downtime, data loss, or both will certainly occur. To calculate the number of predicted failures for these components alone, first calculate the number of failures for a single network adapter for 26,280 hours:

0.000025 × 26,280 = 0.657 failures

Next, add the predicted failures in 26,280 hours for all the critical components:

File server	0.875
Hard disk subsystem	1.971
File server network adapter	0.657
Network cable system	0.329
Total	3.832 failures

These 3.8 failures in three years of continuous operation are hardware failures with MTBFs based on an ideal environment. Many studies estimate, however, that hardware failure is the cause of less than half of all system failures. (For this sample analysis, assume that hardware failure accounts for half of all system failures. The total number of failures in three years, therefore, would be 7.6.) Three other factors add to the number of failures: software, environment, and end users. Because of the vast differences in software reliability (system and application), environmental factors, and end-user capability, these factors are difficult to estimate without specific knowledge of a particular site.

Notes on the Worksheet Model

After you complete the last section of the worksheet, you multiply the number of anticipated failures (7.6) by the total cost of the loss of data, downtime, and image ($11,400), which you calculated in the other three sections of the worksheet. The result is $86,640.

The risk worksheet provides a formal and reasonably simple way to estimate how much money is at risk for a particular system over a given period of time. Almost anyone can use the worksheet to make an estimate. You should note, however, that the accuracy of the estimate is highly dependent on the knowledge and experience of the analyst and the care with which the worksheet is completed. For example:

- The value of lost data depends, in part, on the relative importance of the application to overall company operations. This value is something that can be accurately estimated only by someone who understands company operations or who is willing to get that information from people who do know.
- One of the factors in personnel downtime is mean time to repair (MTTR), best estimated by a professional systems integrator. MTTR depends on the availability of spares (on-site or through a reseller) and on various performance guarantees included in service contracts.
- Estimating the cost of failure to company image depends on an understanding of the type of business, the competitive marketplace, and the particular company's relationship with its customer base.

In addition, the risk worksheet is a general model. Many variables, or factors, are omitted because they pertain only to certain businesses. An analyst can use this worksheet as a foundation for risk analysis and continue to add other factors until the desired degree of accuracy is obtained. For most situations, however, the factors in this sample risk worksheet provide a sufficiently accurate estimate.

The purpose of risk analysis is to determine a cost justification for reliability enhancement. Spending an amount of money equal to or even close to the cost of the risk simply to protect against that risk is seldom appropriate. The decision to enhance reliability should be based on a determination that downtime and data loss *must* be avoided because of the operational nature of the application. Alternatively, the decision should be based on value: the costs for reliability enhancements fall well within conservative estimates of potential risk.

Estimating System Reliability

Reliability is a familiar word and a desirable quality, similar to such other positive words as dependability, sturdiness, and so forth. Because of the general familiarity with the term, the subject of reliability in system design can be confusing.

In system design, reliability has a meaning similar to the standard usage but much narrower and more precise. *System reliability* is a measurement of the likelihood that a system will continue to function through a given period of time. The formulas used to measure system reliability are based on this specific definition.

Reliability is a relative concept expressed as a percentage. For example, a system with a reliability rating of 40 percent (.40) is more reliable than a system with a rating of 25 percent (.25). A hypothetical, perfect system would have a reliability rating of 100 percent. Of course, no system is reliable to the point at which it will never fail. The closer a system is to 100 percent reliability, however, the more reliable the system is.

Calculating Reliability of Components

You calculate reliability by using the MTBF of a component and the period of time against which reliability is measured. For example, a disk drive might have an MTBF of 20,000 hours. If the system is run 8 hours a day, 250 days a year, then the annual use is 2,000 hours. To calculate the reliability of this disk drive for a year, you use the following calculation:

$$Rdisk = e^{-t/\Theta d}$$

where

Rdisk = reliability of the disk drive
t = period of time
Θd = MTBF of the disk drive
e = the inverse natural logarithm

This formula says that the reliability of the disk drive is equal to the inverse natural log of minus time divided by the MTBF of the disk drive. To compute the formula, replace t with 2,000 and Θd with

20,000. Next, apply the inverse natural log, noted on scientific calculators as *ln*.

$$\text{Rdisk} = e^{-2000/20000}$$
$$\text{Rdisk} = e^{-0.1}$$
$$\text{Rdisk} = 0.9048$$

The result is 0.9048, which says that the reliability of the disk drive is 90 percent. Stated another way, the likelihood that the disk drive will continue to operate properly for 2,000 hours is 90 percent.

The disk drive by itself, however, is only one component of the disk subsystem. The other component is the disk controller. The formula for calculating the reliability of the disk subsystem (disk and controller) is

$$\text{Rdisk} = e^{-[1/\Theta\text{disk} + 1/\Theta\text{c}]\text{t}}$$

If the MTBF of the controller (Oc) is 40,000 hours, the calculation is

$$\text{Rdisk} = e^{-[1/20000 + 1/40000]\text{t}}$$
$$\text{Rdisk} = e^{-0.00005 + 0.000025 \times 2000}$$
$$\text{Rdisk} = e^{-0.15}$$
$$\text{Rdisk} = 0.8607$$

The result is 0.8607, or 86 percent. The disk subsystem is less reliable than the disk drive by itself, which was rated at 90 percent reliable for the same 2,000 hours. The reason that the two components in a subsystem are less reliable than a single component is based on the fundamental concept that as components are added to a system, the number of failures for a given time increases, and the reliability decreases.

The formula for calculating an entire LAN is simply an extension of the formula used for the disk subsystem. The reliability of each component in the system is multiplied by the reliability of the other components.

$$\text{Rlan} = \text{Rfs} \times \text{Rdisk} \times \text{Rnet} \times \text{Rnicn} \times \text{Rwsn} \times \text{Rsw} \times \text{Rhuman} \times \text{Renv}$$

where

Rlan = reliability of the LAN
Rfs = reliability of the file server

Rdisk = reliability of the disk subsystem
Rnet = reliability of the network
Rnicn = reliability of the network adapter
Rwsn = reliability of the workstations
Rsw = reliability of the software
Rhuman = human factors
Renv = environmental factors

The consideration of the reliability of the software, human factors, and the environment is covered later in this chapter (see "Modeling Other Factors"). For now, examine only the reliability of the hardware in the following system:

File server: MTBF 30,000 hours

Rfs = 0.9355

Disk Subsystem:

Reliability 0.8607 (calculated in previous example)

Network cable system: MTBF 80,000 hours

Rnet = 0.9753

Network adapter: MTBF 40,000 hours (number of adapters: 11)

Rnic11 = 0.5769

Workstations: MTBF 30,000 hours (number of workstations: 10)

Rws10 = 0.5234

Using the results of these reliability calculations, you can compute the reliability of the sample LAN (Rlan) with one file server, one disk subsystem, one cable system, 11 network adapters, and 10 workstations:

Rfs × Rdisk × Rnet × Rnic11 × Rws10 =
0.9355 × 0.8607 × 0.9753 × 0.5769 × 0.5234 =
0.2371, or 24 percent

This reliability figure provides a quantified measurement of the reliability of the particular configuration in the example. From this point, you can begin to consider various configuration options and estimate their reliability. You also can fine-tune the model to get more precise ways of determining reliability based on site requirements and design options.

Fine-Tuning the Model

The example of the 10-workstation LAN says that if any component on the LAN fails, the system has failed. In a theoretical sense, this fact is true. In practical operation, however, few LANs are so sensitive. Most LANs can have a workstation fail, a network adapter fail, perhaps some other components fail, and still the remainder of the system continues to function and provide services as usual.

The most costly failure and, in that regard, the most critical component on the LAN is the disk subsystem. If the disk crashes, data is lost and the whole network stops functioning. To recover from a disk failure, a new disk must be purchased and installed; the operating system must be installed; old data still on backup systems must be loaded onto the disk; and the new data that was lost must be re-created. This process usually is expensive in terms of user downtime, inability to service customers, and recovery costs.

In using the risk analysis worksheet, system failure costs are used to determine whether redundant components or other reliability enhancements are cost-justified. You might logically decide that the only critical component on the system in terms of cost is the disk subsystem. When determining system reliability, you should include the disk subsystem only. You can compare the reliability of one disk subsystem with a given MTBF and cost with the reliability of another disk subsystem.

Looking at the disk subsystem only, however, is inadequate in determining the reliability of most LANs. Most of the time, a file server failure, a failure of the network adapter in the server, or a failure of the cable system are all critical to continuous LAN service. If any one of these systems fails, users cannot use the LAN until it is repaired. All these critical components should be used in determining and comparing system reliability. Although this model has looked at basic network components only, other components may be important for particular LANs. A printer, modem, or gateway may be required. Whatever is critical to a given LAN should be included in estimating system reliability. Whatever is not critical should generally be omitted from the calculations.

Comparing various design options is another use of the reliability model. For example, as mentioned previously, increasing the number of components increases the number of failures and decreases the reliability of the system. One design option, then, is to reduce the overall number of components on a particular network configuration.

If a LAN has two file servers, each with a disk subsystem and 20 workstations, dividing the LAN in half and connecting the two new LANs with a bridge might be feasible. Assuming that the data is divided between the two LANs to create a logical as well as a physical division, each LAN would be more reliable than the previous configuration of one large LAN.

In creating this new configuration, however, a new component has been introduced: the bridge. This component increases the risk of failure just because it is an additional component. How much will adding the component increase the risk of failure? Is the new two-LAN configuration with the bridge significantly more reliable than the old single LAN configuration? If the new two-LAN configuration is more reliable, is the increase in reliability sufficient to justify the cost of the bridge?

All these questions can be addressed through reliability analysis. Define a configuration and calculate its reliability. Then define an alternative configuration and calculate its reliability. If the reliability of one system is much greater than the reliability of the other, you probably should choose the more reliable system. If the reliabilities are similar, however, the other issues such as cost and performance might take precedence.

Modeling Other Factors

In the model of system reliability, three important factors still need to be evaluated: the software, human interaction, and the environment. Any one of these elements can cause system failure. In fact, most studies find that these three factors, collectively, are at least as responsible for data loss and downtime as the hardware factors discussed in the preceding section.

In practical terms, however, software, human interaction, and the environment cannot be modeled quantitatively. Each of these factors is a combination of so many variables that each site is unique as to each factor's reliability impact.

For example, software includes applications software and systems software. Considering the many options in applications software and the relative importance of a software package to a particular site, quantifying software reliability by giving it a numerical reliability rating is nearly impossible. Then, too, individual software packages do not permit the kind of MTBF rating system that can be used with hardware. Software that works will not fail, at least in theory. Failures occur because a package is not free of bugs (the procedure did not work in the first place, but you had not yet encountered the problem). Often an unusual combination of events that were unforeseen by the programmer causes the software to fail. Failures also frequently occur because the software was not designed well enough to prevent a user or hardware error from crashing the program. None of these types of failures would be predicted through an MTBF rating system.

Human interaction is perhaps even more difficult to quantify. User training covers everything from untrained to expert. Add to this element the curiosity factor (people try commands just to see what they do) and the malicious vandal factor. Multiply by the number of users. Obviously, you have no practical way to come up with a rating for human interaction.

Environmental factors include temperature, humidity, cleanliness, and power source. Every site has a different balance of these factors. You can assign a rating to a particular site after an in-depth analysis, but most sites choose to correct a problem—in effect, neutralizing the problem—rather than rating it and waiting for the predictable failure.

This last observation suggests a practical way to handle complex or unquantifiable variables in system reliability: neutralize the problem.

Preventing Software Problems

Although you may not be able to rate the probability of failure of a software program easily, many of the points of failure that are likely to result in data loss or downtime are known. For example, because a new program is more likely than a mature program to have bugs, from a reliability standpoint, the choice goes to mature software. If you are going to use new software, you should use other reliability measures, such as frequent backup. If the new software is an applications package, can you rely on the operating system to save data if the applications software crashes? If the new software is a network operating system, you may want to determine whether stand-alone operation is feasible as a temporary measure.

Software failures may result in the corruption of a database. When a database is being updated, if the transaction is terminated abruptly because of a failure, the database index can be corrupted. The result usually is that the database is lost, although rebuilding may be possible through expert programming and time. The applications software or the network operating system should monitor transactions and be capable of preventing this type of data loss.

Another preventable software system failure is a read/write failure occurring because of media deterioration. As magnetic media ages, it loses its capability to retain retrievable information. To protect against losses caused by media deterioration, the system should provide read-after-write verification and bad-block remapping—a general facility for dynamic disk housekeeping. Disk housekeeping may be performed by an operating system or as part of the disk drive subsystem control program.

Applications software and the workstation operating system can enhance reliability. Applications and workstation operating systems, for example, can monitor activity and provide a range of recovery routines. The application can handle many editing functions related to user or other input. In addition, the application can interact with operating system reliability enhancement services. Currently, most of these features are absent from PC software. Reliability features at the software level are mostly found in the network operating system, although the services vary considerably among the different operating systems. Although reliability enhancements would be valuable at other levels, these services in the network operating system are critical because they controls disk management and network security.

The problems just discussed are common and preventable, and the software features that prevent the problems should be the foundation of a checklist. Selecting software that matches a reliability checklist neutralizes, in large measure, the issue of software reliability. The checklist for software reliability includes the following:

- ❑ Disk cleanup and recovery
- ❑ Transaction monitoring and recovery
- ❑ Automatic reconfiguration
- ❑ Automatic archive/backup function
- ❑ System monitoring with alert capability
- ❑ User profiles
- ❑ Data profiles

Disk media deterioration is almost inevitable over time and, depending on the location of the bad disk blocks, can cause lost data or loss of the entire disk. *Disk cleanup and recovery* is a system of monitoring the disk, marking bad blocks as inactive, and generally preventing data loss from partial deterioration of the media. This function can be handled by the network operating system, the workstation operating system, or even the disk controller's firmware.

Transaction monitoring and recovery is a system for protecting a database from corruption. An entry or update to a database is called a transaction. When transactions occur, the database indexing system also is modified. If something causes the transaction to fail before completion, the indexing system can be corrupted, making the database unusable except through complex and usually unfeasible reconstruction. Transaction monitoring and recovery eliminates this problem by keeping a copy of the information being modified, including the index. If the transaction fails, the existence of backup data enables the database to remain intact, as before the transaction began. This service can be performed by the network operating system or by the application software.

Automatic reconfiguration capability enables the system to re-establish virtual connections that existed before a system failure occurred. This feature reduces the length of downtime and is handled by the network operating system.

Automatic archive/backup function permits a network manager to establish backup procedures that thereafter take place automatically. This function usually is available through a software utility that is not an integral part of the network operating system, but the utility should be written specifically to support the operating system.

System monitoring with alert capability is a diagnostic and maintenance function. No network can be considered reliable (or manageable) without an extensive monitoring and alerting facility. The function is performed as an integral part of the network operating system or through a software utility closely tied to the operating system. (For more information on this function, see Chapter 20, "Maintenance and Diagnostics.")

User profiles enable the manager to define what an individual user can and cannot do within the system. *Data profiles* further define system use: in this case, how specific data can be used. Together these two features can provide the first line of protection against reliability problems caused by human interaction.

Preventing Problems Caused by Human Error

The data loss and downtime caused by human interaction can be neutralized by system planning and by a combination of operating system features and administrative controls. Losses can occur when somebody turns off the power to a file server, drops the hard disk on the floor, flattens or kinks coaxial cable, and so on. The list is infinite for problems caused by physical access. The solution: plan the layout to limit physical access.

Losses can be caused through logical computer access as well as physical access. The reliability threats stem partially from an administrator giving a user access to too much of the system, resources, and commands. Dangers also arise from the operating system's incapability to give necessary access while shielding other key areas. In other words, the administrator may carelessly open the system to the user. The network operating system may offer all-or-nothing access, as impossible to adapt to user needs as adapting to reliability needs.

You can neutralize this problem by using a network operating system that has a broad range of access privileges for the end user and includes access limitations that you can place on particular directories. The way that resources are presented also is important. The standard in modern network operating systems is to create user profiles (see Chapter 21, "Security"). Through user-profile security, the user is shown only those network resources that the individual is authorized to use. Other resources are never seen, reducing the likelihood of the user pushing for unnecessary access privileges or, worse, trying to circumvent the system to access restricted resources.

Protecting against Environmental Threats

To address environmental threats to system reliability, you first need to analyze the present environment. The environment of the network includes nearly everything except for the system itself and its users. Air, temperature, humidity, dust, and dirt are factors that relate to a specific site and can have a significant impact on system reliability. If the air is dirty, the computer poorly ventilated, the room temperature excessive, or the humidity overly high, correcting the problem usually is cheaper than trying to quantify it and waiting for the failures the problem will cause.

When the system is installed, you should measure each of these environmental factors. If the air contains corrosive or other gaseous elements that could harm the system, you need to install air conditioning and a satisfactory filtering system. If you have no choice but to install the LAN in a hostile environment, then you must make the LAN resistant to the environment by adding special covers and filters to the computer equipment and by encasing the cable with appropriate material. If neither approach is practical, keep spares and be prepared to use them.

Excess humidity usually is regulated by air conditioning. Temperature problems often are solved with air conditioning. However, high temperature is frequently caused by factors other than ambient air temperature. If a computer is positioned next to a wall so that the air intake is close, temperatures inside the computer can reach unacceptable levels. The same problem occurs when dust builds up inside a computer, coating the electrical components so that they are no longer properly cooled. Overheating shortens the life span of electrical components and can produce intermittent failures of the components before they fail completely. Cleaning the equipment, making sure that the equipment is well ventilated, and controlling the ambient air temperature are three easy ways of neutralizing a serious potential threat to reliability.

The electricity that keeps the LAN running is one of the most common causes of system failure. All devices that run on electricity are susceptible to fluctuations, but computers are among the most sensitive.

Several types of electrical failure can threaten your system. *Transients*, or spikes, are high voltages that last for a very short duration. *Power surges* also are high voltages, lasting a little longer than transients. At the other extreme are *brownouts*, reduced voltages, and *blackouts*, complete cutoffs of power. Most power supplies have a few of these failures every year. In some locales, where power lines are outside, one or more of these failures occurs during every thunderstorm.

You need two devices to neutralize the problem of power failure. One is a surge suppresser, and the other is an uninterruptible power supply (UPS). A high-quality *surge suppresser* can handle most surges and spikes by filtering out excessive voltages. A surge or spike can damage equipment quickly. To be effective, the surge suppresser should have a response time, or clamping time, of two nanoseconds or less, and should be capable of handling up to 10,000 volts. A fast clamping time or a high-voltage capability alone is not sufficient protection.

Literally every electrical component on the LAN should be protected by a surge suppresser. These devices cost between $50 and $100 but are worth the expense in terms of increased system reliability and decreased maintenance cost.

An *uninterruptible power supply*, or UPS, is a device used to keep critical components operating after a brownout or blackout occurs. Basically three types of UPS are used: the standby power supply, the on-line power supply, and the motor generator.

The *standby power supply* is a device that can be turned on after a power failure, to provide a certain amount of power for a limited period of time. Although typically classed as a UPS, the standby power supply really is not "uninterruptible" because the power switches on after a failure. The computer equipment, therefore, already has shut down, usually with the loss of data and memory-based configuration information (for example, virtual connections). The standby power supply has little applicability for LANs.

The *on-line power supply*, several types of which are available, is a true UPS. Power is fed into the on-line power supply that feeds the computer system. If power fails, the on-line power supply continues to supply power for a limited time. This type of UPS is ideal if the primary goal is to have enough time after a power failure to close files and shut down the system in an orderly manner without loss of data. This type of UPS may supply power for 10 to 20 minutes or more, depending on its size.

The *motor generator* runs on some fuel such as gasoline or diesel and can operate indefinitely. If a system *must* continue to operate without any loss of service, the motor generator is the only choice. In its most basic form, however, the motor generator is a standby power supply; the generator must be started after the power failure. Typically, a motor generator is combined with an on-line power supply. The on-line power supply takes over when the failure occurs, and the motor generator is then started and takes over from the on-line power supply.

The appropriate UPS for most sites is the on-line power supply. Choosing the right capacity—the length of time the UPS can power the system—should be a matter of necessity. Managers should determine how much time is required to shut down a particular application and the supporting system without causing problems. Add some additional time for contingencies, and that figure is the capacity required for the UPS.

Capacity is of course affected by the number and size of devices that must be powered by the UPS. An important rule is that only critical devices should be attached to the UPS. If a printer or a workstation will not damage the application or the system if the unit shuts down because of power loss, then that printer or workstation should not be attached to the UPS. Carelessly attaching extra devices to the UPS reduces its capability to power the system, and may prevent an orderly shutdown.

Considering Cost Factors

After you have developed a plan to neutralize satisfactorily the software, human, and environmental threats to reliability, you can return to focus on the hardware and system design issues. Although the complete model for system reliability includes quantifiable and nonquantifiable risks, as a practical strategy only the quantifiable risks (hardware and design) are calculated. Nonquantifiable risks should be neutralized as far as can be cost-justified.

Neutralizing threats, such as purchasing a UPS to neutralize the threat of power failure, can be expensive. A good UPS may cost several hundred dollars. You may be able to accept that cost easily, but if you need two or three UPSs to go on other critical machines in the system, the cost can become substantial. The only accurate way to justify the expense is to refer to the risk worksheet. The cost of protecting against reliability threats should be significantly less than the losses estimated for an unprotected system.

As noted throughout this chapter, cost-effective reliability control requires that you evaluate every device on the LAN in terms of how the device's operation affects the entire system. UPS selection and use are another instance in which you should apply this information.

Chapter Summary

Most organizations that install LANs are aware of the need to perform a site analysis. At the same time, those organizations also should perform a risk analysis. Risk analysis is the process of estimating the number of potential failures and the total cost of those failures for a given period of time.

In risk analysis, each component of the LAN (for example, workstations, servers, and peripherals) is evaluated as to its importance in system reliability. Components critical to reliability are those that, if they fail, cause loss of data, personnel downtime, and possibly catastrophic failure of the application. (This definition of critical should itself be evaluated for appropriateness to a specific installation.)

The primary elements in risk analysis are lost data, personnel downtime, loss of company image, and total anticipated losses for a given configuration. Quantification of these elements enables you to assign a monetary value to potential risk. After you establish this value, you can measure the cost of reliability enhancements, such as data backup devices and redundant components, against the risk of not having such enhancements.

Certain factors, such as software reliability, human intervention, and the environment, cannot be quantified at a practical level. These factors, however, are typically the biggest cause of system failure. In most cases, the best approach is to neutralize these potential problems with enhancements.

23

Data Protection

Data protection is one of the least appealing of all computing activities. Data protection is extra work, involves cost with no immediate return, and is redundant.

Fortunately, data protection technology has advanced a great deal recently. A properly designed data-protection system can be painless and effective. The right protection system can even enhance normal operations.

Before you examine these advanced techniques and benefits, you probably need to be sold on the need for data protection. Experts often say that people will not get serious about data protection, specifically backup, until they lose a serious amount of data. This chapter, therefore, first examines the ways in which data is lost.

Magnetic data storage is a fundamental part of the efficient, automated office. Freeing the office environment from paper files opened up all kinds of opportunities for increased efficiency. Storing data in the semivolatile medium of magnetic tape, however, also vastly increased the potential for data loss. Now a few keystrokes can wipe out hours or years of accumulated work. For example, you may type *ERASE D:*.** when you meant to type *ERASE E:*.**, or you may make the wrong assumption about your default drive and use the FORMAT command on the wrong drive.

Data loss due to equipment failure is less frequent. A large midwestern bank had a sprinkler system failure that destroyed an entire department's computer equipment: computers, disks, media, and even the backup tapes. Fortunately, the bank had stored one backup tape in another location off-site. The hardware was replaced, and the system was back on-line in 24 hours. The bank brought the tape in and restored the data. Think about what would have happened if the bank had not had that tape off-site. The system was used to manage bank loans, and without the backup, the department would have had to wait for people to send in their checks, and then would have had to begin the long process of recreating the loan data.

Even if data is replaceable, the cost of replacing data can be substantial. Paying a typist whose hourly wage is $10 per hour to enter 60M of data would cost in excess of $30,000. Therefore, data usually is much more valuable than hardware to a company.

Using Backup Devices

Several types of hardware and media can be used for data backup. These items include backup disks, a secondary hard disk, a disk drive with removable hard disk, and a tape drive with removable cartridge.

Of these choices, the tape drive with removable cartridge often is the best choice (see fig. 23.1). Although procedures for backup are similar for all backup devices, this chapter focuses on tape systems. The benefits of tape backup are as follows:

1. Large tape capacity
2. Inexpensive media
3. Off-site tape storage capability
4. Unlimited system storage

Large tape capacity means that the average hard disk can be backed up with a single tape cartridge. Tape drive manufacturers now are offering systems with tapes that hold up to 256M of data. The benefit of getting everything on a single tape is that nobody has to feed successive tape cartridges to the backup unit, and the backup routine can be run unattended.

How important is unattended backup? Suppose that the backup routine takes an average of 15 minutes a day; not a great deal of time. Most backups, however, are done after hours, involving overtime; taking just 15 minutes each day to backup adds up to

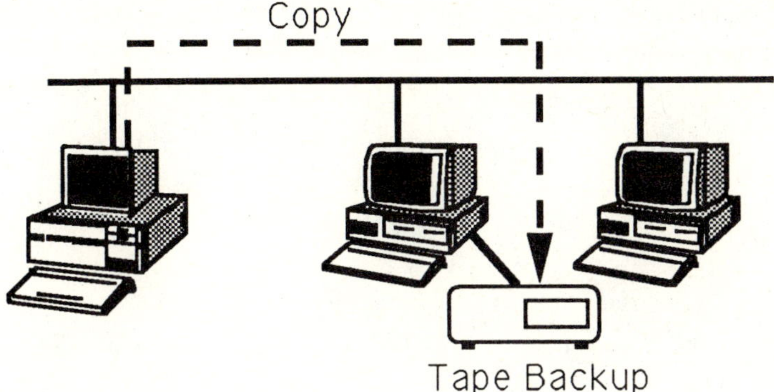

Fig. 23.1. A tape backup device with removable cartridges enables server-based data to be backed up.

approximately 60 hours a year. If the backup can be run unattended, the backup device can be set up in a few minutes during normal working hours.

Tape is the least expensive data-storage medium. Presently, a 60M tape cartridge sells for less than $30. Removable hard disks, in comparison, cost approximately $60 for 20M ($180 for 60M). Disks are in the $1 range for 360K of storage (about $120 for 60M).

Off-site storage is desirable, as demonstrated by the example of the midwestern bank. Backup tapes stored in the same area as the primary data would have been destroyed by the same catastrophe that destroyed the rest of the system.

Unlimited storage capacity in the form of stored tapes is particularly valuable in archiving (a strategy discussed later in this chapter).

One disadvantage of tape is that tape units are slower than other backup systems. If the backup routine is run unattended, however, speed becomes irrelevant.

Selecting a Tape System

To evaluate a tape system, you should first examine the tape cartridge. This cartridge is half the backup device; the other half is the drive itself. Together, they are a system, but because part of the system is removable, precise coordination is difficult.

The variables are the tape's sensitivity, the tape's age, the device's mechanics and their age, the cartridge's manufacturer, the tape's position inside the cartridge, and the alignment of the base plate of the cartridge versus the base plate of the system (warping, bending, and so on).

Tape devices cannot be static; they are not a closed and self-contained unit like most hard disk subsystems. Tape backup devices must adapt to variations in cartridge manufacture, the age of the cartridge, and the age of the recording. With large sites and multiple LANs especially, tapes must be *transportable*; data written on one tape drive should be readable on another tape drive.

On this open medium (the removable cartridge), the system must perform at least minimum realignment and adjustment. Some tape devices are powered by a motor called a stepper motor. A stepper-type motor can realign itself to the position of the tape, performing what is called an *edge seek*. The motor finds the physical location of the bottom edge of the tape and aligns the read/write head accordingly.

The alternative alignment method uses the *servo track*, a block of information recorded on the tape for alignment purposes. With fresh recordings, the servo track system works well. As the recording ages, however, the recording loses its sensitivity, and the drive may not be able to locate the weakened servo track. You can avoid this problem by basing alignment on a physical edge seek.

Automatic gain adjustment is another important feature. The tape drive must align its read electronics to the cartridge. The tape drive must be read through a preformatted key and preformatted data that comes standard on the cartridge, and must adjust itself to handle the sensitivity of the cartridge. Therefore, the tape drive performs a gain adjustment automatically.

A third feature to look for is *automatic retensioning capability*. Tape tension varies according to the length of storage time and tension set during recording or previous reading. If your computer tries to read a poorly tensioned tape, the result can be read errors or a total loss of all data on the tape. The tape should be retensioned before being used.

Correcting Errors

Tape drives should provide a means of error correction. Certain errors are unavoidable on magnetic media and especially on open media such as tape cartridges. (*Open media* refers to devices in which the magnetic media are exposed, rather than completely encased.) The media itself can lose its capability to hold data (a *hard error*), or debris can get on the tape (a *soft error*).

One system of error correction is called *read-after-write verification*. With this system, the data is read after being written initially. If the write is not successful, and the data cannot be read, the write is repeated.

Read-after-write verification usually is sufficient for a hard error (an error caused by faulty media). With tape, however, an estimated 95 percent of all errors are soft errors caused by debris on the tape. Debris does not stay in one place on the tape; debris usually relocates each time you run the tape.

When this kind of soft error is detected and the tape backs up to rewrite the data, the debris is moved to a new location. Rather than solve the problem, the second read merely repositions the debris. Therefore, read-after-write verification tends to be ineffective for soft errors.

A more suitable error-correction scheme for tape cartridges is a system of on-tape backup; a block of data is written once, then written a second time at another location on the tape. If data in the primary location becomes unreadable for any reason, the tape device will go to the secondary, or backup, location and read the duplicate data. The process is automatic and entirely transparent to the end user and requires no user intervention. (This process of on-tape backup is called the *EXCLUSIVE OR* and was developed by 3M in 1980. Since then, the process has been adopted for use in many tape systems.)

Software Considerations

Tape backup systems usually come equipped with software utilities for operation of the system. The best way to test the software is to watch a demonstration and then try the procedure yourself. Copy files to the backup unit, rename the files on the primary hard disk, and then restore the data to the hard disk under its original name. To check the accuracy of the operation, use the DOS compare utility (COMP).

Software should be easy to use, because it often is desirable to have nontechnical people run the backup routine.

A batch file is described in "Performing the Backup Operation" in this chapter. This batch file is a key part of successful data protection. As part of the system evaluation, see whether all parts of the batch file can be implemented on the prospective device and, if so, how difficult the procedure would be.

Tape Backup Systems: Streaming and File-by-File

Two types of tape backup systems are in common use: streaming and file-by-file. *Streaming* tape systems are designed to back up and restore large blocks of data—usually an entire disk drive.

The *file-by-file* method, sometimes called *start-stop*, also can back up large blocks of data but has the advantage of being able to restore individual files. The units go backward and forward, providing random access. These tapes typically are formatted just like a hard disk and can be used like a hard disk, although they run at a slower speed.

Human error causes most data loss, which usually involves only one or two files. Restoring an entire hard disk to recover one file, however, is a waste of time. When you have to restore an entire disk, all users may have to log off the network, which further wastes personnel time.

With a file-by-file tape drive, the end user notifies the supervisor that the file has been lost. The supervisor gets the name of the file and its directory from the end user, then copies the appropriate file from the tape onto the network hard disk. Normal network operation is unaffected.

Performing the Backup Operation

A successful backup operation is one that is extremely easy to perform and requires virtually no attention to operation details. Therefore, backups should be automated through the use of a backup batch routine.

Suppose that it is 5 o'clock in the afternoon, and the supervisor is going to leave the office. Now is the time to run the backup. The supervisor logs onto his workstation, to which the backup device is connected, enters the name of the backup batch file, and leaves. What happens next occurs automatically.

The first routine in the backup process should be to check the condition of the tape. The tape-verify procedure reads the tape and maps bad blocks. This process ensures the quality of the media. The verification may take an extra 30 minutes or more, but because the process is running unattended, the extra time is not a factor.

The next command in the batch file starts a timer that tells the backup when to begin. Running the backup routine after everyone has exited from the system is preferable but not mandatory. The timer usually delays the start of the backup routine until late at night so that everyone is logged off the LAN by the time the backup starts. Most network operating system backup routines skip any open files.

When the backup procedure starts, the program copies files to the backup device, according to specified parameters. The options are to back up all files, to back up all files with a particular extension (DOC or RPT, for example), or to back up files that have been changed since the last backup. Changed files usually are backed up on a daily basis. The whole system is backed up once a week.

After the backup session is completed, the batch file should do a check disk (CHKDSK) of the tape, followed by a compare (COMP). Checking only a sample of the data, such as files with a certain extension, usually is sufficient. In the event of a failure in the tape controller, erroneous data may be written to the tape and probably will affect all the backup files. The compare utility will identify the problem.

Finally, the batch file should direct a log of the backup session to a printer. This hard copy lists any errors that might occur and can be checked quickly in the morning to make sure that the backup is accurate and complete.

If a file is open during backup, the system skips and logs that file as not archived. These files then can be backed up manually. This feature is particularly important for managing a large network on which some files frequently are open.

After the session log is verified, the tape should be labeled and placed in storage.

Several tapes should be used in rotation for the backup system. The system might be based on four tapes, for example, three of which are used for daily backups, and the fourth for a weekly backup. Store your data each day, taking the oldest tape out of the safe to use for the new backup.

If you use three tapes, you will never use the previous day's backup to make the new backup. If a major failure destroyed the primary data, that bad data is copied onto the tape. If the previous day's data is stored safely, however, that data can be used to restore the system.

The weekly full-system backup, or a duplicate of the backup, should be stored off-site because a catastrophe such as a flood or fire could destroy primary and backup data stored at the primary site. Safes usually do not protect against such catastrophes; for example, in a fire, a tape would melt inside most safes.

Normally, a tape can be expected to last for one year. 3M rates tapes as good for 5,000 passes. Many people, however, choose to add an additional safety factor by discarding tapes after six months. Because the data is so valuable, companies choose not to get close to the wear point. Currently, 60M of tape backup costs less than $30, making this precaution cost-effective.

Making Your System Fault Tolerant

Fault tolerance is a another area of data protection that can be used with the backup system. *Fault tolerance* is a scheme based on redundant system components, which prevents data loss or downtime due to the failure of any single component in the system.

Due to their basic architecture, LANs have a high degree of fault tolerance. The failure of an individual workstation does not affect the rest of the LAN, and the failure of the server or other LAN hardware does not prevent the workstation from being used as a stand-alone personal computer.

A good backup procedure, coupled with a LAN's inherent features, reduces the risk of data loss or downtime considerably. In some LANs, this procedure is sufficient protection.

LANs, however, increasingly are used to handle critical data and applications, and in these situations, a higher level of protection is needed. To answer this need, fault-tolerant systems are beginning to be available on some LANs.

Fault tolerance is a system characteristic: if any single part of the fault-tolerant system fails, the system itself can continue to function. You usually can achieve fault tolerance by installing redundant, or backup, components. Then, if the primary component fails, the backup is available to take over.

Novell offers several fault-tolerant products. The product line, called System Fault Tolerant (SFT) NetWare, is divided into three levels of fault tolerance and can be implemented in stages.

Level 1 SFT includes on-disk backup of critical data: specifically, the directory and file-allocation table. The system further provides for dynamic disk monitoring with a read-after-write verification scheme. A read is performed after each write, and if the data is not readable, the data is rewritten to another area of the disk. The first area is marked as bad so that it will not be used again.

In addition to the features of Level 1, Level 2 SFT provides disk mirroring and disk duplexing. (3Com offers a similar product called 3+ Fault Tolerant/Disk Mirroring.) *Disk mirroring* is a scheme that uses two identical hard disks: a *primary disk* and a *mirror-image* disk. When data is written to the primary disk, the data also is written to the mirror-image disk. If the primary disk fails, the mirror image takes over that role without the loss of data or system downtime (see fig. 23.2).

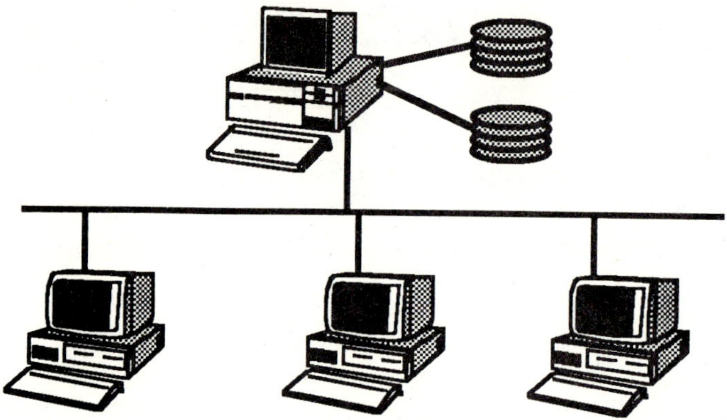

Fig. 23.2. Disk mirroring uses a primary hard disk and a mirror-image disk.

In *disk duplexing*, similar to disk mirroring, the entire disk subsystem—including the disk controller, cable, disk drive unit, and media—is duplicated. If any of the components in the primary system fail, the duplexed system is on-line to keep the system functioning.

Disk duplexing has a beneficial side effect of improving system performance. Read requests go to only one disk subsystem. Simultaneous read requests can be handled in parallel, meaning that two read requests received simultaneously are sent to different drives, the primary and the mirror, to speed execution. This process effectively doubles the bandwidth of the disk channel. Because the disk channel is a primary performance bottleneck in LANs, this increased bandwidth can significantly improve system throughput. Because write operations are duplicated on both disks, no performance advantage occurs with writes. Reads, however, are the principal type of request on most networks.

Level 3 SFT has all the features of Levels 1 and 2 and also supports duplexed network servers. The system is designed so that if one server fails, the other continues to work.

Levels 2 and 3 also include a data-protection scheme called transaction tracking. In a database system, the failure of a single workstation or the software application can destroy your entire database. Suppose that the workstation has initiated a write operation (transaction), during which the database index is updated. If the workstation or the software application fails before the update is completed, the index is corrupted, making the entire database unusable. With *transaction tracking*, a backup of the index is maintained until the entire transaction is completed. If the backup is only partial, the partial transaction is discarded and lost, but the database itself is protected.

The most common type of LAN failure is in the hard disk media. Another common type of failure is in the disk subsystem, because of its electromechanical construction. Probably 95 percent of all failures are media or disk subsystem, and these are covered by Levels 1 and 2. The possibility of network server failure is much more remote, particularly if the network server's power supply is protected by an uninterruptable power supply and a surge suppresser.

Adding Level 3 SFT might reduce the possibility of system failure by another 2 or 3 percentage points. Of course, no system is 100 percent immune to failures.

Fault tolerance should not be considered a replacement for a backup system with removable media. Fault tolerance, for example, cannot protect against operator error. If you mistakenly send the command to erase files, the command will be carried out on the primary and mirror-image disk. Remember that because fault tolerance does not protect against catastrophes such as fires, a backup system with removable media is essential.

The backup system should be regarded as a system requirement. Other types of data protection should be used in addition to the backup system, depending on the particular application.

Saving Hard Disk Space by Archiving Files

Backup systems can be used as on-line archiving devices. With *archiving*, infrequently used data is deleted from the hard disk and stored on tape in an archive library. When you need the files, you can load them back onto the hard disk. This procedure has several advantages, including the reduction of the amount of on-line hard disk space needed.

An archive system usually includes a program that audits the frequency of use for a specific program. When the system finds a program that seldom is used, according to the supervisor's definition—60 days, for example—that program becomes a candidate for archiving.

When a data file is removed from the disk, the file name should be maintained as usual in the hard disk directory. In place of the actual data, however, you should insert a message saying that the file is available from the archive library. You also may include a description of the procedure for loading that file back onto the network from the archive library.

Maintaining archived tapes is similar to maintaining a library. The tapes are numbered and put on a shelf in a suitable storage place. If the material is valuable, you should back up the archive tapes. To perform the backup, run the archive procedure twice before deleting the file.

Archiving also has security advantages. Payroll, for example, can be stored in an archive library instead of on a disk. When used, the payroll is loaded onto the network and, after the work is completed, deleted from the hard disk and put back in the archive library. This procedure adds another layer of security. A person would need access rights to payroll (or know the log-in name and password of a person who has access rights) and access rights to the archived payroll file, to gain access.

Having tape-stored data available on-line is a further enhancement of the archive system. In a network, this practice is supported with a *tape server*, or *archive server*.

Files in the archive server never need to be loaded onto the hard disk; instead, they are accessed directly from the tape device. The drawback is that the tape device runs slower than a hard disk. That disadvantage, however, is overshadowed by the convenience of being able to use the file without going through a restore procedure.

The archive system also functions as the backup device. During the day, the system works as a networked resource; during the night, the system works as a data-protection device. The backup system's role in preventing data loss justifies its cost, but because the system is not used in day-to-day operations, its real value is obscured. People usually resent paying for backup systems (or any other type of insurance) until a disaster occurs. Using the backup system as an archive server, however, makes the system an active operations asset and uses your backup to its fullest potential.

Chapter Summary

Data-protection strategies can effectively prevent data loss. Data loss occurs from many types of failure, and many of these are common. Disk media failure and user error are among the most common.

Strategies used to protect data include backup systems, such as tape backup systems, removable hard disk systems, and even floppy disk systems. The primary characteristic of a good backup system is that the media be removable so that the tapes or disks can be stored off-site where they are less vulnerable to natural disasters, theft, and vandalism.

Fault-tolerant systems also are used to protect data. A fault-tolerant system is characterized by redundant components kept in parallel operation with the primary components. A fault-tolerant system is ready to take over if the primary component fails.

24

Viruses and Inoculations

The issue of viruses in the computer world has become more important today than a year ago. The main reason is that users are now actually suffering from the virus infections.

Viruses have moved out of the realm of theory and into real computer systems. The extent of the problem is hard to gauge, but various studies indicate that viruses are currently affecting between 1 in 1,000 and 1 in 100 sites.

Those sites whose computers have been recently afflicted by viruses can be forgiven for calling themselves unlucky. If a business is aware of the problem and takes no action to protect the computer systems, the organization risks not only financial loss but also the future of the enterprise.

Although computer viruses are being treated with much seriousness, they are in fact only one aspect of a much bigger set of threats—any events, actions, or processes that affect reliability and integrity. Spending a lot of time and effort on anti-virus measures, at the expense of neglecting to address the reliability/integrity issues, is easy to do. The result may be that your business is protected from viruses but highly susceptible to destruction from a simple power failure.

Many existing networks are exposed because of the lack of attention paid to the overall integrity issues. Computer viruses can exploit these weaknesses in system design or simply spread faster and wider because of the increased connectivity.

Understanding the Problems Threatening System Integrity

Data processing has evolved at a staggering pace since the commercial world discovered the business edge that computerization offered. This evolution has resulted in a huge range of hardware, operating software, and applications software as well as architectures that integrate software and hardware into interoperating and intercommunicating data processing systems.

Today's computer systems suffer from three critical system reliability problems: complexity, design, and management.

The level of *complexity* has grown to the point at which no individual can understand a single computer system in total. This difficulty applies to trying just to understand the operating system or the hardware, let alone an intercommunicating network of computer systems.

The lack of effective systems integration in the area of systems integrity and reliability results in computer systems that fundamentally lack robustness, in spite of sophisticated reliability facilities inherent in the computer system.

The lack of *management* at the technical level and at the level of managing users and system organization further weakens the integrity of computer systems. Systems design can simplify management, however, to the point at which poor management is no longer a contributory factor in unreliability.

Design and management problems are so fundamental, and technical, that they are often overlooked. When they are combined with the issue of system complexity, the result is uncontrolled and unreliable systems.

When applied to a stand-alone, single-user computer, the majority of the system may be comprehensible to an individual. The complexity of a stand-alone system is well within the grasp of an individual. Even if the computer is running a multitasking operating system, such as Unix or OS/2, the complexity is manageable.

Design is similarly straightforward. The number of choices that a systems integrator needs to make when assembling a stand-alone system is somewhat restricted. These decisions are focused mainly on the selection and installation of applications rather than management and control facilities.

The issue of how the computer is to be controlled is largely neglected. This fault applies at the information-management level (management is left to the applications) and the corporate level (the individual or department is given the responsibility).

Because a stand-alone, single-user computer is of restricted size, the problems of complexity, design, and management are frequently ignored. The solution to a catastrophe in a stand-alone environment is simply to reconstruct the system.

When a network of computer systems is involved, reconstruction may be impractical, certainly costly, and probably impossible. The only way to construct reliable networks is to adopt a rigorous approach to design supported by thorough, planned systems management and systems auditing.

A network of any kind becomes complex rapidly in direct relationship to its size (see fig. 24.1). This well-understood phenomenon is expressed succinctly by Fink's Fifth Law: "Complexity is the square of the number of components. This means that twins are four times more complex than a single child, and triplets are nine times so."

The key aspect of networks, as the term commonly is used, is that they are dependent on high-speed data links and related technologies. The average computer used in business exists in a network environment just as rich and complex, in spite of the lack of a minicomputer/mainframe host connection. Services such as bulletin boards and mail systems effectively network much larger communities than the majority of high-speed networks. The accessibility may be less, the data transfer rate may be lower, but the complexity is at least as great.

A general description of a network is a group of computers in which client systems are supplied with data, print, system, and communications facilities by server systems. These server systems may be clients of other server systems.

Most sophisticated networks use client/server protocols to support the request/response mechanism. The more sophisticated the

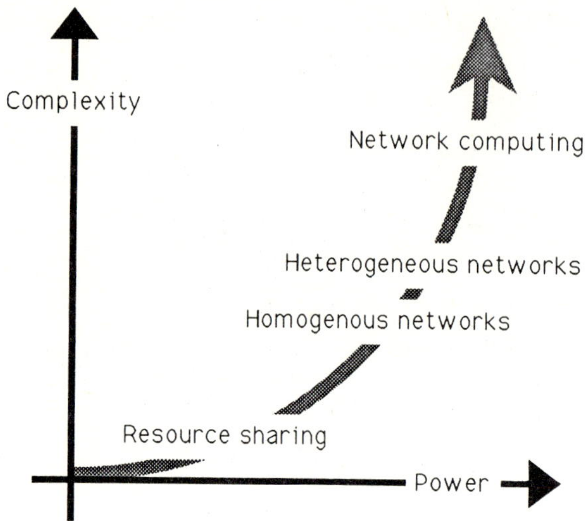

Fig. 24.1. Networks become complex very rapidly in direct relationship to their size.

network, the greater the need for effective security and reliability. Usually, a range of system-level services—such as account control, service access control, alert support, fault tolerance, and redundancy—are supported.

The problem that follows from this rich service environment is the cost and time required to design these services into the implementation and to train the system supervisors and users. The latter is frequently a problem, because training often is considered as an afterthought rather than as an integral part of system design. As a president of the Harvard Business School once said, "If you think knowledge is expensive, try ignorance."

Dealing with Software Problems

Over the last few years, many users have discovered a range of problems that software can cause. These problems stem from two sources: accidental software errors and intentionally rogue programs. The former are caused by random circumstances or human error; the latter are caused by humans specifically creating programs that are intended to act in an undesirable manner.

The next sections detail accidental software errors and intentionally rogue programs. As you will see, the rogue programs are subject to the same problems that create accidental software errors.

Accidental Software Errors

Accidental software errors can be caused by faults in design, incompatible environments, or damaged software and can be difficult to diagnose.

Faults in design, often referred to as *bugs*, are a common problem. These faults can be the result of the program development language. Some languages give the programmer immense freedom in defining a process (a feature of the C language). The complexity and flexibility of the language (for example, with APL) also can cause problems. Wherever complexity exceeds the capacity of the human mind, the opportunity for errors arises.

The size of the program also can cause problems. A small program in assembler can become a huge one if developed in C. As the program source code gets larger, the chance of errors in logic grows exponentially.

Even when a program has been developed, runs successfully, and is in general use, the target operating system may change. The operating system vendors may correct bugs, add new features, or improve existing features. The program that previously ran exactly as intended may, in a new version of the operating system, exhibit new modes of behavior. This new behavior may include actions such as unexpectedly exiting or not saving files in certain situations.

Damaged software, resulting from a change in program code, is a common source of erroneous performance. A change in code can involve addition, deletion, and replacement of code. A frequent cause is other programs accessing the program on disk as if the program file were a data file. For example, program code may be altered if you enable your word processing program to read and save a program file. Many word processors save text data with embedded control characters. By saving the program file, the word processor adds these control characters that effectively corrupt the program.

Another, although less common, source of code damage is caused by other programs overwriting a program that is in the computer's memory.

The biggest problem with program bugs, incompatible environments, and damaged software is that in most cases the program appears to be running correctly. These accidental errors are all difficult to analyze and time-consuming to correct.

Intentionally Rogue Programs

As mentioned previously, intentionally rogue programs are software programs that have been created or modified to do something they should not. These programs are divisible into four categories; logic bombs, Trojan horses, worms, and viruses.

Much has been written on the subject of the *technopath*: one who creates or uses such software. The only conclusion that has been drawn is that you cannot predict who will be the culprit any more than you can predict who will be a shoplifter. Three types of technopaths exist. The first category covers those people whose motives are financial gain. This category can cover activities such as blackmail, fraud, and theft.

The second type of technopath has a motive rooted in revenge. The objective is simply to cause as much damage and inconvenience as possible. This type of behavior has been associated with instances of dismissal and lack of promotion.

The final type of technopath are those people who cause trouble just for fun, with no intention of gain or revenge. This motivation is what created the now infamous "hackers." The perpetrator often is creating such software merely to see whether it can be done. These activities may ultimately cause damage or steal information, if only by accident. This type of technopath has created most of the computer viruses that exist today.

Logic Bombs and Trojan Horses

The *logic bomb* is a section of code intended to carry out a specific impermissible action. This action can be a subtle one, such as a *siphon*—a procedure that transfers money from one account to another in a banking system. This logic bomb ensures that a difficult-to-detect transaction occurs.

A well-known siphon is the collection of rounding-off errors (fractions of cents) that result from calculations of interest for deposit accounts. The rounding-off errors normally are retained by the bank, but the siphon logic bomb diverts the rounding-off errors to another account to be collected in due course.

A more common and unsubtle logic bomb is the much simpler *one-shot bomb*. These bombs execute a task when a cue occurs, such as the date being Friday the 13th or the supervisor having logged onto the system. The task may be a simple deletion of files or other destructive activity but usually is intended to cause damage.

In essence, the logic bomb is a set of codes that somebody attaches to a program. This code is triggered by a cue and then carries out the intended task.

The Trojan horse is similar to the logic bomb but attempts to mimic another program's actions and presentation while carrying out another function. A well-known Trojan horse is a high-quality game with excellent animation—while you play the game, the Trojan horse reformats your hard disk.

Another Trojan horse that has major implications for networks is the *security back door*. This program is a copy of, for example, a log-in program that acts as expected but secretly files away users' log-in data for collection and use by someone else. This same technique might be implemented as a logic bomb.

The difference between a logic bomb and a Trojan horse is that the logic bomb is an included code section in an otherwise "clean" program; the Trojan horse is an emulation of another program and is completely "unclean." A clean program can be, and has been, transformed into a logic bomb. These cases often have been incorrectly referred to as Trojan horses.

Worms and Viruses

Logic bombs and Trojan horses lack the basic attribute of worms and viruses: the capability to replicate themselves. This issue is a key one, because replication ensures that although you may have found one copy of a worm or virus, other copies still may exist.

A *worm* is a program that may perform an action other than replicating but is complete in itself. The worm, therefore, exists within a program file that contains only the worm's code. A worm also may be a Trojan horse. (The worm may appear to be a useful or standard program, doing what the program should do.)

Copies of a worm can be quite easy to detect after you have discovered one copy. The worm program, even if the program renames the copies of itself, usually is of a fixed size and contains sequences of code that act as fingerprints. Note, however, that a worm can evade these detection mechanisms by adding random redundant code blocks to change its size and self encryption to further conceal itself.

The computer *virus*, on the other hand, is a much more subtle program that is hard to detect and complex to remove. Viruses have been known for at least ten years, but only in the last few have they become truly dangerous and common.

The virus differs from the worm in that the virus adds its own code to that of a host program. Several infection strategies have been identified, but only two actually have been seen. These strategies include adding the virus code to the front of the host program (rare), the back of the program (common), or somewhere in the middle (unknown), or finding an area inside the host, such as a buffer, to use instead (also unknown).

The addition of code enables you to detect the virus infection by noting a change in size of the host program—except, theoretically, if the virus overlays a buffer area. You also can detect virus infection by calculating a check sum or cyclic redundancy check (CRC) for the file. These are procedures that perform a calculation on the value of each byte in the program file to produce a value that acts as a fingerprint. By comparing a check sum or CRC value to a previously collected one, you can see whether the program file has been changed.

The possibility of evolving viruses has been the subject of a certain amount of theorizing among computer users. This theory implies that a virus can change its structure according to some random rules and therefore decrease the probability of detection. To date, no such virus has been discovered.

Many people have suggested that given the richness of environments and the number of opportunities that have occurred in the running of systems, computer viruses might have arisen spontaneously. In other words, perhaps code fragments have become corrupted or modified in some way and taken on the viral properties. Various studies have indicated that although this theory is possible, it is highly improbable. As systems get "smarter," the probability may increase, but that development is unlikely within the next decade.

Mainframes and minis are capable of being attacked by viruses, but only a handful of reported cases have occurred. Two theories explain the lack of a virus problem in these types of computer systems. First, getting the resources to develop a virus that can attack the usually superior management of such systems is difficult. Second, those sites affected are reluctant to talk about the infection. Admitting that you have had a virus attack admits that you have experienced a breach of system integrity. This discovery may cause your clients to go elsewhere, particularly if your business is banking.

The truth probably involves a combination of these two theories. Not many technopaths have access and opportunity and can avoid detection. This instance is one in which a system's complexity tends to favor integrity.

Understanding Viruses

The basic operations that characterize a virus follow this sequence:

1. *Invocation:* A file that has been infected by the virus is loaded and begins execution. Control is taken by a virus code at some point, usually before any of the real program code is executed.

2. *Residency check:* This step may be skipped. If the virus is the type that becomes resident in the host operating system, the virus normally checks to see whether it is already resident. If so, the virus does not need to make another copy of itself resident, as that extra copy may make the virus easier to detect and is ultimately pointless. If the virus is resident, the virus code exits (step 6) and

then hands control to the host program or may attempt to initiate the infection of another program file (step 4).

3. *Wait for cue:* The virus usually waits for a cue before performing a function, although some viruses attempt to get action over and done with as soon as possible to decrease the risk of detection. The virus then goes to step 4, 5, or 6, depending on which cue occurs.

4. *Infection:* This phase is when the virus, whether resident or not, accesses other program files and attempts to infect them with a copy of its own code. The virus probably has entered the system attached to a utility or program, usually from a source other than a manufacturer. The virus first checks to see whether the target file is already infected and does not attempt to add its own code if the infection is already present. Note that the virus can detect only if the file has been infected by that particular virus. If another virus already has infected the program file, the new virus probably is not aware of the existing infection. The virus returns to step 3.

5. *Action:* At this phase, the virus does whatever the creator intended it to do. The action or actions may include deleting files, damaging data, displaying messages, or otherwise irritating the user. The virus may now return to step 3 or may exit (step 6). The virus's action may make the computer unusable for one or more reasons, and the flow of control may terminate here.

6. *Exit:* In this step, the virus may hand control to the host program or attempt to clean up first to avoid detection.

The flowchart in figure 24.2 summarizes the majority of the procedures found in computer viruses.

For a computer virus, the main advantage of a network, whether it is a tightly knit, high-speed network or a casual dial-up link, is that the opportunities for replicating and therefore infecting are increased enormously. A network also provides for a much greater rate of infection, and the complexity of network systems effectively masks the existence of a virus. In addition, systems management

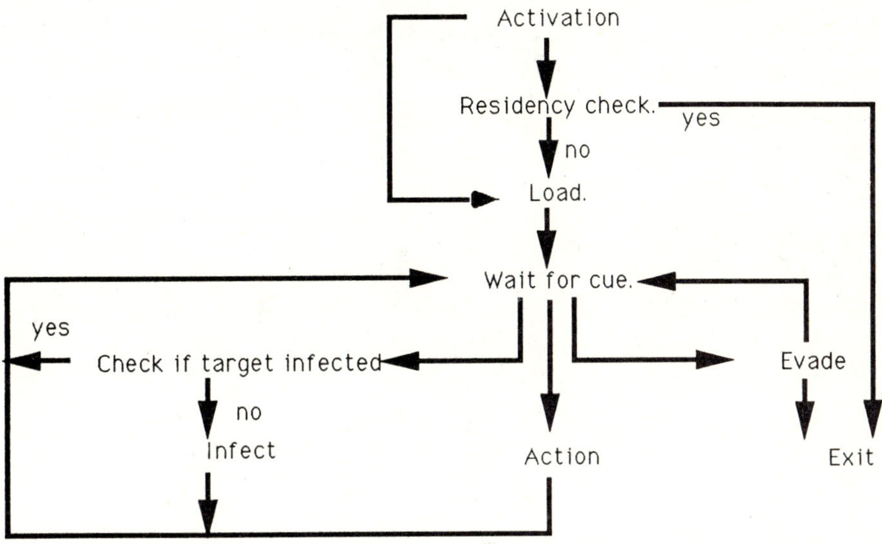

Fig. 24.2. Virus activity summarized.

usually has not been developed with procedures designed for detecting viruses, hackers, and other system threats.

Classifying and Identifying Viruses

Viruses have several attributes by which they may be classified and identified. Behavior is an obvious classification.

Some viruses apparently exist only to replicate, and cause no other apparent problems. This type of virus is a Type A. The obvious problem with this type is that the virus uses system resources. The virus may cause wasted disk space and performance degradation just by existing.

Type B viruses have irritant behavior. The virus may, on cue, display a message or manipulate the screen in some manner, often to show you how clever the author was. The problem that this virus behavior can cause is disruption of services, such as a screen display, simply by acting.

If the virus attempts to cause damage, such as deleting files, then it is a Type C virus. These viruses can perform any action supported by the host operating system and can cause any degree of damage that the system allows. The only limitation on the extent of the damage is the restriction imposed by system facilities.

You should never assume that a virus is anything other than Type C. A virus created in one environment to behave in a specific manner (such as Type A or B behavior) may delete some of the files the virus attempts to infect. A slightly more philosophical reason for looking at viruses as damaging is the fact that all viruses waste system resources—and therefore money.

All the accidental software errors discussed earlier apply to viruses with even greater consequences. You should never assume that viruses are benign or passive. Because of the complexity and often deviousness used in a virus's construction, the "hidden agenda" of the creator is difficult to discover even if you can disassemble the virus.

Most people working in the virus detection and prevention field identify viruses by their length. In addition, many viruses have names that relate to where they were discovered, such as the Italian and Jerusalem viruses.

Knowing How To Stop a Virus

The problem of determining what a virus can do is central to avoiding the virus. The difficulty, however, is that a virus writer needs to obey no rules.

Until recently, any technopath writing a virus for the Apple Macintosh obeyed the Macintosh Developers Guidelines. Therefore, the viruses that appeared were easily identified and, in general, easily removed. The last few months have shown that any technopath interested in the Macintosh market is avoiding these guidelines and producing much more devious viruses.

One topic that has received some press is that of the *anti-virus*, or a virus written to counteract another virus. The anti-virus infects a system and, when the anti-virus detects the fingerprint of the targeted virus, takes steps to prevent the virus from infecting programs—possibly by removing existing infections—and inoculates the system against further attacks from that virus. Using an anti-virus is a dangerous course of action, as accidental program errors may make the anti-virus more dangerous than the original virus.

Inoculation is a practical solution to viruses, but unfortunately can protect you from only viruses that you know about. Inoculation relies on viruses having specific identifiable modes of behavior. Any mode that is not known cannot be prevented. The basic strategy here is to modify potential host program files so that a virus sees them as already infected.

As mentioned earlier in this chapter, the best defense against computer viruses is design and management, including system auditing.

Auditing the System

The most effective method of ensuring that a network is free of and protected against viruses is *system auditing*. Following these audit procedures essentially provides you with a systems quality assurance program.

System auditing involves three objectives:

1. Detect whether a software package is carrying a virus, so that the virus can be prevented from entering and spreading through the network.
2. Protect existing software from infection.
3. Detect infection after the infection occurs.

One major problem exists: system auditing is never going to be 100 percent effective. The reasons for this lack of certainty are partially rooted in the reason that you use application software in the first place—the software performs complex tasks quickly.

Application tasks usually are built with tools built with simpler tools far removed in complexity from the code you execute. The tasks also execute under the control of an operating system, itself a massively complex piece of code. Testing a program to ensure that a specific range of functionality exists requires that you test anything from around 100,000 instructions to 1 or 2 million or more. Because this code usually does not contain a single path, and the creator of the software is unlikely to help you by letting you see the source code, the probability of testing all modes of operation is effectively zero—at least in the time left before the universe ends. You still have not tested the operating system and all the optional bits that most operating systems have.

What is needed is a methodology to help identify the potential dangers inherent in a new software package and assess the risks involved in using that software. The cost of this methodology is the other reason that total certainty is not possible.

Auditing your systems is a time- and money-consuming process. You will have difficulty persuading your managers that, given the current rarity of computer viruses, you need to spend another x days per month and y hours of system downtime to audit for a threat. Management may, however, become more interested after the first major infection at your site. Additionally, systems auditing covers more than viruses. Systems auditing ensures that you have a real picture of your system and requires that you collect information on how that system is constructed and what measurements can be taken to assess integrity.

In short, systems auditing is a key management and organizational strategy that protects systems against viruses and ensures integrity from a range of threats. The key to organizing this mass of information is the site log.

A *site log* is a simple idea. Rather than keep the information about the system in general filing, you reserve a specific document or file for use. Enter all relevant and related data about the system into the log. System design notes, suppliers' meetings, site data, and copies of software registration forms, therefore, are retained. The site log is one of the most powerful tools for diagnosing any problem with your network.

Following the Three-Phase Process

Systems auditing involves three phases: auditing new software, auditing the environment, and auditing existing systems.

The following prescription is not the only way to partition the auditing process. You can perform these processes piece-by-piece when you need them. Alternatively, you can adopt them wholesale as a fundamental systems management strategy. You also can do something midway between the two extremes. Whichever strategy you choose, consistency of approach and strict control are the tactics that will ensure that your auditing is successful.

These basically simple, but unfortunately time-consuming, auditing phases comprise the basic auditing process. You may devise more comprehensive tests that are unique to the local conditions of your user environment (such as the operating system, communications links, special input/output subsystems, and so on).

If you observe any peculiar, unexpected, or undocumented performance of the system or applications software, you need to evaluate the consequences carefully and, if possible, query the supplier. When in doubt, do not use the software. If you are in doubt and do not need the software, throw the software out. If you must keep the program, make sure that it is controlled and not available for use by people who are not aware of the potential failures or other virus-related problems and how to avoid them.

Phase 1: Auditing New Software

You typically acquire new software from one of the following sources:

- ❑ Original authors
- ❑ Commercial supplier
- ❑ Public sources

Each source has associated risks that depend in part on what sort of software you are getting: source, executable, or a combination of the two.

The reliability of supplied software can be graded as follows:

Grade A	The supplier's reputation relies on the software being reliable and of high quality.
Grade B	The supplier can only exercise best efforts in ensuring that the software is virus-free.
Grade C	The software is from suppliers of totally unknown reliability and motives.

Because the supplier is unlikely to grade their own software, the purchaser must determine the grade.

Beware that programs supplied from a highly reputable source may be compromised by the very technology that supports them. Viruses may be embedded in a compiler, in a run-time system that is linked to the compiled code, or in an interpreter.

The greatest danger comes from the vast amount of software supplied by public sources such as bulletin board systems, shareware dealers, and friends. The latter are particularly dubious, because the software programs often are pirated copies of commercial games. However, games are not the only means of transmission in public source supply. Utilities are freely available from all sorts of authors to do everything from displaying file contents to enabling communications to mainframes.

The rule, therefore, should be to acquire software from reputable sources and carefully audit new software to the extent that time, money, and common sense allow. The following steps provide a model of how to audit new software of any grade:

1. Protect the original master disks. Write-protect the original disks, especially the operating system disks, when you first take them out of their package.

2. Copy the original master disks to make a backup master set and working master set. Write-protect the backup master set; then put the original and backup master sets in different storage locations.

   Do not use the original or backup master sets unless you are reconstructing a system from scratch. You therefore ensure that you have a guaranteed untouched master set for reference.

3. Test the software, using the working master set. If possible, test the software in a clean and sealed environment (a network or computer system without links to other systems). A clean environment is one as free from contamination and other software as possible. A sealed environment ensures that, if the software is carrying a virus, your other operational systems are not affected.

This environment also should be completely erasable so that you can erase all storage after testing. (You should even erase the nonvolatile RAM that contains configuration information if you want to be thorough.) Erasing all storage enables the stated functionality to be tested without the software being influenced by other programs or influencing any subsequently tested software.

4. When you have tested the software in this clean environment, you can add other software with which the new program will operate, and then repeat the testing. An interesting aspect of thorough testing is the need to read the software manuals carefully. Although this procedure goes against the grain for many computer professionals, reading the manual can give you a great insight into what the software *should* do rather than what you *think* the software should do.

5. If you can afford it, acquiring and using all the available virus diagnostic tools is highly advised. These tools usually are reasonably priced and perform a useful function. Remember, however, that diagnostic tools are created after a virus has been discovered and can rarely detect a new virus.

6. Record the specifications and parameters. When testing has been completed, the specifications of the software should be recorded for future auditing in phase 3. You should note the following data:

    - ❑ File sizes (program and, where appropriate, data)
    - ❑ File check sums (program and, where appropriate, data)
    - ❑ File creation and modification dates
    - ❑ File owner/creator information, if available
    - ❑ Any other descriptive data
    - ❑ Repeatable performance measurements
    - ❑ Response to test data

The objective is to generate a document that describes the software as completely as possible. This record is vital if you are to have a reference against which to test for integrity.

Phase 2: Environmental Auditing

Auditing the operating environment is a simple exercise in determining what is in the system and what vectors of infection are available.

1. Document the environment. Record the configuration and size of device drivers and other system components (such as system control files), bad block tables, and the operating system itself. Check sums for all components are essential. This procedure again ensures that you have a base from which to assess whether changes have occurred in your system.

2. Back up the system. With a backup, you ensure that if the software becomes infected or develops some other problem you can perform a complete reinstallation as quickly as possible.

   Another important step is to check whether your backup systems work. You may have heard the story of the user who had been assiduously making backups for over a year. When he had a disk crash, he went to his backups only to discover that oxidation on a connector had corrupted the data transmission and ruined every tape. Therefore, he had no backup.

3. Install the software and, if the system supports it, set the attributes of all files that are not altered by normal operations to the minimum set of access rights that can be used.

   No reports are available of viruses that modify network file attributes, but these types of culprits will undoubtedly appear. If your network system allows for execute-only files or access rights set on subdirectories, then use those facilities. A common mistake made with networks is ignoring the security services that exist. Giving every user supervisory access rights is guaranteed to lead to trouble.

4. After installation, check all software and system statistics and parameters for any changes. If any unexpected changes have occurred, start investigating immediately. Refer to the specifications you assessed in phase 1, step 3 for the software and phase 2, step 1. Begin by examining the installation process, checking with the vendor, restoring the system to the uninstalled state, and trying again.

5. Evaluate all virus transmission vectors. Do not allow an unneeded path between files, processes, or machines. This safeguard is particularly important in local area networks. Once again, you need to use the existing security services effectively and apply common-sense principles to the management of your system.

6. Back up the system with the software installed before the system is used for normal operation.

By following phase 2 carefully, you ensure that your system is restorable to its state prior to the software installation, that the software itself is protected to the greatest degree possible, and that the infection vectors are understood and minimized or eradicated.

Phase 3: Auditing a Live System

After a system has been in use, viruses that were not found in the first two phases of auditing or were introduced after those phases start replicating. The purpose of auditing a live system is to attempt to spot irregular conditions, events, or parameters that might indicate the existence of a virus problem.

1. Verify all recorded statistics. Referring to the statistics gathered from phases 2 and 3, look for changes. Research the cause of any change that cannot be accounted for.

   If you discover software that has not been subjected to phase 1 auditing, take immediate action to audit the software and assess all consequences of the use of the program. An optional action is to fire the person who introduced the software. If the unauthorized software is pirated, and particularly if the person who introduced the software to the system obviously knew that the software was pirated, dismissal is strongly recommended as a company policy. The danger to your systems and the basic illegality of the action warrants this drastic measure.

2. Run all virus diagnostic utilities you have. Research all indications that arise before doing anything else with the system.

3. Check transmission vectors. Verify that only the vectors identified in phase 2 exist. If new vectors exist, determine how they were created and what risk they provide. Close or restrict any vector that is not appropriate or needed for current operations.

   If several people have the ability to change the system, you should be keeping a log of all activity that affects the organization of the computers. This log gives you an audit trail that, particularly when you are dealing with many machines or users, can provide clues that may reduce your research time.

4. Record allowable changes. For future reference, document any change that has occurred for an allowable reason. Phase 3 should be an ongoing quality-control check. Not only do you increase the chance of detecting and being able to take action early in the infection of a system, but you also validate the integrity of your system.

Table 24.1 provides a checklist that you can use to audit your system.

Using Alternative Methods

You can accomplish some of the steps within each phase by using batch files and custom software. Because a complete phase 3 auditing carried out on a large system—for instance, a 50-user LAN with 400M of storage—can take a long time, automating the process is a valuable exercise.

If the total system is not available for a long enough period for the purpose of auditing during any phase, you need to identify the

Table 24.1
Systems Audit Checklist

Pre-Audit Checklist

1. Review suppliers. [ ]
2. Test all system components. [ ]
3. Implement a site log. [ ]
4. Audit schedule (fill in frequencies):

	new	days	weeks	months
Phase 1: New software	Y	-	-	-
Phase 2: Environmental	Y	[ ]a	[ ]b	[ ]b
Phase 3: Live system	Y	[ ]c	[ ]d	[ ]d

a - key environmental features only
b - all environmental features
c - key system features only
d - all system components

Phase 1: Auditing New Software

1. Protect the original master disks. [ ]
2a. Make a backup master set and working master set. [ ]
2b. Write-protect the backup master set. [ ]
2c. Store the original and backup master sets. [ ]
3. Test the software, using the working master set. [ ]
4. Test with other software. [ ]
5. Use all available virus diagnostic tools. [ ]
6. Record the specifications and parameters. [ ]

Phase 2: Environmental Auditing

1. Document the environment. [ ]
2. Back up the system. [ ]
3. Install the software. [ ]
4. Check all system statistics and parameters. [ ]
5. Evaluate all virus transmission vectors. [ ]
6. Back up the system with the software installed. [ ]

Phase 3: Auditing a Live System

1. Verify all recorded statistics. [ ]
2. Run all virus diagnostic utilities. [ ]
3. Check transmission vectors. [ ]
4. Record allowable changes. [ ]

sections that can be audited in isolation, or devise a method for dynamic auditing.

Dynamic auditing involves taking a snapshot of a portion of a live system and auditing the snapshot. As this procedure is extremely technical, the procedure is possible only as a function of systems design. Dynamic auditing is a specialist's job and must be built into the system.

Each system manager is responsible for implementing each phase to the extent that is practical and cost effective for that system. In many cases, the compromise you reach allows for a minimal amount of auditing, but anything is better than nothing. "How often should I audit?" is a difficult question. A lot depends on what kind of system you are running, the number of computers and the links between them, and the cost involved. A rule of thumb is that you should do an audit every time you do a major backup of the system.

Chapter Summary

Computer viruses in a network system are a potentially more dangerous and costly combination than in any other computer system. The faster and more complex the network, the more opportunity for catastrophe. Conversely, many sophisticated networks offer far greater environmental control and often much more secure access control than the vast majority of single-host systems.

Many LANs, in particular, offer significant advantages in having embedded (system-level) network management and control services. Additionally, the LAN market is supported by a large number of third-party products that significantly extend the options and techniques available.

If you ignore these issues and institute inadequate (or no) auditing procedures, hoping that your networks will remain unaffected and uninfected by computer viruses, you had better be able to afford the cost of an attack. If you are managing such a system for someone else, you should start writing your resume as soon as possible—no network system professional, however, should be prepared to give you a reference.

25

Disaster Recovery

Disaster recovery is a topic often discussed, frequently claimed to be built into a system, and usually ignored. You will find a great difference between being able to reconstruct your PC if the hard disk fails and re-establishing the services provided by a 50-user network.

Disaster-recovery planning involves identifying the potential sources of catastrophic failure and estimating their likelihood, the ways to recover from single or multiple catastrophes, and the cost of each recovery method. When you finish planning, you are in a strong position to evaluate the cost-effectiveness of each strategy available to you.

What Is a Disaster?

You can classify each kind of network disaster catastrophic to the functioning of the system. Catastrophes are events that cause a complete failure of the network.

Failure of a single critical node may be a disaster in terms of the functioning of a network. A network server system may fail completely, for example, causing a total loss of network service. In such a situation, however, one or more workstations may be capable of functioning as stand-alone machines.

Disaster is relative to the use of the system and its importance to the organization. One man's disaster is another man's catastrophe; an event is judged to be a disaster by different people on different scales. Disasters, therefore, can be classified only by the network manager who knows what failures cause a major loss of service. The scale of a problem is defined by its context; if the event prevents the overall functioning of the system, the event probably is a disaster.

A disaster can be the result of natural forces or man-made events, including the following:

Natural

- Fire
- Lightning
- Power supply failure/surge
- Component failure
- Flood

Man-made

- Arson
- Data deletion
- Theft
- Computer viruses

Developing a Disaster Recovery Plan

The object of a plan to overcome a disaster is to restore service as fast—and as comprehensively—as possible. Recent surveys have shown that more than 50 percent of computer installations have inadequate provisions for recovery from a disaster.

Following are the elements of a disaster-recovery plan:

- Identification of critical programs/functions
- Damage assessment
- Disaster-action plan

- ❑ Emergency processing
- ❑ Client/public relations handling
- ❑ Permanent site restoration
- ❑ Salvage operations
- ❑ Disaster plan review and simulations

These elements are fairly straightforward and form the basis for a cost-justification argument where one is required. The first part in developing a disaster-recovery plan is to analyze the facilities. Analysis involves documenting all machines on the network and determining their usage. Machines with other machines dependent on them (such as file servers, application servers, and gateways) are obviously critical components. Also analyze the support service and facilities, such as the network cabling and power supply.

At this point, you should review your backup and restore facilities. The location of the backup and archive media is critical if you want to have any hope for disaster recovery. For large sites, the daily backup may have to be duplicated and taken off-site for storage. Archival systems such as optical storage may involve such huge volumes of data that duplication is impractical. In such a case, provision of an ultra-secure and disaster-proofed environment may be required. For all system storage of backups off-site, a monthly backup is advised.

Carefully examine your plan for backup and recovery. The testing of the plan is mandatory; assess the time required for the recovery. The issue of the time involved in completing a restoration can be important. If the system implements a total monthly back-up and an incremental daily backup (that is, only the changed items are backed up daily), restoration may be time consuming.

Restoration may involve, at worst, restoring the monthly image of the system and restoring 30 incremental backups. Assume that a backup/restore subsystem can restore at a real rate of 0.25 megabytes per second and that the incremental changes on a 1000-megabyte server involve 30 megabytes per day. Recovery in the worst case would take $(1000/0.25)+((30\times30)/0.25)$ seconds, or just over 2.5 hours, excluding handling and bringing the backups to site.

When you have a breakdown of the components of the network, you can identify critical and noncritical components. The definition of *critical* depends completely on the perception of the system manager. A network providing an SNA terminal service as its prime function may not require the file server to operate. In this case, the critical unit is the gateway; the file server is noncritical.

A damage-assessment plan requires that you use a crystal ball to classify all types of failure for each item and whether the item is critical or noncritical. Tie this information into the disaster-action plan so that the response is planned and achievable for each type of failure.

The disaster-action plan is a directory of what should be done in response to a particular catastrophe. Each action should be well detailed. The staff who will be in charge during a disaster must all have access to a copy of the plan (ideally, each staff member should have a copy) and be thoroughly familiar with the plan. You may want to implement a training program with regular updates and reviews.

One of the easiest tactics to overcoming a catastrophe is to set up emergency-processing facilities. This tactic also is costly. Setting up emergency facilities usually is more important for financial applications, particularly accounts systems. The emergency facilities can be on-site or off-site. On-site emergency facilities can be provided by allocating a spare system or another system to be loaded with a backup of the failed system. Alternatively, arrangements can be made to hire enough equipment to build a minimal system. You will need a stock of cabling and other sundries if costs are to be kept within reasonable bounds.

The problem with on-site emergency-processing facilities is the assumption that the site is still there. Loss of site can be caused by several events: fire, flood, structural failure, and total power loss are all possible. In the case of total power loss, generators can be brought in; if it is winter, however, renting enough generators to provide power for the network and the environmental services may be difficult.

Total power loss also can occur as the result of lightning strikes and other events that cause power surges. The problems of supplying power cabling around a site of even modest size may make on-site emergency processing unfeasible. Most problems with on-site emergency processing stem from the hazards to health and safety. Power cables trailed through a building must conform to local laws; violations can be dangerous and have severe legal consequences.

Carrying out the major repairs necessary to restore the network can be difficult if the site is still in use. In the case of power or network cabling loss, the process of replacing the systems can be extremely disruptive even in a modern building with well-designed cabling support.

Off-site emergency processing is often difficult to arrange. Any agreement with another company to supply facilities that enable you to resume processing should be covered by a contract. Contracts are a good idea even when the agreement is with another part of your own company. Many instances occur where informal agreements have not been honored when the need arose. Regular reviews of the arrangements and dry runs should be carried out to assure both parties of the feasibility of the arrangements.

In the event of a failure, one of the greatest mistakes is to not inform clients and other interested parties of the crisis. A client who receives poor service because of a situation that he or she was never told about may view the disaster, and possibly your company, negatively. Keeping clients informed of a problem and the progress your company is making, as well as flagging any potential service losses, demonstrates professionalism and builds corporate image. In effect, the disaster can be an exercise in public relations for your company.

Restoration of a permanent site requires a well-researched plan to ensure that the restoration is done optimally and within a known cost range. The basic activities involved in site restoration are presented in the following list:

- ❑ Clean-up. After a disaster, you must restore the fabric of the building to a state suitable for further work. A fire, for example, causes smoke and structural damage that must be fixed before anything else can be done. A flood presents other challenges such as drying out the building—a major task that can take considerable time.

- ❑ Removal of damaged installation. After the clean-up is done, the damaged components of the system must be removed. The removal process is straightforward for components like printers and workstations, but removal of network and power cabling can be major tasks. In the case of damaged cabling, carefully test the cabling to ensure that it still meets specification. If you doubt the functionality of a component, discard that component.
- ❑ Refitting. When the site is clean and all damaged equipment is removed, the process of reinstalling and refitting the network systems and support services can begin. Refitting can be based on the original installation plan; however, if an architectural review has not taken place recently, a review at this time might be appropriate. The architectural review includes an analysis of the physical site, the applications and users, and current technologies.
- ❑ Reinstallation and commissioning. The final step to restoring the site is to reinstall the software and commission (approve) the setup. Testing and commissioning time varies depending on the scale of the disaster.

As part of the disaster-recovery plan, you should consider whether to conduct salvage operations. Salvage operations require a cost-benefit analysis of what can be salvaged from a particular disaster. If the disaster was a flood, recovery of cabling—particularly if the cable is robust such as plenum or fiber optic—may provide major cost savings.

In the case of fire, the extent of the damaged area is a variable that affects the cost benefit of cable salvage. If the disaster was lightning, you may want to throw away all copper cable; the cost of salvage and retesting can be uneconomical in view of the probable unreliable state of the cable.

Although you may have created a disaster-recovery plan, review the plan on a regular basis. Regular reviews ensure that changes in the functions of the network are echoed in the plan and planned for effectively. Staff training also requires review and verification for effectiveness.

Walk-throughs, simulations of scenarios, and dry runs are great confidence builders. These suggestions are particularly important if off-site emergency-processing facilities are to be used. Make a plan for how the disaster review should be carried out. For large sites, the issues of damage assessment, carrying out the disaster action plan, emergency processing, client/public relations handling, permanent site restoration, and salvage operations are interrelated. A structured review is vital if recovery is to be efficiently and effectively done.

Disaster Planning Costs and Benefits

The degree to which you should develop a disaster-recovery plan depends on how much your business has invested in the network and the proportion of your business based on network services. If you cannot operate without the network, you must have a disaster-recovery plan.

The cost of developing such a plan can be high for large network systems. Ideally, the disaster-recovery plan should be related to, and be part of, the design process that generated your system configuration. The benefits of planning can be enormous, and not only when you have a disaster. Insurance companies may be more amenable to reductions in premiums if the degree of risk they are insuring is quantifiable.

The organizational benefits of a disaster-recovery plan are that more comprehensive management is developed for the network system.

For smaller networks, the existence of a simple disaster-recovery plan is very useful. At least your staff will have an idea of what to do in an emergency and the recovery response will be organized.

Chapter Summary

Disaster is a relative term, but for most computer sites the loss of systems and associated services qualifies as a disaster. Disasters come from such causes as theft, vandalism, fires, floods, and electrical surges.

A disaster recovery plan is a list of actions to minimize the period of downtime following a disaster. Such a plan inevitably reduces the cost of a disaster.

Glossary

Access. To retrieve data from permanent magnetic storage and bring that data into electronic memory. Computers can manipulate data only when in electronic memory.

Algorithm. A problem-solving method. On a contention network, for example, an algorithm is used to reschedule transmissions after a collision.

Analog. A system based on a continuous ratio, such as voltage or current values. (See also Digital.)

Analog transmission. A communications scheme that uses a continuous signal, varied by amplification. Broadband networks use analog transmissions. (See also Digital Transmission.)

API. Application Programming Interface. The calls in an operating system used by application programs to access operating system services.

APPC. See LU6.2.

Application Programming Interface See API.

Application server. A server that processes a particular application, usually for multiple clients; for example, a database server.

Applications software. A program or set of programs that performs a specific task for the user. Word processor and spreadsheet programs are applications software.

ARCnet. Attached Resource Computer Network. A local area network scheme designed by Datapoint. ARCnet provides intercommunication among networked devices at a rate of 2.5 Mbits/sec.

Architecture. In data communications, a definition of components and their relationships within a communications network.

Archive. In data processing, to place data on removable media for long-term, off-line storage.

ASCII. American Standard Code for Information Interchange. This coded character set is used internally by the IBM PC and most other microprocessors.

Asynchronous (Async). A method of data communication in which transmissions are not synchronized by a clocking signal. Sets of data are defined by start-stop bits. Local area networks transmit asynchronously.

Attenuation. Loss of signal strength. On a local area network, attenuation prevents successful communication when cable lengths exceed their maximum range.

Backbone-and-cluster. An internetwork design with small workgroup or departmental networks (clusters) attached to a single common network that carries traffic among the clusters.

Background task. A job processed in a subordinate status to foreground tasks. Some network operating systems enable a microcomputer to function as a network server and workstation. The network duties often are carried out as background tasks while the local user's instructions are executed in foreground.

Backup. A duplicate copy of a program or data file. A backup of data should be made as protection against corruption or loss of the original.

Bandwidth. The capacity of a communications channel. Bandwidth typically is stated as bits per second (bit/sec) or cycles per second (Hertz). As a measure of the rate at which information can be passed across a network, bandwidth is an indication of network speed.

Baseband system. A communications method in which the information-bearing signal is placed directly onto the cable in digital form. Because the I/O of the microcomputer also is digital, no translation is necessary for a baseband system at the sending or receiving end.

Baseband coax. A single channel medium for carrying baseband transmissions.

Batch mode. Running a program without user interaction. In networking, batch mode often refers to batch transfers whereby an entire file is downloaded from a central machine, such as a network server or host mainframe computer. The file is manipulated locally, then returned to the central device.

Baud. An imprecise unit of measure, roughly equivalent to bits per second.

Bisynchronous (Bisync). Binary synchronous. A protocol developed by IBM for mainframe data transmissions. The transmission method is controlled by a clocking signal.

Bit. Binary digit. The basic unit of information used in computer systems. A bit is 0 or 1.

Bridge. A device that matches circuits and is used to connect identical local area networks through store-and-forward buffers that check addresses and may regulate bandwidth.

Broadband system. A communications method characterized by a large bandwidth. The bandwidth usually is split, or multiplexed, to provide multiple communications channels. A broadband system uses analog transmissions. Because the microcomputer is a digital device, a modem is required at either end of the transmission cable to convert the digital signal to analog and back again.

Broadcast. A transmission technique in which all attending stations receive the transmission. Messages are broadcast onto local area networks by the sending workstation, but only the addressee accepts and reads the message.

Buffer. A temporary data storage facility.

Bug. A segment of computer code that fails to perform as intended or expected.

Bus. A path for electrical signals; also a type of network topology with a single cable onto which all devices attach. The cable ends are terminated with resistors.

Byte. A unit of measure, usually eight bits. (Ten-bit bytes occasionally are used, but should be predefined.)

Cache. A buffer between the CPU and the magnetic storage device. Data can be retrieved from magnetic storage and held in the cache in anticipation of the data's use by the CPU. A cache increases the speed of system operations because data acquisitions are faster from the cache than from magnetic storage.

Carrier Sense Multiple Access (CSMA). A contention network access scheme. Workstations monitor the network and may transmit any time the cable appears to be clear—when no carrier is sensed, or "heard," on the network.

CCITT. International Telegraph and Telephone Consultative Committee. A standards committee.

Central mass storage. A shared hard disk on a network.

Central processing. See Shared processing.

Chip. Slang for a silicon wafer imprinted with integrated circuits. Often used to mean CPU.

Client-server protocol. A data communications environment comprised of intelligent machines (not terminals) in which machines have defined roles. Certain machines (typically PC workstations) request services from other machines known as servers. Client-server is the standard environment for local area networks.

Client. An intelligent machine that makes requests to other machines known as servers. Clients usually are PC workstations on a local area network.

Client-based application. An application that runs in a network client (usually a PC workstation).

Coaxial cable. Two-conductor cable in which the conductors have the same axis. The center conductor carries the signal and the outer conductor, a tubular braid of wire, provides the ground. The outer conductor also shields the signal against electrical interference.

Collision. A garbled transmission that results from simultaneous transmissions by two or more workstations onto the same network cable.

Communications link. An electrical and logical connection between two devices. On a local area network, a communications link is the point-to-point path between sender and addressee.

Contention. An access method for sharing a network cable, based on a first-come, first-served policy.

Controller. A device that communicates with the host computer and relays information between the host computer and terminals.

Cooperative processing. A technology that permits different tasks within the same application to be processed on different computers.

Coprocessor. A microprocessor installed in a system to handle specific tasks, reducing the workload of the CPU.

CPU. Central Processing Unit. The microprocessor that provides processing capability, or intelligence, for a microcomputer.

CRC. Cyclic redundancy checking. A common method of checking for errors in a received message.

Cross talk. Signal interference created by emissions passing from one cable element to another.

CSMA-CD. Carrier Sense Multiple Access with Collision Detection. A contention scheme that includes a method of recovery in the event of a collision. When a collision is detected, transmitting stations cease transmission and wait a predefined interval before retransmitting.

Daisy chain. A linking of components in a series. A daisy chain internetwork links one network to another, which attaches to another network.

Data. Information. (See Data communications.)

Database. An organized compilation of data.

Database management system (DBMS). A software program designed to facilitate entry, organization, and retrieval of data in a database.

Database server. A process that manages record handling, indexing, disk I/O, and other back-end functions for a database application. Front-end functions, typically the user interface and query mechanism, are processed within client workstations.

Data communications. The passage of information in the form of electrical impulses representing alphanumeric characters. Data communications contrast with voice and video communications.

Datagram. A message comprised of packets of information.

Data integrity. The condition in which data (information) is uncorrupted and usable. Computer data normally is stored and transmitted in volatile form for easy manipulation. Such storage, whether electrical or magnetic, is subject to a number of threats, and great care must be exercised to maintain data integrity.

DECnet. Digital Equipment Corporation's communications network architecture. Classes of network computers and other devices and how these devices communicate are defined within this architecture.

Dedicated. Reserved for a single function. A dedicated network server, for example, cannot be used for any purpose other than network serving.

Default value. A definition selected when no other definition is specified. Default values are used for disk drives, printers, programs, and many other software and hardware variables as a convenience to the user.

Diagnostics. Programs or routines that test computer hardware and software to determine whether they are operating properly.

Digital. A system based on discrete states, typically the binary condition On or Off.

Digital transmission. A communications system that passes information encoded as pulses. Baseband networks and microcomputers use digital transmissions.

Direct connect. In local area networking, the process of attaching a workstation to the network cable without an intervening multiplexer. Direct connect is accomplished via a network interface card.

Disk server. A software program that enables multiple users to directly access a shared hard disk.

Disk subsystem. The set of components in a hard disk drive, typically including the hard disk, drive unit, connecting cable, and interface card.

Distributed database. A database, parts of which are resident on different hard disks and managed by different computers.

Distributed processing. A technology in which processing occurs in multiple machines on the network. Distributed processing is typical on most local area networks.

DMA. Direct memory access. A high-speed method of transferring data from a peripheral device directly into the microcomputer's memory.

DOS. Disk operating system. On microcomputers, the workstation operating system developed by IBM and Microsoft. PC DOS from IBM and MS-DOS from Microsoft have minor differences but are essentially the same system.

Download/upload. The transfer of an entire data file (or program) between computers. Transferring a file from a host to a remote computer is downloading. Transferring from a remote computer to a host or LAN is uploading. (See Batch mode.)

ECMA. European Computer Manufacturers Association.

Emulation. The duplication of the functional capability of one device in another device. For example, an IBM PC may be made to emulate a dumb terminal for communications with a host mainframe computer.

EtherNet. A local computer network protocol designed by Xerox. EtherNet is a baseband, contention network that runs on coaxial or twisted-pair cable and has a bit rate range of 1 Mbit/sec to 10 Mbits/sec, depending on the implementation.

Expansion bus. A set of slots in a computer that enable additional circuit boards to be attached, effectively expanding, or increasing, the capabilities of the computer.

FDDI. Fiber Distributed Data Interface. A high-speed (100 Mbits/sec) data transfer method.

FDM. Frequency division multiplexing. A technique in which a communications medium is divided into parallel channels. Each channel is allocated a different frequency band. This technique is used to give broadband coax its multichannel capability.

Fiber optics. Glass or plastic fibers that carry information by modulating a visible signal.

Field. A range of data within a record denoting a category of information.

File locking. A scheme that prevents a file from being used by more than one user at a time.

File server. A software program that provides central management for a hard disk subsystem on a local area network. In common usage, file server software also performs user-management and communications functions. File server often is used to mean a computer running file-server software.

File transfer. At a user's request, the copying of a data file from one system onto another.

Finder. The operating system for Apple Macintosh computers.

Foreground task. A job done in priority status before subordinate, or background, tasks are executed. In multitasking, a network server usually performs local workstation routines in foreground while executing network tasks in background.

Gateway. A device that connects two dissimilar networks. A gateway has its own processor and memory and may perform protocol and bandwidth conversion.

Gigabyte. 1,000 megabytes.

GOSIP. Government Open Systems Interconnection Profile. A suite of protocols, called a profile, that follows the OSI Reference Model. Many governments have their own GOSIP committees whose purpose is to standardize data communications and practices.

Groupware. Application software that performs group management and coordination functions in addition to various application functions such as electronic mail, scheduling, and project management.

Hard disk. Also called a fixed disk or Winchester disk.

Host computer. A machine that provides the processing power for attached terminals. The host computer usually is a mainframe or minicomputer.

Host-to-terminal. A network scheme in which a central controlling machine, the host, serves multiple dumb terminals. Also known as a master/slave scheme.

Hub. A wiring concentrator on an ARCnet network. An active hub performs the additional service of regenerating the signal.

IEEE. Institute of Electrical and Electronic Engineers. One of several groups whose members are drawn from industry and who attempt to establish industry standards. The IEEE 802 committee has published numerous definitive documents on local area network standards.

Integration. The merging of separate environments.

Interprocess communications (IPC). Communications protocols that enable programs to talk to each other.

IPX/SPX. Internet Packet eXchange/Sequenced Packet eXchange. Transport (subnet) protocols developed by Novell.

Intelligent workstation. A PC used as a workstation on a network.

Internetwork. Between networks, or the process of sending traffic from one network to another. Also, a network comprised on two or more individual networks that can communicate with each other.

Interrupt. A signal that can break into the execution of a program with a new command.

Interface. The point at which systems communicate with each other. An interface may be hardware-to-software or software-to-software.

I/O. Input/output.

I/O port. A circuit that receives data from the main processor or provides data to the processor.

ISDN. Integrated Services Digital Network. A network capable of using the same communications equipment for all types of communications traffic, with special emphasis on voice, data, facsimile, and video.

K. Kilobyte. A unit of measure for computer memory equal to 1,024 bytes.

Jumper. An electrical conductor that connects two points in a circuit.

LAN. Local area network.

LAN hardware. Communications components of a LAN. Cables, topologies, and network interface cards are the primary pieces of LAN hardware.

Layer. A discrete set of communications functions capable of interfacing with adjacent sets in a hierarchical structure. (See OSI Reference Model.)

Local area network. A geographically confined computer-based communications system. The network may be used to indicate any combination of hosts, terminals, microcomputers, and other attached devices. In this book, unless otherwise noted, the term is used to mean a microcomputer local area network.

Lock. A method of preventing simultaneous access of data. A lock may be advisory, as with a semaphore, in which case the user may override. Such advisory locks warn the user that a file is in use but do not prevent access. Most network operating systems support physical locks that cannot be overridden.

Log on/log off. The process of activating or deactivating a local microcomputer as a network entity. Log-on procedure for a local area network requires the starting (booting) of a network user program, often followed by keyboard entry of a log-on name and a password. Same as log in/log out.

Logical. A functional description that may differ from the physical description. A network, for example, may be configured so that a logical local drive C for one workstation is physically volume F on the file server's hard disk.

LU6.2. Logical Unit 6.2, an IBM designation for machine type. LU6.2 is an identity that a machine assumes from running LU6.2-compatible software. The LU6.2 identity is that of an intelligent machine, typically a PC-type workstation. LU6.2 also defines a communications link between two intelligent machines. This link often is referred to as Application Process to Process Communications (APPC).

Mapping. Assigning a hard disk volume to a particular logical disk drive.

Megabyte. A unit of measure equal to 1,000 kilobytes.

Memory dump. A captured image of part of the internal memory of a microcomputer. Memory dumps generally are used for software diagnostics.

Menu. A display that lists the choices available to the user.

Menu-driven. A software program in which all information necessary for its operation is displayed in a menu. This type of program restricts the available options but makes the program easier for a novice to use.

Microcomputer. A microprocessor-based computing system with enough power to perform computations, including the capability to modify its own programs. The microcomputer has its own memory and I/O circuitry. Processing power usually is limited to one CPU.

Migration. In computing and data communications, the movement from one technology to another. Migration often is needed to add functionality or to remain compatible with evolving or new standards.

Migration path. The procedures required to move from one technology to another.

Minicomputer. A host-type computer, smaller in size and capacity than a mainframe.

Modem. MOdulator/DEModulator. A device that converts digital signals from a computer to modulated signals for transmission over a telephone line. At the receiving end, another modem converts the modulated signals back to digital signals and passes them to a receiving computer.

Motherboard. The main circuit board of a computer system, into which smaller boards may be plugged to expand the functions of the system. Same as system board.

Multitasking. The concurrent handling of multiple jobs by one CPU. On a network server, multitasking usually means that the server can be used in the foreground as a local workstation while network tasks are carried out in the background.

Multiuser. A system in which multiple users share one CPU. Multiuser commonly indicates a host-to-terminal system.

Multiple access. The condition in which multiple users can open the same file simultaneously. Same as concurrent access.

Multiplexing. Supporting simultaneous multiple transmissions on one medium.

NetBIOS. Network Basic Input/Output System. A transport level (subnet) protocol from IBM.

Network. A communications system that consists of attached devices.

Network adapter. See Network interface card.

Network computing. A strategy for network design that places the emphasis on managing distributed resources and supporting heterogeneous environments.

Network interface card (NIC). A circuit board that permits direct connection of a microcomputer to a network cable. The network side of the NIC usually has a connector for the LAN cable and a plug that fits into the computer expansion bus. NICs often have a transmitter, encoder/decoder circuitry, memory buffer, and sometimes a coprocessor. Same as Network adapter.

Network operating system. A set of software programs that manage a network of users, resources, and services. Network operating systems attach to a communications subnet that establishes and maintains links among network devices.

Network server. See server.

Non-shareable. Available for only one user at a time. One of the possible characteristics with which a file can be labeled to control its access.

Office automation. The practice of using technology, usually in the form of a computer system, to perform tasks that previously were handled manually.

Operating system. A software program that manages the hardware/software interface of a computer.

OSI Reference Model. The International Standards Organization's Open Systems Interconnection model. A set of guidelines for network design, divided into seven distinct layers. Same as ISO Model.

OS/2. Operating System/2. A multitasking, microcomputer-based operating system developed jointly by IBM and Microsoft.

Overwrite. To write (store) data on a magnetic disk in the same area where other data is stored. In the process, the original data is destroyed. In a local area network, overwrites occur most often when two people access the same data, update the data, then attempt to write the updates to disk. The network operating system may be unaware that the data has been modified and may store the two updates in the same space. The last person to store data overwrites the first person's data.

Packet. A set of data with addresses and control codes attached so that it may be transmitted on a computer network.

Packet switching. The transmission of data packets across a shared medium. The circuit is available to other transmissions as soon as the packet has been sent. Other packets, though part of the same message, may be transmitted across different circuits if necessary. This transmission method commonly is used on local area networks.

Parameter. A definable variable.

Parity. An error-detection scheme for data communications based on an odd or even number of 1 bits. If odd parity is specified, an extra bit is added to make the total number of 1 bits odd. If even parity is specified, the extra bit is used to make the total even. Parity is checked after a transmission is received and, if parity is inconsistent, a transmission error has occurred.

Password. A security tool used to identify authorized network users and to define their privileges with the network. Passwords normally are requested during the log-on procedure after the log-on name is entered by the user.

PBX. Public Branch eXchange. A central control unit for telephone systems.

Peer-to-peer. A network scheme that assumes that connected devices have local processing power. Typically used in host-to-host transfers of data.

Peripheral. A device, such as a printer or disk drive, that is connected to and controlled by a computer.

Personal computer (PC). A microcomputer small enough and inexpensive enough to dedicate to a single user.

Platform. A computer or operating system that supports a function or set of functions. The term platform is used to place emphasis on the support capabilities of the computer or operating system.

Polling. A system of regularly checking the status of attached devices. When the polled device has a request, that request is accepted and executed.

Premises network. A data communications network that covers an entire building, but does not extend beyond the building to a campus or wide-area network.

Protocol. A set of defined parameters for establishing and controlling communications. In a local area network, major protocols cover the hardware level (EtherNet, ARCnet, and so on), and transport level (XNS, TCP/IP, and so on).

Queue. A waiting line in which jobs are stored, pending processing. A common queuing device is a print spooler that holds data sent for printing. The spooler feeds the data to the printer as the printer can use it.

RAM. Random-access memory. A read/write memory space, any area of which can be accessed in a nonsequential manner. RAM normally refers to electronic memory.

RAM disk. An area of electronic memory configured by a software program to emulate a disk drive. Data stored in a RAM disk can be accessed more quickly than data stored on a physical disk drive.

Read. To access a data file and examine its contents without making a modification.

Read-only. An access privilege designation that permits a user to open, but not modify, the file.

Read/write. An access privilege designation that permits a user to open and/or modify the file.

Record. An entry in a database.

Record locking. A scheme to prevent multiple users from simultaneously updating a record.

Redirector. See shell.

Repeater. A network device used to amplify and pass along an attenuated signal.

Requester. A software component of the network operating system that runs in the workstation and manages calls to network resources. Used in conjunction with workstation operating systems that are network-aware, such as OS/2.

Resident program. A program that, once loaded into memory, remains there until the system is powered down or reset. The resident program is readily available to the user or other programs. Same as terminate and stay resident (TSR).

Response time. The interval necessary to answer a request, usually measured at the user interfaces; the time from the issuance of a keyboard request until the receipt of the answer on the display.

ROM. Read-only memory. Often designated as firmware, a ROM is a memory chip with a software program permanently embedded in its circuits.

RPC. Remote Procedure Call. A mechanism for sending executable requests from one computer to another.

RS-232-C. A common protocol for connecting microcomputer system components. On the IBM and Apple microcomputers, an RS-232-C is the serial data interface to modem-based communications.

SAA. Systems Application Architecture. An IBM-defined set of standard interfaces and protocols that eventually will be implemented across much of IBM's product line. A primary goal of SAA is to achieve compatibility and connectivity among IBM products.

Screen buffer. A memory area that contains the screen characters and attributes.

Scrolling. The process of adjusting the display upward or downward.

Serial transmission. A data transmission method in which each bit in a byte is sent sequentially, one at a time. When the data arrives at its destination, the bits are reassembled into 8-bit bytes.

Serial port. A computer data channel, usually an RS-232-C interface, on a computer. A serial port allows serial data into and out of the computer. The port converts parallel data generated by the computer to outgoing serial data and serial data to incoming parallel data.

Server. A hardware and software device that acts as an interface between a local area network and a peripheral device. The server receives requests for peripheral services and manages the requests so that they are answered in an orderly, sequential manner. Same as Network server.

Server-based application. An application that runs partially in a server machine and partially in a client.

Shareable. Available for use by multiple users. One of the possible characteristics with which a file can be labeled to control access.

Shared processing. A technology in which one processor is used by several end users or other computer processes. Same as central processing.

Shell. A component of the network operating system that runs in the workstation and traps calls to the network before they reach the local operating system.

SNA. Systems Network Architecture. IBM's communications network architecture. As part of this architecture, classes of network computers and other devices and how these devices communicate are defined.

SNA/SDLC. Systems Network Architecture/Synchronous Data Link Control. A communication method commonly used to transmit data from an IBM host computer to a 3274 or 3276 controller.

Software. The instruction programs that tell a computer what to do.

Spooler. A software program that stores data addressed to a peripheral in memory. The spooler will release the data to the peripheral as the data can be used. After the spooler is loaded, the CPU is free to continue processing while the peripheral is served by the spooler. Print spoolers that hold files for printing are the most common type of spoolers.

SQL. Structured Query Language. SQL is a standard (widely-used) language for relational database manipulation that was developed by IBM.

Stand-alone. In computing, a condition in which a computer (often a PC) operates without connections to a network.

Star. A local area network topology in which cables radiate from a central network processor or wiring concentrator. Workstations are attached to the cables, one workstation per cable.

Star-wired ring. A network topology with the physical layout of a star network (workstation cables radiating from a central point). The star-wired ring is a logical ring because of the traffic pattern that circles around through the attached devices.

Store-and-forward. A technology that enables messages or requests to be created, held for a period of time, and then sent to the addressee.

Structured Query Language. See SQL.

Subnet. The transport level of the network, usually including Layers 3, 4, and 5 of the OSI Reference Model.

Synchronization. In multiuser environments, the process of coordinating multiple requests received by one resource, such as a file server.

Synchronous. A transmission controlled by a clock pulse acted on by the sender and receiver.

Systems Application Architecture. See SAA.

TCP/IP. Transmission Control Protocol/Internetwork Protocol. A transport level (subnet) protocol that is widely used, especially for wide-area communications among networks.

Terabyte. 1,000 gigabytes.

Terminal. A user interface device that lacks built-in processing capability. Terminals normally have a keyboard and a display and attach to a host computer for processing and data storage facilities.

Token passing. A network access scheme in which a special packet is circulated among workstations. Any workstation wanting to transmit captures the token by modifying and addressing a message to it. When the workstation has completed its transmission, the station releases the token and control of the network by resetting the token to "free" status.

Token ring. A network hardware protocol that uses a token-passing access scheme and is configured in a star-wired ring topology.

Topology. The physical layout of a local area network. Some common topologies are Bus, Ring, and Star.

Transient program. A program that is loaded into memory, executes a specific function, then releases the memory space occupied by the program. Unlike a resident program, the services of a transient program are no longer available after the program has been exited.

Traffic. The volume of messages sent over a shared medium. Traffic often is used as a rough measure of the amount of cable use (such as heavy, light, etc.).

Transaction. In data processing, a complete operation involving one or more records. A transaction usually involves a modification to an existing record or the creation of a record. If a modification affects multiple records, the transaction is not complete until the changes to all effected records are completed.

Transparent. Refers to actions or services that take place automatically as a service of the application or the operating system without user intervention or even user awareness that the specific actions or services are occurring.

TSO. Time-sharing option. A widely used multiuser system on large IBM host computers.

TSR. See Resident program.

Unix. A multitasking, multiuser operating system developed by AT&T's Bell Laboratories.

User. A computer operator.

User profile. A set of defined rights to network resources. A user profile usually is defined for each user or group of users on the network.

Virtual. The effective condition. Virtual memory, for example, may function as main memory but provides greater storage capacity by using a portion of disk storage as if the data was in electronic memory.

Virtual circuit. A logical data transmission path between sender and addressee. The virtual circuit exists only during the transmission.

Virus. A program that, after being introduced to a system, attaches to an executable file and then replicates itself, attaching to other files and entering other systems at every opportunity. Computer viruses cause problems ranging in severity from inconvenience to destruction of data and total system failure.

VM/CMS. Virtual Machine/Conversation Monitor System. A widely used multiuser system on IBM host computers.

Twisted pair. Transmission cable composed of two braided wires, commonly used for telephone systems and increasingly popular for local area networks because of its low cost.

Volume. In a local area network, a partitioned area of a shared hard disk. Volumes are similar to local disk drives and may be used similarly.

WAN. Wide-area network. A data communications system that typically uses telephone and leased lines to connect sites to other sites and data resources.

Wide-area network. See WAN.

Winchester. A hard disk.

Window. An area of display screen, not taking up the entire screen, used by an application. A window typically is displayed as an overlay of an application on the full screen, or with one or more other windows.

Workgroup. A natural division of employees based upon activity. People within a workgroup share projects, applications, and data and tend to communicate mostly within the workgroup.

Write. To store data to disk.

X.25. A transport level (subnet) protocol defined by the CCITT and primarily used for wide-area communications.

X.400. A standard protocol for message handling that covers layers 5 through 7 of the OSI Reference Model. X.400 is focused primarily on electronic mail, store-and-forward communications. X.400 is defined by the CCITT.

X.500. A standard protocol for message formats and address definition. X.500 is defined by the CCITT.

Index

B

C

D

E

F

G

H

I

K

L

M

N

O

P

Q

R

S

T

U

V

W

X

More Computer Knowledge from Que

Lotus Software Titles

1-2-3 QueCards 21.95
1-2-3 for Business, 2nd Edition 22.95
1-2-3 QuickStart 21.95
1-2-3 Quick Reference 7.95
1-2-3 Release 2.2 Quick Reference 7.95
1-2-3 Release 2.2 QuickStart 19.95
1-2-3 Release 3 Business Applications 39.95
1-2-3 Release 3 Quick Reference 7.95
1-2-3 Release 3 QuickStart 19.95
1-2-3 Release 3 Workbook and Disk 29.95
1-2-3 Tips, Tricks, and Traps, 2nd Edition 21.95
Upgrading to 1-2-3 Release 3 .... 14.95
Using 1-2-3, Special Edition 24.95
Using 1-2-3 Release 2.2, Special Edition 24.95
Using 1-2-3 Release 3 .... 24.95
Using 1-2-3 Workbook and Disk, 2nd Edition 29.95
Using Lotus Magellan 21.95
Using Symphony, 2nd Edition 26.95

Database Titles

dBASE III Plus Applications Library 21.95
dBASE III Plus Handbook, 2nd Edition 22.95
dBASE III Plus Tips, Tricks, and Traps 21.95
dBASE III Plus Workbook and Disk 29.95
dBASE IV Applications Library, 2nd Edition 39.95
dBASE IV Handbook, 3rd Edition 23.95
dBASE IV Programming Techniques 24.95
dBASE IV QueCards 21.95
dBASE IV Quick Reference 7.95
dBASE IV QuickStart 19.95
dBASE IV Tips, Tricks, and Traps, 2nd Edition 21.95
dBASE IV Workbook and Disk 29.95
dBXL and Quicksilver Programming: Beyond dBASE 24.95
R:BASE User's Guide, 3rd Edition 22.95
Using Clipper 24.95
Using DataEase 22.95
Using Reflex 19.95
Using Paradox 3 .... 22.95

Applications Software Titles

AutoCAD Advanced Techniques 34.95
AutoCAD Quick Reference 7.95
CAD and Desktop Publishing Guide 24.95
Introduction to Business Software 14.95
PC Tools Quick Reference 7.95
Smart Tips, Tricks, and Traps 24.95
Using AutoCAD 29.95
Using Computers in Business 24.95
Using DacEasy 21.95
Using Dollars and Sense: IBM Version, 2nd Edition 19.95
Using Enable/OA 23.95
Using Excel: IBM Version 24.95
Using Generic CADD 24.95
Using Managing Your Money, 2nd Edition 19.95
Using Q&A, 2nd Edition 21.95
Using Quattro 21.95
Using Quicken 19.95
Using Smart 22.95
Using SuperCalc5, 2nd Edition 22.95

Word Processing and Desktop Publishing Titles

DisplayWrite QuickStart 19.95
Microsoft Word 5 Quick Reference 7.95
Microsoft Word 5 Tips, Tricks, and Traps: IBM Version 19.95
Using DisplayWrite 4, 2nd Edition 19.95
Using Harvard Graphics 24.95
Using Microsoft Word 5: IBM Version 21.95
Using MultiMate Advantage, 2nd Edition 19.95
Using PageMaker: IBM Version, 2nd Edition 24.95
Using PFS: First Choice 22.95
Using PFS: First Publisher 22.95
Using Professional Write 19.95
Using Sprint 21.95
Using Ventura Publisher, 2nd Edition 24.95
Using WordPerfect, 3rd Edition 21.95
Using WordPerfect 5 .... 24.95
Using WordStar, 2nd Edition 21.95
Ventura Publisher Techniques and Applications 22.95
Ventura Publisher Tips, Tricks, and Traps 24.95
WordPerfect Macro Library 21.95
WordPerfect Power Techniques 21.95
WordPerfect QueCards 21.95
WordPerfect Quick Reference 7.95
WordPerfect QuickStart 21.95
WordPerfect Tips, Tricks, and Traps, 2nd Edition 21.95
WordPerfect 5 Workbook and Disk 29.95

Macintosh and Apple II Titles

The Big Mac Book 27.95
Excel QuickStart 19.95
Excel Tips, Tricks, and Traps 22.95
HyperCard QuickStart 21.95
Using AppleWorks, 2nd Edition 21.95
Using dBASE Mac 19.95
Using Dollars and Sense 19.95
Using Excel: Macintosh Verson 22.95
Using FullWrite Professional 21.95
Using HyperCard: From Home to HyperTalk 24.95
Using Microsoft Word 4: Macintosh Version 21.95
Using Microsoft Works: Macintosh Version, 2nd Edition 21.95
Using PageMaker: Macintosh Version 24.95
Using WordPerfect: Macintosh Version 19.95

Hardware and Systems Titles

DOS QueCards 21.95
DOS Tips, Tricks, and Traps 22.95
DOS Workbook and Disk 29.95
Hard Disk Quick Reference 7.95
IBM PS/2 Handbook 21.95
Managing Your Hard Disk, 2nd Edition 22.95
MS-DOS Quick Reference 7.95
MS-DOS QuickStart 21.95
MS-DOS User's Guide, Special Edition 29.95
Networking Personal Computers, 3rd Edition 22.95
Understanding UNIX: A Conceptual Guide, 2nd Edition 21.95
Upgrading and Repairing PCs 27.95
Using Microsoft Windows 19.95
Using Novell NetWare 24.95
Using OS/2 .... 23.95
Using PC DOS, 3rd Edition 22.95

Programming and Technical Titles

Assembly Language Quick Reference 7.95
C Programmer's Toolkit 39.95
C Programming Guide, 3rd Edition 24.95
C Quick Reference 7.95
DOS and BIOS Functions Quick Reference 7.95
DOS Programmer's Reference, 2nd Edition 27.95
Power Graphics Programming 24.95
QuickBASIC Advanced Techniques 21.95
QuickBASIC Programmer's Toolkit 39.95
QuickBASIC Quick Reference 7.95
SQL Programmer's Guide 29.95
Turbo C Programming 22.95
Turbo Pascal Advanced Techniques 22.95
Turbo Pascal Programmer's Toolkit 39.95
Turbo Pascal Quick Reference 7.95
Using Assembly Language 24.95
Using QuickBASIC 4 .... 19.95
Using Turbo Pascal 21.95

For more information, call

1-800-428-5331

All prices subject to change without notice. Prices and charges are for domestic orders only. Non-U.S. prices might be higher.

Que®

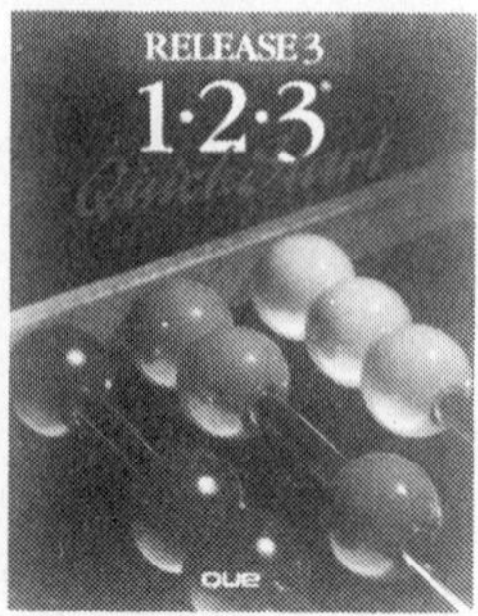

1-2-3 Release 3 QuickStart

Developed by Que Corporation

More than 100 two-page illustrations help users learn the fundamentals of 1-2-3 Release 3. This is a graphics-based approach to 1-2-3 worksheets, reports, graphs, databases, and macros.

Order #973
$19.95 USA
0-88022-438-X, 450 pp.

Using PFS: First Choice

by Katherine Murray

An excellent introduction to this popular integrated program. A series of **Quick Start** tutorials leads readers step-by-step from First Choice fundamentals through coverage of each module. Shows how to use First Choice as an integrated system, as well as how to interface with other programs.

Order #984
$22.95 USA
0-88022-454-1, 500 pp.

Using PFS: First Publisher

by Katherine Murray

From word processing basics to advanced layout features, this text is power-packed with program and design tips. One of Que's best-selling titles!

Order #937
$22.95 USA
0-88022-401-0, 500 pp.

Using Harvard Graphics

by Steve Sagman and Jane Graver Sandlar

This well-written text presents both program basics and presentation fundamentals to create bar, pie, line and other types of informative graphs. Helps users put a professional polish on business presentations.

Order #941
$24.95 USA
0-88022-407-X, 550 pp.

For more information, call

1-800-428-5331

All prices subject to change without notice. Prices and charges are for domestic orders only. Non-U.S. prices might be higher.

Free Catalog!

Mail us this registration form today, and we'll send you a free catalog featuring Que's complete line of best-selling books.

Name of Book ______________________

Name ______________________

Title ______________________

Phone ( ) ______________________

Company ______________________

Address ______________________

City ______________________

State ____________ ZIP ____________

Please check the appropriate answers:

1. Where did you buy your Que book?
   - ☐ Bookstore (name: ________)
   - ☐ Computer store (name: ________)
   - ☐ Catalog (name: ________)
   - ☐ Direct from Que
   - ☐ Other: ________

2. How many computer books do you buy a year?
   - ☐ 1 or less
   - ☐ 2-5
   - ☐ 6-10
   - ☐ More than 10

3. How many Que books do you own?
   - ☐ 1
   - ☐ 2-5
   - ☐ 6-10
   - ☐ More than 10

4. How long have you been using this software?
   - ☐ Less than 6 months
   - ☐ 6 months to 1 year
   - ☐ 1-3 years
   - ☐ More than 3 years

5. What influenced your purchase of this Que book?
   - ☐ Personal recommendation
   - ☐ Advertisement
   - ☐ In-store display
   - ☐ Price
   - ☐ Que catalog
   - ☐ Que mailing
   - ☐ Que's reputation
   - ☐ Other: ________

6. How would you rate the overall content of the book?
   - ☐ Very good
   - ☐ Good
   - ☐ Satisfactory
   - ☐ Poor

7. What do you like *best* about this Que book?

   ____

   ____

8. What do you like *least* about this Que book?

   ____

   ____

9. Did you buy this book with your personal funds?

   ☐ Yes ☐ No

10. Please feel free to list any other comments you may have about this Que book.

    ____

    ____

    ____

QUE

Order Your Que Books Today!

Name ______________________

Title ______________________

Company ______________________

City ______________________

State ____________ ZIP ____________

Phone No. ( ) ______________________

Method of Payment:

Check ☐ (Please enclose in envelope.)

Charge My: VISA ☐ MasterCard ☐

American Express ☐

Charge # ______________________

Expiration Date ______________________

Order No.	Title	Qty.	Price	Total

You can **FAX** your order to **1-317-573-2583.** Or call **1-800-428-5331, ext. ORDR** to order direct.

Please add $2.50 per title for shipping and handling.

Subtotal ________

Shipping & Handling ________

Total ________

QUE

NO POSTAGE
NECESSARY
IF MAILED
IN THE
UNITED STATES

BUSINESS REPLY MAIL
First Class Permit No. 9918 Indianapolis, IN

Postage will be paid by addressee

11711 N. College
Carmel, IN 46032

NO POSTAGE
NECESSARY
IF MAILED
IN THE
UNITED STATES

BUSINESS REPLY MAIL
First Class Permit No. 9918 Indianapolis, IN

Postage will be paid by addressee

11711 N. College
Carmel, IN 46032